D0858901

SERVICES

THE EXPORT OF THE 21st CENTURY

A Guidebook for US Service Exporters

DISCARDED

Property of
The Public Library of Nashville and Davidson County
225 Polk Ave., Nashville, Tn. 37203

WORLD TRADE PRESS
PUBLICATIONS

General References

Importers Manual USA
Exporting to the USA
World Trade Almanac
A Basic Guide to Exporting
Dictionary of International Trade

Country Business Guides

ARGENTINA Business   KOREA Business
AUSTRALIA Business   MEXICO Business
CANADA Business   PHILIPPINES Business
CHINA Business   SINGAPORE Business
HONG KONG Business   TAIWAN Business
JAPAN Business   USA Business

Passport to the World Series

Passport Argentina   Passport Korea
Passport Brazil   Passport Mexico
Passport China   Passport Philippines
Passport France   Passport Russia
Passport Germany   Passport Singapore
Passport Hong Kong   Passport Taiwan
Passport India   Passport Thailand
Passport Israel   Passport UK
Passport Italy   Passport USA
Passport Japan   Passport Vietnam

CD-ROMs

Importers Manual USA CD-ROM
Exporting to the USA CD-ROM
World Trade Almanac CD-ROM

SERVICES

THE EXPORT OF THE 21ST CENTURY

A Guidebook for US Service Exporters

Joe Reif
Janet Whittle
Alexandra Woznick
Molly E. Thurmond, J.D.
Jane Kelly

Originally Compiled by:

Kirsten M. Ditterich
Mitch G. Larsen
Robert A. Ostrea, Jr.

A Joint Publication of

The Northern California Export Council

and

WORLD TRADE PRESS®

Professional Books for International Trade

World Trade Press
1505 Fifth Avenue
San Rafael, California 94901
USA
Tel: (415) 454-9934
Fax: (415) 453-7980
USA Order Line: (800) 833-8586
email: WorldPress@aol.com

Cover design: Peter G. Jones
Text design: Edward G. Hinkelman, Peter G. Jones, Joe Reif

Copyright © 1997 by World Trade Press. All Rights Reserved.

No part of this book may be reproduced, transmitted, or copied in any manner whatsoever without written permission, except in the case of brief quotations embodied in articles and reviews with full credit given to this publication. For information, contact the publisher.

The name *World Trade Press* and the representation of the world map imprinted on an open book appearing in this publication are registered trademarks and the property of World Trade Press.

This publication is designed to provide general information for businesses preparing to export their services. It is sold with the understanding that the publisher is not engaged in rendering legal or any other professional services. If legal advice or other expert assistance is required, the services of a competent professional person should be sought.

Promotional trade events and professional associations included in this book are provided solely as an informational source and, excluding US government-certified and organized events, are not necessarily endorsed by the US Department of Commerce, the International Trade Administration, or the Northern California Export Council.

Services--the export of the 21 century: a guidebook for US service
    exporters / compiled, edited and revised by Joe Reif and Janet Whittle
        p.   cm.
    "A joint publication of the Northern California Export Council and World Trade Press
        Includes bibliographical references (p.).
        ISBN 1-885073-41-0
        1. Service industries--United States--Marketing. 2. Export marketing--
    United States. 3. Foreign trade promotion--
    United States. I. Reif, Joe. II. Whittle, Janet.
    HD9981.5.S448   1996   96-33514
    658.8'48--dc20   CIP

Printed in the United States of America

Foreword

The Department of Commerce is deeply committed to helping US companies become more competitive in the global economy. From the establishment of the Trade Promotion Coordinating Committee and the development of a "National Export Strategy," to dynamic advocacy for American firms overseas and the expansion and reorganization of export assistance centers here at home, we are moving to increase the US share of the US$5 trillion our trading partners are forecast to import in the year 2010.

The dominant role that services play throughout the US economy translates into leadership in technology advancement, growth in skilled jobs, and global competitiveness. Service sector jobs come from an enormous range of industries, including banking and insurance, travel, entertainment, wholesale and retail trade, legal and other business services, information, telecommunications, health care, education, transportation, energy and environmental services, and architectural, construction and engineering services. US services exports more than doubled over the last seven years—increasing US$100 billion since 1987, and US$51 billion just since 1990. In 1994, US services exports exceeded imports by US$60 billion (offsetting 36 percent of the deficit on merchandise trade), despite relatively open access to US markets.

The Department of Commerce has recognized the importance of services to the future of the US economy through the establishment of the "Services Initiative" of the National Export Strategy. We welcome your contribution to that effort, your guidebook, *Services: the Export of the 21st Century*, covering 20 service sectors from accounting to wholesaling. It will be a most valuable resource. I highly recommend it for those American service providers entering the export market.

We thank members of the Northern California District Export Council, and the 50 other councils throughout the country, who generously share their international expertise with aspiring US exporters and this Department.

Michael Kantor
Secretary of Commerce

Secretary of Commerce Michael Cantor (left) with former Secretary of Commerce Ronald Brown

Acknowledgments

As chairman of the Northern California Export Council of the US Department of Commerce's Santa Clara Export Assistance Center, I am pleased to present *Services: The Export of the 21 Century,* the third edition of our successful 1982 and 1987 publications. We sincerely hope that this guide will assist US services exporters to enter and compete effectively on an international level in what has become known by many as the "services economy."

This edition has been completely rewritten, and as is appropriate for the dynamic services export sector, is more than twice the size of the previous edition.

This guidebook is just one example of the pro bono work performed by over 1,500 members of the 51 Export Councils throughout the country. These councils are organizations of community leaders from business, universities, and local government, whose knowledge of international business provides a source of professional advice, assistance, workshops, and publications to firms seeking to expand their international sales. Closely affiliated with the US Department of Commerce, they provide specialized expertise to the Department and its clients.

We are grateful for the leadership of the Northern California Export Council Chairpeople who launched the previous editions: J.H. Dethero and John Leitner. We also appreciate the assistance of the International Trade Administration Center Director, James Kennedy; the Regional Director, Michael Liikala; and of course the strong support of the Secretary of Commerce, Ronald H. Brown, who launched the National Export Strategy Services Initiative in 1995, and of Secretary Michael Kantor, who pursued services opportunities as US Trade Representative, and has continued to do so as Secretary of Commerce.

We thank the many individuals who gave us time, patience, and assistance throughout the course of preparing this guidebook. Special thanks also go to Kirsten M. Ditterich, Mitch G. Larsen, and Robert A. Ostrea, Jr., who teamed to compile, edit, and revise the initial draft of this edition. In addition, we would like to recognize Jason A. Klein, who did a wonderful job updating statistical portions of this textbook. We also want to thank those who worked most closely beside them: John Dunning, Jeannine Seremi, and Eduardo Perez, research assistants; and Elizabeth Givens, editorial assistant.

Jerry Levine
Chairman
Northern California Export Council

About This Book

Over a decade ago, the San Francisco Export Council of the US Department of Commerce, recognized the unique needs of those involved in the service industry and the lack of export resources available to them. In response, in February of 1982, the San Francisco office held its first conference addressing the needs of a particular group of service exporters, entitled "Marketing Engineering and Technical Consulting Services Overseas." This conference served as a catalyst for the publication of our service export manual, *Services: How to Export, A Marketing Manual,* the first of its kind. Now, over a decade later, services remain the largest and fastest-growing sector of the US economy. Between the introductions of the services manuals in 1982 and 1987, total private sector service exports increased an impressive 46 percent. This fact alone underscores the need for our third and most comprehensive edition of this service export manual, now entitled *Services: The Export of the 21st Century.*

Objective

This book's objective is to provide US service exporters with the basic concepts of service exporting and to assist companies entering international markets in utilizing the resources of the US Department of Commerce, International Trade Administration, professional and trade associations, and private and non-profit institutions. *Services: The Export of the 21st Century* aims to assist the increasing number of service exporters by providing a one-stop source to service exporting resources.

Who Should Read This Book?

The primary focus of this text is to assist service firms that: 1) are taking an incremental approach to expanding business internationally; 2) have a shortage of capital and/or human resources that preclude foreign direct investment; 3) prefer to export; and 4) would prefer to participate in foreign direct investment, but are disabled by market barriers to entry. Additionally, this book can serve as an excellent resource for students and others who are interested in learning more about the US export of services. *Services: The Export of the 21st Century* does cover foreign direct investment although it will not be a major focus of this text.

Special Thanks

The editors of *Services: The Export of the 21st Century* would like to thank the following people for their help and expertise:

Brad Smith
Director of Member Services
International Insurance Council
1212 New York Avenue, NW, Suite 250
Washington, DC 20005
Tel: (202) 682-2345
Fax: (202) 682-4187

Jamie Born
American Marketing Association
250 South Wacker Dr.
Suite 200
Chicago, IL 60606-5819
Tel: (312) 648-0536

Robert Ostrea
LA Trade, c/o The Los Angeles Area COC
350 South Bixel Street
Los Angeles, CA 90017
Tel: (213) 580-7528

Raphael Baron
Polyglot International
340 Brannan Street, Fifth Floor
San Francisco, CA 94107
Tel: (415) 512-8800
Fax: (415) 512-8982
www.polyglot.com

L. Neal Amidei
The Amidei Group
230 California Street
Suite 601
San Francisco, CA 94111
Tel: (415) 956-2830
Fax: (415) 956-4525
Email: 102374,3313@compuserve.com

Felix Braynin
Intercapital Trust, Ltd.
50 California Street, Suite 3165
San Francisco, CA 94111
Tel: (415) 433-9450
Fax: (415) 392-0117

Ed Anderson
Lil' Orbits
2850 Vicksburg Lane
Minneapolis, MN 55447
Tel: (612) 559-7505
Fax: (612) 559-7545
www.lilorbits.com

Maria Solomon
US Agency for International Development, West Coast
One World Trade Center, Suite 1670
Long Beach, CA 90831
Tel: (310) 980-4550
Fax: (310) 980-4561

Also thanks to the trade specialists that have contributed to US Department of Commerce publications and made these service industry analyses possible.

Patricia Anderson
Robert Atkins
Richard Barovick
Wray O. Candilis
Achamma Chandersekaran
J. Marc Chittum
Patricia Cooper
Karla Dancy
Janice Dessaso
William R. Evans
Daniel W. Edwards
Fred Elliot
Simon Francis
Colleen Flannery
Linda L. Gossack
Bruce Harsh
Melissa Harrington
William Hurt
Mary C. Inoussa
Scott C. Johnson
Loretta S. Jonkers
Terry Smith Labat
Robert L. Lurensky
Bruce McAdam
Stephanie W. McCullough
Julie Heizer Rhodes
John R. Shuman
Jenifer Talarico
Patrick Thompson

Table of Contents

Chapter 1:

AN OVERVIEW OF SERVICE EXPORTS

The Service Economy

A fundamental shift has been taking place in the world's economy over the past 25 years. For most developed economies and multinational firms, competitiveness in the global marketplace no longer strictly lies on the assembly line in the production of consumer durables or in heavy manufacturing. While economic well-being will always be closely linked to the efficient production, consumption and trade of goods, it is also increasingly being determined by the productivity, application, and utilization of information, as well as other less tangible business services—either throughout the industrial process, or as a separate activity. Just as "muscle and manpower" were the forces that drove the manufacturing sector in the first part of this century, "knowledge" is increasingly the engine that will fuel many of the most rapidly growing service industries. In global trade, most of the industries in which America maintains a strong competitive lead—such as telecommunications, aerospace, bioscience, and computers—are accompanied by sophisticated services support.

The growth in services in our economy is intimately tied to the rate of technology development over the past few decades. Due to the explosion of communications technology and an increasingly liberal global trading environment, various services markets are now reaching across national borders to become truly global. Technological change—knowledge or information development, if you will—has fostered the growth of specialized business service firms that can interact over large geographic distances. Technology has also reduced the cost of providing services on a large scale, and allowed them to be produced at a much greater distance from the customer. Many services have become more "tradable" over the past decade, over and above the traditional services that the US has always exported, such as shipping and travel. Some of the services that have grown most rapidly from technology development include communications, financial services, software development, database management, computer services, royalties on proprietary products, accounting, architecture, construction, and engineering (ACE), advertising, legal services, and management consulting. And even travel, still the largest single service category, has been bolstered by technological advances in air and rail, as well as computer and communications technologies, the globalization of business, and increased leisure time.

The Importance of Services in the US Economy

With America's persistent merchandise trade deficit, it is sometimes possible to overlook the country's enormous "white collar" successes abroad. But since 1971, the US service sector has enjoyed a growing trade surplus. The US is the world's leading producer and exporter of services, which now account for 70 percent of US GDP—or roughly US$4 trillion in 1995—and roughly 75 percent of non-farm private jobs. In fact, American services now comprise about 20 percent of the world's total cross-border sales in services. In the trade of true "privately produced" services (which excludes receipts and payments on investments and government transactions), the US racked up a record US$185.4 billion in services export trade in 1994, and US$173 billion in 1993, up from US$86 billion in 1987. In addition, in 1994 service exports exceeded imports by US$62 billion, offsetting 37 percent of the deficit on merchandise trade (in 1993, the US$56.9 billion surplus in private sector service trade offset over 40 percent of the year's US$133 billion goods trade deficit).

The percentage of services as a portion of total world trade in goods and services has remained relatively constant since 1970—about 21 percent, or US$976 billion of US$4,484 billion total goods and services in 1994—but this figure is rather deceiving. The growth in exports of certain kinds of traditional services, such as transportation and travel, has been slower than the growth rates for services trade overall; this has kept this percentage constant (the cost of transportation services fell sharply from 1970 to 1994, reflecting the use of bulk cargo, very large tankers, and the lower costs of moving people). The fact is that there has been tremendous growth in the trade of most kinds of knowledge-based, business services over the past twenty five years. By 1994, business services had become the second largest component of global services trade, accounting for over 42 percent of the total value of world trade, about US$410 billion, or 9.1 percent—up from 6.2 percent in 1980.

One needs only to look at the relative growth rate in services employment vs. manufacturing in the major developed economies to understand better what importance services has and will take in the world economy. Between 1980 and 1993, the percentage increase in employment in the United States in trade, restaurants, and hotels was 22.7 percent; for finance, insurance, and real estate (FIRE), 55 percent; and 34 percent for community, personal, and social services, according to UN

Private Service Transactions by Type, 1986 - 1995
(millions of dollars)

US Exports	1986	1990	1993	1994	1995*
Total Private Services	77,378	137,219	274,207	185,419	196,411
Travel	20,385	43,007	57,875	60,406	61,137
Overseas	15,650	30,806	45,298	49,225	n/a
Canada	2,701	7,093	7,458	6,251	n/a
Mexico	2,034	5,108	5,119	4,930	n/a
Passenger Fares	5,582	15,298	16,611	17,477	18,534
Other Transportation	15,784	22,745	23,983	26,078	28,063
Freight	4,651	8,063	8,755	9,836	10,780
Port Services	10,574	13,662	14,222	15,213	16,091
Other	559	1,020	1,005	1,029	1,193
Royalties and License Fees	8,113	16,634	20,637	22,436	26,953
Affiliated	6,174	13,250	16,095	17,628	21,619
US parents' transactions	5,994	12,867	15,275	16,611	20,180
US affiliates' transactions	180	383	820	1,017	1,439
Unaffiliated	1,939	3,385	4,542	4,808	5,333
Other Private Services	27,514	39,535	55,101	59,022	61,724
Affiliated	8,385	13,622	16,191	17,215	19,458
Unaffiliated	19,129	25,913	38,910	41,807	42,265
Education	3,495	5,126	6,732	7,140	7,517
Financial Services	3,301	4,417	6,606	6,962	6,109
Insurance, Net Premiums	1,970	572	1,380	1,640	1,395
Telecommunications	1,827	2,735	2,784	2,757	2,848
Business, Professional, and					
Technical Services	4,428	6,951	13,294	14,813	16,264
Advertising	94	130	338	399	n/a
Computer and Data Processing	985	1,031	2,306	2,546	n/a
Database and Information Services	124	283	694	823	n/a
Management Consulting	306	354	849	986	n/a
Legal Services	97	451	1,446	1,558	n/a
ACE	759	867	2,358	2,704	n/a
Installation, repair of equipment	1,033	2,031	2,990	3,394	n/a
Medical Services	490	630	750	794	n/a
Other Unaffiliated Services	4,648	7,285	9,676	10,104	8,132

*full detail not available
Source: Survey of Current Business, September 1995

statistics. Manufacturing employment, on the other hand, decreased by 6.2 percent. This employment trend can be seen throughout the developed countries and in many of the less developed countries, as well. In China, manufacturing employment from 1985 to 1989 fell 12.3 percent, while employment for the same years in FIRE grew 46 percent, and in community, personal, and social services, 19.1 percent.

In the US, the service sector is creating jobs at about three times the rate of manufacturing. In fact, by the early 1990s services were creating about 90 percent of all new jobs in this country. Interestingly, many of these new jobs being created are not the archetypal low-wage, low-skilled service jobs in restaurants and retailing that have materialized in the past. Nearly half of the newly created service jobs are going to people with managerial, professional, or technical skills, which has helped to raise the average income of all service workers to levels close to those in manufacturing.

These trends in job growth are mirroring the fact that now more than ever, job creation in the US is skewing along educational, and high-skill lines. The "middle ground" may be losing way, especially in traditional manufacturing. The fastest growing employment sectors in services are now educa-

Private Service Transactions by Type, 1986 - 1995
(millions of dollars)

US Imports	1986	1990	1993	1994	1995*
Total Private Services	65,576	99,333	115,448	125,902	129,655
Travel	25,913	37,349	40,713	43,562	45,855
Overseas	20,311	28,929	31,859	34,585	n/a
Canada	3,034	3,541	3,692	3,912	n/a
Mexico	2,568	4,879	5,162	5,065	n/a
Passenger Fares	6,505	10,531	11,313	12,696	14,313
Other Transportation	17,817	25,168	26,558	28,373	29,205
Freight	11,888	14,353	14,846	16,444	17,089
Port Services	5,254	9,920	10,817	11,011	11,215
Other	674	895	895	919	902
Royalties and License Fees	1,401	3,135	4,863	5,666	6,312
Affiliated	917	2,206	3,462	3,852	5,148
US parents' transactions	118	239	234	248	430
US affiliates' transactions	799	1,967	3,228	3,604	4,718
Unaffiliated	484	931	1,401	1,814	1,163
Other Private Services	13,941	23,150	31,999	35,605	33,970
Affiliated	3,915	9,118	10,606	11,602	13,723
Unaffiliated	10,026	14,033	21,395	24,003	20,247
Education	433	658	753	791	877
Financial Services	1,769	2,475	5,558	6,835	1,707
Insurance, Net Premiums	2,201	1,910	3,107	3,405	4,481
Telecommunications	3,253	5,583	6,193	6,828	6,773
Business, Professional, and					
Technical services	1,253	1,891	4,046	4,227	4,502
Advertising	77	243	644	736	n/a
Computer and Data Processing	32	44	304	386	n/a
Research, Development, and Testing	76	210	247	281	n/a
Management consulting	60	135	280	283	n/a
Legal Services	40	111	317	428	n/a
ACE	301	170	336	296	n/a
Installation, repair of equipment	467	714	837	739	n/a
Medical Services	1,053	1,627	2,965	3,149	n/a
Other Unaffiliated Services	1,317	1,780	2,817	2,994	8,132

*full detail not available
Source: Survey of Current Business, September 1995

tionally based—in high knowledge, high technology sectors such as computer software, legal and advertising services, and telecommunications. These areas are becoming the United States' comparative advantage in trade overseas.

The world is already taking advantage of America's technical reserve, as evidenced by the fact that the US has been the global leader in the production and export of services. To remain competitive in a sophisticated and competitive international marketplace, firms will require superior service inputs—and that translates into human capital. The United States is endowed with a dynamic and highly-educated pool of workers with a widely varying range of knowledge and skills that serve as valuable inputs into the world economy.

Services and Economic Restructuring

Historically, investment in services overseas by US firms has involved the establishment of a subsidiary in a host country in order to sell the service to the local market. In today's global economy, services investment is also run along industrial lines as well, with export trade being a key part of the story. The growing role of services overseas arises not only from a growing demand for services by local (foreign) consumers, but also from the increasing demand by large US multinational firms for services related to their industrial production overseas. Now when a large US firm produces abroad, it is accompanied by an array of in-house and outside service support-related activities as well.

Developing economies are also replacing imports of government (e.g. public sector or transnational) services with the use of private business services. This bodes well for US exporters of these services, especially in such areas as architectural, construction, and engineering, and management consulting.

The United States is, slowly but surely, continuing to replace traditional manufacturing industries such as automotive, apparel, mining and metals with high tech manufacturing industries that, in turn, have a lot of "services spin off." In this economic restructuring and technology shift, there is now a direct link between manufacturing's well-being and services growth. Many high tech manufacturing jobs need sophisticated services support—for example, computer hardware needs software development, marketing services, distribution, and finance. Application/engineering products need skilled consultants to adapt products to specific customer requirements. And fully modernized plants need sophisticated maintenance and facilities support. Is IBM a manufacturer of computers or a service provider? The answer is both. In the economy of the future, the enmeshment of goods with services will become even more obvious.

In fact, the companies that survive at home and expand successfully overseas will be the ones that successfully combine services and goods. The growth industries of the future will be semiconductors, computers, optical equipment, biotechnology, medical equipment, electronics, pharmaceuticals, and industrial and scientific instruments. Related services include banking, health and medical services, information services, insurance, legal services, management consulting and public relations, with many of these now enjoying annual growth rates of 8 to 10 percent. Services industries now outpace America's goods producers not only in employment, but in capital spending, corporate profit rates, and trade growth.

The new manufacturing also is contracting out more and more of its services outside the company. The temporary employment sector in part mirrors the growing diversity of service-based employment. No longer do temporary personnel agencies send out only secretaries and receptions. Now, professional agencies are contracting out lawyers, accountants, technicians, and human resource people. Over the last ten years, the increase in the number of high skilled, high paying service jobs held by women in such fields as education and health care has increased, helping to lower the wage gap in median earnings between women and men. In this sense, then, the new knowledge-based services and their international competitiveness will rest substantially on how this country continues to invest in its capital and human resources, especially in education, itself a service industry.

Government Policy

Compounding the excitement of the service sector's phenomenal growth is the prospect for increased trade liberalization. Inaugurating the past decade of negotiations was the 1985 US-Israel Free Trade Agreement, which recognized the importance of free trade in services for the first time. In 1989, the US-Canada Free Trade Agreement (CFTA) incorporated a comprehensive international understanding of the service sector.

Top Five Destinations for US Service Exports — 1995

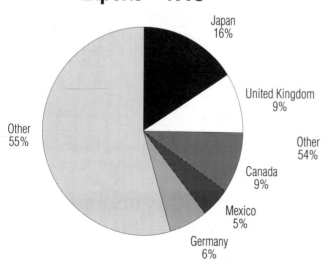

Japan 16%
United Kingdom 9%
Other 54%
Canada 9%
Mexico 5%
Germany 6%
Other 55%

Top Five US Service Imports by Country of Origin — 1995

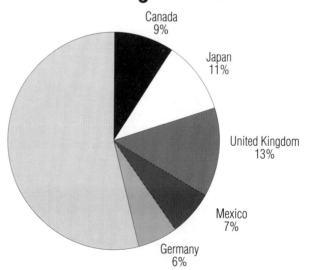

Canada 9%
Japan 11%
United Kingdom 13%
Mexico 7%
Germany 6%

Note: 1994 imports totalled $126 billion. Exports totalled $185 billion.

Source: Survey of Current Business, September 1995

The 1993 conclusion of the Uruguay Round on the General Agreement on Tariffs and Trade (GATT) and the subsequent formation of the World Trade Organization (WTO) resulted in a much larger inclusion of agreements helping to expand worldwide services trade. GATT's General Agreement on Trade in Services (GATS) has specific rules that will give many US service companies better access to foreign markets and guarantee fair treatment by their governments. The rules apply to specific services, including tourism, wholesale distribution, systems consulting, ACE, and accounting. Improved protection of intellectual property rights will also benefit software industries. Discussions are also continuing for some industries that were not included in the Uruguay Round—entertainment, for example. Most GATT signatories have also agreed to end payments restrictions—such as exchange controls or limits on access to hard currencies.

These developments in international trade negotiations are just beginning to reflect the requirements of a contemporary world economy, and thus bolster the prospect for continued high growth in the trade of services into the 21st century. And as of January 31, 1994, US negotiating efforts also came to fruition with the implementation of the North American Free Trade Agreement (NAFTA), again including rules governing trade in services. Because the CFTA had already dealt

Principal Means of Exporting Services

There are different ways of selling services across borders. Direct selling is by no means the primary method for residents of one country to provide services to residents of another. The establishment of a subsidiary in one country by a foreign firm is still in many sectors a more typical means, as when a foreign owned banking affiliate provides retail banking services in a second country. In the past, direct investment was the primary means of foreign participation in markets that were once local; now trade is often the major means of delivering services abroad. The following list samples some of the typical routes for selling services:

International Consulting

International consulting, also termed transient service export, occurs when a US businessperson renders a service to a foreign client on a short-term basis. International consulting is considered an export because a US citizen exports their skills temporarily and, upon completion of a project, the US citizen is compensated by a foreign national.

Direct Exporting

Because the value of some services is embedded in the tangible products associated with these services, the export of a service sometimes can be shipped much like a manufactured good. Examples of this type of service export include books, pharmaceuticals and software. Interestingly, these "service-derived" exports fall in the merchandise balance of payments, not in the services balance of payments.

Telematic Trading

Telematic trade is another means of exporting a service and is one which involves the transfer of knowledge and information abroad via telecommunications. This includes technical information and data transferred (or exported) over the telephone, by facsimile, electronic mail and via the Internet.

Royalties and Licensing Agreements

According to the Bureau of Economic Analysis, royalties and licensing fees consist of receipts and payments for the use of patented techniques, processes, formulas, and other intangible property rights used in goods production, as well as copyrights, trademarks, franchises, rights to broadcast live events, and other intangible rights. Licensing and other agreements for the use of intangible property rights provide an important means for transferring technology and for marketing goods; thus, they provide an important alternative or complement to direct exporting.

Franchising

A franchise is a business arrangement in which an established business gives an independent party (the franchisee) the rights to use its brand names or trademarks, and transfers knowledge which is essential to running the business. These franchises also qualify as "exported services." The reason for this is that a foreign franchisee pays the US franchisor for the use of trademarks, knowledge, and marketing and merchandising know-how. Foreign franchises fall under the export classification for the same reason licensing agreements do: a resident of the US sells a proven idea (service) to a resident of another country.

Providing Services to Foreign Visitors

This export can be simply defined as a service performed and completed in the United States and sold directly to a foreigner while in the United States. For instance, a German citizen may pay a visit to a barber while on vacation in the United States. Although the service provider, at the time of provision, may not be aware he is involved in a service export transaction, this is precisely what is occurring. This kind of export is very common in the travel and health care industries, when foreigners visit the cinema or utilize medical facilities while in the US. Specifically, the reason this transaction is considered an export in that it follows the balance of payments definition of a service export, where the services produced by residents of one country and paid for by the residents of another.

US International Sales of Private Services, 1986 –1995

* Note: There was no information available for the sales to foreign persons for 1994 and 1995.

☐ Cross border exports   ◆ Sales to foreign persons by foreign affiliates of US companies

Source: Survey of Current Business, September 1995

with services, much of the benefit to service providers from NAFTA will involve trade with Mexico. Major benefactors will be small and minority-owned firms, entertainment, finance, insurance, and trucking. Limitations on foreign ownership in certain industries such as insurance and retailing and wholesaling will be phased out. Importantly, NAFTA also guarantees intellectual property protection by extending national treatment to foreign owners of trade secrets, patents, and copyrights. In Mexico, US service providers will be able to establish businesses on an equal footing with national firms and will no longer be required to hire additional nationals, utilize local content, limit the types of products offered, or restrict the size of the firm.

For the past several years, services exports have been a major focus of US trade policy, as articulated by the Services Initiative of the National Export Strategy. This initiative is spearheaded by the Secretary of Commerce through a coordinating committee of 17 agency members. The Services Initiative creates a business-government partnership that is seeking to reduce or eliminate foreign government roadblocks to market access; focus trade-promotion efforts on the most promising foreign markets and sectors; enlist the entire US government in an effort to win more overseas contracts; and make trade finance more readily available. Other trade negotiations in recent years that have focused on services include TRIPS—Trade Related Intellectual Property Rights; the US-Japan Framework agreements, and the agreement with China on intellectual property protection. Also in March, 1996, a working group on services was established in Cartagena as part of the current Free Trade Area of the Americas (FTAA) process.

The US Foreign Commercial Service has a team of trade specialists dedicated to helping service firms exports. The team leader can be contacted at the US Export Assistance Center in Long Beach, telephone (310) 980-4550.

Services Defined

There is no one true accepted definition of just what comprises the services sector in our economy today. Some analysts broadly define services as the "residual" category that includes all output not originating from goods producing sectors: these being agriculture, mining, manufacturing, and construction. Definition is also difficult because many goods producing activities now contain a large and growing service component, as we've explained earlier.

The economist Simon Kuznets stated that the basic attribute of a service industry was the absence of a good: none of the activities' outcomes results in any significant way in the production of commodity, rendering a different kind of product that is intangible and not easily measured. Under this very broad definition, service producing industries encompass retail and wholesale trade, finance, insurance, real estate, transportation, utilities, communication, miscellaneous services, and government, while manufacturing, mining, construction and agriculture comprise the goods producing sectors.

The government service sector is generally excluded from the service sector, separating public and private services. In its national income and product accounts, the Bureau of Economic Analysis (BEA) classifies the government sector separately. The BEA also excludes transportation, utilities, communications, wholesale and retail trade, classifying them as distributive industries. It is interesting to note that under current practice,

US Purchases of Services from Foreigners, 1986 – 1995

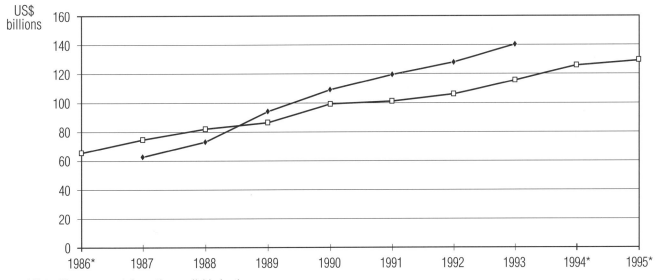

* Note: There was no information available for the
sales to US persons for 1986, 1994, or 1995.

─□─ Cross border imports   ─◆─ Sales to US persons by US affiliates of foreign companies

Source: Survey of Current Business, September 1995

government statisticians include services in the value of goods if they are performed internally, but report them separately as services, if they are purchased or contracted out.

This simple and somewhat fuzzy non-goods definition is far too broad; concurrently, the narrowest definition of services as described by the BEA does not include many intangible outputs that are relevant to international trade. Increasingly, the service sector also includes a segment of service providers that are highly specialized or technologically advanced, such as health care specialists, software designers, lawyers, business consultants, entertainers, educators and a number of other service providers with specialized know-how. The chief providers of these services are small- and medium-sized private firms (those with fewer than 500 employees). The following is the US government's definition of services:

> *"All economic activities of private firms whose outputs are other than tangible goods, as enumerated in the Trade and Tariff Act of 1984, that include, but are not limited to, banking, insurance, transportation, communications, data processing, retail and wholesale trade, advertising, accounting, construction, design and engineering, management consulting, real estate, professional services, entertainment, education, health care, and tourism."*

For the purposes of this book, services will include all privately sold services in the US (including unaffiliated and affiliated). The major categories are travel (including tourism), passenger fares, other transportation, royalties and license fees on branded or trademark products, other private services, and unaffiliated services, which includes education,

finance, insurance, telecommunications, business, professional and technical. Excluded are military transactions and government receipts and expenditures (the cost of maintaining US embassies overseas, for example).

The following listing provides additional classifications of the various service industries. Included are examples of service providers and activities associated with these providers within each grouping.

Travel, Tourism and Leisure Services

The largest single category within the US service sector, the travel and tourism industry involves, quite simply, all businesses involved in its related services. Recreational and cultural services are also included. The industry is diverse and includes services in transportation, lodging, food and beverage service, recreation, purchases of incidentals consumed while in transit and traveling on commercial airlines. An increase in business travel has created the need for various services, such as "sky phones" and "red-carpet" clubs for businesspeople in airports. Other common travel services involve taxi cabs, campgrounds, automobile rental, travel agents, and commercial air, rail, and ocean transportation services.

Royalties and License Fees

Royalties and licensing fees include payments for the use of copyrights, trademarks, patents, technology, franchises, and manufacturing rights. Other fees can include charges for special services, rental payments under operating leases, and research and development costs. US exports of royalties and license fees far surpass imports. Direct and other investment income is not generally discussed here; neither is real estate income and workers' remittances.

Business Support Services

This group includes firms that render services to other business establishments. These services include work which is performed by individuals with higher specialized knowledge and who commonly possess special qualifications or even professional licensing. Examples include: advertising agencies, security guard services, credit reporting agencies, marketing consultants, management consulting and employment agencies.

Financial and Insurance Services

Financial services cover a range of offerings that manage capital, invest funds, and extend credit to individuals, governments and businesses. Financial services include: investment advice, securities brokerage, credit card services and collection management, and public offerings. Financial institutions include: commercial and investment banks, venture capital firms, and securities firms.

Entertainment Services

Entertainment services satisfy needs for social and recreational activity. Examples include: motion picture and television production, movie theaters, and amusement parks.

Health Care Services

This group includes businesses and practitioners engaged in furnishing private medical, surgical, and other health services to individuals. Examples include: medical and dental offices, nursing homes, primary care medical clinics, hospitals, laboratories, and blood banks.

Educational Services

Includes schools, colleges, and private learning institutions. Academic or technical institutions which provide instruction or assistance by providing libraries, student exchange programs, and curriculum development programs also encompass the educational services category.

Information and Data Processing Services

Development in new areas of high technology have created a demand for services that either "invent" or complement these technologies. The providers in this growing category concentrate their efforts primarily in the computer, multimedia, and related technology industries. Examples of services and technologies that underpin them are: systems integration services and software, turnkey systems and hardware, pilot training and flight simulators, business presentations and multimedia capabilities enabled through CD-ROM technology.

Transportation and Distributive Services

Distributive services facilitate the movement of goods, services, and people. Such services involve trucking, railroads, shipping, postal services, couriers, freight forwarders and ports. Retailing and wholesaling functions also support the distribution of services by circulating goods into the hands of customers.

Science-based Services

This group includes commercial establishments which are primarily involved in physical and biological research and development on a contract or fee basis. Science-based services could also be considered technological but are distinguished by having a natural science basis. Examples include: water and sanitation services, commercial food research, agricultural, and rural development and biotechnology services.

Architecture, Construction and Engineering Services (ACE)

Construction services include the building and renovation of homes, manufacturing facilities, hospitals, office buildings, hotels, and site preparation. Quite often construction is considered a "good" rather than a service because the end-product results in physical building.

Repair and Leasing Services

A service can also replace or repair a manufactured product on a temporary or long-term basis. A repair service fixes the existing product, thus eliminating the need to purchase the identical item again. Other common examples include refrigeration and air-conditioning services and the repair of watches, clocks, and jewelry.

Leasing involves the temporary use of a manufactured product for rent, sometimes with the potential of owning it in the future. Most end-users of leasing are businesses. Commonly leased goods include: trucks, aircraft, computers, containers, furniture, and fixtures. Other rental services not commonly recognized as such are laundromats, hotel rooms, and temporary employment services.

Communications Services

Communications services involve broadcast and point to point transmission of voice, images, and data, facsimile machines, news services, radio, and television. Telecommunications can also be considered a distributive service in the sense that telecommunications can now be used to send documents.

Personal Services

Less relevant to trade, this category includes businesses primarily involved in providing services directly to the individual consumer. A common characteristic of personal services is that the customer usually visits the place of business for the service to be rendered. Examples include: dry cleaning plants, barber shops, funeral parlors, and shoe repair shops.

Chapter 2:
GETTING READY TO EXPORT

Deciding to Export

The decision to export a service is a serious one, whether you are an individual or a large firm. Nonetheless, many companies make the decision to export their services haphazardly, without carefully screening markets, conducting research, considering costs, or weighing alternatives. Some companies succeed in their export operations despite these oversights, but many more fail, perhaps needlessly. When early export efforts are unsuccessful because of poor planning, the company will probably be misled into abandoning exporting altogether. But, with the proper preparation, exporting can become a positive strategic move to increase profit margins, stimulate innovative service ideas, and reduce dependence on a single market. The key lies in making a knowledgeable and well thought-out decision about what, when, where, and how to export.

There are several ways to gauge the overseas market potential of a company's services—not the least of which is to assess the success of the service in domestic markets. If a service sells successfully in the US, there is a good chance that it will also be successful in markets abroad, at least wherever similar needs and conditions exist. If a service is successful in the US, a careful analysis of why it sells well will greatly aid in the determination of if and where it will be successful abroad. And, even if US sales of the service have begun to decline, sizable export markets may still exist, especially if the service once did well in the US but is now losing market share to competitive services, or facing declining market growth due to saturation. This will be especially true for expansion into developing markets which did not have early access to, or resources for, the particular service.

In markets that differ from the US market, services may need some modification before they become marketable. Differences between markets may be due to climate and environmental factors, local availability of raw materials or capital inputs, lower wage costs, lower purchasing power, the availability of foreign exchange (lack of hard currency), government import controls, and many other factors. Each of these factors must be examined and considered in making the decision to export. Market research can aid this process greatly.

In this regard, the availability and quality of market research becomes an important factor in the determination of whether or not to export. If the service is not new or unique, low-cost market research may already be available to help assess its overseas market potential. If, however, it is new or unique, or the target country is only newly developed or developing, market research will be largely unavailable or prohibitively expensive.

If the service is unique or has important features that are hard to duplicate abroad, however, there are compensating factors which may override the lack of research in making the decision to export. For a unique or specialized service, the chances are good for finding an export market despite any hard data indicating firm demand. Competition for a unique or specialized service may be nonexistent or very slight, while demand may be quite high.

In short, to ensure the success of a new export venture, the potential exporter must be clear about both the realities of the targeted international marketplace and its own internal capabilities. International expansion will put new demands on the firm due to the shuffling of existing resources or the procurement of entirely new personnel into export-related activities. Increased demands will also likely be placed on the company's production capacities and its finances, and consideration of how these demands will be met must be made. A thorough internal analysis should be performed before a service firm explores international markets. A careful examination of management objectives, international experience, service capability, and financial capacity are important. The firm must be certain it is equipped with appropriate in-house capabilities to meet the demands of exporting.

Analysis of Internal Capabilities

A practical examination of a firm's internal capability is important in assessing its potential to expand internationally. A prospective exporter must be confident of in-house capabilities before it seriously considers exporting. Below are some important questions to ask in making this assessment:

- What is the motive to export? Is the motive sound (e.g. increasing sales volume or developing broader customer base) or is it frivolous (e.g., the decision maker wants an excuse to travel)?

- How committed is top management to an export effort, and is it ready, willing, and able to commit the necessary resources to support international expansion.

- Will international expansion be at the expense of profitable domestic operations, and will current customers be neglected in the export process?

- What does the company hope to achieve through exporting, in respect to financial gain, business growth, and long-term development?

- What current in-house international expertise does the company have (international sales experience, language capabilities, etc.)?

- What organizational structure is required to ensure that export sales are adequately supported and serviced, and are there current or reasonably expected resources available to allocate to export operations?

- Who will be responsible for the export organization and staff development, and who will follow through after the planning is done?

- What special training or staff development will be required to successfully expand internationally?

- What is required in the way of adaptation or modification in order to successfully export and can these requirements be reasonably met?

- What amount of capital can be committed to export and marketing, and how much of export operations costs can be currently supported?

- Does the company have any experience at all with exporting, or have inquiries from abroad already been received?

- Who are the primary domestic and foreign competitors to be faced when exporting the service?

The Export Qualifier Program (EQP) of the US Department of Commerce's International Trade Administration can help a US firm decide if it should export. The EQP is a computer program that provides a preliminary view of a firm's organization and strengths. The program analyzes five aspects of a firm: its business background, motivation for going international, top management's commitment to exporting, and assessment of both overall strengths and market-specific strengths. Based on responses to a series of questions, a matrix graphically illustrates the firm's organizational and product "readiness" to export. The EQP can provide an unbiased, clear-cut evaluation of a service firm's strengths and weaknesses as they affect its export potential. The EQP is an effective tool to aid in the decision of whether or not a service firm should export and to identify strengths and weaknesses to improve a firm's present export performance.

Analyzing External Factors

Even if a company decides it has the internal capacity and capability to expand internationally, it must also research and evaluate external factors before making the decision to export. Many of these factors will be outside the company's immediate control, and they must therefore be carefully considered in the export decision.

- Which services or portions of service packages are most likely to be exportable, and what modifications, if any, must be made to adapt them for overseas markets?

- What particular barriers lie in each of your target markets, and is it reasonably possible to break through these barriers?

- In each targeted country, what is the basic customer profile, and what marketing and distribution channels are available to reach these customers?

- What are the sales and profit potential for each service in each foreign market?

- What special challenges pertain to each market with regard to competition, cultural differences and import controls, and what strategy will be used to address them?

- How will the service's export sales price be determined and will it be competitive and profitable?

Developing an Export Strategy

If a company is comfortable with its internal resource capability and the potential for success in foreign markets, the next step is to construct an export strategy. Formulating an export strategy based on good information and proper assessment increases the chances that the best options will be chosen, that resources will be used effectively, and that efforts will consequently be carried through to completion.

An export strategy's objective is to set forth goals for operations, marketing, human resources, and control. The goal of a strategic plan is to organize your export effort efficiently in order to maximize your chances of success in foreign markets while minimizing disruption of the quality of your day-to-day domestic business. An effective export plan must assemble facts, constraints, and goals, then create an action statement that takes all of these into account. It sets forth time schedules for implementation, and it marks milestones so that the degree of success can be measured and assessed. The written plan that details a company's export strategy will describe the export venture on a short- and long-term basis. The formal export plan will enforce the commitment of everyone involved and clarify each person's role.

The first time an export plan is developed, it should be kept simple. It need be only a few pages long, since important market data and planning elements may not yet be available. The initial planning effort itself gradually generates more information and insight that can be incorporated into more sophisticated planning documents later.

Implementing the Plan

From the start, the plan should be viewed as a management tool, not as a static document or strategy. For instance, objectives in the plan should be compared with actual results as a measure of the success of different strategies. Furthermore, the company should not hesitate to modify the plan and make it more specific as new information and experience are gained.

The way a company exports its services can have a significant effect on its export plan and specific marketing strategies. Different strategies and methods must be tried and compared to determine the company's optimal level of involvement in the export process. Companies considering export strategies must decide whether to fill orders from domestic buyers who then become the actual exporters; to seek out domestic buyers who represent foreign end users or customers; export indirectly through intermediaries; or to export directly themselves. A more detailed plan is recommended for companies that intend to export directly as this method is the most difficult and requires the most commitment of management time and attention. Companies choosing to export indirectly require much simpler plans as not so many resources are devoted specifically to export operations.

Despite the unquestioned value of planning for export, however, many companies begin export activities haphazardly, without carefully screening markets or options for market entry. While these companies may nonetheless have a measure of success, they may overlook better export opportunities. In the event that early export efforts are unsuccessful because of poor planning, the company may even be misled into abandoning exporting altogether. In many cases, this is an unnecessary loss of growth opportunities.

Creating a strategic plan will allow you to continue to deliver your services domestically, while simultaneously launching an export campaign balanced with your internal goals associated with human resources, costs and capacity.

Finding Service Export Advice

For companies making initial plans to export or to export in new areas, considerable advice and assistance are available from the US government. It is easy to overestimate the problems involved in exporting or to get embroiled in difficulties that can be avoided. For these and other good reasons, it is important to get expert counseling and assistance from the beginning. Do not be overwhelmed by the number of sources of advice available. It is not necessary to go to all of them, although it is valuable to know that they exist and to pursue at least a few of them. Each individual or organization contacted can contribute different perspectives based on different experience and skills.

While having many sources to choose from can be advantageous, deciding where to begin can also be difficult. Some advice from experienced exporters may be helpful in this regard. Thus, the best place to start is the Trade Promotion Coordinating Committee (TPCC), which harnesses all the resources of the federal government to serve American exporting business. The TPCC conducts export conferences, coordinates trade events and missions that cut across federal agencies, and it operates an export information center that can help exporters find the right federal program to suit their needs. The telephone number of the TPCC is 1-800-USA-TRADE.

The local US Department of Commerce Office can not only provide information about the TPCC and what it offers, but can give export counseling advice in its own right and can direct companies toward other government and private sector export services. There are 41 District and 21 Branch offices located throughout the United States, staffed with trade specialists who can provide trade-related information as well as information about several of the sources listed below.

US Export Assistance Centers (USEAC)

USEACs are customer-focused, federal export assistance offices. USEACs streamline export marketing and trade finance assistance by integrating together in a single location the counselors and services of the US&FCS, the Export-Import Bank of the US, the Small Business Administration (SBA), and the US Agency for International Development (USAID). In addition, through cooperation with local public and private export service partners, USEACs increase the depth and range of export services available to clients and promote a more rational and integrated delivery network. USEACs target export-ready businesses, particularly small- and medium-sized firms.

USEACs provide firms with one-on-one counseling to identify target markets and develop marketing strategies. They also offer guidance in various areas relating to export finance, such as export credit insurance and pre- and post-export financing.

Export Councils

USDOC District Offices work closely with 51 Export Councils (ECs), comprising nearly 1,700 business and trade experts. ECs host export seminars and educational programs on various aspects of trade and members of the EC provide counseling and advice to new entrants to the international trade arena. For more information regarding Export Council activities, contact the Office of Public & Private Programs at (202) 482-2975, or your local US Department of Commerce Office.

International Economic Policy (IEP)

This is the DOC source for information on trade potential for US products in specific countries. IEP specialists look at the needs of an individual firm wishing to sell in a particular country in the full context of that country's economy, trade policies, and political situation. Desk officers collect information on a specific country's regulations, tariffs, business practices, economic and political developments, trade data, market size, and rate of growth, keeping a current pulse on the potential markets for US products, services and investments.

Trade Development (TD) Industry Specialists

TDs work with manufacturing and service industry associations and firms to identify trade opportunities and obstacles by product or service, industry sector, and market, as well as develop product marketing plans and programs.

American Chambers of Commerce

These are non-governmental entities which support communication and business relations between foreign country firms and US companies, and monitor bilateral business and political relationships between the two countries. Contact: The Chamber of Commerce of the United States, International Division, 1615 H Street, NW, Washington, DC 20062; telephone (202) 463-5460; fax (202) 463-5836.

Small Business Administration (SBA)

Provides several consulting services to help new exporters. Exporters eligible for SBA assistance include manufacturers and service providers with a maximum of 1,500 employees; wholesalers with maximum annual sales of US$9.5 million; and service providers with maximum average annual sales of US$2 million over the last three years. Call (800) 827-5722.

Minority Business Development Agency (MBDA)

Identifies minority business enterprises in selected industries and provides information on market and product needs worldwide. Call (202) 482-3237; fax (202) 482-5117.

Office of Service Industries (OSI)

OSI provides trade promotion, industry analysis, and export marketing advice. Service trade specialists keep abreast of industry trends overseas and trade barriers unique to service industries, and maintain relevant statistics on service exports. Contact: Office of Service Industries, 14th & Constitution Avenues, NW, HCHB Room 1124, Washington, DC 20230; telephone (202) 482-3575; fax (202) 482-2669.

Export Legal Assistance Network (ELAN)

Qualified attorneys will provide free initial consultations to small companies to answer basic legal questions concerning international trade and investment. Call (800) 827-5722.

State Assistance

Several state agencies throughout the country have a wide range of export assistance programs available. Contact: The National Association of State Development Agencies, 750 First Street, Suite 710, Washington, DC 20002; telephone (202) 898-1302; fax (202) 898-1302.

Office of Minority Small Business and Capital Ownership Development

Encourages minority small business participation in international trade through its management and technical Assistance Program. Contact: Division of Management and

Technical Assistance; telephone (202) 205-6420; fax (202) 205-7549.

Agent Distributor Service (ADS)

A fee-based service which locates qualified foreign import representatives, agents and distributors suited to a company's specific needs. The charge for an ADS search is approximately US$250 and results take between four and six weeks. Contact your nearest USDOC Office for further information.

Matchmaker Trade Delegations

Enable new-to-export and new-to-market firms to meet prescreened prospects who are interested in their products or services in overseas markets. For further information, call Export Promotion Services, International Trade Administration; telephone (202) 482-3119.

Gold Key Service

Provides pre-scheduled business appointments with prospective trading partners in a target market, including agents, distributors, joint venture partners or licensees. Orientation briefings, market research, and assistance in developing a follow-up strategy are standard features of each Gold Key package. Any US firm offering technical expertise, consulting services, manufactured products or components that are at least 51 percent US-made are eligible for the US&FCS Gold Key Service. The fee varies from country to country. Contact your nearest DOC Office for more information.

Foreign Traders Index (FTI)

Database retrieval service provides US exporters with names, addresses, products, company size and other relevant information on foreign firms interested in importing US goods and services. Contacts are collected and maintained by Commerce Offices and Commercial Officers at foreign posts. Contact your nearest USDOC Office.

Investment Missions Program

This Overseas Private Investment Corporation (OPIC) program is designed to give businesspeople the opportunity to meet with key business leaders, potential joint venture partners, and government officials of a host country. Contact: Investor Services; telephone (202) 336-8662; fax (202) 408-5145.

Trade and Professional Organizations

Service firms should always be active members of international trade and industry specific professional associations as they can serve as key resources for service exporters. Please see the industry analyses in the back of this book for professional service-related organizations.

Chapter 3:
MARKET RESEARCH

Once a firm decides to do business internationally, the next step is to perform the necessary market research to determine the best locations, markets, and techniques for exporting or investing. Adequate market research is perhaps more important with services firms due to the ways which business is transacted, since providing services overseas can require customer contact and a long-term presence inside countries.

Extensive study of overseas markets and specific sales opportunities can decrease the possibility of serious and expensive problems in the long run. Service firms should therefore have a clear assessment of their targeted foreign business environments and potential customers prior to committing themselves to the international marketplace. Adequate market research will help to find new markets, hold on to the ones already cracked, fight the competition, and react quickly to sales opportunities.

Market research includes all the methods that a company uses to determine which foreign markets have the best potential for its products. Results of this research inform the firm of such important things as the largest markets for its services, the fastest growing markets, market trends and outlook, specific market conditions and practices, and companies competing to sell the same service.

International Research

Generally, the tools and techniques for research are the same for both foreign and domestic marketing, but the extent and availability of market information in foreign countries can be quite different than that available in the United States. The quality of information available to a foreign marketer varies from country to country and from service to service. International marketers are usually called upon to develop the ability for imaginative and deft application of tried and tested techniques in sometimes totally strange environments. The overall objective, however, remains the same—to answer questions with current, valid information that a company can use to design and implement a successful export strategy for a particular country.

The primary difference between domestic and foreign market research is that researching foreign markets is much broader is scope and requires all types of information essential to conducting business abroad. Researching a foreign market can involve general information about the country or area; specific market information used to make advertising, pricing, or distribution decisions; or information about social, economic, and consumer trends within specific markets or countries. A comprehensive market research program in a foreign country usually involves all three types of research.

Scope of Research

Market research should include topics such as market structure, culture, economic trends, and consumer behavior. Unlike the goods sector, numerous reports or detailed statistics are often not available with the service sector trade. However, market intelligence can always be gathered, and it is up to the supplier to connect with all possible sources of information, both firsthand and secondary. It's best not to rely solely on an agent or distributor for this information for service-related products (such as software, for example). Their understanding of the local marketplace is important, but should always be verified. In many cases, this may not even be an option. The intangibility of a service product makes ongoing personal contact a basic component of the research process as well as the sale.

Country-specific research entails researching broad, country-level characteristics, such as per capita GNP, regulatory environment, system of government and law, inflation rate, currency controls, major business cities and regions, development plans, foreign aid, and import and export trends. After several countries have been identified as potential markets, specific industry research must be conducted to identify relevant regulations affecting the industry, competition, market share, industrial and technological sophistication, distribution channels, business practices, professional licensing requirements, and primary competitors. This will probably narrow the potential markets somewhat so that more in-depth research can be conducted on end users (or consumers). Market research on consumers analyzes the end users of a given service and identifies a pool of customers with similar characteristics and consumption habits. A consumer population can be segmented according to any set of criteria: by age, income, education level, family size, or preferences. This involves identifying different categories of customers, potential market size, consumer demand for the service, and channels of distribution.

Since markets are always changing, market intelligence should be continual. The size of the firm, its capabilities, and the strategic importance of the market will often determine the resources devoted to front-end research. Eric Wiklund in his book *International Marketing Strategies* cites specific factors in successful research which can be applied to services:

- Identify target countries. Even a very large international operation with ample resources must prioritize overseas markets and know where to apply sales power.

- Stay alert to political and economic trends in the priority markets. This is especially important now that some trade barriers in services are breaking down and deregulation is occurring.

- Decide what field and logistic resources you will need to break into new markets or expand existing ones.

- Plan promotions geared to sales objectives and budgets. Learn all about local promotion schemes; possibilities for trade fairs and conventions, where and how to advertise.

- Budget the funds needed to accomplish reasonable marketing objectives.

- Learn about the competition: their policies, staffing, sales forces, and methods. Estimate what your competitors are doing in the local market.

- Evaluate end users and consumers and decide how best to get to them. How you market a service may differ in each country.

Wiklund also stresses key pitfalls to avoid when doing your research:

- incomplete fact gathering, or ignoring facts when they don't agree with the opinion of management;

- over-reliance on statistics that may be dated, and often will not reflect the most recent developments;

- letting the intelligence information sift through several layers of people before it arrives at the hand of the decision-maker; and

- excessive emphasis on countries, companies, and products, but not enough on people. Knowing who your competitors are—as people—their strengths and weaknesses, can be critically important, particularly in the service industries.

Methodology

A company may research a market by using either primary or secondary data resources. Micro-oriented market intelligence is found through on-site and in-person marketing research efforts, otherwise known as primary research. Information about the inner workings of a foreign business, such as their corporate culture, daily operations, and purchasing behavior is difficult to acquire without a local presence. Even with the latest and most reliable market intelligence, market segments are mobile and are perpetually changing. Primary market research has the advantage of being tailored to the company's needs and provides answers to most questions, but the collection of such data is time-consuming and expensive.

When conducting secondary market research, a company collects data from compiled sources, such as trade statistics for a country or a product. Working with secondary sources is less expensive and helps the company focus its marketing efforts.

Although secondary data sources are critical to market research, they do have limitations. The most recent statistics for some countries may be more than two years old. Product breakdowns may be too broad to be of much value. Statistics on services are often simply not available, or statistics may be distorted by incomplete data-gathering techniques. A common problem is that different governments use different definitions for product categories or use different measurement techniques, which results in data impossible to compare.

Yet, even with these limitations, secondary research is a valuable and relatively easy first step for a company to take. It may be the only step needed if the company decides to export indirectly through an intermediary, since the other firm may have advanced research capabilities. Because of the expense of primary market, many firms rely on secondary data sources.

When relevant research questions cannot be answered by secondary data, however, the researcher must collect primary data. Although the methods of collection are similar to those used to collect primary data in the US, researchers encounter added problems when attempting to collect this type of data abroad.

Strategic Market Research Issues

As more companies begin to export their services and more countries become viable export markets effective market research increasingly requires some method of standardization to ensure that results can adequately be compared between different countries. When researching different cultures it is inevitable that some standards will have different reliabilities in different cultures, and even have different reliabilities when utilized by the same individual in evaluating seemingly identical data from different cultures. Marketers have developed a variety of research techniques to address these issues, but there are three traits that any international marketer must employ in order to effectively conduct and analyze market research in a foreign country: a high degree of cultural understanding and sensitivity about the country in which research is being conducted; the ability to adapt available research findings to conditions and circumstances as they exist in the target country; and a high degree of skepticism in evaluating both primary and secondary data, with the ability to recognize discrepancies or unrealistic skews.

In general, the success of a survey depends on the willingness of those questioned to provide the desired information, or their ability to articulate what they know. Cultural differences and language nuances and idioms complicate this process. An additional level of analysis is often required to ensure that the questions were indeed relevant, the respondent understood the questions as the surveyor intended them to be understood, and that both questions and answers were translated accurately.

A recurring problem with cross-national research is that many companies insist on forming issues and evaluating results with reference to their own domestic experience.

While this will certainly take away some of the difficulty of foreign market research, it also limits the effectiveness of this type of research. The process should begin, therefore, with development of specific research objectives relevant to the service intended for export and free of self-reference criteria that will cloud the issue at hand. Market characteristics across diverse cultures must be compared for similarities and differences, and a determination made as to whether standardization or adaptation of research will result in the most reliable data upon which to base an export strategy. Isolating and abandoning self-reference criteria and asking instead the "right" questions are crucial steps in embarking on an effective market research campaign.

This is admittedly difficult. Cross-national research will always give rise to questions of reliability and comparability, but a company should not dismiss its importance nor neglect to engage such research simply because of the difficulties. Rather, it is important to isolate the relevant criteria, assess the difficulty of obtaining the desired information, determine its level of reliability in each market researched, and objectively evaluate the results without reference to domestic standards or cultural norms.

Creating an objective checklist covering a range of issues is the first step to obtaining effective market research. The following is a sample checklist of research issues:

Target Countries

- Which countries offer the best prospective market according to company goals?

Political Environment

- system of government
- government stability and continuity of policies
- internal and external political risk
- current and historical attitudes toward business and more specifically, their business relations with the United States
- national economic and development priorities and goals

Demographics and Economic Conditions

- population size, growth, and distribution
- literacy rate and educational level, availability of labor, and indigenous management potential
- national and per capita income, and distribution of income
- economic growth, gross domestic product (GDP), and industrial sector growth
- role of foreign trade in the economy-percentage of GDP, balance of payments, and debt-service ratio on foreign loans
- foreign exchange risk—inflation rate, controls on the local economy, currency controls, difference between parallel and official exchange rates, and credit regulations

Development Level and Infrastructure

- natural resources
- industrial and technological development
- infrastructure—physical distribution and communication networks

Regulatory Environment

- limitations on trade tariff levels, quotas, non-tariff barriers, and restrictions on payments
- foreign standards, accepted industrial practices, measuring systems, and certification procedures
- export licensing requirements
- hiring practices

Legal Considerations

- code of law vs. common law
- investment and licensing regulations
- employment practices
- anti-trust law
- intellectual property rights, patents, trademarks, and copyrights
- multilateral and bilateral agreements
- reality of the law vs. the letter of the law

Government Assistance

- united States government assistance
- foreign government aids and attitudes toward the specific service being sold
- development incentives, and tax holidays for foreign investors

Customer Profile

- types of customers
- potential market size
- customer need/desire for the service
- buying process and channels of distribution

Business Travel

- customs regulations
- immigration procedures
- professional licensing requirements

Sources of US-Based Market Research

US Department of Commerce

The US Department of Commerce offers several forms of market research. The best country-specific reports are known as country marketing plans (CMPs), and are prepared annually by the commercial sections of US Embassies located in 67 countries. CMPs analyze an individual country's business and economic climate, emphasizing marketing and trade statistics, relative development, and other issues.

Other DOC reports that include information particular to market research for services are: overseas business reports, industry subsector analyses, and best market reports. Some of these are also available on the National Trade Data Bank (see below).

National Trade Data Bank (NTDB)

The NTDB, accessible on-line or on CD-ROM, carries international trade and export data from over 15 US government agencies. The NTDB contains over 100,000 documents covering basic export information, including the DOC's Basic Guide to Exporting, the CIA World Fact Book, and the US Industrial Outlook. The NTDB is available at more than 600 public libraries nationwide and can be purchased for US$35 per single CD-ROM disc or US$360 for a 12-month subscription. Contact: US Department of Commerce, Office of Business Analysis, Room 4885, Washington, DC 20230; telephone (202) 482-1986; fax (202) 482-2164.

The Economic Bulletin Board

The EBB is an on-line service which contains over 3,400 files from all the major economic agencies of the federal government. The EBB contains foreign trade information and daily Trade Opportunities (TOPS), which is an excellent source for service firms interested in bidding opportunities. EBB can be reached from most personal computers equipped with a modem and standard communications software. For further information, call the EBB staff at (202) 482-1986.

The Automated Trade Library Services (ATLS)

The ATLS is a computer-based, comprehensive information system available to all California companies. The program allows California exporters immediate access to a network containing market research, trade leads, trade event listings and other valuable information. For additional information, telephone (310) 590-5965; fax (310) 590-5958.

Customized Sales Survey (CSS)

The CSS is a USDOC custom-tailored research service that provides firms with specific information on marketing and foreign representation for their individual products in selected countries. Research specialists in the targeted country interview distributors, retailers, wholesalers, end-users, and local producers of comparable products and inspect similar products on the market. CSS can provide critical customized marketing information such as: marketing channels for a service, price points, customer preferences, local regulations, and potential representatives and licensing partners. The cost can range from US$800 to US$3,500. Contact the nearest USDOC Office for more information.

Feasibility Studies

Feasibility studies are generally conducted by private firms located in the foreign market who poll the target market, survey potential competition and study target customers. The specifics of a company's service are matched against the realities of the foreign marketplace, providing an approximation of actual service introduction. Information on private firms capable of conducting feasibility studies can be gathered from industry trade associations, US embassies, and foreign embassies in the United States. Funding assistance for feasibility studies is sometimes available. Contact: US Trade and Development Agency, SA-16, Room 309, Washington, DC 20523-1602; telephone (703) 875-4357; fax (703) 875-4009.

Publications

US Industrial Outlook

This practical resource and desk reference for planners, researchers and decision makers analyzes more than 350 industries. It contains a summary of industry highlights, short-term forecasts, narrative analysis and authoritative statistical data for corporate strategists, investors and marketers. Contact: The Department of Commerce or The Reference Press, 6488 Highway 290 E., Austin, Texas, 78723; telephone (512) 454-7778; fax (512) 454-9401.

International Business Practices

This book provides the latest information on business practices in 117 countries within five geographical regions: North and South America, Europe, Asia and the Pacific Rim, the Middle East, and sub-Saharan Africa. It covers types of business organizations, exporting, commercial policies, foreign investment, intellectual property rights, taxation, regulatory agencies and useful contacts for each country. Contact: Department of Commerce.

Journal of Commerce

This daily newspaper offers a data bank with information from the compilation of water borne manifest data. Service exporters can use the Journal of Commerce to trace manufactured products of a particular company with the intention of eventually servicing that firm. This information service can be relatively expensive. As the Journal of Commerce also publishes Trade Opportunity Program (TOPS) leads, it is best to check these first. For information about the Journal of Commercial's services, contact: Journal of Commerce, 2 World Trade Center, 27th Floor, New York, NY 10048; telephone (800) 223-0243.

Other Resources

US Department of State

The USDOS supplies information on bilateral treaty agreements, foreign market reports from US embassies and consulates, and general socioeconomic information of foreign nations. The Department has an extensive publication program which includes background notes on 164 countries and territories. These 6-10 page pamphlets give a brief overview of the society, history, geography, government and economy of foreign countries. For information on Department of State's resources, contact: International Trade Administration, Office of Public Affairs (202) 482-3808. To contact the Department of State directly, call their public information number at (202) 647-4000.

National Technical Information Service (NTIS)

NTIS is a government research clearing house which operates under the aegis of the Department of Commerce. NTIS publishes market share reports which contain both US and selected countries broadly categorized, industry market shares in manufactured goods. These statistics can assist service providers in analyzing complementary products in various markets.

NTIS also publishes country market surveys. These are detailed market studies prepared in-country by foreign or US research firms under contract to the USDOC. Only the leading 10 to 15 overseas markets are covered for individual product categories. The product list includes: communications equipment, electronic components, electronic production and test equipment, food processing machinery, agricultural equipment, computers and related equipment, machine tools, industrial process controls, medical equipment, and laboratory instruments. For information, contact National Technical Information Service, 5285 Port Royal Road, Springfield, VA 22161; telephone (703) 487-4650.

Organization for Economic Cooperation and Development (OECD)

The OECD is made up of Western Europe, the United States, Canada, Japan, and Australia. The organization's members produce the majority of the world's goods and approximately one-half of world trade is intra-OECD. OECD publishes statistics on member countries and at times studies on LDCs (lesser developed countries). Unlike international banking institutions and UN agencies, both of which provide market information and contact leads, the OECD maintains only market data. For further information, telephone (202) 785-6323.

Public Libraries

Many public libraries maintain foreign business directories which have been published by both private and foreign government organizations. If translation is not a problem, some business libraries have foreign telephone books that are useful for researching potential businesses contacts.

Private Consultants

Foreign and US-based consultants can provide in-depth analysis of markets, competitors and technology trends. Consultants often specialize in industry sectors, geographic regions, or functional areas such as finance, law, and taxation.

World Trade Press

World Trade Press publishes a series of Country Business Guides which give detailed information in 25 categories about doing business in the subject country. The company also publishes the "Passport to the World" series on the business, culture, and etiquette of countries of the world. While these are not statistical in nature they do help understand the cultural aspects of doing business in a particular country. Catalog available. 1505 Fifth Avenue, San Rafael, CA 94901; telephone (415) 454-9934; fax (415) 453-7980.

Polyglot International

Matching Service and Market

Raphael Baron, CEO of Polyglot International, feels that adjusting a service to fit a particular market is probably the most important step to success.

"Companies should try to fit their service into a market, not the other way around," Baron said. "They should study a market before entering, find out what is needed, and how they can provide it."

The San Francisco-based localization and multilingual communications firm translates all languages with offices in London, Berlin, and Tokyo, as well as Moscow, Beijing, and Almaty (Kazakhstan). In each case, they have had to adjust their service to find success.

In more advanced countries, Polyglot often provides "localization" of software, a combination of translating and reprogramming applications so they can be successful in other countries. Localization includes "checking the graphical interface, icons, and even re-recording sounds, to make sure nothing in the program is inappropriate or offensive to a particular culture," said Katharine Whipple Vestri, marketing manager for Polyglot.

Software localization is a smaller market in developing countries, however, and Polyglot had to provide other services if they wanted to succeed there. "Polyglot provides legal and technical translating services to developing markets, and interpreters for on-site assignments or meetings," Baron said.

Entering the Country

Polyglot has stayed away from the risky tactic of entering a market "cold," without any awaiting clients.

"Every time we set up an office, it was in response to a specific client," Baron said. They opened up shop in Kazakhstan, for example, by providing interpreters to help Chevron Corp. negotiate and start up deals in the Tengiz oil fields.

Baron said businesses also need a great deal of patience when entering a market, particularly when dealing with the bureaucracies of some countries.

"We had a number of difficulties entering China, for example," Baron said. "The approval process is slow there, plus the government had serious issues about a foreign translating firm entering their country."

Although translating is considered a worthwhile service in the West, the Chinese government has suspicions about what they consider "transfers of information."

"We basically had to explain to a number of people in the government that we were going to provide a useful service to the country," Baron said.

Overcoming Barriers

Polyglot met some other barriers in Russia. "They are constantly changing their taxation and foreign company laws," Baron said. "In order to meet thir requirements, we are constantly staying informed of local laws."

Cultural barriers will exist no matter where a business wants to set up shop. "The best way to beat any cultural differences is to hire local employees," Baron said, "plus you have to follow and have respect for local customs."

"Probably the most difficult barrier for us to break through, especially in Japan, is the overall wariness from local companies," Baron said. "Some companies will just naturally not want to use you." Baron believes the best way to get around this barrier is to offer a needed service and be professional, and businesses will eventually come around.

Help is always around from the local Export Council, as well as from US Commercial Offices at home and within the various countries. "Export Councils are very helpful for networking and giving information about a country," Baron said. "Commercial Offices and embassies are also useful, though, because they are in the countries and can offer direct assistance."

> "Companies should try to fit their service into a market, not the other way around," Raphael Baron said. "They should study a market before entering, find out what is needed, and how they can provide it."

Raphael Baron, CEO (l), Holger Otto Reiter, CFO

Chapter 4:
MARKETING

Services versus Goods

US service exports are highly competitive in the global economy. Primary markets for US services are the European Union, Japan, and Canada, and exports of services to these regions have been growing at 10-15 percent annually. Significant opportunities for export growth also exist in Latin America and Asia, and Central and Eastern Europe. In addition, US service exports to Mexico are expected to grow at an amazing 19 percent annual rate in the years ahead. Historically, many service firms started doing business overseas by following large US multinationals abroad, and then developing a more proactive approach to marketing internationally. With the globalization of goods has often come the globalization of the services needed to support them: In fact, it is now estimated that the six largest US accounting firms now realize over 40 percent of their revenues from overseas; in addition, the 400 largest US construction companies realize over 25 percent of their revenues internationally.

Unique Service Feature	Resulting Marketing Problems
Intangibility:	Services cannot be stored. Services cannot be protected through patents. Services cannot be displayed or communicated. Prices are difficult to set.
Inseparability:	Consumer involved in production. Other consumers involved in production. Centralized mass production of services difficult.
Perishability:	Services cannot be inventoried.
Heterogeneity:	Standardization and quality control difficult to achieve.

Source: "Marketing Services Internationally: Barriers and Management Strategies," *Journal of Services Marketing*, Summer 1991

The US has a strong edge in services that place a premium on know-how, technology, and capital. US firms are also making inroads overseas in industries that have a strong customer service component, such as food franchising and retailing.

When making marketing decisions, the service exporter should keep in mind some universal characteristics of services that set them apart from goods: intangibility, degree of inseparability, human intensiveness, proprietary knowledge, perishability and heterogeneity. Depending on the service, one particular quality may be more applicable than others. The following table highlights some of the distinct marketing issues which can arise from these characteristics. These inherent qualities can sometimes make marketing a service more challenging or complicated, with the result that a different kind of marketing approach is often required.

Characteristics of Services

Intangibility

The intangibility in a service means that, unlike a good, the service cannot be lifted, transported, felt, or seen. This quality can make the service more difficult to assess or evaluate, and being able to supply the service promptly can be more difficult since the service, unlike normal inventory, cannot be "stored."

Intangibility introduces a certain element of risk for purchasers of a service. When a customer buys a manufactured product, such as an automobile, the customer can see it, touch it, "kick the tires," and take it for a test drive. Conversely, when a customer buys a service, such as legal advice, it may not be visible-and the buyer cannot see it, touch it or for that matter, have a firm idea of what the results of the service will be. Service providers must consider this as a real marketing issue.

Advertising and promotion can play a large part in soothing the perception of risk for a customer. Intangibility can mean that clients have less information, causing the customer to be especially apprehensive. For this reason, customers or users are likely to search for tangible evidence that will give them an insight into the caliber of the service they intend to purchase. As a service provider, it is important to make as many elements of the service as tangible as possible. By doing this, a service provider articulates the actual service delivery and creates a perception of existence. This can be achieved, at least partially, by supplying the customers with tangible sales tools such as high quality brochures, effective presentations, and dedicated facilities.

Inseparability

Inseparability in services means that the production and consumption of the service often occur simultaneously, not sequentially, and are embodied in the transaction of the service. This means that the production (creation) and consumption of the service are often at the same site, technology notwithstanding. Many services are, to certain degree, inseparable from location, although the degree of separation may vary. Certain professional services, such as accounting, environmental science, or consulting, are knowledge-intensive, and are provided by transfer of "know-how" from one person to another. For that reason, they can have a greater separation from an actual good or product.

There are, too, services whose basic value is embodied in some tradable form—such as a piece of software or legal document, often created (produced) in one country and shipped to another. "Knowledge-based" services such as architecture and engineering can also be exportable when the consultant travels to one client's site but develops the plans at home.

If the service is embodied in a shippable form, it gains some of the marketing elements of a shelf product. For instance, software is embedded in an application which can be packaged and marketed as a good. Hence, the service firm must be aware that the marketing strategy requires methods of distribution that reflect the degree of inseparability in the service product. In general, the closer a service is related to a good, the more it can follow a marketing pattern similar to the manufacturing sector.

Many other services—retailing, airline services, entertainment, hotels, and tourism—are completely inseparable and thus require local production and consumption. Because of this, these kinds of service firms often enter foreign markets through licensing, franchising, joint venture, or direct investment.

Human-Intensiveness

One important difference between marketing a service and marketing a good is the role of people. Consumer or industrial products can be sold with a fairly high degree of anonymity. Conversely, some services are highly human-intensive in their delivery, and are sold based upon an individual's actions and performances. The delivery of a service can demand greater cultural sensitivity on the part of marketers since the anonymity of indirect communication does not exist. Ultimately, until a service provider has developed a solid reputation, all judgment is placed on the deliverer or performer of the service. As service providers, employees of that firm become the personification of the product, and many service firms have found it expeditious to staff their operations with nationals of the host country. This may even be essential in industries where an extremely high degree of customer contact is required.

Perishability and Homogeneity

Perishability relates to the ephemeral nature of services. If they are not consumed on site and immediately, they may be "lost." They cannot be inventoried, or stored for use after production, which presents a unique set of marketing issues.

In addition, services may vary in their heterogeneity. Each time a service is provided, it may be unique. Standardization and quality control are not really achievable in the traditional sense, since the product is not tangible.

Other Marketing Factors

Certain factors can be said to promote the successful trade of services. One is mobility, which has, in recent years, become related to the speed of travel and the rate of technological change. Most successful business service exports have taken advantage of the rapid changes in the speed of international travel, either to deliver the service or to sell it. The ability to be mobile in exporting services is also often related to the presence of a firm's global technological or distribution network, which can respond to the needs of customers instantaneously. From a distribution point of view, the commonality of a global technological standard can lessen the likelihood for deviations in quality which can impact the service firm's performance.

Cultural transferability is another factor important to a firm's success. Some foreign markets may be more culturally indifferent to some services than others. World financial markets, for example, are relatively indistinct in their need for financial capital to provide loans to growing businesses. Airline travel operates in much the same way in every country. Other services, such as entertainment, lodging, or software, must be more adapted to local markets.

Questions often arise in a multinational service firm about the degree to which internal policies, procedures, and performance requirements should reflect local customs and needs. Successful service providers have found the correct balance between tailoring their product to the local operating environment, while at the same time maintaining the proper level of standardized control. A firm may compensate or manage their employees based on local practice; however all overseas managers might receive the same type and level of training.

Market Entry Considerations

The combination of services' intangible characteristics, along with these other qualities, expand both the possibilities and obstacles for international market entry strategies of service providers, and any market entry strategy must be accompanied by a clear understanding of what delineates the difference between a service and a goods export. Service exports not only expand the possibilities for market entry, they also require different methods of servicing the consumer. It is, therefore, essential to develop a system that supports a service's unique market entry needs.

The intangibility of many services creates the need for an entirely different export infrastructure. For example, a service firm is less likely to ship their product overseas, hire a freight forwarder or fill out an Export Declaration Form. The fundamental difference between a service and a goods producer's infrastructure is that the infrastructure that facilitates the movement of goods is an organized international system including shipping, postal services, export management, freight forwarding and port services. On the other hand, the export infrastructure that moves a service is a consciously developed network of international business relationships. A service exporter often crafts a customized marketing system by persuading other firms and partners to market and distribute the service. A tangible good has marketing value on its own by virtue of its physical presence. Once a service is delivered to an international market, it is difficult to maintain visibility. If an international network is to be implemented successfully, an existing infrastructure of business relationships will continue to exist, allowing the momentum of the service's original presence to perpetuate.

There are several proven market entry methods and channels that a service exporter can utilize without the resource commitment necessary for foreign direct investment. Every service provider must decide which method of market entry will provide the greatest chance of market penetration. A service firm's success will depend on four factors: alliances with local companies, the ability to protect intellectual property, advertising and marketing strategies and access to financial resources. What marketing venue the firm decides to take will ultimately depend upon its internal capacity and the creativity, drive, and tenacity of its overseas partners.

Regardless of a firm's market entry decision, the particular strategy that drives a services firm must correspond with the legal framework for business that exists in a targeted country, and requirements concerning the scope of practice and legal structure of businesses should be carefully examined. Choice of market entry also depends greatly on variable factors such as current regulatory policy and the extent of domestic competition. These factors will be discussed more fully in the Marketing Barriers chapter.

Market Entry Methods

Market entry methods consist of all the possible alternatives to developing a business presence in a foreign market. Three major market entry strategies available for the service provider are exporting, contractual agreements and foreign direct investment. Underlying these market entry strategies are a host of arrangements or platforms on which a service can be promoted, marketed and sold. Market entry methods include, but are not limited to, the following:

Project Consultancy

Project consultancy is the purest form of service export and entails the temporary export of specialized human capital. As long as this movement is for less than one year, the practice is to classify the transaction as an export. Project consultancy takes place when a foreign client abroad requests that a service be performed from a US service provider. Architectural, engineering, and design firms typically sell this way.

US-Based Agents

A number of US companies specialize in forming international marketing networks and alliances which assist client companies. The US agent serves as a value-added intermediary, creating a total market entry package, including: financing, pricing, and legal considerations; signing on foreign representatives; and establishing an after-sales support structure for the package.

Electronic Commerce

This method of exporting a service involves the transfer of knowledge and information abroad via telecommunications. The availability of computerization and networking has brought about a great increase in transborder data flow. Telematic trade covers a wide array of channels, including technical information and data transferred over the telephone, facsimile, electronic mail, and the Internet. Although telecommunications is not commonly thought of as an export, it is an increasingly efficient and prevalent method of exporting services and products. Firms may not even be cognizant that they are engaging in a telematic export (for instance, the release of a single report to an affiliate in Germany qualifies as a service export). Furthermore, some firms, such as data retrieval services, depend on telecommunications as their sole method of distribution.

Representatives

Service providers, like goods providers, can hire distributors to market their service in a foreign country. This form of market entry is not used frequently in the service industry because services usually need to be transferred directly from one person to another. This method is similar to project consultancy but introduces an intermediary as an additional layer to the distribution channel. US service exporters can hire individuals to represent their service in a "local" foreign market.

Because a service representative can't take title to a product, the representative's role is to monitor market conditions firsthand, sift through and pursue potential sales leads, and advertise and assure reliable after-service maintenance and communication. The official sale and delivery of the service, however, still takes place in the foreign producer's own country. Subsequent to a local representative identifying a strong sales lead, the US service provider often then travels abroad and handles the final sales negotiations. Representatives are key to the provision of a service by maintaining the morale, communication and momentum of the relationship after the US provider returns home. The US Department of Commerce's Agent Distributor Service can be an effective tool for finding service representatives.

Client-Firm Representation

Another way a service firm can enter foreign markets is through an agreement with a foreign firm to market some of the US firm's services. The overseas entity may be a one-person operation or it may be a multimillion dollar, multinational company; size differential is not necessarily a factor. The relationship between a US service exporter and his representative firm is agreed upon contractually between the parties. In the client-firm relationship the US service provider compensates the agency with a commission or predetermined form of payment upon signing a contract with a buyer.

The client-firm relationship exists when the US service exporter contracts with or arranges for a local firm to represent or market a US service that is complementary to a foreign firm's line of products or services. Representation can take shape in various ways. For example, an insurance company could arrange for travel agents in another country to market its tour packages. Foreign retailers could showcase a firm's service in a product or service catalog or newsletter, complementary to the retailer. This is similar to a "piggyback arrangement," in which a manufactured product is added to the product line and marketing strategy of a non-competing firm.

Subcontracting

Subcontracting occurs when a US firm contractually provides its independent services to a foreign firm. The client-firm representation relationship is distinct from subcontracting in that the US service provider is allowed to use its service mark while contracting with the foreign firm to market its service. The foreign firm promotes the US exporter's name to its entire client base. This arrangement is conducive to promoting name recognition. However, in a subcontracting relationship, the contracting foreign firm is the end-user of the US exporter's services. For example, the US exporter may simply contract to do part or all of a large project for a foreign company under the foreign company's name. An example of this is an independent software developer contracting with another larger software developer working on a project that is too large to handle individually. The contracted developer creates only a part of the program. If the job is done well, the programmer will likely gain future jobs from the contractor but the developer will not be known to the buyers of the end-product to which they contributed.

Management Contracts

An international management contract is a non-equity agreement in which a US management firm will take over all or key areas of relevant operations for a foreign firm lacking management expertise. This relationship exists when a foreign firm requires the assistance of a US consultant to apply its specialized know-how to train employees, streamline an entire business or provide a specific business function. The US firm is usually compensated in the form of fees over the life of the contract.

Turnkey Contracts

Under a turnkey project, a US service firm provides services and takes full responsibility for a capital-intensive project, such as a factory or construction project, through to the point of operation. Once the project is completed, the contractor turns the project over to the buyer. Quite often, a turnkey project requires the transfer of an entire service package, which can include training both employees and management. Major turnkey projects often involve development bank financing, as well as subcontractors and teaming arrangements, in order to complete the project.

Alliances

An alliance is an informal or formal, equity or non-equity working arrangement, negotiated between a US firm and a foreign firm having mutually beneficial strategic business purposes. Alliances can consist of two firms or can require a consortium of companies to piece together a major project. There are many benefits that partners of alliances can bring to the table, including: geography, human resources, finance, language, and marketing skills. Alliance partnerships are developed based on core competencies and can result in informal (project-by-project), or formal contractual arrangements, comprising distribution, knowledge, cross-licensing, outsourcing, and joint marketing agreements.

Licensing Agreements

Licensing agreements allow the export of intellectual property or technical knowledge. In a licensing arrangement, intellectual property rights are licensed allowing the licensee to acquire rights to patents, trademarks, copyrights and other "know-how." In return for the right to use a technology, the licensee compensates the licensor in the form of royalties or cash payments. A service firm may wish to license a technical service when adequate capital, human resources and/or local knowledge is not available to effectively exploit the technology in the foreign market. Keep in mind that each foreign government has its own set of laws and regulatory agencies governing the licensing process. It is important to investigate all avenues before signing any licensing agreement.

Technology Brokers

A technology broker is an intermediary who can formulate market entry strategies for firms interested in transferring their technologies. Technology brokers use an established international network of business contacts to deploy US technologies through international commercialization. Some brokers also help US firms acquire foreign technologies. US licensors should be certain that the agent has adequate overseas contacts and technological competency. Technology brokers usually specialize by technology category and by specific regions of the world. A broker's services include, but are not limited to: evaluating licensable intellectual property, identifying potential markets, determining the value of technology assets, extracting profits from non-strategic technologies, developing a start-to-finish licensing package, managing intellectual property issues, and negotiating royalty payments.

Franchising

Franchising is a growing form of technology licensing used by many consumer service industries, including restaurants and apparel stores. Retail franchising typically involves the license of a trade or service mark, a business format for the sale of products or services, and the use of related know-how. There are two different types of franchise arrangements: product distribution arrangements in which the dealer is to some degree identified with the manufacturer/supplier; and the business format franchise in which the franchise offers not only a trademark and logo, but an entire business system.

In franchising, the franchisor (licensor) expands a business by permitting the franchisee (licensee) to employ the parent company's trademark or service mark in a contractually specified manner for the right to market goods and services. Often,

Promoting Your Service

When entering a new market, it is important to identify the most effective methods of promotion in order to give a service maximum exposure. At the bottom of any promotion strategy is the basic goal of capturing the customer's attention and creating a need for the service. To do this effectively, a service provider should attempt to make their service appear more "tangible."

There are several mechanisms that can be implemented to merchandise a service, and options will range widely depending on the type of service sold. Publishing a newsletter on a monthly or bimonthly basis provides an ongoing awareness of the firm's service and the industry itself. Written materials are an absolute must for the service firm because they help articulate the service delivery and create perceptions of existence. Trade shows can also highlight a service and improve or confirm the customer's perception and confidence in the service. The following outlines a few promotional techniques that a firm might consider before launching a service package abroad.

Trade Exhibitions

International trade shows are effective tools for entering new overseas markets. There are many excellent international trade fairs, both privately-run and government-supported. Foreign trade exhibitions provide a number of benefits to service exporters: 1) a company can announce its entrance into a new market, 2) it is a good way to solidify market identity and commitment to the industry and users of the service in that country, 3) market research data can be gathered by talking to potential buyers and complementary service suppliers, 4) the firm can meet and screen potential agents and partners on a firsthand basis, and 5) it is an opportunity to test and train representatives and check out the competition.

It is wise to check the overall reputation of the trade show. The US Department of Commerce has a Certified Trade Fair Program that ensures basic organizational qualities. To receive certification, the organization must demonstrate that the fair is a leading international trade event for an industry, and the fair organizer is capable of recruiting US exhibitors and assisting them with freight forwarding, customs clearance, exhibit design, set up, public relations and overall show promotion. The local USDOC Office can tell if a certain trade fair appears on the official Export Promotion Calendar.

Video and Catalog Exhibitions

US firms may test foreign markets, develop sales leads and locate agents or distributors through catalog and video exhibitions sponsored by the US Commercial Service. Catalog exhibitions feature displays of a large number of US product catalogs, sales brochures and other graphic sales aids at US embassies and consulates or in conjunction with trade shows in a region. Alternatively, a video of your service can be displayed as a promotional tool. Commercial staff provide each participant with sales leads and a visitors' list of all foreign buyers attending the event. Because it requires the exporter to make a much smaller investment than a trade mission or other personal visit, this program is particularly well-suited for use in developing markets.

These promotions are low-cost exhibits that offer small, less-experienced companies an opportunity to test overseas markets for their products without traveling overseas. ITA promotes the exhibitions, provides staff who are fluent in the local language, and forwards all trade leads. For more information contact a USDOC Office.

Foreign Buyer Program

The Foreign Buyer Program (FBP) is a USDOC program that assists exporters in meeting qualified foreign purchasers for their product or service at trade shows held in the United States. FBP selects leading US trade shows in industries with high export potential. Each show selected for the FBP receives promotion through overseas mailing, US embassy outreach and other promotional techniques. ITA trade specialists advise participating US exhibitors. For more information contact your local USDOC Office.

Commercial News USA

Ten times a year, the Department of Commerce advertises new products worldwide in Commercial News USA. Under the Department's New Product Information Service (NPIS), this monthly magazine compiles short promotional descriptions and photographs of products which are then sent to US embassies and consular posts abroad. About 250,000 foreign firms receive these Commercial News bulletins. Commercial News also has a specific section reserved for the promotion of a wide variety of services including licensing, investment and technical literature advertisements. Information on this program may be obtained from a USDOC Office.

US Information Agency (USIA)

The USIA produces a "Doing Business" television program, a half-hour, monthly business program sent by satellite to more than 100 countries, highlighting innovation and excellence in US business. The program consists of segments on new products, services, and processes of interest to overseas buyers. Contact: Worldnet Television; telephone (202) 501-8450; fax (202) 501-6076.

the franchisor will supply signature facilities, product sourcing and supply, management training, advertising, and capital assistance to the franchisee. The trademarks and the patents remain in possession of the franchisor; the franchisee only has the right to use them. For this privilege, the franchisee pays the franchisor a flat fee or royalty, and assumes the right to manage the business.

International Associations

An international association has many similar characteristics of retail franchising, but is organized to offer a group of professional business services. The association can involve independent companies with a mutual referral service, or it can establish common standards and offer common administrative services to its members. Usually, a franchisee must adopt the service mark of the franchisor as a trade identity, though in some cases the franchisee retains the original trade name as a secondary, or even predominant, trade identity. In addition, members may agree to conduct business in accordance with the franchisor's specifications and standard operating procedures, to pay fees to the franchisor, to maintain certain standards, and to share common costs. The strength of the affiliation relationship lies in the prestige and financial backing of a well-known firm. Simultaneously, the licensor often acquires new market geographies and a wider knowledge base and competency, enhancing the firm as a whole. Most major CPA firms have an international arm which sets standards for the firms bearing their name around the world. Furthermore, many international professional firms in law, consulting, executive recruiting and real estate are legally international associations of national partnerships.

Foreign Direct Investment

Foreign direct investment (FDI) occurs when a US firm establishes a physical overseas presence. Foreign direct investment is important to the service industry, since many services require on-site production and delivery. Forms of FDI include joint ventures, wholly-owned subsidiaries and branch offices. Service firms that are more likely to require foreign direct investment are those that require simultaneous client and seller interaction, such as retail stores, educational services, and restaurants. Foreign direct investment is the dominant mode of market entry for international transactions generated by large service companies.

Joint Ventures

A joint venture is a method of market entry in which two or more firms share in the ownership of a business. Joint ventures are an important market entry method for the service industry and often represent an entry solution to markets that otherwise restrict the pure export of services or wholly-owned subsidiaries. If a service is deemed essential to the foreign government's economic plans, foreign direct investment is regarded positively; however, 100 percent US ownership is often prohibited. A foreign country may require that a certain percentage of a service firm be owned by nationals of that country, possibly requiring US firms to operate in a minority investment position. A joint venture can have similar elements found in an alliance, such as distribution agreements, cross-licensing, and joint marketing, but a joint venture requires an equity stake.

Chapter 5:

BARRIERS TO TRADE

Market and Trade Barriers Unique to Service Industries

The existence of discriminatory regulatory policy by governments is perhaps the largest single barrier to international trade in services, and can have an adverse impact on the ability of foreign entities to provide services in any country. Barriers to doing business overseas can include restrictive trade and investment rules, controls on the transfer of technology, government procurement policies, prejudicial tax structure, incompatible environmental and health policies, and more. In addition, difficulties in marketing overseas are also related to services' intangible qualities, as discussed earlier. The difficulty in liberalizing trade in services often goes beyond physical distribution and can appear in the very relationship that has been built up over time between the society itself and the services it provides (such as banking or legal advice).

Barriers to trade in goods are fairly straightforward, and often begin and end at the border (with a tariff or quota, for example). Trade barriers in services are often less visible to the international marketer since they can be embedded in complex domestic industry regulations, as well as in the overall business environment of that country. The banking, insurance, telecommunications, and transportation industries have tended to have more regulatory barriers imposed on them than other services. For example, in the early 1980s, before the Economic Union of 1992, an average of 22 non-tariff barriers per country were imposed on service industries in EU countries, primarily in these four industries.

Government monopoly and control of many basic services has also worked to create market distortions in the pricing and delivery of services that are difficult for foreign providers to supercede. In the past, many governments limited imports of certain kinds of services on the grounds that they were protecting their domestic consumers from foreigners that offered services of a differing technological standard, or of a lesser quality. Lesser developed countries (LDCs) often kept their service industries insulated on the grounds that they were "infant industries" that needed trade protection. National governments have also limited access to services providers on the grounds of national security.

There is now a much greater acceptance on the part of national governments on the need to open up markets to foreign competition and include services under the rubric of international trade treaties. To a large extent, this has come about due to the growing trend towards inter-country deregulation and privatization in many countries, especially in key service industries—such as telecommunications, transportation, and health care.

The US economy was perhaps the first to push forward with this in the 1980s, with the deregulation of banking and aerospace, the break-up of telecommunications monopolies, and interstate commerce. Within the last ten years, countries in Asia, Latin America and Europe have gone a long way towards privatization, making for far greater trade growth and market opportunity. This global push towards deregulation has allowed many US service firms to sell more actively overseas, and at the same time, it has allowed foreign service providers wider access to the US market.

Services and Trade Agreements

Until the last decade, the lowering of tariff or non-tariff barriers to services trade was often negotiated on a bilateral basis for specific industries. For example, in 1990 the US negotiated with the government of Korea for increased US corporate participation in the Korean insurance industry. Multilateral trade policy was about tariffs—whether to raise, lower, or eliminate them. Once governments became convinced of the efficacy of freer trade, and with the advent of the first post-war GATT Round, the issue was primarily: how much should tariffs be reduced on goods and to what extent should goods be allowed to move freely across borders?

In fact, trade negotiations did not even begin to consider services until Punta de Este in 1986, when the US began to push for inclusion of services into the GATT framework; there are still relatively few international rules of fair play governing trade in services.

One of the most substantial regional trade initiatives to date for services involved the final integration of the European Common Market in 1992. This represented significant opportunity for individual European companies to sell regionally. Integration highlighted a key focal point that will arise with future trade pacts: As trade in services continues to expand, resolving the issue of harmonization vs. simple deregulation will be crucial in some industries, such as telecommunications. The EU uses a mixture of harmonization and liberalization in its attempts to mesh country-specific standards with regional ones. However, reciprocity and harmonization, key concepts used in the EU, can also conceivably be used to curtail the entrance of outside service industries into Europe. Non-discriminatory rules and fair treatment are a basic component of trade liberalization, and the EU is still attempting to set policy for non-members.

Inroads

GATT During the Uruguay Round of GATT negotiations, the US pushed for increased market access and national treatment of services as one of the major issues for negotiation. Progress during the Uruguay Round on negotiations in services was generally slower than had been anticipated; by the close of the Round in December, 1993, trade negotiators had reached agreement on a services framework under the newly created General Agreement on Trade in Services—or GATS. GATS negotiations, which are being approached on an individual industry basis, will be ongoing over the next several years. Resultant rules and commitments are to be incorporated into sectoral annexes and attached to the GATS framework and national schedules. There are now GATS working committees on maritime transport, finance, professional services, telecommunications, the movement of natural persons, and others.

The GATS framework attempts to set out overall principles and rules designed to help integrate multilateral trade into services. The framework, along with the national schedules of commitments, is working to incorporate basic obligations regarding the following:

- total coverage, where participants agree to include in principle all traded services and their suppliers;

- national treatment, where foreign firms supplying services are treated no less favorably than domestic firms supplying services;

- most favored nation treatment (MFN), where foreign firms supplying services are treated the same as any other foreign firm supplying services;

- transparency, where regulations governing services trade will be published and administered impartially, and will include enquiry points where foreign firms can secure information on necessary national qualifications, etc.;

- payment transfers, where there will be no restrictions on the international transfer of payments for services for current accounts except for temporary balance of payments difficulties;

- progressive liberalization, with selective negotiations at five year intervals;

- market access, with commitments on granting access clearly set out in national schedules; and

- dispute settlement, where a procedure for resolving disputes between GATS participants concerning trade in services would be available for the first time.

Several principles fundamental to GATT may apply differently under GATS. For example, under GATT guidelines, concessions to one trading partner under MFN must be made to others receiving MFN treatment. With services this may need to be done on a conditional basis, since some developing countries are very sensitive to their infant industries.

Another GATT protocol involves national treatment, whereby imported products once cleared are treated the same

as national firms. With some services, the degree of market presence may need further definition. In banking, for example, international banks are allowed to enter the US, but only to open retail or consumer accounts. If national treatment towards finance were enacted, what would their operating constraints be? "Barriers at the border" is another important trade principle which needs clarification. When barriers to marketing goods are imposed, they are done at the border. Many obstacles to marketing services are internal or cultural, as we have mentioned; GATT as yet has no umbrella mechanism to deal with this.

NAFTA The North American Free Trade Agreement's provisions opened previously closed or restricted Canadian and Mexican markets by eliminating many barriers to cross border trade and investment in finance, insurance, and entertainment. Other accomplishments included: the right to sell across borders; the right to invest; the right of professionals to cross the border following streamlined procedures; the right to access Mexico's professional services market by US professional, technical, and managerial personnel; the right of public access to information on any law or regulation regarding service trade; the right to effective protection and enforcement of intellectual property rights; and the right to provide services to Canadian or Mexican government entities.

Several other agreements concluded over the past three years will open new market opportunities for services exporters. These include the Trade Related Intellectual Property Rights (TRIPS); the US-Japan framework agreements; a new agreement with China on intellectual property protection; and more recently, the Free Trade Area of the Americas (FTAA) negotiations. The FTAA process includes the establishment, at the March 1996 Trade Ministerial meeting in Cartagena, of a working group on services. The working group's mandate will be to undertake preliminary work in preparation for FTAA services negotiations.

Currently, the US is engaged in international discussions to promote competition, provide open access, and create a flexible regulatory framework for the development of a global information infrastructure (GII). The GII will consist of global, regional, and national networks and will facilitate worldwide access to information, interconnection, and communication.

Specific Barriers to Services Trade

The United States Trade Representative has classified trade barriers into five general categories: the rights to establish and operate a business, national treatment, repatriation of royalties, intellectual property protection, performance requirements and standards, and legal limitations. Listed below are some of the most common foreign trade barriers that restrict the international export of services. This list was adapted (with permission) from the California State World Trade Commission's publication, *California Service Exports: Emerging Global Opportunities,* one of the most comprehensive studies done on service sector exports:

Practical Issues and Barriers to Trade

Intellectual Property Rights and Trademarks

Computer design and software, trademarks, brand names, and other intellectual properties are easy to duplicate and difficult to protect. Countries seldom have adequate, or any, legislation; any laws they do have are difficult to enforce. Sensitivity to piracy, bootlegging and replication varies from one service industry to another. In some cases, professional services are very difficult to reproduce because they are tailored to a specific end user and contain a unique knowledge base that takes years to develop. On the other hand, some services and knowledge are embodied in material products and can be easily copied, such as software, musical recordings, and books.

A commonly accepted definition of an intellectual property right (IPR) is a firm's ownership of the right to possess, or otherwise use or dispose of, products created by human ingenuity. Also important to all service industries is the protection of a firm's trade or service name. A service mark can be one of the most influential devices a service firm can obtain to distinguish itself on an international basis. Careful research into a target country's laws and attitudes toward IPRs is necessary in order to protect a firm's competitive advantage.

Most intellectual property rights are country-specific, unless that country conforms to international agreements. Applications for patent protection must be filed in each country in which the patent owner desires protection. Often, a foreign patent agent or attorney is necessary in order to file an application in another country. The US Department of Commerce recommends that US service exporters with intellectual property concerns consider taking the following steps: 1) obtain protection under all applicable US laws for their inventions, trademarks and copyrights, 2) research the intellectual property laws of countries where business is conducted, 3) secure the services of competent local counsel to file appropriate patent, trademark or copyright applications within priority periods, 4) adequately protect trade secrets through appropriate confidentiality provisions in employment, marketing, distribution, licensing and joint venture agreements and 5) find out how effectively intellectual property regulations, laws, and rules are being enforced.

International Mobility

Because the value of a service is often embedded in people, the provision of a service often requires the service provider to stay and work in a particular country for an extended period of time. Just as the provision of a manufactured product entails sending the product via air or ocean and getting the product into the safe hands of a subsidiary or a distributor, a service firm must be aware of visa requirements, work permits, immigration procedures, and special professional licensing requirements to ensure the smooth provision of a service abroad. Harmonization of professional standards and licensing requirements are not only desirable, but a prerequisite to transborder trade in professional services. Unfortunately, at this time, immigration laws are determined country-by-country and there is no central organization or document that outlines visa and work regulations for each country worldwide.

Visas

A US passport is required for most countries. Passports are good for 10 years and can be obtained through 13 offices located in major cities in the United States. Certain countries require a visa in addition to a US passport. For information regarding entry requirements into a foreign country, contact the US Department of State. The Government Printing Office publishes a booklet entitled *Foreign Entry Requirements,* which lists addresses of embassies and consulates in over 238 countries where visas may be obtained, along with any special requirements. Contact: Visa Services, Public Inquiries, Department of State, Washington, DC 20520; telephone (202) 663-1225.

Trans-World Visa Service offers a free, one-page chart outlining current tourist visa requirements for US citizens traveling abroad. Copies are available from Trans-World Visa Service, 790 27th Ave., San Francisco, CA 94121; telephone (415) 752-6957.

Work Permits

Typically, the prospective employer, not the employee, must apply for a foreign work permit. The permit is usually for a specific overseas worker and for a specific job. A permit quite often will not be issued if, in the opinion of the government, suitable resident labor is available. However, it still may be granted if the work is of a short term nature and will not disadvantage a local resident. The prospective employer is often required to advertise the position to employment offices, newspapers or trade journals, and allow a specified time for a suitable resident worker to be found.

Permits are typically determined on an individual basis. Individuals who are commonly accepted include: professionals, highly qualified technicians having specialized experience and workers with scarce qualifications in an industry or occupation requiring specific expert knowledge or skills. Applications for work permits can take months to process, so it is important to plan far in advance. The service exporter is expected to provide full details of the proposed work, together with supporting documentation from the prospective employer.

Inquire at the nearest foreign consulate about work conditions, professional requirements and immigration laws of the country. Consulates also have information about application procedures.

International Payments

Service firms sometimes experience difficulty repatriating fees, royalties, and profits to their home office. This may occur when foreign repatriation procedures are ambiguous or poorly publicized or when governments fail to comply with their own regulations, effectively limiting, delaying, or discouraging repatriation. Currency exchange controls are often a major consideration also.

Access to Public Sector Markets

In certain countries, service sectors are still regulated by governments that restrict foreign firms from obtaining government contracts. In such situations, local service firms will receive preference for government contracts, except in cases where they are unable to carry out the required services.

Preferential Purchasing Requirements

These are especially important for architects, accountants, and management consultants who work for government and public entities. Foreign architects may be excluded from bidding on government projects and enterprises are sometimes reserved for national firms. For example, this "buy national" policy occurs when the US government decides to buy training services only from US firms, impeding foreign suppliers.

Importation of Tools of the Trade

Service firms needing to import materials related to their service are often hindered by questionable customs valuations, excessive delays and outright prohibitions. A particularly troublesome problem involves the importation of training material for in-house use. Many countries impose customs duties on such materials even though they constitute communication among affiliates rather than salable merchandise.

Establishment

US service firms often encounter difficulty in obtaining permission to establish a branch or subsidiary in a foreign country. These kinds of barriers are not really trade barriers, but rather direct investment barriers. In addition, firms initiating franchises (a form of export through licensing) may face establishment barriers, and many nations explicitly restrict foreign access to certain industries (such as advertising) or impose strict limits on what constitutes a legal form of operation. Some countries limit the percentage of foreign ownership in a local service firm, often requiring that majority ownership be held by nationals.

Licensing Standards and Domestic Employment Requirements

Professions such as accounting, law, medicine, engineering, and teaching are often heavily licensed and regulated in order to protect local practitioners. Regulations often discriminate against foreign professionals, either on the grounds that citizenship is required or local expertise and language proficiency are needed. Consultants are often forced to collaborate with local firms in order to practice. The overall development of service industries in some countries may be limited through a prohibition on hiring foreigners, since adequately trained personnel in the host country may not be readily available.

Further Information and Resources

NAFTA Flash Fax

The NAFTA flash fax is a 24-hour, automated information system that transmits, directly to your fax machine, the most current information on NAFTA. Information sourced from this system includes export counseling services available from the US Department of Commerce, market research reports, tariffs, professional licensing requirements, trade statistics and drafts of the original NAFTA agreement. For more information, telephone (202) 482-4464 for Mexico issues; (202) 482-3101 for Canada issues.

GATT Hotline

A telephone hotline provides current information received from the GATT Secretariat in Geneva, Switzerland on proposed foreign regulations which may significantly affect trade. The recorded message is updated weekly and gives product and country facts as well as details on technical barriers. For more information, telephone (301) 975-4041.

GATT National Enquiry Points

GATT also has a network of central contact points that can provide information on trade-related technical standards, regulations, and rules of certification for 70 countries. These offices, although specifically tailored toward product-related standards, can often help determine professional requirements for technical fields or direct one to the appropriate agency.

Professional Associations

Professional Associations quite often have international chapters which are in tune with international professional requirements. For example, the Federal Bar Association has a subcommittee on international law that addresses the issue of US lawyers practicing abroad.

Professional and Occupational Licensing Directory (POLD)

Another source for the professional desiring to work abroad is the Professional and Occupational Licensing Directory. The POLD provides complete national and state information on licenses and licensing procedures required for about 250 occupations (and hundreds of more specific job titles) in the United States. The POLD covers professional- and vocational-licensed careers, from acupuncturists to well drillers, and is arranged and cross-referenced by occupational title. In addition to federal and state requirements and regulations, full contact information for licensing and certifying organizations is provided. Information includes: type of license required, duration of license, nature and prerequisites of examination, auxiliary procedures such as fingerprinting or bonding, continuing education requirements needed to maintain a license, reciprocity with other states or countries, exemptions, waivers and exclusions, fees involved, licensing boards (name, address, phone, contact) and governing statutes. For more information contact Gale Research Inc. at 1-800-877-GALE.

Trade Remedy Assistance

US International Trade Commission

The Trade Remedy Assistance Office, a component of the US International Trade Commission (USITC), provides technical assistance and legal support to certified small businesses pursuing remedies under international trade laws. If a US firm is adversely affected by a competitor's practices, a complaint may be filed with the Trade Remedy Assistance Office. In addition to information and assistance on anti-dumping laws, this office also provides remedies for countervailing duty laws (where subsidized foreign goods are sold in the US); intellectual property laws (where articles imported into the US infringe patents, trademarks, or copyrights); and investigation of situations where US exports are subject to unfair restrictions in overseas markets. Contact the Trade Remedy Assistance Office, US International Trade Commission, 500 E Street, SW, Washington, DC 20436; telephone (800) 343-9822.

Intellectual Property Rights

Office of the US Trade Representative (USTR)

USTR is responsible for administering trade cases that provide relief from unfair trade practices under Section 301 of the Trade Act of 1974. Individual exporters should contact USTR concerning procedures for filing a trade complaint. For more information telephone (202) 395-3432; fax (202) 395-3639. The USTR issues an annual report on 45 countries, describing the trade barriers that exist in each country and estimating the impact on US exports. *Foreign Trade Barriers* may be obtained through: Office of the US Trade Representative, Executive Office of the President, 600 17th Street, Washington, DC 20506; telephone (202) 395-3230. It may also be ordered through the Government Printing Office (GPO); telephone (202) 512-1800; fax (202) 512-2250.

United States Trade Representative

The "301" legislation, signed by Congress in 1988, requires the United States Trade Representative to report the trade status of trading partner countries. It also requires the USTR to review the condition of intellectual property protection among US trading partners. Submissions are accepted from industries after which the USTR, weighing all relevant information, makes a determination as to protection of intellectual property. If the USTR makes a positive determination, a country may be named to one of three lists: Priority Foreign Countries, the Priority Watch List or the Watch List. These ratings are important to review, especially before making decisions to enter foreign markets with an intellectually sensitive service sector. For more information, contact: Winder Building, 600 17th Street, NW, Washington, DC 20506; telephone (202) 395-3150; fax (202) 395-3639.

US Patent and Trademark Office (PTO)

The US Patent and Trademark Office administers laws relating to patents and trademarks in order to promote industrial and technological progress in the United States and to strengthen the national economy. It develops and advises the Secretary of Commerce on intellectual property policy, including copyright matters. The PTO also advises the agencies of the US government, such as the USTR, on the trade-related aspects of intellectual property. For more information, contact: 2021 Jefferson Davis Highway, Arlington, VA 22202; telephone (703) 308-4357. For general information or to order books, call (703) 557-4636.

International Trademark Association (INTA)

The International Trademark Association is dedicated to promoting trademarks as essential to world commerce. A not-for-profit organization, INTA takes a lead role, not only in serving members, but in actively pursuing public policy matters concerning trademarks. It also educates business, the press and the public on the proper use and importance of trademarks. INTA's membership includes over 2,600 organizations in nearly 100 countries. These include both major multinational corporations and smaller companies that recognize the importance of trademarks to their continued marketing success. For more information, contact: 1133 Avenue of the Americas, New York, NY 10036-6719; telephone (212) 768-9887; fax (212) 768-7796.

Copyright Office

The Copyright Office is primarily an office of record: a place where claims to copyright are registered when the claimant has complied with the requirements of copyright law. The Copyright Office furnishes information about the provisions of copyright law and the procedures for making registration. It explains the operations and practices of the Office and reports on facts found in the public records, but it does not give specific legal advice. Enforcement of copyright and defense against unauthorized use, infringement or piracy, must be pursued in court. For more information, contact: Library of Congress, Subcommittee on Intellectual Property; telephone (202) 707-3000.

World Intellectual Property Organization (WIPO)

The World Intellectual Property Organization (WIPO) is part of the United Nations system of organizations headquartered in Geneva, Switzerland. WIPO is responsible for the promotion of the protection of intellectual property throughout the world. Service firms will find within WIPO's catalogue of publications documents such as: *The International Classification of Goods and Services for the Purposes of Registration of Marks, Introduction to Trademark Law and Practice* and *100 years of Industrial Property Statistics*. For more information, contact: World Intellectual Property Organization, 2 United Nations Plaza, Room 560, 5th floor, New York, NY 10017; telephone (212) 963-6813.

Case Study:

Intercapital Trust Limited

ITL often advises clients to invest in countries where the market is more secure. "Countries like the Ukraine are quite risky, for example, because they don't have an advanced communication system," Felix Braynin said. "Russia is for many industries a safer market to invest in."

Felix Braynin

Barriers? What Barriers?

Intercapital Trust Limited (ITL) doesn't work around international trade and investment barriers; it knocks them down. The San Francisco-based diversified holding company is actually a conglomeration of several businesses, all with one goal in mind: helping people invest in countries.

"For a consultation fee, we help companies get around the hurdles they would normally face when investing in a country," said Felix Braynin, ITL's Chairman of the Board. ITL helps companies in a variety of industries, such as banking, real estate, and project finance.

Companies like Braynin's often assist businesses looking to enter a particular region. ITL primarily helps firms or people who wish to invest in the former Soviet Union. Many of the employees are familiar with the culture there and know what to expect. Braynin, for example, graduated from the University of Minsk and was a professional hockey and soccer player in Belarus before moving to the US. He has several connections throughout the former USSR, and was instrumental in helping Boris Yeltsin's re-election campaign during the summer of 1996.

"Dealing with these countries is particularly easy for us," Braynin said. "For companies planning to enter a country on their own, however, the best advice I could give is for businesspeople to make themselves as familiar with the country in question as they can."

Braynin said any company should expect at least a few barriers when entering a market on their own. "Preparation will keep problems to a minimum, though," he added.

Play it Safe

Rather than trying to enter a risky market, ITL often advises clients to invest in certain countries where the market is more secure. "Countries like the Ukraine are quite risky, for example, because they don't have an advanced communication system and their economy is still a few years away from being secure," Braynin said. "Russia has more advanced communication and economic systems, however, and for many industries it is a safer market to invest in."

Braynin also said developing countries have a more unstable political system, and it creates a greater risk for businesses, no matter how much potential a market may have.

"Companies may enter a market with a weak political system and discover there are things they weren't told," he said, "or they may invest in a company and suddenly it changes ownership." In cases like these, Braynin said companies are almost powerless because there are no laws to protect them, or the existing laws are never enforced. "In more developed countries, however, there are laws set in place to protect foreign businesspeople," he said.

For companies who want to enter a developing market, Braynin said patience is a key. "I think in about two years, a country like Ukraine, with a beginning legal and political system, will be about where Russia is today, in terms of political stability." The Ukraine is much better off than a country like Belarus, however. "Their political system is almost totally unstable," he said, "it may take a long time before people can safely invest there."

Export Councils and other government groups are helpful for beginning companies, and Braynin felt they work, although their methods are different from companies such as his. "Our approach is very different," he said, "but they get results just the same."

Chapter 6:
US GOVERNMENT REGULATIONS

Export Administration Regulations (EAR)

Although export licensing is a basic part of exporting, it is one of the most widely misunderstood aspects of government regulations for exporting. The export licensing procedure may appear complex at first, but in most cases it is a rather straight-forward process. Export controls are administered by the Bureau of Export Administration (BXA) in the US Department of Commerce. This chapter in no way covers all the material necessary to make an educated licensing decision. Instead, this work endeavors to address basic regulation issues facing a service exporter. Anyone considering the export of a service should consult the BXA and associated reference materials to make real export licensing decisions.

The majority of US exports are not limited by the US government and are only restricted for reasons of national security, foreign policy or short supply. Under the US Export Administration Act of 1979 and Amendments of 1985, the President of the United States is empowered to control the export and re-export of certain commodities and technical data to prohibited countries. In practice, this power is only exercised to limit or prohibit exports to recalcitrant countries or for purposes of embargo. Because services are invisible and intangible, many firms are inclined to assume that services are not regulated. However, services do fall within government export regulations and licensing requirements, and these must therefore be studied to determine whether the export of a particular service product or service is restricted or requires special licensing.

The export of technical knowledge, ideas, systems and processes, falls under controls embodied in the Export Administration Regulations. In the past, US export regulations for technology were quite extensive but they have been streamlined and minimized in recent years. The export of controlled technological data requires a validated export license. The requirement to file for a license does not mean that the export will be denied; it only means that the US government has the right to review potential sales on a case-by-case basis and deny those that conflict with present US foreign policy goals. The licensing requirements apply to the export of controlled data regardless of the means of export.

Controlled technological data is generally defined to include information of any kind that can be used or adapted for use in the design, production, manufacture, utilization, or reconstruction of articles or materials. The data may take a tangible form, such as a model, prototype, blueprint, or an operating manual, or it may take an intangible form such as a technical service. Technical information can be exported in a number of ways: via modem, facsimile, mail, electronic mail, Internet, software, or through information disclosed during instructional conferences and business trips.

Export Licenses

All necessary information required to determine a service's licensing eligibility is found in the Export Administration Regulations (EAR), the official US government publication that lists the rules and regulations controlling the export of US commodities by Export Control Classification Number (ECCN).

Regulated services are those that provide information that are associated with a restricted manufactured end-product. If a service encourages the production of a controlled end-product, the service will be regulated accordingly. When consulting the EAR for export licensing determination, the end-product of the service must be identified to determine if the related service is controlled.

Finding out if a validated license is required for a service export is a process of elimination. To classify a service, the exporter needs to look for the service that closely relates to the end product's technical specifications in the Commodity Control List (CCL) found in the EAR. The CCL identifies items that are restricted for export. If the commodity is not listed, the service may be performed with a general license.

Commodity descriptions in the EAR are very technical. To be absolutely certain a service does not require a validated license it is best to consult with the Bureau of Export Administration. The review of pertinent sections of the CCL by an in-house technician or engineer who has an intimate knowledge of the service or technology is also advised.

Technical data and software can be exported under the following types of licenses depending on the technology and destination:

General Technical Data Available (GTDA) License

The General Technical Data Available (GTDA) license is covered in Section 779.3 of the EAR and is a general license for technical data to all destinations. Technical data that is freely available to the general public can be exported under GTDA. This includes information published or placed in libraries accessible to the public, in government record open to the public (such as the Patent and Trademark Office) made available to the public free or at no more than the cost of reproduction and distribution, released as educational information by instruction (in catalog courses) and associated teaching laboratories of academic institutions or disclosed in the context of fundamental research that will be published.

General license GTDA is perhaps the most important, general license for technology. Initially, GTDA is the only general license that is in no way affected by technical limitations, country restrictions, end-use restrictions or end-user restrictions. Secondly, there are several different means to qualify for and benefit from GTDA. Thirdly, GTDA pertains to the technology and not to the transaction. Therefore, under GTDA, you may export information published by someone else.

Exporters do not need to apply for general licenses, since such authorization is already granted through the EAR. If your export does not qualify then you should investigate the availability of GTDU general licenses.

General Technical Data Unrestricted (GTDU) License

The General Technical Data Unrestricted (GTDU) license is covered in Section 779.3 of the EAR and is valid for all except a select group of destinations for reasons of national security or foreign policy (see EAR for country-specific details). There are five separate authorities of GTDU under which technology or software may qualify for this general license. These include items authorized in the Commodity Control List, mass-market software, sales technical data, operation technical data and software updates.

Technology/Software Specifically Authorized in the Commodity Control List (CCL)

Check the CCL under the appropriate ECCN to determine if the item is specifically listed as eligible for GTDU. If the ECCN for the technology or software indicates "GTDU: yes," then the technology or software can be exported to all countries except a select group of destinations (specified in the EAR). Exports may be made without a validated license and without obtaining written assurance. If the ECCN for the technology or software indicates "GTDU: no," then it may not be exported solely based on the ECCN authority of GTDU. However, the technology may qualify for GTDU as mass-market software, sales technical data, operation technical data or as a software update.

Mass-Market Software

Software that meets the requirements of the General Software Note (GSN) may be exported under General License GTDU to all destinations except a select group of destinations (specified in the EAR manual). The GSN applies to all categories in the CCL and is available for the export of software that is generally available to the public, designed for installation by the user without further substantial support by the supplier and distributed from stock at retail. The GSN prevails over the language of the CCL entries.

Sales Technical Data

GTDU authorizes the export of "sales technical data" to all destinations except a select group (specified in the EAR). Sales technical data is information supporting a prospective or actual quotation, bid, or offer to sell, lease, or otherwise supply any item controlled by the EAR. To qualify for this authority, the information must be of the type customarily provided to customers under established business practices and the information must not disclose the detailed design, production, manufacture, or means of reconstruction, of either the quoted item or its product.

Operation Technical Data

GTDU authorizes the export of the minimum necessary technology to install, operate, maintain (check) and repair those products that have been legally exported. It also authorizes the export of the minimum necessary software to operate a commodity authorized for export by either a general or validated license. Such authority does not permit the export of software or technology that increases the performance level of the related products beyond those authorized in the relevant validated or general licenses for the related product.

Software Updates

GTDU authorizes the export of software updates limited to the correction of errors in software previously exported. The export of the update must be to the consignee of the original software export and may not enhance the functional capabilities of the software initially authorized for export.

G-Temp for Software and Technical Data

If an export fails to qualify for GTDA or GTDU treatment, it still may be eligible for general license G-TEMP. G-TEMP authorizes various temporary exports of software such as exports for demonstration, use as tools of the trade and use in news-gathering. G-TEMP provides authorization of the commodity and software export for a period of up to one year from the date of export and must be returned to the United States.

General Technical Data Restricted (GTDR) License

If technical data is not eligible for GTDU there is a possibility for eligibility under GTDR supplemented with a letter of assurance. Technical data under restriction is found in Section 779.4 of the EAR and may only be exported to a specific set of countries (specified in the EAR). GTDR is a specific grant of authority from the US government to a particular company to export a product if a general license is not available. GTDR requires a letter of assurance from the consignee, prior to export, assuring that neither the data nor the end-product will be sent to high-risk countries. If the ECCN for technology or software indicates "GTDR: yes," then after receiving the required written letter of assurance, the export of the technology or software to the appropriate countries is allowed. If such written assurance is not received in advance of the export, a validated license is required.

End-use and end-user limitations only apply to the GTDR with written assurance and GTDU General License. For example, many of the proliferation controls restrict the use of these general licenses based upon the end-use and end-user. If the export does not qualify for one of these general licenses, then an Individual Validated License must be obtained prior to effecting the export.

Validated Licenses

Service exporters, just like manufacturers, must determine if their service requires a Validated License. It is the sole responsibility of the exporter to find out if a service that releases technological data is controlled. If a service is controlled, an exporter must obtain an Application for Export License, Form BXA 622P, from the BXA. A potential exporter can also apply for validated licenses electronically. Validated Licenses are granted on a transaction-specific basis or for a number of transactions within a specified period of time. In most cases, an application will need to be accompanied by two supporting documents: a letter of explanation which clearly states the intent to buy a service, and a letter of assurance from the consignee prior to export assuring that neither the data or the end-product will be sent to high-risk countries.

Special Validated Licenses

In order to facilitate the export of a commodity requiring a validated license, a series of special licensing procedures have been established that may be used, when appropriate, in lieu of the individual validated license (see Section 773.3 of the EAR). Special licenses generally allow for the export of pre-approved commodities and technical data to pre-approved consignees or destinations. They are usually used to replace several individual validated licenses and therefore minimize multiple licensing burdens.

Distribution License

A distribution license is designed for repetitive sales to pre-approved consignees. It allows exports under an international marketing program to at least three pre-approved foreign distributors/end-users. This license is a privilege, not a right, and the exporter and distribution license consignees must demonstrate reliability to the US Department of Commerce.

Project License

Projects that require the transfer of a number of licensable products over an extended period of time, i.e. turnkey projects, can be licensed under a special project license. A project license authorizes exports for one year for use in specified activities, such as capital expansion, supply maintenance, and supply materials used in promotion. Service firms engaged in the sale of products, services and technological data may apply for this type of license when a variety of licensable commodities and technical data is exported.

Service Supply

The service supply license/facility license (Section 773.7 of the EAR) assists US exporters in servicing investment commitments abroad. This special license allows firms in the US or abroad to provide prompt service for equipment exported from the US produced abroad by a subsidiary, affiliate or branch of a US firm or produced abroad by a manufacturer who uses parts imported from the US in the finished product.

Laws and Regulations

Anti-Boycott Regulations

The US government has promulgated a number of regulations that define the actions US firms can take and what statements they can make in compliance with foreign boycott requirements. In general, these laws prohibit US persons from participating in foreign boycotts or taking actions that further or support such boycotts. The anti-boycott provisions apply to all US persons, including intermediaries in the export process, as well as foreign subsidiaries that are "controlled in fact" by US companies or officials.

Most exporters need not worry about US anti-boycott rules since most boycott compliance statements are set forth in the letter of credit. US banks usually screen documents for unacceptable language. Yet, if the banker misses or misreads the statement or if the customer goes directly to the US exporter for specific affirmation, the exporter must check on the lawfulness of foreign boycott compliance before making a move. When US service exporters see a statement which they interpret as applying to a foreign boycott, they should contact: US Department of Commerce, Office of Anti-boycott Compliance, telephone (202) 482-2381.

If a US exporter is requested to provide a "reportable" boycott statement by an overseas customer, one may be obtained through ITA Form 621P, "Report of Request for Restrictive Practice or Boycott," from the BXA. Even if the exporter has not complied with the boycott clause, a report must still be made regarding the request to make a statement.

Antitrust Laws

US antitrust laws reflect this country's commitment to an economy based on competition, and are intended to foster the efficient allocation of resources by providing consumers with goods and services at the lowest price that efficient business operations can profitably offer. Under US antitrust laws, some types of trade restraints—such as price-fixing agreements and conspiracies, divisions of markets by competitors, and certain group boycotts and tying arrangements—are illegal. Other unspecified activities may also be found to violate the antitrust laws if their intent or impact results in an unlawful restraint of trade.

Although the great majority of international business transactions do not pose antitrust problems, antitrust issues may arise in various types of transactions, including:

- overseas distribution arrangements;
- overseas joint ventures for research, manufacturing, construction, and distribution;
- patent, trademark, copyright, and know-how licenses;
- mergers and acquisitions involving foreign firms; and
- raw material procurement agreements and concessions.

By writing a business letter to the Antitrust Division describing the business transaction contemplated, the Department of Justice can determine the legality of the proposed transaction. For more background on antitrust enforcement policies, refer to the Department of Justice's *Antitrust Enforcement Guidelines for International Operations.*

Antidiversion Clause

The US government requires a control statement on shipping documents. Under this requirement, the commercial invoice and bill of lading for nearly all commercial shipments leaving the US must display a statement notifying the carrier and all foreign parties that the US material has been licensed for export only to certain destinations and may not be diverted from that those destinations.

Sources of Assistance

Office of Export Trading Company Affairs, ITA, USDOC

Administers the Export Trade Certificate of Review program, which provides exporters with an antitrust "insurance policy" intended to foster joint export activities where economies of scale and risk diversification are achieved; promotes export trading companies and export management companies; and offers information and counseling to businesses associations regarding the export intermediary industry. For more information, telephone (202) 482-5131; fax (202) 482-1790.

The US Bureau of Export Administration (BXA)

Performs the bulk of validated export license processing for the US government. BXA's services also include:

System for Tracking Export License Applications (STELA)

Three weeks after submitting an application, STELA allows the potential exporter to track the status of a license application over a touch-tone phone. For more information, telephone (202) 482-2752.

Export License Application and Information Network (ELAIN)

Allows potential exporters to apply electronically for a validated export license. MS-DOS, with a Hayes-compatible modem, is required for connection. Contact the Exporter Counseling Division, P.O. Box 273, Washington, DC 20044; telephone (202) 482-4811; fax (202) 482-3617.

Export Licensing Voice Information System (ELVIS)

Automated telephone attendant which contains valuable information on the latest regulation updates, special licenses, information about STELA and ELAIN, seminar updates and commodity classification assistance. Telephone (202) 482-4811.

Export Licensing Seminars

Seminars that cover the basics of export licensing for technical data, software, the implementation of export management systems and other licensing issues. For more information telephone (202) 482-6031; fax (202) 482-3617.

BXA Contacts

Exporter Counseling Division (ECD)
P.O. Box 273
14th Street and Pennsylvania Ave., NW
Washington, DC. 20044
Tel: (202) 482-4811
Fax: (202) 482-3617

BXA West, Headquarters
3300 Irvine Avenue
Suite 345
Newport Beach, CA 92660-3198
Tel: (714) 660-0144
Fax: (714) 660-9347

BXA West, Santa Clara Branch Office
5201 Great America Parkway
Suite 333
Santa Clara, CA 95054
Tel: (408) 748-7450
Fax: (408) 748-7470

Other US Government Regulatory Agencies

Commission of Patents and Trademarks

Controls the export of unclassified technical data. Contact: Commission of Patents & Trademarks, US Patent and Trademark Services, Washington, DC 20231; telephone (703) 308-4357.

The Department of State

Controls the export of munitions. Contact: Department of State Defense, Space and Trade Control Department, PM-DTC Room 228, SA-6, Washington, DC 20522-0602; telephone (703) 875-6644; fax (703) 875-6647.

The Drug Enforcement Administration

Controls the export of narcotics and dangerous drugs. Contact: Drug Enforcement Administration, 700 Army Navy Drive, Arlington, VA 22202; telephone (202) 307-7977; fax (202) 307-7965.

The Nuclear Regulatory Commission

Governs exports of nuclear equipment and materials. Contact: Office of International Programs, US Nuclear Regulatory Commission, Mailstop O17F2, Washington, DC. 20555-0001; telephone (301) 415-1780; fax (301) 415-2400.

The Department of Energy

Governs exports of natural gas and electric power. Contact: Department of Energy, Office of Fuels Programs, 1000 Independence Avenue, SW, FE-53, Washington, DC 20555; telephone (202) 586-9482; fax (202) 586-6050.

The Department of Treasury, Office of Foreign Assets Control

Controls assets of and some exports to countries which have been embargoed by the United States. Contact: Department of Treasury, Foreign Assets Control, 1500 Pennsylvania Avenue, NW, Washington, DC 20220; telephone (202) 622-2500; fax (202) 622-1657.

The Amidei Group

> "There are going to be times when you won't be prepared to do business in a particular market," Neil Amidei said, "and you have to learn from them so you don't make the same mistake twice."

The Learning Curve

Exporting services is a learning experience. Just ask Neil Amidei, President of the Amidei Group. The San Francisco-based public relations firm promotes clients like American Express, Dean Witter, Arthur Anderson & Co., and First Nationwide Bank around the world. Amidei says every company is going to make mistakes when exporting their service.

"There are going to be times when you won't be prepared to do business in a particular market," he said, "and you have to learn from them so you don't make the same mistake twice."

Amidei points to his company's venture in Japan as an example. Hired to promote one of their clients, they were unprepared for the higher costs in the Far East. "Frankly, we didn't know it would be that expensive to get materials and to participate in seminars," he said. "We now try to be constantly aware of changes in methods and costs between country."

"In public relations, particularly, you have to make sure your language and cultural aspects are correct," said Vi Cooper, Account Executive at the Amidei Group. "We learned the color blue isn't as welcome in many markets, for example, because of its association with Israel and the Star of David."

Although some errors are inevitable, Cooper said the best way to prepare for them is research. "You'd be amazed how much you learn just by talking to people, and getting their ideas," she said.

Technology

Amidei said the Internet is a boon to any service group, because it makes advertising on a global scale that much easier. Now, just about anyone in the world can read about a company on the World Wide Web.

"The great thing about the Internet is that it's accessible to so many people," Amidei said. "We can put news items on the wire and it's instantly seen by people we couldn't reach before."

Because of the Internet's capabilities, Amidei says more than one Web-site may be needed for a single company. "You can't do one Web-site that will appease everyone around the world," he said, "there are too many cultural and language differences."

Advice

The Amidei Group has always made a point of following clients into other countries rather than trying to create their own market in a country.

"We've never just opened an office in another country or tried to solicit foreign clients," Amidei said. "Our international experience has come about because of domestic clients that have wanted to branch out into other markets. I think there is a lot less risk that way."

Amidei feels that the greatest thing a company can do to get integrated into another market is begin or join a network of other similar firms.

"We actually began our own network called the Pinnacle Group," Amidei said. "It allows us to sit down with other professionals and learn how to provide services in those countries."

Amidei also feels that, if possible, a firm should incorporate other professionals as consultants. "That allows them to get over any cultural differences that may pop up," he said.

Neil Amidei

Chapter 7:

EXPORT FINANCE

Financing Export Transactions

In general, exporters want to get paid as quickly as possible, and importers prefer delaying payment at least until they have received and resold the goods or services. Being able to offer good payment terms is often necessary to make a sale and definitely will give a seller an advantage over other suppliers. Exporters should be aware of the many financing options open to them so they may choose the one that is most advantageous to both buyer and seller.

An exporter may need financing to produce or purchase the product or provide a service, or need postshipment financing of the resulting accounts receivable, or both. Some factors to consider in making a decision about export financing:

How necessary is financing to make the sale?

Favorable payment terms may make a product or service more competitive or may actually make the difference in winning the contract. Sometimes, financing is necessary for promotion or other selling expenses and shipping costs.

What are the different costs of various methods of financing?

Since interest rates and fees vary greatly, total costs and their effect on the entire transaction should be well understood before financing terms are finalized.

For what length of time is financing required?

Costs usually increase with the length of financing, and this can have an impact on the overall costs of any transaction.

What is an acceptable level of financial risk?

The greater the transaction risks, the greater the costs to the exporter as well as the more difficult financing will be to obtain. The creditworthiness of the buyer is one factor to consider, but it is not the only criteria upon which to evaluate risk. Political and economic stability in the buyer's country, as well as volatility of currency, also have some bearing on the risks associated with an international transaction.

Does the exporter have financial resources available?

Companies may be able to extend the credit necessary for an international transaction without seeking outside financing, or the company may have sufficient resources to establish a commercial line of credit to carry the costs.

In addition, there are several sources which provide assistance in determining which financing options are available and which are best suited to the transaction at hand:

- the exporter's international or domestic banker
- the exporter's state export promotion or export finance office
- the Department of Commerce District Office
- the Small Business Administration
- the Export-Import Bank in Washington, DC

Extending Credit to Foreign Buyers

Foreign buyers often press exporters for longer payment periods. Although longer credit periods increase the risk of default for which the exporter may be liable, it is also true that liberal financing is a means of enhancing the competitiveness of a product or service. Exporters must therefore carefully consider financing arrangements and the terms of payment which are acceptable to them in their foreign transactions.

In extending credit to foreign buyers, exporters should carefully follow the same credit principles they employ for domestic customers. A useful guide for determining the appropriate credit period is the normal commercial terms in the exporter's industry for internationally traded products or services. Buyers generally expect to receive the benefits of such terms. With few exceptions, normal commercial terms range from 30 to 180 days for non-specialized products or services, and financing for custom or specialized products ranges from cash on receipt to one year or more. Most exporters absorb interest charges for short-term credit unless the customer pays after the due date.

One thing exporters may need to allow for that is not a consideration in domestic transactions is the longer shipping time required for foreign purchases. Allowances may have to be made for longer shipment times because foreign buyers are often unwilling to have the credit period start until they have actually received the product or service. Remember, credit terms extended to a buyer tend to set the precedent for future sales, so the exporter should carefully consider any credit terms extended to first-time buyers.

Generally, it is a good idea to check a buyer's credit even if credit risk insurance or relatively safe payment methods are employed. Banks are often able to provide credit reports on foreign companies, either through their own foreign branches or through a correspondent bank.

The Department of Commerce's world traders data

reports also provide useful information for credit checks. For a fee, a WTDR may be requested on any foreign company. Although the WTDR is not a credit report, it does contain some financial information and also identifies other US companies that do business with the reported firm. The exporter may then contact those companies directly to find out about their payment experience.

Private credit reporting services also are available, many of which have extensive reporting services in foreign countries. Dun & Bradstreet offers three services to evaluate the risk of doing business with an overseas company. The *Business Information Report* contains a variety of information such as payment experience, company summary, finances, history, operations and corporate structure. The *Payment Analysis Report* provides a comprehensive analysis of a company's payment habits. The *Financial Profile* provides detailed financial information on a company, plus key business ratios calculated for both the company and its industry.

Dunn & Bradstreet also has a full range of collection services to collect domestic and international past-due dollars quickly. For more information call (800) 234-DUNS.

Reliable evaluations can also be obtained from foreign credit reporting services, many of which are listed in The *Exporter's Guide to Foreign Sources for Credit Information,* published by Trade Data Reports, Inc., 6 West 37th St., New York, NY 10018.

Methods of Payment

US service exporters must address a number of financial considerations when operating in the international marketplace. Increasing international competition makes the role of export finance even more important to foreign buyers, exporters and project bidders, and negotiating appropriate financial arrangements can be the key to the transaction's feasibility and profitability.

There are four common methods of international payment, each providing the buyer and the seller with varying degrees of protection for getting paid and for guaranteeing shipment. Ranked in order of most security for the supplier to most security for the buyer, they are: cash in advance, documentary letters of credit (L/C), drafts drawn of foreign buyers (documentary collections), and open accounts.

Cash in Advance

In cash in advance terms the buyer simply prepays the supplier prior to shipment of goods. Cash in advance terms are generally used in new relationships where transactions are small and the buyer has no choice but to pre-pay. These terms give maximum security to the seller but leave the buyer at great risk. Since the buyer has no guarantee that the goods will be shipped, he must have a high degree of trust in the seller's ability and willingness to follow through. The buyer must also consider the economic, political and social stability of the seller's country, as these conditions may make it impossible for the seller to ship as promised.

Cash in advance terms hold virtually no risk for the exporter. However, in a competitive environment it is also difficult to get buyers to agree to these terms. A buyer of services might be willing to make a partial cash payment in advance but usually buyers are reluctant to pay 100 percent up front.

Documentary Letters of Credit (L/C)

A letter of credit is a bank's promise to pay a supplier on behalf of the buyer so long as the supplier meets the terms and conditions stated in the credit. Documents are the key issue in letter of credit transactions. Banks act as intermediaries, and have nothing to do with the goods themselves. The primary advantage of the letter of credit is that the exporter can receive payment when the service has been carried out or is near completion.

Letters of credit are the most common form of international payment because they provide a high degree of protection for both the seller and the buyer. The buyer specifies the documentation that he requires from the seller before the bank is to make payment, and the seller is given assurance that he will receive payment after shipping his goods so long as the documentation is in order. Letter of credit documentation problems occur when documents presented do not agree with the terms and conditions of the letter of credit.

It is the responsibility of the buyer to arrange for the letter of credit. The cost of obtaining a letter of credit varies from country to country. Letters of credit are almost always irrevocable and may be unconfirmed, confirmed, commercial, or standby in nature. With an irrevocable letter of credit, there can be no cancellation or modification of the conditions stated therein, without the mutual consent of both the buyer and seller. An unconfirmed letter of credit carries only the undertaking of the opening bank. A confirmed letter of credit carries both that commitment as well as that of the confirming bank in the country of the seller.

Commercial Letter of Credit

A commercial letter of credit is a commitment on the part of the issuing or confirming bank to hold an agreed sum at the disposal of the seller, on behalf of the buyer, provided that the seller submits documents in strict accordance with the requirements of the credit and on time. A service can complicate a letter of credit as the contract is likely to involve various phases of a project rather than the simple delivery of a product.

Documents requested under a commercial letter of credit usually consist of a draft, commercial invoice, inspection certificate and other evidence to prove that the service has been performed according to the terms of the credit. Banks pay against documents only and most banks negotiate documents in accordance with the rules set forth by the International Chamber of Commerce in Paris, known as the Uniform Customs and Practice for Documentary Credits. These rules insure uniformity of interpretation in international trade and have been adopted in over 180 countries. The rules can be found in ICC Publication 500.

In order for the seller to maintain the protection that a letter of credit affords, the letter of credit must be scrutinized upon receipt for any deficiencies, such as documents that cannot be provided or performance deadlines that cannot be met. The letter of credit can be amended when discrepancies are uncovered. This is accomplished when the buyer, upon request of the seller, instructs its bank to amend the L/C. Any amendments to the L/C must be mutually agreeable to buyer and seller.

Standby Letter of Credit

A standby letter of credit is generally obtained by the exporter, and held in reserve or paid out only as a penalty for noncompliance with some other underlying contract between the parties involved.

Payment under this type of L/C is effected against a draft accompanied by a written and signed statement by the buyer of the service that compliance has occurred. Exporters may be asked to provide a standby letter of credit when bidding on a project abroad or as an assurance under a contractual obligation that they will perform as agreed. If the service is performed accordingly, the standby letter of credit will expire unused. The exporter must also be certain that the documents submitted are exactly as required in the letter of credit.

Performance Bonds

Performance bonds protect the foreign buyer against the seller's default, and represent an alternative to a standby letter of credit. Performance bonds can be extremely difficult to obtain. When an exporter is unable to obtain a performance bond, a standby letter of credit can usually be used in lieu thereof. The main difference between a performance bond and a standby letter of credit is that a bond is issued by an insurance company, while a standby letter of credit is issued by a bank. Companies required to obtain a performance bond should contact an international insurance company.

Private firms and foreign governments often require the posting of a bond in order to insure the completion of quality work done by a service supplier. Most bonds for projects range from one percent to five percent of the total cost of the job. The bonds are commonly issued on a buyer-renewable or indefinite time basis, although some may be allowed for a set time period—usually around 36 months for a major project.

Documentary Collection

A documentary collection is like an international cash on delivery (COD), but with a few twists. The exporter ships goods to the importer, but forwards shipping documents (including the title document) to his bank for transmission to the buyer's bank. The buyer's bank is instructed not to transfer the documents to the buyer until payment is made (documents against payment), or upon guarantee that payment will be made within a specified period of time (documents against acceptance). After the buyer has the documentation for the shipment it is able to take possession of the goods or receive the service. Documentary collection terms are also called "drafts" or "bills of exchange" and are analogous to a foreign buyer's check. Like checks, however, drafts sometimes carry the risk that they will be dishonored.

Documents against payment and documents against acceptance are commonly used in ongoing business relationships and provide a measure of protection for both parties. The buyer and seller, however, both assume risk in the transaction, ranging from refusal on the part of the buyer to pay for the documents, to the seller's shipping of unacceptable goods.

Sight and time drafts are employed as the basis for payment in many export transactions. They are drawn by the seller on the buyer and are generally forwarded by the seller through his/her bank to the buyer's bank for collection. Some banks have a form known as a "direct collection letter," which is provided to the seller or his agent and is forwarded with documents directly to the overseas bank. A sight draft calls for payment when it is presented to the buyer, whereas a time draft calls for payment within a period of time after a date established by "sight," "arrival" or "date." Usually this is expressed in multiples of 30 days, up to 180 days.

An in-country agent can be named by the seller in the collection letter as an "in case of need" party to whom the local bank can refer for assistance or instruction regarding the collection process. In establishing a sight or time draft, it is important for the seller and buyer to establish the responsibility for collection expenses and charges to avoid misunderstanding.

Sight and time drafts are less secure than the letter of credit. Unlike a letter of credit transaction, a sight or time draft is not supported by the credit of a bank. The buyer may decide the service provided is not acceptable and refuse to pay the draft, thus leaving the service provider empty-handed.

There is also risk associated with payment of a time draft versus that associated with a sight draft. The latter is payable upon presentation to the buyer, whereas a time draft need only be accepted upon presentation and is actually paid at its later maturity date. An accepted draft has the same status as a promissory note. The seller agrees to await payment until the draft matures, which can be several months if a time draft is used.

Open Account Terms

An open account is an agreement by the buyer to pay for goods within a designated time after their shipment, usually in 30, 60, or 90 days. Open account terms give maximum security to the buyer and greatest risk to the seller. This form of payment is used only when the seller has significant trust and faith in the buyer's ability and willingness to pay after the goods have been shipped. The seller must also consider the economic, political, and social stability of the buyer's country as these conditions may make it impossible for the buyer to pay as promised.

Although open account financing carries the most risk, it is the least complicated in terms of the involvement of paper work, documentation, bank charges and fees. However, it affords virtually no safeguard for the seller since it provides only a billing process. Little evidence of obligation makes it difficult for the seller to collect if the buyer defaults. And, if the exporter must pursue collection, it must be done abroad, which is often difficult and costly.

Sources of Financing and Insurance

There are many private and public institutions that provide financial assistance to small- and medium-sized creditworthy service exporters. Trade organizations offer two important finance services under various terms and conditions that are extremely valuable financing tools. Some are guarantee programs that require the participation of an approved lender; others provide loans or grants to the exporter or a foreign government. Government guarantee and insurance programs are used by commercial banks to reduce the risk associated with loans to exporters. Lenders concerned with an exporter's ability to perform under the terms of sale, and with an exporter's ability to be paid, often use government programs to reduce the risks that would otherwise prevent them from providing financing.

Exporters who insure their accounts receivable against commercial credit and political risk loss are usually able to secure financing from commercial banks and other lending institutions at lower rates and on a more liberal basis than would otherwise be the case. This enables exporters to extend credit on more favorable terms to overseas customers without tying up working capital needed for internal operations. Some US exporters find that the low premium charge for insuring their exports is largely offset by the more favorable terms under which they are able to secure accommodation from their bankers.

Credit insurance is not based on the premise that the seller can grant credit without exercising normal prudence and business judgment, nor should it substitute for the seller's own credit department. Its value to the buyer and seller is the protection provided against political and economic contingencies beyond the control of the parties to the contract.

Commercial Banks

The same type of commercial loans that finance domestic activities—including loans for working capital and revolving lines of credit—are often sought to finance export sales until payment is received. However, banks do not usually extend credit solely on the basis of an order.

A logical first step in obtaining financing is for an exporter to approach its local commercial bank. If the exporter already has a loan for domestic needs, then the lender already has experience with the exporter's ability to perform. Many exporters have very similar, if not identical, preshipment needs for both their international and domestic transactions. Many lenders, therefore, would be willing to provide financing for export transactions if there were a reasonable certainty of repayment. By using letters of credit or export credit insurance, an exporter can reduce the lender's risk.

For a company that is new to exporting or is a small or medium-sized business, it is important to select a bank that is sincerely interested in serving businesses of similar type of size. The exporter should ensure that its bank's charges for export-related transactions are reasonable, that it has foreign branches or correspondent banks, and that it has experience with US and state government financing programs that support small business export transactions.

If the exporter's bank lacks an international department, it will refer the exporter to a correspondent bank that has one. The exporter may want to visit the international department—of the exporter's own bank or a correspondent bank—to discuss its export plans, available banking facilities, and applicable fees.

Government Agencies

Export-Import Bank of the United States (Eximbank)

Eximbank's main function is to provide protection against foreign defaults so that exporters may offer more attractive terms to their overseas customers. Eximbank provides an insurance tool enabling US exporters to extend terms and protect themselves against unforeseen adverse global economic conditions.

As the export credit agency of the United States, Eximbank provides a range of financing services aimed at facilitating US exports. The bank's most widely used program is its foreign credit insurance coverage. Under this program, Eximbank assumes all liability for political risks, including: hazards of war, revolution or similar hostilities, unforeseen withdrawal or nonrenewability of a license to export, requisition, expropriation, confiscation or intervention in the business of the buyer by a governmental authority. Eximbank also covers transport or insurance charges caused by interruption or diversion of shipment and certain other government acts that may prevent or unduly delay payment and are beyond the control of the seller or buyer. Contact: US Export-Import Bank, 811 Vermont Ave., NW, Washington DC. 20571; telephone (800) 565-3946; fax (202) 565-3380.

Small Business Administration (SBA)

The SBA provides business development and financial assistance for exporters through three main programs: regular business loans, international trade loans and export revolving line of credit loan guarantees. For more information about SBA financing call the SBA Answer Desk at (800) 827-5722.

California World Trade Commission (CWTC)

The CWTC's Export Finance Office provides working capital loan guarantees to financial institutions on behalf of small- and medium-sized California companies in support of export transactions. CEFO's guarantees cover 90 percent of an export loan allowing for a maximum guarantee of $750,000 (or a loan of $833,000). Guarantees support short-term working capital loans, single or multiple transactions and direct loans and/or standby letters of credit. For more information, contact the California World Trade Commission, 6 Enterprise Drive, Suite 760, La Palma, CA 90623; telephone (714) 562-5519; fax (714) 562-5530.

Developing Country Markets

There are numerous organizations, both private and public, whose missions are to support economic development through international trade. US development assistance emphasizes long-term development objectives for agriculture, rural development and nutrition; population planning, health, child survival fund; AIDS prevention and control; education and human resources development; private sector, energy, environment and science and other assistance. Because of the highly technical and diverse nature of economic development programs consultants with specific, specialized expertise are frequently utilized on a short-term basis for larger long term projects.

United States services have high sales potential in developing economies, especially education, training, technology and business management services. Several major multi- and bilateral development banks (MDBs & BDBs) fund projects exclusively intended for less developed countries, that increase the opportunities in developing regions for US service providers.

Because major projects generate the need for a variety of ancillary services, many opportunities for small service firms do not necessarily lie in the actual financial support of an MDB. Quite often a small service provider can subcontract with the principal contractor of a multimillion dollar MDB bid.

Multilateral Development Banks

The underlying purpose of multilateral development banks is to assist in the development of lesser developed countries (LDCs). Multilateral development banks play an important role in the transfer of technology and services between countries. The World Bank, UN Development Programme and Inter-American Development Bank all contribute funds and management expertise to less developed regions of the world lacking capital, human resources or research and development capabilities.

Most multilateral banks finance in three ways: 1) reimbursement—when the borrower first pays expenditures and subsequently requests MDB for reimbursement; 2) direct payment—when the borrower transmits an invoice received after verification to the bank, and requests that MDB pay the supplier, contractor or consultant directly, and 3) commitment—when the borrower opens a normal commercial letter of credit for the supplier, contractor or consultant. Subsequently, the borrower requests the bank to inform the credit negotiating bank in the seller's country that, subject to certain conditions specified in the commitment, they promptly reimburse payments made under the letter of credit.

To compete for MDB-funded projects, a US service firm must: 1) register with the development bank—this assists the bank in linking US services to the lesser developed countries that need them most, as well as providing project leads for US firms and 2) bid for the project which allows the development bank to find the best qualified and least expensive service firm. MDBs and BDBs have strict regulations and application processes to which the service firm must adhere to become eligible for the bidding process.

Multilateral Development Bank Operations (MDBO)

The Office of Multilateral Development houses the five offices of the African Development Bank, Asian Development Bank, European Bank for Reconstruction and Development, Inter-American Development Bank and the World Bank. The common goal shared by the MDBO is to help raise standards of living among the people of developing nations by channeling diversified financial resources to them. MDBO has responsibility for providing information and assistance to US companies interested in supplying goods and services to overseas construction, engineering, manufacturing and investment projects that are supported by each of the independent offices. In an effort to encourage, inform and assist US companies seeking to become more familiar with opportunities available through MDB-supported projects, the MDBO staff reports on projects being considered by these financing institutions, counsels companies on decision making and procurement processes of each MDB, and provides assistance in developing competitive strategies on behalf of US firms. The following section details services offered by individual development banks, however, all have the same common contact point. When contacting the Office of Multilateral Development by phone or letter, simply specify the bank of particular interest. Write to: Office of International Operations, Office of Multilateral Development Bank Operations, US Department of Commerce, International Trade Administration, 14th & Constitution Avenues, Washington, DC 20230; telephone (202) 482-3399; fax (202) 273-0927.

African Development Bank (AfDB)

The AfDB mobilizes efficient funding and technical resources to economic and social development projects aiding African countries. The AfDB has two project departments: 1) the African Development Fund (ADF) is responsible for providing financing to member countries and promoting sub-regional cooperation and increased international trade; 2) the Nigerian Trust Fund (NTF) focuses on development projects to those in more needy circumstances by extending loans on terms and is more flexible than other AfDB terms. Both ADF and NTF loans are restricted to countries with a per capita GDP of no more that US$500.

Asian Development Bank (ADB)

The ADB promotes economic development and cooperation in developing Asian countries through conventional and concessional loans, technical assistance and investment promotion. The ADB sources millions of dollars of goods and services each year from the United States. The Bank's capital is distributed on highly concessional terms and almost exclusively to the poorest of borrowing nations. Financing comes in the form of loans and co-financing. The ADB primarily focuses on projects related to economic development emphasizing energy, industry, education, health, population, urban development, water supply and sanitation, telecommunications, transportation, agriculture and other infrastructure concerns. Two useful publications provided by ADB are *Guidelines for Procurement under Asian Development Bank Loans* and *Guidelines on the Use of Consultants by the Asian Development Bank and Its Borrowers*.

Inter-American Development Bank (IDB)

The IDB was established to accelerate the social development and economic growth of Latin America and the Caribbean. The bank provides funding for technical assistance to low-income countries for the preparation, financing and implementation of development plans and projects in such areas as agriculture, industry, environment, public health, education, urban development, energy and transportation. The IDB's service industries and finance representatives can be particularly helpful in providing business consulting, project procurement advice, business leads, information on specific projects, and assistance with procurement disputes.

European Bank for Reconstruction and Development (EBRD)

The EBRD operates in Albania, Estonia, Lithuania, Bulgaria, the Czech and Slovak Federal Republic, Hungary, Poland, Romania, Slovenia and the former Soviet Republics. EBRD combines merchant and development banking to help restructure both the public and private sectors, and offers advice, loans, debt guarantees and equity investment projects.

The World Bank

In most cases, procurement to the World Bank and its affiliates is based on international competitive bidding rules. For the most current information on World Bank projects, subscribe to *Development Business*, which contains a monthly operational summary of projects pending Bank approval. A subscription to *Development Business* also includes projects pending at the Inter-American Development Bank (IDB) and a quarterly summary for the African Development Bank as well as invitations to bid on projects funded by the IDM, the AfDB, the Asian Development Bank, the European Bank for Reconstruction and Development, the Caribbean Development Bank and the United Nations system.

Inquiries may be addressed to *Development Business,* United Nations, G.C.P.O., Box 5850, New York, NY 10163-5850; telephone (212) 963-1515; fax (212) 963-1381. Sample copies of *Development Business* may be obtained by calling (201) 476-2497.

International Bank for Reconstruction and Development

The IBRD extends loans on conventional terms for specific high priority projects. Recipient eligibility is given to member governments, their political subdivisions and public or private entities in their territories. The focus of IBRD projects is towards improving education, ensuring environmental sustainability, expanding economic opportunities, strengthening population planning, improving health and nutrition services, developing the private sector and building roads, railways, telecommunications networks and port and power facilities.

International Development Association (IDA)

The IDA provides assistance primarily to poorer, non-industrialized countries with an annual per capita GNP of US $635 or less. IDA offers "soft" lending terms that are less stringent than regular IBRD loans. No interest is charged and only a minimal administrative service charge is levied against recipient countries.

International Finance Corporation (IFC)

The IFC encourages growth of productive private enterprise in developing countries by extending loans and non-controlling equity, providing underwriting and standby commitments and attracting and acting as a catalyst for outside financing. Interest rates on loans are keyed to the IBRD rate. Possible recipients include private firms in developing member-countries.

Multilateral Investment Guarantee Agency (MIGA)

MIGA encourages equity investment and other direct investment flows to developing countries. The agency offers investor guarantees against non-commercial risks, and advises developing member-governments on the design and implementation of policies, programs and procedures related to foreign investment and sponsors dialogue between the international business community and host governments on investment issues.

The United Nations

Various organizations within the UN maintain rosters of interested subcontractors for a wide spectrum of service projects and include both qualifications and specifications. For UN procurement information and opportunities, ask for the free publication, *General Business Guide to the United Nations System*. For DACON registration information, contact: DACON Information Center, 1818 H St., NW, Washington, DC 20433.

United Nations Development Programme (UNDP)

The UNDP is one of the most important contact points available to service providers. Advance notice on business opportunities emanating from UNDP-assisted projects to potential procurement sources is transmitted on a regular basis through the biweekly Development Forum Business Addition. Contact: Senior Director, Office for Project Services, United Nations Development Programme, One United Nations Plaza, New York, NY 10017; telephone (212) 906-6100.

United Nations Industrial Development Organization (UNIDO)

UNIDO is one of the central international agencies in the field of technology transfer. Service firms receive business leads from this institution regarding project identification, design and implementation. Through the studies, conferences and declarations of UNIDO, service/technology exporting firms can evaluate the general climate and planning trends in technology acquisition occurring in the LDCs. Contact: Head, Purchase and Contract Services, UNIDO, One United Nations Plaza, New York, NY 10017; telephone (212) 963-6882; fax (212) 963-7904.

US Assistance

International Development Cooperation Agency

The IDCA is an umbrella organization housing three separate agencies: the Agency for International Development (AID), Trade and Development Agency (TDA) and the Overseas Private Investment Corporation (OPIC). These sister agencies have the unified purpose of supporting developing nations, yet work independently of each other.

Agency for International Development (AID)

The Agency for International Development (AID) manages a wide variety of economic and humanitarian assistance programs in more than 100 countries in the developing world, Central and Eastern Europe and the Newly Independent States (NIS) of the former Soviet Union.

AID administers most US bilateral foreign economic assistance programs. Grants and concessionary loans are extended through AID to foreign governments and their related institutions in developing countries. AID is required to procure products and services from US sources. Annually, the agency procures millions of dollars of consulting services, social services, building and construction equipment, engineering designs, education, etc. from US suppliers. Leads are publicized in the *Commerce Business Daily,* which offers a synopsis of federal agency contacts worth $25,000 or more and is issued by the US Department of Commerce. In addition, AID information bulletins announcing procurement opportunities are sent to firms that register with the Agency.

Service firms, such as research, architect/engineering, consulting and construction firms interested in bidding on AID-financed projects, should register in the AID Consultant Registry Information System (ACRIS) to compete for technical service contracts. ACRIS is a computerized database listing American firms and their technical capabilities. Foreign firms can contact ACRIS free of charge to identify American firms with matching capabilities. For more information, contact USAID, Washington, DC 20523-0229; telephone (800) USAID4U; fax (202) 663-2670.

The Infrastructure Division

The US Department of Commerce's Office of Major Projects (OMP), located in Washington, DC, is the best contact point for questions and counseling for US firms wishing to compete on major foreign projects. The OMP receives early notices of foreign projects from the US embassies abroad, helps link foreign projects to US firms and assists US firms on bidding procedures. One of the best ways the USDOC assists prospective international project bidders is by publishing these early contacts through the *Commerce Business Daily,* a newspaper that lists government procurement invitations and contract awards, including foreign business opportunities and foreign government procurements. The OMP primarily focuses on overseas construction, engineering, industrial systems and infrastructure projects, including turnkey installations in excess of 25 million dollars. Contact: The Infrastructure Division, Room 4314, Trade Development, International Trade Administration, US Department of Commerce, Washington, DC 20230; telephone (202) 482-4642; fax (202) 482-3954.

US Trade and Development Agency (TDA)

TDA has an exclusive mandate to promote US exports for major projects, that are economic development priorities of host governments in middle income and developing countries. TDA provides grants to fund feasibility studies and other planning services for major projects. TDA-funded studies must be performed by US companies. More than 65 percent of TDA's 1992 funds were allocated to development of energy and natural resources, transportation and telecommunications projects, all deemed essential for establishing an efficient infrastructure to support modern economic development.

TDA funds orientation visits to familiarize foreign officials with US technologies and services, including technical symposia and trade-related training programs. TDA also publishes a newsletter called the *TDA Biweekly,* which provides US suppliers and manufacturers with up-to-date information on TDA-supported projects. Those firms that would like leads on potential TDA-funded projects should subscribe to the *Early Bird,* which lists the current projects under consideration that have not yet received any funding from TDA. Once TDA commits funds to a project, it is tracked in the *TDA Biweekly.* Call (703) 875-4246 for a subscription.

For information on opportunities to bid on TDA-funded projects, call the Definitional Mission hotline at (703) 875-7447. Consultants also should inquire about being included in the TDA consultant database. Contact: US Trade and Development Agency, Room 309, SA-16, Washington, DC 20523-1602; telephone (703) 875-4357; fax (703) 875-4009.

Overseas Private Investment Corporation (OPIC)

OPIC facilitates US private investment in 140 lesser developed nations by providing three principal programs: 1) financing of investments through direct loans and loan guaranties; 2) insuring investments against political risks and 3) providing a variety of investor services. OPIC's investor services program is designed to assist small- and medium-sized US firms, as well as new-to-market companies, with their overseas investment planning and implementation needs. OPIC's fee-based services involve counseling to American firms on business plan development, project structuring, joint venture partner identification and location of project financing sources. For more information, contact: Overseas Private Investment Corporation, 1100 New York Avenue, 12th Floor, Washington, DC 20527; telephone (202) 336-8400; fax (800) 424-OPIC.

Trade and Investment Services (TIS)

This organization engages the resources of the International Executive Service Corps (IESC) to support a range of industry-specific, trade and investment services designed to link businesses in the US, developing countries, and emerging democracies worldwide. TIS activities are designed to assist in the expansion of US and developing country business through development of joint venturing alliances and co-ventures, including the sale or licensing of US equipment and technology, long-term sales and co-production agreements. Contact the Office of International Business Development: telephone (202) 663-2680; fax (202) 663-2670.

Lil' Orbits

> "Every market is different," Ed Anderson said. "Many countries, particularly France, had difficulty pronouncing 'Lil,' so we also registered 'Orbie' as an additional trademark."

The Match Game

Ed Anderson, founder and president of Lil' Orbits, knows all about adjusting one's service to fit a market. The Minneapolis-based company sells donut-making equipment and ingredients, so users can set up their own shops and become entrepreneurs. They also train users how to make and sell the snacks, and share marketing tips with their users.

"We do much more than just sell them the equipment," Anderson said. Lil' Orbits only began exporting their service in 1987, and already they have become enormously successful. They received the President's Award for Merit in Export in 1992, and they have over 20,000 dealers operating in 78 countries. That means a lot of markets, and a lot of different types of customers.

"Every market is different," Anderson said. "Many countries, particularly France, had difficulty pronouncing 'Lil,' so we also registered "Orbie" as an additional trademark."

Lil' Orbits also changes its recipe for several countries. "We developed a concentrate of our special donut formula which can be blended with local ingredients," Anderson said. "We have to alter the flavor in certain countries to suit the local taste."

Communicating

Staying in touch with all his licensees can be difficult, but Anderson feels it is worth the effort. "We have a newsletter that comes out twice a year and is sent to all Lil' Orbits dealers," Anderson said. "It features some selling tips and examples of how other licensees have found success." He also regularly faxes out a communique to the network to keep them updated on the latest developments.

Anderson makes sure to include examples from Lil' Orbits licensees in other countries in his newsletter. "It is a huge portion of their business," Anderson said, "plus they offer tips that can be helpful to licensees in the United States."

Lil' Orbits also has a book that helps beginners set up, with sections like "starting your business," "running your machines," and "financing your business."

"Our licensees have a great deal of freedom with our product," Anderson said, "but we try to help them, especially when they're just starting out."

Email is another great way to keep communication lines open. "Email allows you to talk back and forth without spending a fortune," Anderson said.

In the Beginning...

Anderson feels that forwarding companies can really help service companies looking to export. "They did all our paperwork in the beginning," he said. "We eventually learned how to do it ourselves, but they were very helpful when we were just starting out."

Export groups such as Export Councils can also be of tremendous use, and Anderson said not to forget about other business groups. "SCORE (the Service Corp Of Retired Executives) can really help because they've been there," Anderson said. "Try to contact a representative whose field of expertise is close to what you want to accomplish."

Advertising is essential for any starting business. If people don't know you, they won't try your product. "We started advertising with the *Commercial News,* a publication of the Department of Commerce," Anderson said.

Web pages are also tremendously helpful. "They are a great way for people to get their name out to markets for very little money," Anderson said. He advises other companies to list their web-site address with search engines abroad, to help get the address out.

Chapter 8:

SERVICE INDUSTRY ANALYSES

The United States is home to a multitude of service industries that are increasingly moving into new foreign markets and entering them with a variety of market entry strategies: foreign direct investment, project consultancies, franchising and alliances.

This chapter examines 20 selected US service industries and their basic functions. It also highlights marketing strategies, pinpoints common market barriers and offers a number of key public and private resources for each industry.

The trade associations and events included in these analyses are provided solely as an informational source and, excluding US government-certified and organized events, do not represent an endorsement.

Information in this chapter was compiled with permission from a variety of US government resources: The *US Industrial Outlook,* the *Office of Service Industries' Competitive Analysis,* and *Business America.* Market barrier information found at the end of many of the analyses was extracted from the USDOC Office of Services Industries' report analyzing the service industry's competitiveness. The export intermediary industry analysis was excerpted from *Business America.* See bibliography for further information.

Service Analyses:

Accounting

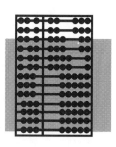

Defined

Accountants, auditors, and bookkeepers have been referred to traditionally—and usually lightheartedly—as "bean counters." They are routinely employed by clients in both the public and private sector to prepare, examine, and verify financial accounts and records, provide tax return preparation services and organize and maintain books of money transactions. They monitor, and often chart the course for, the movement of a client's money and are essential to the daily operations of their clients.

However, modern accounting has recently become a much broader and analytical field than its auditing and bookkeeping counterparts. Accounting is now regarded almost as an art form in the business world. Modern accountants are being called upon more often to provide consulting and estimation services. They are being asked to look beyond the "beans" and evaluate the bigger picture. Today's accountants are economic forecasters and have become essential to investors seeking information about a company's visibility.

Much of this accounting revolution has evolved from the savings and loan crisis of the late 1980s. The crisis triggered feelings of fear and dread throughout the corporate world as the threat of extensive professional audits grew. As a result, US corporations now expect—and demand—that their accountants be able to confront problems associated with various legal and ethical issues. This includes addressing the quality of corporate governance and accountability. These expectations make examining and monitoring various other aspects of a company's internal structure an unavoidable responsibility for today's corporate accountants.

Domestic Market Overview

There are more than 150,000 accounting firms in the United States. The industry is dominated by the so-called "Big Six," which includes Certified Public Accounting (CPA) powerhouses Ernst & Young, Deloitte and Touche, KPMG Peat Marwick, Coopers & Lybrand, Price Waterhouse and Arthur Anderson & Co. These companies constantly battle to secure big clients, or even capture accounts from one another, by offering special rates and services peppered with a good deal of marketing and self-promotion. The "Big Six" are in a position to exercise this "lowballing" approach among themselves because they are financially powerful enough to take big risks and can easily recoup losses from failed deal attempts. Unfortunately, this practice of flexing financial muscle leaves almost no opportunity for smaller accounting firms to court big clients.

However, the industry is slowly changing. Many US accountants have discovered that their key to success is operating in niche markets that the "Big Six" do not effectively serve. Smaller CPA firms are in an excellent position to offer a hands-on and personalized approach to accounting, specifically seeking those companies that prefer to avoid bigger accounting firms. This includes specializing in certain aspects of accounting or catering only to one type of industry, such as retail or construction. Some accountants deal only with clients who speak a particular foreign language.

Software applications designed to streamline operations and increase profitability are in great demand by the corporate world, and accounting firms of every size are working to develop and provide this technology to their clients. CPA establishments are also expected to install the software for their clients, as well as teach a company's employees how to use it. Accounting firms that are Internet and World Wide Web savvy and exhibit an understanding of Local Area Networks (LANs) also become the toughest competitors for new clients.

Top CPA firms are also starting to refuse or drop clients that fall into so-called "high risk" categories. This attitude coincides with a trend in the accounting industry toward streamlining internal operations to remain competitive. Potential client risks include fledgling companies preparing for an initial public offering (IPO), or small banks and savings and loans that are easy takeover targets in this era of bank mergers and takeovers. CPA firms outside the "Top 100" would not typically take on clients which pose such risk. However, this risk category attracts little competition for the moment and client relationships established now in this category could prove profitable in the long run.

Another recent and significant cost-cutting trend in the US accounting industry is the utilization of paraprofessionals by both small and large CPA firms. US firms are turning to paraprofessionals to accommodate their staffing needs because it keeps billing rates low, and allows them to remain competitive. Accounting firms save considerable money paying the salaries of part-time paraprofessionals instead of shelling out the cash needed to hire and pay new staff professionals. This method of operation frees up the cash needed to support the domestic and international expansion of many US accounting firms.

International Market Overview

The "Big Six" also preside over the international accounting world and their domination is the result of operating on a global scale for decades. The top ten CPA firms recorded worldwide revenues of US$34.6 billion in 1992.

These and other top CPA firms that are internationally significant have at least 60 overseas offices. Many have established between 150 and 200 offices worldwide.

It is tough for smaller CPA firms to compete effectively with these accounting powerhouses because they have left an indelible mark on so many international markets. Their names alone have become synonymous with international accounting, and they have almost no difficulty moving into new global markets and attracting new business. In fact, the industry's top players have been slashing their rates recently to make sure they do remain the international leaders, especially in emerging markets.

The "Big Six" have been pouring money into Eastern Europe for several years now, knowing they will have to wait to recoup their initial investment. Eastern European countries lack a lot of basic infrastructure, as do indigenous companies in this region of the world. But the top international accounting firms have deep pockets and can afford to bide their time while Eastern Europe catches up with the rest of the world technologically and becomes more politically and economically stable.

Just like the US market, small and medium-sized companies are seeking to invest whatever is most cost-effective. This leaves plenty of opportunity for boutique accountants to edge their way into the international marketplace.

Today's US accountants are more willing to investigate relationships with foreign companies looking to set up operations in the United States. While more small- and mid-sized US companies work to stake their claim in international markets, there are countless foreign companies of similar size looking to this country to expand their business. These companies usually don't have the cash to attract the "Big Six," but look instead to hire smaller US accounting firms and individual CPAs to meet their needs. And many foreign companies with the cash to spare for bigger CPA firms are spending it on CPA firms that can provide the "boutique" approach.

Market Barriers

US accountants and accounting firms must remember that no matter which international market they choose to enter, they will be competing with established local accountants. Foreign governments favor their countries' accounting firms and work aggressively to protect and promote their interests. The General Agreement on Tariffs and Trade (GATT) does support the concept of "national treatment," which is the belief that foreign firms should be treated equally with indigenous companies in any market. But national treatment is more suggestion than law at this time, and discrimination against foreign-owned and operated businesses freely abounds. Therefore, US accounting firms must accept that they are playing on an uneven field.

Global market access for the majority of US-based CPA firms is greatly influenced by this preferential treatment for local accountants. However, the situation is not hopeless. For example, Greek accountants recently lobbied for creation of a law that would require any company with operations in

Greece to employ only Greek firms for their auditing needs. The World Trade Organization (WTO) blocked this movement by citing its obvious violation of national treatment and the Greek government concurred. Situations and conflicts like this constantly arise, but are now being dismissed more frequently by countries looking to keep or earn the Most Favored Nation (MFN) trade status with the United States.

Standards, Certification, Fees, and Taxes

Licensing requirements for foreign and domestic accounting firms vary from market to market. In Finland, a permit is not needed for founding an accounting or auditing firm, although the Finnish government will closely monitor a firm's operations afterward. It should be noted that accounting and auditing firms are regarded as two separate business areas in Finland, and are divided according to a recently implemented Finnish auditing law. Professional degrees in accounting are not required to practice in Finland, but are regarded as a measure of quality by clients.

Across the globe in Brazil, the accounting industry is regulated by the Federal Accounting Council and several regional councils. These councils are regulated by Brazil's Ministry of Labor. Accountants in Brazil typically specialize in bookkeeping and tax return services for self-employed individuals and small companies. Accountants are not qualified to audit accounts. As in Finland, there is a distinct and enforced division between the two areas of accounting and auditing.

The above references to Brazil and Finland provide a glimpse of how standards for and expectations of accountants and auditors vary throughout the world. US accounting firms face countless hurdles when entering a global market. There are also fees, taxes, and joint venture requirements to be observed in different markets. In Mexico, a US accountant is required to establish a joint venture partnership with an established domestic accounting firm. By law, the US company can only participate in 30 percent of the venture. According to many joint venture agreements, US accounting firms are also required to sell off their interest to their partners after a certain period of time.

US accountants entering foreign markets can also expect to take one or more tests to prove their qualifications. These tests, unfortunately, are used more to discourage foreign firms from doing business in particular markets than to establish credentials. Some examples are even reportedly more difficult than tests taken by domestic accountants and auditors. The Working Party on Professional Services, a division of the World Trade Organization, is working with thousands of foreign accountants and governments to develop a mutual recognition of credentials. It will be years before standardized accreditation will come into being, but it is already clear that the global door is slowly opening for international accountants.

Market Channels

Decide on an Area of Expertise

A key step in achieving success in a global market is specializing in a particular area of accounting. For US firms, this means using elements of their existing client base to chart their new international course. Accountants with a background in serving wholesalers or retailers, for example, should pursue similar clients in other countries. This focusing will also help determine what regions, countries and cities have the highest demand for these services and present the greatest opportunity for success. Narrowing the point of entry in a global market gives any foreign accountant an edge over other firms operating with a generic or less specific marketing program.

Follow US Clients Abroad

Be willing to follow clients expanding into new international territory. Accountants should make it absolutely clear to their clients that they are ready and able to support them in their efforts to set up offices in foreign countries. US accountants should never assume that their clients will look to them first for the task. Many executives are unaware that they can place their own accountants in foreign offices. Savvy accountants will also offer to do the necessary research on their limitations and expectations abroad.

Establish Alliances with Foreign Companies in the US

Approach foreign companies operating in the United States. Winning their business here can lead to easy access to markets abroad. One of the main reasons foreign executives turn to the "Big Six" and other large international firms for their accounting needs is name recognition. In most cases, international companies would rather not employ a large accounting firm due to the cost. Most businesses will gladly choose smaller US accounting firms to handle their worldwide projects, provided these firms have already proved themselves worthy on the US front. No matter how large an international company may be, saving money and building strong alliances with quality service providers is always at the top of global executives' minds.

Learn the Language and the Culture of a Target Global Market

It cannot be stressed enough that global thinking opens doors to global markets. An accounting firm—no matter how small—that exhibits international savvy will always have an advantage over any size firm lacking the same global intelligence. Again, the "boutique" marketing approach can be applied. For example, if a US accounting firm wants to break into Mexico, a key player at said firm should know how to speak and write in Spanish. It should never be assumed that English is an acceptable form of communication for global businesses. International executives may hire a US accounting firm because it needs to do business with English-speaking clients. But that does not mean that the same executives want to conduct their business in any language but their own.

Focus on Netting Smaller Clients First

US accountants operating abroad should seek out small- or mid-sized clients to establish operations in a foreign country. In many cases, accountants and their foreign clients will be learning together and from each other. If a US accountant

is serious about being a success in a particular foreign market, and spends the time and effort needed to do a great job, the word will eventually spread throughout that market's business community.

It is very important to establish a good reputation and serious work ethic in a foreign market, especially when dealing with the smaller players. US accounting firms must remember that more weight is given to their professional reputation in other countries than it might in the United States. There is also less opportunity for a professional rebound when any company has been blackballed by a foreign business community. There are also plenty of domestic and foreign companies to take over for another's failure.

Regional Opportunities

Note: These are only examples of regional opportunities and in no way constitute a complete list.

According to a recent report on the international accounting industry by the US Department of Commerce's Office of Service Industries, the accounting industry's Big Emerging Markets (BEMs) are not tied to one particular global region. The ten BEMs, based on research gathered this decade, include India, Indonesia, South Korea, Mexico, Brazil, Argentina, South Africa, Poland, and Turkey. The latter three BEMs exhibit opportunity primarily because they are more politically stable now than in years past. Their economies are also in an upswing and new small- and mid-sized businesses are rapidly developing. However, these countries lack critical infrastructure and are still perceived as risky ventures by many US accounting firms.

Asia

The markets of South Korea, India, and Indonesia are also budding with opportunity. But US accounting firms can expect to face off with their Japanese counterparts in these markets. Japan has a strong foothold in these regions due to its location and its similarities in culture. Many Japanese firms have been operating in these countries for more than a decade and have the trust of small and large clients alike. Still, US accounting firms can find success by following their own clients into these countries.

The number one emerging market for accounting is the so called "Chinese Economic Area." This consists of China, Hong Kong, and Taiwan. But their status in Hong Kong will be in question once British rule ends there in 1997.

Central and South America

Mexico, Brazil, and Argentina may be the most accessible emerging markets for US accounting firms. Geographical location is a key factor in accessibility. However, the demand for computer software is even greater. The "boutique" marketing approach is essential for doing business in Brazil and Argentina. Many firms seek the advice and expertise of US accountants willing to act as economic consultants. Software applications are also in great demand by growing companies in these countries. US accountants must be prepared to tailor and install software for, and teach their Brazilian and Argentine clients how to use, these programs.

There remains a good deal of red tape for US firms entering Mexico because of that country's established domestic accounting community. However, the North American Free Trade Agreement is slowly helping to smooth the path for US firms attempting to enter the Mexican market. But it will be years before US accountants are recognized as equals with Mexico's domestic firms.

Sources of US Assistance

International Federation of Accountants
117 West 47th St.
Ste. 2410
New York, NY 10036
Tel: (212) 302-5952
Fax: (212) 302-5964

Independent Accountants International
9200 South Dadeland Blvd., Ste. 510
Miami, FL 33156
Tel: (305) 670-0580
Fax: (305) 670-3818

American Institute of Certified Public Accountants
1211 Avenue of the Americas
New York, NY 10036
Tel: (212) 596-6200
Fax: (212) 596-6213

Publications

Accounting Horizons
American Accounting Association
5717 Bessie Dr.
Sarasota, FL 34233
Tel: (813) 921-7747

Accounting Professionals Product News
Accounting Professional Product News, Inc.
4210 W. Vickery Blvd.
Ft. Worth, TX 76107
Tel: (817) 738-3356
Fax: (817) 731-9704

Accounting Systems for Law Offices
Matthew Bender & Co., Inc.
11 Penn Plaza
New York, NY 10001
Tel: (212) 967-7707

International Accounting and Auditing Trends
CIFAR Publications, Inc.
3490 US Hwy. 1
BL012
Princeton, NJ 08540-5920
Tel: (609) 520-9333
Fax: (609) 520-0905

International Accounting Bulletin
Lafferty Publications
2970 Clairmount Rd.
Ste. 800
Atlanta, GA 30329
Tel: (404) 636-6610

Internet Sites

American Accounting Association
http://www.rutgers.edu/accounting/raw/aaa/aaa.html

Association of International Accountants
http://www.a-i-a.org.uk/

Global Interact Network (GINLIST)
International business and marketing—services and products
http://ciber.bus.msu.edu

Infomage International
Global business information by region
http://www.commerce.com/net2/business/business.html

Advertising

Defined

Advertising is a paid announcement or sale offer in a public area or medium, with the intent to present or promote goods, services, or ideas. It is designed to inform, persuade, and remind. Advertisements are paid for by an identifiable individual or organization, called a sponsor. An advertisement can be either a print or broadcast message, directed to a general or targeted audience.

Advertising includes media messages, direct marketing, trade promotions, displays at trade fairs, and sponsoring. The primary means of advertising are through newspapers, magazines, radio and television. When advertising is through a newspaper, magazine, or other print media, it is called an advertisement; when it is broadcast on radio or television, it is called a commercial or spot.

Advertising is often used with other marketing tools such as public relations, sales promotions, and personal selling strategies to create an effective overall marketing strategy. An advertising campaign is that part of an overall marketing strategy that uses diverse media and advertising methods to gain acceptance of an idea or item or to increase the sales of a product or service. Many advertising campaigns are undertaken by advertising agencies on behalf of the seller of the product or idea. Advertising agencies specialize in producing advertising campaigns and strategies to help sellers target their customers and promote their products. There are three types of advertising agencies:

Full Service Agencies

Full service agencies oversee all phases of a marketing campaign, including creative services, public relations, marketing research, promotion advice, media buying, and publicity. Most full service agencies charge a commission for their services, based on a percentage of the media purchases they make for a client. In addition, clients are charged for direct costs incurred for public relations and publicity.

Specialty Service Agencies

These agencies offer limited, specialized services relating to advertising. Specialty agencies are often referred to as boutique agencies. Many specialty agencies provide only research, copy, or media services, and they often operate only within a single industry.

In-House Agencies

An in-house advertising agency is actually part of a client company and it oversees most or all aspects of the company's marketing campaign. While an in-house agency performs most or all the services of a full service agency, it often works with an outside agency on certain projects.

Domestic Market Overview

The advertising industry is by nature volatile; advertisers must constantly keep pace with changing trends, products, markets, and demographics. The US advertising industry is currently undergoing significant structural changes as well, with competing products and services increasingly coming from newly opened international markets, and the implementation of new technology radically changing the way advertisers assess and reach their markets. There has been a noticeable trend away from traditional media advertising and towards direct mail, telemarketing, and computer on-line advertising.

Although newspapers still account for over half of all media advertising, television about 20 percent, and periodicals about 15 percent, these traditional primary means of mass advertising have been squeezed in the past decade as direct-mail operations, cable television, community-based shopper newspapers, radio, Yellow Pages, and on-line computer services increasingly compete for advertising dollars and audiences. Total newspaper circulation has remained flat over the past few years—newspaper advertising rates rise about five percent each year, while the number of advertising pages declines by one percent. Periodicals have suffered pretty much the same fate as newspapers, with the exception of periodicals that cater to special interests, which have witnessed an increase in total advertising pages, although the circulation of each remains limited. The most profound change can be seen in the reduced role broadcast television commercials play in a company's advertising campaign. The choice of three network channels has evolved into nearly 100 cable choices, with more to come. Many of these cater to specific groups of patrons, which removes a large number of people from the general audience of traditional television.

Overall, traditional advertising is expected to continue to decline in importance (it has already reduced its share of every marketing dollar from two-thirds in 1982 to one-third in 1992), as technology continues to provide more efficient ways to target a specific audience. However, over the next several years, when the domestic business climate is expected to remain healthy, advertising spending is forecast to increase by between five and seven percent each year. Most of the growth will come from direct mail and promotions rather than from more traditional forms of advertising.

Direct mail advertisers will account for much of the increase. Computer technology allows sophisticated and highly detailed profile and spending analyses of consumers, and direct mail advertisers are thus able to reduce redundant or ineffective mailings. Television infomercials, generally 30 minutes in length, and interactive advertising which is emerging on computer on-line services, are currently the major growth areas in advertising. Several companies are already spending significant advertising dollars to create and run compelling, high-quality advertisements that will appeal to this sophisticated market.

The Internet and World Wide Web has brought a whole new level to advertising. There are many benefits to the Web, including smaller firms putting up Web-sites and competing on an even playing field with large companies. Web-sites are relatively inexpensive and have the potential to be seen by millions. Unfortunately, the World Wide Web has become inundated with sites, and the difficult part is not impressing people with your site, but getting them to see it.

In order to remain competitive in this rapidly changing industry all advertisers must pay close attention to their markets to learn the preferences and needs of consumers—both as to products and services, and media preferences. Database marketing is essential, as is flexibility and the ability to reconfigure or reposition according to data analysis. Emphasis is placed on a sophisticated advertising approach that communicates a product's use, and which maintains or improves the consumer's perception of the product. Advertising agencies are working hard to become comprehensive one-stop business service shops for their clients.

International Market Overview

The US advertising industry is well-represented and highly competitive in international markets. US agencies enjoy a reputation for creative, high quality advertisements of both US and local domestic products. In fact, most advertising concepts have historically come primarily from the West, and the presence of large multinational advertising agencies throughout the world has been the result of the expansion of their clients overseas rather than the rise of significant local markets. In most countries advertising agencies generally work through small local offices (employing less than 20 people), although US-owned agencies are almost always the largest.

Due to cultural and regulatory concerns, many US advertising agencies work in partnership with a local agency or representative to ensure that local preferences and customs are considered before creating or exporting any advertising material. Advertising and marketing methods and styles that are successful in the US may or may not be suitable for direct application in another country. Successful US companies operating internationally have learned to tailor not only their products, but also their advertising to appeal to local consumers, and local agencies can provide valuable advice in this area. US companies should make full use of local advertising agencies, marketing consultants, and other experts in the region to determine the suitability of a particular advertising approach.

Sub-contracting is common practice in many countries. Larger firms will often contract creative work—photography, design, copy, or computer graphics—to a smaller agency that specializes in the field. Smaller agencies and individuals trying to establish themselves abroad should build solid relationships with the large multinational agencies for this reason.

The international advertising industry is expected to grow rapidly over the next few years, as many governments are in the process of implementing liberalization policies that will open their markets to foreign investment and foreign products and services. These policies are likely to yield strong economic growth, with a resulting rise in the county's middle class, which will create ever larger consumer markets. This will generate increased demand for new advertising strategies and innovative media planning, especially in the consumer products and services industries.

In general, the advertising industry in most countries will increasingly need to address more than the mere advertising needs of its clients; it must also actively participate in evolving brand strategies and providing vital marketing inputs to clients. Many multinational agencies carry out brand mapping exercises, work out communication packages, suggest alternative media, and evolve positioning strategies for their clients. With competition in all areas of the industry increasing, clients now expect advertising agencies to be innovative at providing comprehensive services which complement the company's product management.

Market Barriers

Many governments impose barriers on advertising by foreigners in local markets. Market barriers can consist of anything from heavy taxation, to outright restrictions on foreign operations or investment. They often include high customs duties or quotas on entry of products and heavy regulation of professional licensing in order to limit the services foreigners may provide.

There may well be restrictions placed on the type of advertising or on the products or services which may be advertised. For example, many countries now prohibit or restrict advertising of tobacco and liquor products, as well as firearms, chemicals and other potential weaponry, and pharmaceuticals. Advertisement of professional services is also heavily restricted in many places.

Several countries require that advertisements of certain products or within certain industries be approved prior to broadcast or publication. There will often be a regulatory agency or department set up just for this purpose, or a governmental official designated as liaison. The approval process can be quite lengthy, involving a comprehensive examination of style, content, and method; or it can require merely filing a copy of the proposed advertisement prior to broadcast or publication.

Barriers can also be erected by industry insiders and officials. Trade organizations, professional groups, unions and enforced queueing are all methods of maintaining a market closed to outsiders. Also, some cultures have a strong tradition of doing business only with family or close friends, and foreigners are not likely to make major inroads in these areas.

Regional Opportunities

Note: These are only examples of regional opportunities and in no way constitute a complete list.

Hong Kong

Hong Kong represents one of the strongest opportunities for US advertisers and advertising agencies. The Hong Kong advertising industry is rapidly becoming one of the most dynamic business services in the region. US ad agencies are well-represented in Hong Kong (eight of the ten largest agencies are US-owned); they enjoy an excellent reputation for both creativity and reliability. Furthermore, US products are much sought after; they convey a sense of affluence and quality that Hong Kong purchasers look for.

The influence of the large and rapidly growing Chinese consumer market is contributing significantly to the growth of Hong Kong's advertising industry. It is undoubtedly the base from which goods and services from all over the world are traded with China. Marketing and advertising campaigns are generated in Hong Kong, and there has already been a noticeable influx of advertising business from China in the past few years. Much of it falls to US-owned agencies.

US sellers and advertisers must be particularly aware, however, of the strong traditions and cultural influences which affect the purchasing decisions of the Chinese. Chinese are very "brand" conscious, and the purchases they make heavily influence their sense of self-esteem. In addition, superstitions still play a big role in everyday life—the color white traditionally represents death, while black print on white is used at funerals, and gold lettering on red is common only at Chinese New Year. American advertisers must also be aware that Chinese clients are demanding; they want fast quality service and they push for polished ads that sell.

India

The advertising market in India, which includes broadcasting, print media, outdoor advertising, sales promotion, and production grew by nearly 30 percent in 1994. One of the major reasons for the high growth rate of the Indian advertising industry is the government of India's liberalization policy which is substantially opening the Indian market to foreign investment. In addition, India possesses one of the fastest growing consumer markets in the world. With liberalization and economic development, new consumers are developing in nearly all industries, driving companies to spend significantly higher amounts on advertising.

Indian advertising companies with foreign collaborations have a 30 percent share of the Indian advertising market. When considered together with Indian companies with less formal foreign affiliations the market share increases to over 58 percent. With the increase in the number of multinational corporations in India, the Indian advertising industry is expected to witness more affiliations and collaboration agreements with foreign agencies over the next three years. While European agencies currently dominate these relationships, Indians are generally amenable to US participation and US firms do enjoy a reputation for high quality and reliable service.

Mexico

The Mexican Foreign Investment Law allows 100 percent foreign ownership of direct marketing and advertising services. Many US firms are successfully doing business in Mexico and growth has been strong over the past few years, despite the economic slowdown and currency crisis. The most effective firms have obtained a Mexican partner to handle cultural differences and arcane regulations.

The best opportunities for US firms are in telemarketing and direct mail, which are fledgling sectors of the Mexican advertising industry. Advanced technology will increase media options in these sectors and will permit better targeting. The infrastructure, while still incomplete, is developing quickly and it is a good time to become established with a local joint venture partner before these sectors become saturated. Products which are not readily available in stores, such as telephone sets and accessories, telephone answering machines, and fitness equipment represent especially good opportunities for direct mail and telemarketing advertising.

Europe

Television is the fastest growing media for advertisers in Europe, growing by about 20 percent in 1995. Newspaper advertising increased by 14 percent, and outdoor and movie theater advertising also showed strong growth. Although there are several large European advertising agencies that control a large percentage of the market, many sellers are open to US representation, especially for services requiring innovation and creativity. In general, US advertisements need not be modified significantly to sell well in Europe. Europeans are well accustomed to US products and services, and most US marketing methods work well throughout Europe.

Best Bet Opportunities

Note: These are only examples of industry opportunities and in no way constitute a complete list.

Telemarketing

While the US market has grown accustomed, weary even, of telephone marketing this has proved an effective and cost-efficient means of advertising. Telemarketing has not yet caught on in many countries and there are good growth opportunities throughout the world. Potential telemarketers must be cautioned, however, that many countries (such as the Philippines) do not yet have adequate or reliable telephone services, while others (such as Australia and Japan) charge exorbitant rates for telephone services. These would not be the ideal places to undertake a telemarketing advertising campaign.

Direct Mail

Direct mail advertising is proving an up-and-coming industry in many European countries, which have reliable and inexpensive postal services, widespread rural populations, and efficient delivery mechanisms. Direct mail offers the advantage of targeting (not available through television or general circulation newspapers), accurate results assessment and low cost. In many areas where other sophisticated means of advertising have become worn, direct mail is only now beginning to come into widespread use.

Local cable television advertising "spots" are possible on several stations when dealing with a cable operator. A local seller can peddle a product to a specific target audience by using the same commercial on different cable stations carrying shows that appeal to the target market. Cable television stations can sometimes produce commercials for local advertisers on a tight budget.

On-line Computer Advertising

It is too early to tell whether this sector of the advertising industry will prove the boon its proponents hope it will be. To date, few claim to have made any money in this area. However, on-line computer services are actively looking for ways to generate revenues and, unless on-line users want to pay exorbitant rates for the services they use, advertising looks to be the answer. Some advertisers have already jumped in with slick, up-to-date, sophisticated advertisements targeting the young, affluent, educated on-line user. There is probably a large market to be found here for those who can keep pace with this rapidly developing industry.

Sources of US Based Assistance

Advertising Council
261 Madison Ave.
New York, NY 10016-2303
Tel: (212) 922-1500

Advertising and Marketing International Network (AMIN)
c/o B. Vaughn Sink
Sullivan Higdon & Sink, Inc.
801 E. Douglas
P.O. Box 11009
Wichita, KS 67202
Tel: (316) 263-01124

American Advertising Federation (AAF)
1101 Vermont Ave. NW, Ste. 500
Washington, DC 20005
Tel: (202) 898-0089

American Association of Advertising Agencies
666 3rd Ave., 13th Fl.
New York, NY 10017
Tel: (212) 682-2500

International Advertising Association (IAA)
342 Madison Ave., 20th Floor, Suite 2000
New York, NY 10173-0073
Tel: (212) 557-1133

International Federation of Advertising Agencies (IFAA)
1450 E. American Ln., Ste. 1400
Schaumburg, IL 60173-4973
Tel: (708) 330-6344

Mail Advertising Service Association International (MASA)
1421 Prince St., Ste. 200
Alexandria, VA 22314
Tel: (703) 836-9200

Affiliated Advertising Agencies International (3AI)
22800 S. Xanadu Way, Ste. 300
Aurora, CO 80014
Tel: (303) 671-8551

Transworld Advertising Agency Network
866 United Nations Plaza
New York, NY 10017
Tel: (212) 759-7900

Western States Advertising Agencies Association (WSAAA)
6404 Wilshire Blvd., Ste. 1111
Los Angeles, CA 90048
Tel: (213) 65501951

Publications

Advertising Age
Crain Communications, Inc.
740 rush St.
Chicago, IL 60611
Tel: (312) 649-5200

Journal of Advertising Research
641 Lexington Ave.
New York, NY 10022
Tel: (212) 751-5656

Internet Sites

Advertising & Marketing International Network
http://www.commercepark.com/amin/

American Advertising Federation
http://www.aaf.org/

American Association of Advertising Agencies
http://www.commercepark.com/AAAA/index.html

Architecture, Engineering, & Construction

Defined

Architecture, engineering, and construction are three different fields that work together to create structures for public use. Architecture is the design and formation of a structure, taking the project from abstract idea to calculated plan. Engineers oversee a project and perform a number of duties, making sure a structure is completed correctly. They perform feasibility studies, finding the most efficient methods to get a structure built. They also investigate different sites and the different tools that would be used to build a structure. Then a construction crew will assemble a structure. Projects can take years and can cost millions of dollars to complete.

Architectural, engineering, and construction firms are hired to build houses and buildings, but they also design and construct a country's infrastructure (its transportation or public works system). Some specific projects that firms may be called to assist upon include:

- office buildings
- residential structures
- hotels
- resorts
- railroads
- public transportation systems
- dams
- sanitary systems
- factories
- roads
- bridges
- harbors
- power stations
- electricity distribution systems
- communications networks

Domestic Market Overview

Architecture, engineering, and construction services have hit hard times recently domestically, due to the recession of the early 1990s. Growth is expected to continue by only small amounts in the near future, although repair and remodeling work will grow at a slightly faster pace. The most promising markets appear to be home improvement, hospitals, telecommunications systems, and highways. The weaker markets are expected to be office buildings, hotels, public service build-

ings, military facilities, and federal industrial plants. Some reasons for the slow growth include the relatively modest economic growth rate, high interest rates, and high vacancy rates for apartments and commercial buildings, depressing prices and the demand for new construction.

Private residential construction has become the most prosperous sector, although the relatively healthy growth rates are expected to diminish somewhat in the near future. Greater construction of multifamily owner and rental units may occur as more people find it difficult to afford a single family home. Remodeling will probably become more popular and will continue to outpace the construction of new homes.

The total value of new private nonresidential construction has been falling lately, reflective of the aftermath of the phenomenal commercial building boom of the 1980s. The declines were most severe for office buildings and hotels, while the construction of hospitals and electric utility plants registered solid increases. Lower interest rates have tempered the decline in commercial construction, but availability of credit has been tight. Lenders have been reluctant to provide credit for real estate development because of poor loan experiences and government regulations. In contrast to the weak outlook for construction, the non residential repair and renovation markets will probably continue to grow in the future.

Publicly owned construction increased slightly, primarily because of gains in highways, water works, and federal industrial facilities. This sector will probably post only modest growth rates in the near future, although there will be some bright spots, including highway, water works, and prison construction. The biggest declines are likely to be in military construction and other public buildings. School construction will likely be unchanged. As in the private sector, maintenance and repair will likely increase faster than new public construction spending primarily because the public works infrastructure is steadily becoming older and will need repairs.

Many of the world's largest contractors have entered the US construction market, but have found success only in a few specialized sub-markets. Although construction firms from nearly a dozen nations compete for the US market, the bulk are from the United Kingdom, Germany, and Japan.

International Market Overview

About 40 percent of the 200 top international design firms are from the United States. In contrast to a slowly recovering domestic market, those firms that ventured into international activities found a thriving and expanding business environment. Renewed opportunity has resulted from the North American Free Trade Agreement, privatization in

Eastern Europe and the countries of the former Soviet Union, and high growth in the Pacific Rim economies.

Companies should emphasize long-range planning. Executives are increasingly aware that early market entry and a strategic approach must be essential components of their plans. Forward-looking companies identify projects at an early stage, establish networks in the host country, assist in the development of pre-feasibility and feasibility studies, and exercise creativity in the development of financial packages.

Financing will take on added importance for architecture, engineering, and construction companies. Certain large, commercial banks are beginning to show renewed interest in developing country projects. They are now more concerned about a stronger financial base for repayment, however, and give more attention to the underlying assumptions and financial details of projects. In many cases, they claim equity participation in the projects they finance.

Different areas of a country could have vastly different construction needs. In Germany, for example, firms will face different markets depending on whether they choose to promote their services in the eastern or western area of the country. Western Germany has seen favorable economic conditions along with reviving residential construction. The public sector, however, has cut back construction in the west to aid the slumping east. In the east, bureaucracies are trying to catch up with western laws and regulations, but there are still a number of hurdles and the red tape is thick.

Patience and a great deal of money to invest is crucial. It often takes years to build a reputation or acquire the contacts needed to be an "insider." Most local firms are not interested in simply providing contracts for US "competitors," but seek to create a true partnership. This may turn out to be a benefit. In Japan, for example, competition is extremely fierce, and the possibility of cooperation with rival firms is great. Particularly for large projects, consortium arrangements are common. US firms can also work in Japanese markets through "tie-ups" with local competitor firms, where US firms offer the expertise that Japanese firms need.

To be competitive in international markets, US firms need to carefully reassess their marketing strategies. Much of their success abroad will depend on their willingness to pursue joint ventures with local companies, their ability to develop and implement advanced technologies, and their demonstration skills in effectively promoting, marketing, and obtaining project financing.

Market Barriers

US firms can be at a severe financial disadvantage with respect to major foreign competitors, who often have significant financial backing from their governments. This takes a number of forms, including outright subsidies, various kinds of tax relief, generous insurance and guarantees against risks, and the financing of feasibility studies. Except for limited insurance and guarantees from Eximbank and minimal funding of feasibility studies by the US Trade and Development Program, this type of assistance is limited in the United States.

Government Barriers

Some bureaucracies are slow to move, if they move at all. Responsibility is often divided among several departments. Diverging interests between local, state, and federal governments often result in decisions being delayed beyond the capacity of the investor to wait. Local laws can also be a hindrance for US firms. In Germany, for example, laws and professional ethics prohibit architects and engineers from advertising or publicly promoting their services. This obviously makes it difficult for new firms to gain recognition.

US firms may find the negotiation process of foreign countries unusual. Bribery is an accepted practice in many, as is one country openly showing favoritism toward another. Many governments favor local firms and workers, giving them priority in the selection and hiring of consultants for certain government jobs. In the Philippines, for example, laws state that Filipino consultants shall be employed whenever the services required for a locally-funded project are within the expertise and capability of Filipinos.

Many countries do not recognize foreign university degrees, so US architects and engineers cannot be responsible for projects. In these cases, projects must be supported and signed for by a local Engineer or Architect. The best way to enter these markets is through local companies in charge of the major projects. This means hard work to secure a suitable partner with a good position in the market.

The best (and perhaps only) way around these government barriers is to cooperate with a local firm. Without a good local partner or agent, many US firms will find it nearly impossible to win contracts.

Social Barriers

Nonmetric labeling continues to be a barrier to the entry of many US products into foreign markets. Conversion to metric standards has become a prerequisite to full participation in the international construction market. Since 1992, the European Community has required metric labels on all products. Canada and Mexico are now largely metric as well. To fully penetrate these markets, US firms must "go metric."

Cultural Barriers

Many US construction techniques and materials are not accepted in foreign markets. In Mexico, for example, people are accustomed to traditional construction of blocks and cement, and wood houses are not as popular. This barrier is beginning to ease a little in some markets, because the demand for housing is growing and the money supply is tightening, leaving many governments looking for fast, inexpensive construction that US firms can supply regardless of the materials they use.

Market Channels

For most countries, there are two markets: public and private. The public sector is still the major force in many countries, providing opportunities for architectural, engineering, and construction firms. Some examples of projects sponsored by governments include transportation, power generation, and pollution control. These are somewhat advanced technologies, not available locally, that must be imported. Many government agencies look to foreign firms with projects whose scope or magnitude requires a level of expertise or attention beyond the agencies' optimum in-house capability.

The private sector also has a need for architectural, construction, and engineering services in many countries. Land development corporations, manufacturing and mining companies, and resort and hotel owners are some private entities that engage the services of architecture, engineering, and construction consultants. Some projects include industrial estates, townhouses, condominiums, subdivisions, industrial plants, and commercial and building complexes. Reputation and cost are the major considerations of the private sector in selecting consultants.

Governments are now giving more attention to private infrastructure financing. To obtain this type of financing, the project must be supported by user fees or through government or public agency service contracts. Relatively small projects, such as sewage sludge disposal, water treatment, wastewater treatment plants, and other environmental facilities will likely be privately financed in many countries in the future.

Regional Opportunities

Note: These are only examples of regional opportunities and in no way constitute a complete list.

Asia

Some experts predict that infrastructure spending in Asia could total hundreds of billions of dollars annually by the year 2000. Most Asian countries have large projects in various stages of development. The combination of rapid economic growth, relatively stable governments, substantial foreign exchange services, low levels of foreign debt, and an extensive need for infrastructure present tremendous opportunities for US engineering and construction firms.

Taiwan has been a relatively open market for US firms. Taiwan end-users and engineering consultants frequently require proposals to be written in English, creating an advantage for US companies. Many local engineers have been educated in the US and understand English.

Japan's construction market remains largely inaccessible to foreign companies. This may change, however, under Japan's new and more open administrations. The US and Japanese governments exchanged diplomatic letters in 1994 to ensure the openness of Japan's publicly-financed construction market.

Latin America

Latin America is emerging as a good market for engineering and construction services, although it still maintains a hearty overhang of external debt. Some countries have yet to implement economic stabilization policies. Nevertheless, there is increased political stability and governments are moving toward privatization of public enterprises.

As a result of the NAFTA, Mexico has accelerated its infrastructure development. Project opportunities in Mexico abound in pollution control, water purification and other areas. The annual housing demand of 580,000 units is far in excess of production, and the total shortfall is estimated at more than seven million units. Here, as elsewhere, partnership with a local firm can be an important part of a company's market development strategy.

Eastern Europe

Despite continuing needs in Eastern Europe and the countries of the former Soviet Union, economic constraints in most of this region prevent substantial construction growth. Problems include unresolved land ownership issues, lack of project development capabilities and antiquated construction techniques and technology. The primary constraint is a lack of investment capital. Therefore, companies prepared to structure creative financial packages are the most likely to find opportunities in these markets.

Best Bet Opportunities

Note: These are only examples of industry opportunities and in no way constitute a complete list.

Infrastructure

Global population projections indicate a large future demand for infrastructure. By the year 2025, there will be an estimated eight billion people on the planet (as compared to five billion in 1987), most of them in developing countries. The United Nations reports that 100 million people move annually to cities around the world, which requires immense investments in transportation, communications systems, sewers, and roadways, all increasing the demand for architectural, construction, and engineering services. A significant number will offer opportunities for US firms, particularly as prime contractors or subcontractors for design engineering.

Housing

Housing production is becoming a major concern in developing countries, as their populations explode and many people are moving into urban areas to find work. US firms will probably have to adjust their techniques and may have to change the materials they use to succeed in foreign markets. In many countries there is only limited land available, meaning suburban and town developments are usually designed to maximize the utilization of space, and land prices are very high.

Environment

The global environment will continue to present unusual opportunities for US companies. During at least two decades of domestic environment cleanup activity, US firms have acquired a unique expertise in lessening or preventing air, water, and soil pollution. US engineers, contractors, and equipment suppliers will find lucrative environmental management markets overseas. Some environmental problems can be solved on a global basis and in partnership with governments and companies in both developed and developing countries.

Sources of US Based Assistance

American Institute of Architects
1735 New York Avenue N.W.
Washington, DC 20006-5292
Tel: (202) 626-7300
Fax: (202) 626-7421

The American Architectural Manufacturers Association
1540 East Dundee Road, Suite 310
Palatine, IL 60067
Tel: (708) 202-1350
Fax: (708) 202-1480

National Society of Architectural Engineers
700 S.W. Jackson Street, Suite 702
Topeka, KS 66603-3758
Tel: (913) 232-5707
Fax: (913) 357-6629

Construction Association of Michigan (CAM)
500 Stephenson Highway, Suite 400
Troy, MI 48083
Tel: (810) 585-1000
Fax: (810) 585-9785

American Consulting Engineers Council (ACEC)
1015 Fifteenth Street, N.W.
Washington, DC 20005
Tel: (202) 347-7474
Fax: (202) 898-0068

International Federation of Professional and Technical Engineers
8630 Fenton Street, Suite 400
Silver Spring, MD 20910
Tel: (301) 565-9016
Fax: (301) 565-0018

American Institute of Constructors
9887 North Grandy
St. Petersburg, FL 33702
Tel: (813) 578-0317
Fax: (813) 578-9982

Publications

Engineers World
Engineers Australia Pty Ltd
2 Ernest St.
P.O. Box 588
Crows Nest NSW 2065
AUSTRALIA
Tel: (02) 438-1533
Fax: (02) 438-5934

International Directory of Engineering Societies and Related Organizations
American Association of Engineering Societies
1111 19th St. NW, Ste. 608
Washington DC 20036-3603
Tel: (202) 296-2237
Fax: (202) 296-1151
Editor: Gordon Davis

International Directory of Practices (Year)
Royal Institute of British Architects
RIBA Publications Ltd.
Finsbury Mission
39 Moreland St.
London EC1V 8BB
UK
Tel: 0171-2251-0791
Fax: 0171-608-2375

International Journal of Engineering Science
Elsevier Science Ltd.
Pergamon
P.O. Box 800
Kidlington, Oxford OX5 1DX
UK
Tel: (914) 524-9200
Fax: (914) 333-2444

International Journal for Numerical Methods in Engineering
John Wiley & Sons, Inc.
605 Third Ave.
New York, NY 10158
Tel: (212) 850-6645
Fax: (212) 850-6021

Internet Sites

American Association of Cost Engineering International
http://www.pair.com/aaceets/index.html

American Consulting Engineers Council
http://www.acec.org/

American Institute of Architects/American Architechtural Foundation
http://www.aia.org/

Institute of Industrial Engineers
http://www.iienet.org/

International Association for Continuing Engineering Education
http://www.dipoli.hut.fi/org/IACEE/

International Facility Management Association
http://www.ifma.org/

Banking

Definition

A bank is a company authorized under federal or state law to engage in any or all of the following financial activities:

- accepts custody of money
- lends money
- extends credit
- issues currency
- exchanges currencies of different countries
- facilitates the transfer of funds by means of checks, drafts, bills of exchange, or other instruments of credit
- invests

The US commercial banking system includes the Federal Reserve System, the central bank consisting of 12 federal reserve banks; nationally chartered banks; state chartered banks; state governed trust companies; private banks; and cooperative exchanges.

All banks are subject to government regulation. National banks are chartered and regulated by the Comptroller of the Currency. State chartered banks are regulated by the appropriate state regulatory agency along with the Federal Deposit Insurance Corporation (FDIC), if the bank is insured. A state bank may elect to become a member of the Federal Reserve System, in which case it is also regulated by the Federal Reserve authorities. If a bank is federally chartered, the name "National" or "N.A." appears in its name.

Most consumer commercial banking is done through state chartered banks. Although each state maintains its own laws and regulations, most state banking laws allow:

- **Unit banking** Bank may operate in a single location.
- **Limited branch banking** Bank branches located only within a specifically defined geographic area within a single state.
- **In-state multibank holding company** A large corporate holding company exercises control over several banks, but only within a single state.
- **Multistate holding company** A large holding company exercises control over several banks in one or more states.

There are also non-commercial bank institutions, including savings and loan associations, mutual savings banks, and credit unions. In general, these "thrift" institutions have authority to diversify into fields of commercial banking. The largest system of non-commercial bank institutions which engages in deposit banking is the Federal Home Loan Bank System (FHLBS), which links mortgage lending institutions to the capital markets by issuing consolidated obligations and discount notes in large denominations. It serves as a source of secondary liquidity to its members in meeting heavy withdrawal demands. All federally insured savings and loan associations are required by law to belong to the FHLBS, and qualified state-chartered mutual and stock savings and loan associations, mutual and stock savings banks and life insurance companies may join if they wish.

Domestic Market Overview

At one time a bastion of security and stability, the US banking industry has in the past couple of decades been buffeted by wildly fluctuating interest rates, unstable economic conditions—both in the US and throughout the world—and an almost uncontrollable urge to diversify into new and unusual financial markets. There has been an accelerating shift away from traditional lending and borrowing activities, and a definite trend toward a blurring of the lines between commercial and non-commercial banks, and between banks and non-bank financial institutions.

Both commercial banks and thrifts have been affected by the myriad new products and services developed by securities firms, including money market funds and cash management accounts. They have responded to these threats by merging into super, "department store" financial institutions engaging at once in many kinds of banking and related services. Many have found the going tough, however, because securities firms and other non-bank financial institutions are able to offer products and services which banks and thrifts are not permitted to offer. Increasingly, banks are acting as middlemen in markets for financing backed by securities. This has transformed banks from "lenders"—originating loans which are retained on the balance sheet as assets—into mere sellers of somebody else's money. While traditional corporate lending has not disappeared entirely, it has certainly been overshadowed by activities that look more like investment banking than commercial banking.

Although each state retains control over banking within its borders, nearly all states now allow interstate banking, and the banks are responding in droves. The past decade has witnessed the emergence of regional superbanks, born to compete in this era of deregulation. There has been a significant consolidation and concentration of banks. The number of commercial banks has already declined from 14,481 in 1984, by 31.4 percent (or 4,540 banks) in 1995, with a reduction of 110 banks in the fourth quarter of 1995 alone. Additions from new charters and savings institutions converting to commercial banks charters were far outweighed by commercial banks absorbed through mergers.

Although the past decade has been a turbulent one for the banking industry, it has now begun to emerge, with definite patterns indicating long-term profitability. Insured commercial banks registered their second-highest quarterly net income ever in late 1995, with earnings increasing 13.3 percent over the prior year. Almost two-thirds of the banks reported an overall increase in quarterly earnings from December 1994 to December 1995, with 97 percent of commercial banks reporting positive earnings in 1995. In addition, bank failures, which had plagued the industry for several years, have begun to decrease significantly; there were no significant commercial bank failures in 1995.

Banks have concentrated on increasing the net interest-rate margins—the spread between interest income and interest expense—and reducing their commercial real estate loan portfolios to regain their profitability. In addition, customer use of automated teller machines (ATMs) has been rising significantly over the past few years with the result that branch operating costs have been falling, and banks have further reduced branch costs simply by closing many unprofitable neighborhood branches.

Foreign banks operate in the US as branches, agencies, commercial banks, and edge corporations (chartered by the Federal Reserve to engage in international banking). Subsidiaries of foreign banks which are chartered by the state or federal government are examined and supervised by federal or state banking authorities similar to other state or federally chartered banks. Assets of foreign bank offices in the US have increased significantly in recent years, rising from under $200 billion in 1980 to over $1 trillion today—approximately one-fourth of total US banking assets.

Foreign banks are a significant part of the US banking system. Of the nearly 50 banks that have received approval to deal in government securities, most are foreign banks. In addition, several other foreign banks have used grandfather status under the International Banking Act of 1978 to deal in both commercial banking and securities underwriting activities in the United States. Almost 50 percent of the foreign banks operating in the US do so in New York (the effective capital of US business and finance), with most of the rest in California (the center of ties with the Pacific Rim), Illinois (the center of foreign business activity involving the US heartland), and Florida (the seat of business with Latin America). Japan, Canada, France and the UK have the largest number of bank offices in the United States.

International Market Overview

In contrast to the continued growth, both in size and in number, of foreign banks in the US, US banks abroad have been restructuring and consolidating their activities during the past several years. By the end of 1992, only 120 Federal Reserve member banks were operating 774 branches in foreign countries and overseas areas of the US, a decline from 916 branches at the end of 1985. Of the 120 banks, 88 were national banks operating 660 branches, and 32 were state banks operating the remaining 114 branches. Indeed, the entire US international banking presence has been contracting since the heyday of the 1980s. Following several years of disastrous results in overseas markets—especially for the smaller banks—primarily due to loans to developing countries in the early 1980s, fewer have been interested in international operations, most of which require banking on a relatively large scale to provide adequate returns.

The banks that do operate overseas, however, are quite competitive in their markets, especially when offering account management, credit card operations, collection management, and other innovative items at which they are particularly skilled. US bankers are especially welcome in the areas of financing and facilitation of international trade. Trade financing, in fact, is a growing field in many countries. Because the economic growth of most countries increasingly depends on exports and because there is some risk associated with international trading, the ability to effectively finance exports is becoming more important to businesses. Trade financing is expected to become as important to businesses in foreign countries, which are entering the export arena in increasing numbers, as it has traditionally been to US businesses.

Banks in developing countries, and especially where governments are undertaking liberalization programs, are looking for new types of deposits and services to offer their customers, deposits and services that are already well established and familiar to the US banking industry. They are also seeking to reshape their loan portfolios to raise the volume of credits offered to private sector borrowers while decreasing financing available to the public sector. This process requires new methods and procedures which are simply not yet entrenched in many places, and US banks are well positioned to take advantage of these opportunities. US banks are also well represented in the growing securities markets of many countries.

Before Entering a Market

Throughout the world the banking industry is heavily regulated, and in many countries it is also rigidly controlled by the government. Extensive research of a country's banking laws, its currency controls, regulations governing other financial institutions, and limitations on company structure is absolutely essential prior to conducting any banking operations.

In addition, the economic health and stability of a country, and the growth or decline of individual sectors will greatly effect the country's banking industry. Inflation is an important factor in banking, and a country's central bank will often attempt to control inflation through use of the banking industry. Currency volatility can make or break a commercial bank, so it is also essential to be aware of trends and limitations in this regard.

In short, the banking industry often operates within relatively rigid parameters and under heavy scrutiny by the government. There will probably be a regulation regarding any enterprise within the industry, and vast limitations on an entrepreneur's ability to conduct any business relating to banking free from restraint.

In addition to evaluating the logistics of entering a market, make certain the product or service (especially bank automation equipment) you intend to sell is compatible with or will complement existing products and systems in operation in the country. Also, make certain you are able to provide adequate after sales technical support and assistance, as this is often an important factor in the success or failure of foreign endeavors.

Market Barriers

In some countries the barriers to entry may be as fundamental as restrictions on imports and foreign participation in general, while in others, restrictions aimed specifically at the banking industry may preclude foreign participation.

Many governments impose onerous capital or reserve requirements on foreign banks, or restrict the opening of branch offices. Several countries simply prohibit outright foreign participation in this industry. Also, the banks in some countries remain nationalized, and there are no private enterprises at all, foreign or domestic. In any event, be assured there will be numerous legal and/or financial barriers to be overcome in the operation of banking enterprises in foreign countries.

Regional Opportunities

Note: These are only examples of regional opportunities and in no way constitute a complete list.

Canada

Until fairly recently, Canadian government policy placed limits on the ability of foreign banks allowed to operate (either directly or through Canadian-domiciled subsidiaries) in the country. Since the deregulation of the industry, foreign banks have been granted a greater ability to engage in banking and other financial services. The Bank Act permits foreign banks to engage in very restricted forms of business in Canada. Specifically, a foreign bank may not directly or indirectly undertake any banking business in Canada, or maintain a branch or automated banking machine in Canada for any purpose. They may, however establish "Schedule II" subsidiaries, which have virtually identical powers as domestic banks, subject to additional scrutiny and regulation.

Foreign banks may maintain properly registered representative offices in Canada. Representative offices have limited ability to carry on business in Canada other than to promote the foreign bank and its relationship with its customers.

Foreign banks may also establish a head office in Canada, subject to the approval of the federal cabinet. From that head office, the bank may issue directions and manage operations for its business outside of Canada.

Mexico

Mexico is underbanked, underbranched, undermortgaged, underinsured, and desperately in need of foreign financial and securities services. The government has in the past few years begun issuing new banking licenses, the first after several decades of nationalization. Its official goals include the encouragement of better regional coverage; the diversification and decentralization of ownership; and the encouragement of the growth of strong, balanced financial conglomerates—not to mention the generation of revenue.

The implementation of NAFTA has meant that Mexico must accord US financial institutions the same treatment as national institutions. It has to a large extent done so; although it stringently requires them to abide by all rules to which national entities are subject, and these can be quite cumbersome. Mexico also places strict restrictions on branching. Although the major Mexican banks have large networks of branches nationwide, there are especially cumbersome requirements for opening branches, and foreign banks have some difficulty negotiating this type of expansion. In 1996, foreign bank acquisitions of partial ownership in Mexican banks have been increasing.

Foreign banks are allowed to operate representative offices which are for the most part free of Mexico's prohibitive banking regulations. Representative offices can promote business or negotiate contracts and trade deals that are concluded and fulfilled overseas. There are nearly 200 such offices operating in Mexico, and the number seems to be growing.

Foreign banks are also allowed to operate offshore banking facilities physically located in Mexico but dealing exclusively in extraterritorial activities, although such operations receive no particular incentives and US institutions have so far shown little interest.

Singapore

Foreign penetration of the banking system of Singapore is high compared to most countries. Foreign banks account for almost half of all nonbank deposits from residents and more than half of all loans to nonbank residents.

The government does impose restrictions on foreign banks, however. In addition to a long-standing freeze on the number of full banking licenses granted to foreign, as well as domestic, banks, those banks that already have full licenses do not enjoy full market access. Foreign banks cannot open new branch offices, freely relocate existing branches, or freely operate off-premises automated teller machines. However, Singapore does actively encourage foreign participation in the offshore market in which US banks have a substantial presence.

Korea

Foreign banks continue to face numerous obstacles which impede their operations in Korea. Foreign banks are permitted to establish branches, only after one year has passed following the establishment of a representative office and subject to onerous individual branch capitalization requirements. Foreign banks face issuance limits for CDs based on branch versus global capital, limiting their ability to obtain local currency funding. Foreign banks also face discriminatory treatment in the interbank market. In short, foreign banks are disadvantaged by a relatively non transparent regulatory system, and must seek approval for introducing new products and services.

Taiwan

Taiwan has made significant progress of late in liberalizing its banking sector. The Taiwan authorities lifted the ban on investment in local banks, rescinded numerical and geographical limits on branching, removed the ceiling on local currency deposits, and shortened the representative office requirement for new branches. The authorities did, however, onerously raise the capital requirement for new branches. Banks are also subject to foreign exchange liability ceilings, which will soon be replaced with reserve requirements. US bankers are optimistic that further liberalizations are underway and will significantly lighten the burden of operating within Taiwan's banking industry.

Thailand

For some time, foreign banks had been prohibited from entering Thailand through a moratorium on new offshore licensing although the authorities have announced that five foreign banks will be granted branch licenses by 1997. Generally, however, the Thai government has limited foreign banks to a very small share of the total Thai banking market largely by restricting foreign bank entry, branching and acquisition of Thai banks.

Foreign bank branches are also legally precluded from establishing new sub-branches in Thailand. Recently however, regulations were changed to permit foreign banks to participate in the local ATM network, although foreign banks have been unable to negotiate satisfactory agreements to participate in the ATM network with domestic banks. Foreign banks are precluded from opening their own ATM systems.

US banks do, however, participate eagerly in the offshore markets. Seven US banks have received offshore licenses which enable them to make loans to Thailand and to third countries using funds from abroad, but they have not been permitted to take domestic deposits or to fund domestic lending from domestic sources.

India

Most Indian banks are government-owned. However, five new private sector banks have been established and five more have been approved. Approval has been granted for operation of several new foreign banks or bank branches.

Foreign bank branches and representative offices are permitted based upon reciprocity and India's estimated or perceived need for financial services. As a result, access for foreign banks has traditionally been quite limited. Four US banks now have a total of 15 branches in India. They operate under restrictive conditions including tight limitations on their ability to add sub-branches or automated teller machines.

Arabian Gulf States

Banks are variously restricted from entering Gulf markets. In Saudi Arabia, Saudi nationals must own 60 percent of any bank. Banking is currently closed to foreigners in Kuwait; however the Central Bank of Kuwait has recommended amendments to Kuwait's commercial law which will allow foreign firms to hold minority shares in joint venture banks in Kuwait.

Bahrain has not issued licenses for new commercial banks since 1983, though the majority of commercial banks in Bahrain are foreign bank branches; Bahrain does encourage the establishment of offshore of representative offices of foreign banks.

Oman, Qatar, and the U.A.E. technically allow foreign banks to operate, but have refused new foreign banks from establishing operations on the grounds that their countries are "over-banked" (the U.A.E. did, however, allow one US bank to open a representative office in 1993).

Czech Republic

The Czech Republic actually offers several opportunities for foreign participation in its fledgling banking industry. The Banking Act provides for universal banking where commercial banks carry out investment banking and brokerage activities in addition to traditional commercial transactions and lending, subject to the issuance of a license by the State Bank. The State Bank controls application requirements, minimum capital and reserve requirements and is in charge of bank supervision. Banking supervision is a new concept in the Czech Republic, and initial bank examinations are just beginning to be carried out.

The difficulties associated with the Czech banking system relate to human resources, outdated and inadequate computer systems and a dearth of products to meet customer needs. There is little or no notion of credit analysis, risk assessment or customer service. Although banks are beginning to modernize their computer systems, there is still no nationwide checking system and banks do not yet offer checking accounts. Inadequate telecommunications links also hinder the system.

Foreign banks can take two forms: representative offices or full-fledged branches. The representative office can offer advice and inform clients of services available through the parent bank, but are not authorized to perform services such as opening accounts or lending. Branches can handle any transactions authorized by the parent bank. All foreign banks having branches in the Czech Republic must agree to take over the assets and liabilities if the branch experiences financial problems, effectively guaranteeing the financial health of the branch.

So far, foreign banks in the Czech Republic have concentrated on international payments services, and transactions with western clients. Foreign banks are subject to stricter requirements than Czech banks with respect to collateral, documentation and interest rates.

Best Bet Opportunities

Note: These are only examples of industry opportunities and in no way constitute a complete list.

Banking Automation Equipment

The market for banking automation equipment and know-how is growing at a tremendous rate, and is expected to pick up even further over the next several years as countries develop and modernize their banking systems. Banking automation equipment includes all equipment capable of performing a procedure with little human participation, but is primarily automatic teller machines and check processing equipment.

The primary markets for this type of equipment will be in countries that are liberalizing or privatizing their banking industries, as government-run institutions rarely purchase this type of equipment.

US manufacturers are the dominant suppliers of bank automation equipment in most regions, with the primary competition coming from Japan, Germany, and the UK.

Merchant Banking

Merchant banking is a growing industry in many countries which are beginning to develop sophisticated financial sectors, where it is becoming increasingly important to manage new issues and their underwriting. In the past few years there has been a virtual stampede to operate merchant banking services in such economically promising countries as India and the Philippines. US merchant bankers have a tremendous advantage in these areas due to their superior experience in undertaking portfolio management, venture funding, mergers and acquisition, project financing, and handling Euro-issues, and exotic financial instruments. Many local bankers are actively looking for tie-ups with US investment banks which can bring in sophisticated technology, expertise, research facilities, innovation and general experience.

Merchant banking activities are fund-based and non-fund based. Fund-based include underwriting of equity and preference shares, bonds and debentures in new issues, dealing in money market instruments such as commercial papers, certificates of deposits, equipment leasing, and venture capital activities. Non-fund activities include public issue management and private placement of securities, loan/credit/fund syndication, corporate counseling, trusteeship management, portfolio management, management of mergers and acquisition, capital restructuring and reorganization.

Sources of US Based Assistance

Bank Information Center
2025 Eye St. NW, Ste. 522
Washington, DC 20006
Tel: (202) 466-8191

Bankers Association for Foreign Trade
2121 K St. NW, Ste. 701
Washington, DC 20036
Tel: (202) 452-0952

American Bankers Association
1120 Connecticut Ave. NW
Washington, DC 20036
Tel: (202) 663-5000

Savings and Community Bankers of America
1709 New York Avenue NW
Washington, DC 20006
Tel: (202) 637-8900

Publications

Yearly Industrial Outlook
US Dept. of Commerce
Superintendent of Documents
P.O. Box 371954
Pittsburgh, PA 15250-7954

Brown, Richard, Industry and Trade Summary Commercial Banking
US International Trade Commission
Washington, DC 20436
Tel: (202) 205-1819

ABA Banking Journal
American Bankers Association
1120 Connecticut Ave., NW
Washington, DC 20036
Tel: (202) 620-7200

American Banker, volume CLVIII
(Various issues)
One State St. Plaza
New York, NY 10004
Tel: (212) 9443-6700

Internet Sites

American Bankers Association
http://www.aba.com/

Financial Management Association International
http://www.webspace.com/~fma/

International Economics and Finance Society
http://www.rtpnet.org/~iefs/

International Society of Financiers
http://www.insofin.com/

Biotechnology

Defined

Historically, the definition biotechnology has included animal and plant breeding and the use of micro-organisms to leaven bread or brew beer. However, modern biotechnology has evolved into a sophisticated industry which draws on many scientific and engineering disciplines. It consists of several biological processes and technologies that are used to produce goods for several fields, including medical, agriculture, and cosmetic. Some steps in the biotechnology process, which can also be considered needed services, include:

- initial creation of the product
- clinical testing after the product has been created
- helping the drug pass any government regulations
- marketing the product
- training local users in how to best use the product

Domestic Market Overview

Biotechnology is still considered a rising industry, and it has already become a strong force in the domestic economy. The industry generated nearly US$8 billion in product sales between 1982 and 1994, according to the Biotechnology Industry Organization. Despite these healthy numbers, the biotechnology industry is one that is extremely competitive and difficult to survive in.

Taking drugs or other chemicals from creation to marketing is often a time-consuming process. Only a small percentage of the drugs developed ever survive the rigors of clinical trials, and only about 5 to 10 percent of these are ever approved for sale. According to the Congressional Office of Technology Assessment, the entire process—from the discovery of a new drug through its clinical trials and approval by the FDA—costs approximately US$359 million per drug.

Nevertheless, the biotechnology industry remains strong. It has already made notable contributions to areas such as medical diagnosis and therapeutics. Older forms of drug discovery and development are being replaced by the techniques and methodology of biotechnology research.

The biotechnology industry's research and development (R&D) expenditures are expected to reach US$7 billion in 1995, making it one of the most expensive US industries. Except for a few large firms, such as Amgen and Genentech, the industry is made up mostly of mid-size companies that constantly must find new money for research. Many of these smaller companies find they must link up with a corporate partner or be swallowed in the US biotechnology market.

International Market Overview

US manufacturers and service providers account for nearly half of the major biotechnological services marketed worldwide. While consistently maintaining a positive trade balance, the industry faces increasing international competition. To maintain competitiveness, the industry must overcome international obstacles such as price controls, illegal use of patents and copyrights, and foreign regulations on marketing and R&D.

Industry experts predict that in Europe alone two million more jobs will be created by the year 2000 because of the enormous growth projected in the world market for biotechnological goods. Competition will keep out all but the strongest US firms, however.

The new markets of Russia and other countries in the Commonwealth of Independent States provide particularly strong potential, but at the same time present formidable challenges as a result of registration, testing, and licensing requirements. China is also a large potential pharmaceutical market, but is increasing its own pharmaceutical production. The Japanese market remains one of the best for the United States, but in reaction to slumping domestic pharmaceutical prices, the Japanese industry is developing new markets in the United States and Europe and acquiring foreign firms.

The North American Free Trade Agreement is expected to increase US exports of biotechnological products–particularly through the reduction of tariffs, the improvement of intellectual property rights protection, and the opening of the government procurement markets in Mexico and Canada. These countries represent approximately 15 percent of total US exports of pharmaceutical goods and services.

Biotechnological service companies will continue to focus on developing new vaccines, particularly for AIDS. However, the biological products industry will be affected by stringent regulations, which tend to increase production costs. Research expenditures are high, yet there is a demand for lower prices. As with all sectors of the biotechnology industry, the development of innovative technology will depend upon the amount of R&D money available.

Agents who can provide quick after-sales service will retain an edge over the competition. A successful agent of biotechnology equipment is one who keeps a 40 percent inventory of spare parts on stock to satisfy his client's needs. Furthermore, credit facilities also serve as an incentive to boost sales. Many laws require that foreign firms retain a local commercial agent to submit bids on public tenders. Although governments are often less stringent about dealings with private companies, most foreign firms have found it advantageous to engage a local agent who can deal with problems related to communications, bureaucratic procedures, local business practices, and marketing. A firm can appoint multiple agents on a geographical or product basis.

Market Barriers

Government Barriers

Government regulations and restrictions regarding the biotechnology industry are usually strict. US firms are often not able to obtain, on their own, import licenses for their biotech services. They must be imported through qualified domestic pharmaceutical companies. Some ways around these barriers include:

Acquisition of a local company

A US company may be able to acquire a local company. In so doing, the US company benefits from direct access to the market, an established supply infrastructure, and available and experienced sales staff.

Independent set-up of direct sales subsidiaries

This is generally undertaken when there is an immediate market opportunity.

Economic Barriers

Although US biotechnical services are well known and highly regarded worldwide, competition between firms from other countries can be fierce. US firms could compete through more competitive pricing, frequent advertising, and good after-sales support. Sales presentations with local agents/distributors are strongly recommended. American suppliers must be able to address the problems and concerns of the users in an expeditious manner.

Some biotechnology firms indicated dissatisfaction with financing terms offered by present US suppliers and would welcome increased competition from other firms. Finance problems in Mexico, for example, have caused many third-country firms to think of opening their own laboratories there to be closer to large pharmaceutical and processed food manufacturers and to penetrate other Latin American markets.

Regional Opportunities

Note: These are only examples of regional opportunities and in no way constitute a complete list.

The United Kingdom

The United Kingdom, which currently has the largest biotechnology industry in Europe, also offers the brightest opportunities for American companies wanting to benefit from cross-fertilization between the biotechnology and the pharmaceutical sectors. The market for biopharmaceuticals in the UK parallels that of the United States more closely than any other country in Europe. There is a strong research base, with an emphasis on basic mainstream research.

Both the expanding private health care sector and the increasingly cost-conscious National Health Service (NHS) are fueling the demand for more price competitive pharmaceutical products. Products developed for medical applications in the United Kingdom are not subject to a regulatory regime as strict as that imposed by the FDA. Clinical tests in the United Kingdom can be performed more rapidly than would be possible in the United States, accelerating development of new drugs and diagnostic kits.

Because of a common language and a similar business culture, the UK offers US companies the best opportunity in Europe to understand the EC's changing regulatory environment for biopharmaceutical products. Moreover, UK corporate taxes are relatively low, and once products are in this market they enjoy duty free access to the rest of the European Community.

Germany

Germany has outstanding research capabilities and renowned facilities that can benefit any biotechnology firm wanting to export there. The country's reputation for scientific know-how derives from its excellent universities, the well-known Institute for Biotechnological Research (GBF) in Braunschweig, the Max-Planck-Institutes, the Frauenfeld Institutes, and the European Molecular Biology Laboratory (EMBL) in Heidelberg. At these facilities, research breakthroughs and innovative developments provide an excellent source for new products and concepts. Over the past several years, German companies have turned toward American companies to form strategic alliances, receive venture capital, and gain production sites.

Mexico

In the last ten years there has been a growing interest among processed food manufacturers in Mexico in biotechnologically-developed products. Now at least 700 companies are using some type of bio-developed product. This number is expected to increase in the next five years to 1,500 companies producing more than 7,500 products including cereals, snacks, soups, confectionery, milk and beverages. Mexico is a leading country in biotechnology R&D in Latin America and is a good country for US firms to enter the Latin American market through. Business visitors from the US can enter the country very easily, and conduct activities related to research and design; manufacture, and production, marketing, sales, and distribution; after sales service (e.g., warranty services and repair, sales-service (e.g, warranty services and repairs) of equipment exported by US producers; and certain other activities related to trade.

Taiwan

The scientific research base in biotechnology is fairly well developed in Taiwan, but the industrial sector is still weak. Taiwan depends mostly on imports of biopharmaceuticals for human health care. Due to the lack of technology and insufficient research and development, local manufacturers are primarily producing hepatitis-B vaccine and medical diagnostic kits.

Best Bet Opportunities

Note: These are only examples of industry opportunities and in no way constitute a complete list.

Ag-bio

Biotechnology being used to improve agriculture is an important issue in this era of international overpopulation. There has been an ongoing debate about whether or not to label food products, and many countries prefer a requirement to label all genetically-treated foodstuffs. Others only order foods to be labelled if they have been "substantially" changed. Nevertheless, this is a huge market for US R&D firms.

Gene Therapy

Gene therapy has become a popular industry, particularly in the health care sector. One focus of gene therapy research is cardiovascular disease since almost one out of four people in industrial nations suffers from heart disease.

Environmental Warning Systems: Biosensors

The biosensor field is a new area with a great deal of potential for US firms. Biosensor systems use micro-organisms as early warning systems for environmental pollution. Test results are rapidly obtained through biosensors, and the devices can be built to fit specific needs such as reacting to a specific pollutant or toxic substances in general. Companies in Germany are currently making great strides with biosensors. They have built cost-effective devices which measure oxygen content and monitor water quality at purification plants.

Sources of US Based Assistance

Biotechnology Industry Organization
1625 K Street, N.W.
Suite 1100
Washington, DC 20006-1604
Tel: (202) 857-0244
Fax: (202) 857-0237

International Society of Pharmaceutical Engineers
3816 West Linebaugh Avenue
Suite 412
Tampa, FL 33624
Tel: (813) 960-2105
Fax: (813) 264-2816

National Association of Pharmaceutical Manufacturers
320 Old Country Road
Garden City, NY 11530
Tel: (516) 741-3699
Fax: (516) 741-3696

Pharmaceutical Research and Manufacturers Association
1100 15th Street, N.W.
Suite 900
Washington, DC 20005
Tel: (202) 835-3400
Fax: (202) 835-3414

Publications

Biotech Reporter
Freiberg Publishing Company, Inc.
Box 7
2302 W. First
Cedar Falls, IA 50613
Tel: (319) 277-3599
Fax: (319) 277-3783
Current scientific and business news in the field of agricultural biotechnology.

Biotechniques
Eaton Publishing Co.
154 E. Central St.
Natick, MA 01760
Tel: (508) 655-8282

Biotechnology at Work
Biotechnology Industry Organization
1625 K St., NW
Ste. 1100
Washington, DC 20006
Tel: (202) 857-0244
Covers the latest development of biotechnology in environmental, agricultural, and medical fields.

Biotechnology and Bioengineering
John Wiley & Sons, Inc. Journals
605 Third Ave.
New York, NY 10158-0012
Tel: (212) 850-6645
Fax: (212) 850-6021
Presents original research on all aspects of biochemical and microbial technology.

Biotechnology Software
Biotechnology Software Report
Mary Ann Liebert, Inc. Publishers
2 Madison Ave.
Larchmont, NY 10538
Tel: (914) 834-3100
Fax: (914) 834-3688
Email: Liebert@pipeline.com
Acts as an interface between computers and researchers who are not computer scientists. Aims to prevent the unnecessary duplication of effort that occurs when a new computer application is designed that has already been devised in another laboratory.

Biotechnology Techniques
Chapman & Hall
Journals Promotion Department
One Penn Plaza
41st Floor
New York, NY 10119
Tel: (212) 564-1060
Fax: (212) 564-1505
Provides rapid publication and permanent record for new techniques in biotechnology.

Biotechnology Therapeutics
Marcel Dekker Journals
270 Madison Ave.
New York, NY 10016
Tel: (212) 969-9000
Fax: (212)685-4540
Covers both preclinical experimentation and clinical trials of therapeutic agents produced by biotechnological processes. Emphasizes the utility of a broad array of emerging products from molecular biology for potential and actual medical practice.

Biotherapy
Box 358
Accord Station
Hingham, MA 02018-0358
Tel: (617) 871-6600
Fax: (617) 871-6528
Covers immunology, molecular biology, cytology, and gene therapy.

Bioventure Stock Report
BioVenture Publishing
32 W. 25th Ave.
Ste. 203
San Mateo, CA 94403-2236
Tel: (415) 574-7128
Fax: (415) 574-8319
Tracks the performance of the top 100 biopharmaceutical companies by technology focus, leading product status, market capitalization and financial profile.

Guide to Biotechnology Products and Instruments
American Association for the Advancement of Science
1333 H Street, NW
Washington, DC 20005
Tel: (202) 326-6417
Lists the manufacturers of scientific instruments and laboratory equipment.

Food Biotechnology
Marcel Dekker Journals
270 Madison Ave.
New York, NY 10016
Tel: (212) 969-9000
Fax: (212) 685-4540

International Biodeterioration & Biodegredation
Elsevier Science
660 White Plains Rd.
Tarrytown, NY 10591-5153
Tel: (914) 524-9200
Fax: (914) 333-2444
Presents original research papers and reviews on the biological causes of deterioration or advantageous biological upgrading of all types of materials.

Computer Services

Defined

Computer professional services consist primarily of three activities: systems integration (setting up and maintaining computer systems), custom programming, and consulting and training. Providers advise and train customers on such issues as:

- the design, selection, and installation of computer systems
- computer and telecommunications linkages
- systems and network management
- Internet set up and management
- telephony systems

Domestic Market Overview

The computer services industry experienced record profits in the 1980s, but the 90s have seen mixed results. Many domestic companies have failed to meet their own growth projections in recent years. In response to sluggish market conditions, managers were more willing than usual to reduce employment and inventory levels.

Computer services must continually adjust to keep up with the constant changes in computer technologies. Customers for systems integration services are required to a much greater degree today to comply with industry standards ranging from integrated systems digital network (ISDN) protocols to the new ISO 9000 series of quality system technical standards. This trend toward compliance with technical standardization is expected to accelerate for the next few years.

Despite slower growth than in the past, the domestic market for computer services remains one of the faster growing segments of the US economy. This market is expanding as organizations in both the public and private sectors strive to increase productivity and quality in the workplace by "reinventing government" or "reinventing the corporation." These organizations rely on outside help in designing, installing, and operating automated information and management systems.

Computer services continue to benefit from steady growth in the numbers and performance features of personal computers, workstations, and network terminals. Since 1990, the use of electronic mail systems (including digitized voice mail) and services has been the fastest growing source of revenues from professional services. Such services will expand with the installed base of computers and computer networks.

A recent problem has been the widening time lag between purchases of computer equipment and revenues for professional services. For many years, most equipment sales were additions to the installed base, creating demand for new services after a fairly constant interval. Increasingly, however, equipment expenditures are for replacements and upgrades, and the installed base is growing less dramatically. This trend, together with a slowdown in the growth of sales of computer equipment, is expected to hold down revenue growth in computer professional services for the next five years.

Foreign ownership of US-based service firms, particularly by companies headquartered in the United Kingdom, is expanding. The most common method of entry is acquisition rather than start-up. Firms in developing countries such as India and Pakistan are more likely to enter the US market as subcontractors providing custom programming for US firms involved in fulfilling multinational contracts.

Customers have become increasingly hesitant to make purchases as the time lag has increased between announcements of new products, such as computer hardware and prepackaged software, and the products' release and customer acceptance. This time lag increased throughout the 1980s and into the 1990s, and computer services firms are concerned that it will hold down their growth rates for the rest of this decade. The problem was typified by the delayed release, and customer acceptance, of Windows® products.

International Market Overview

US companies have continued to move from joint ventures to full service subsidiaries in many foreign markets, especially in western Europe and Latin America. An increasing share of revenues for custom programming comes from abroad.

Mergers and acquisitions in Western Europe's computer professional services have significantly accelerated, beginning in 1990 in anticipation of the creation of the European Community's single market. In contrast, mergers and acquisitions have not been as significant a factor in the restructuring under way in Japan's computer services industry, although some of the recent reorganizations within Japan's industrial families have had analogous outcomes.

Broad social and economic changes have also created important advantages for US providers of computer services. One example is US managers' superiority to their foreign counterparts in computer literacy. In addition to buying more existing services, this large, technically-oriented customer base encourages services providers to develop innovative products that give them competitive advantages when offering services abroad.

In Western Europe, Japan, and South Korea, it is more common for computer services firms to be subsidiaries of corporate conglomerates, despite attempts at fostering entrepreneurship, especially within the European Community (EC).

US firms have begun joint ventures in central and eastern Europe, and revenues began to appear in 1992 because contracts for services can generate sales and profits quickly. So far, these markets are considerably smaller than expected, however, and competition from EC firms is intense.

This forecast is consistent with other estimates, including one by the Marcar Management Institute in Washington DC, for a more broadly defined "information market." Marcar wrote: "Global information markets will rise dramatically to the year 2000. By the end of the decade, equipment and services will total US$3,010 billion, averaging 9.1 percent annual compound growth." North America, with sales totalling US$1,470 billion, will constitute nearly half the world market, according to Marcar. Western Europe will spend US$910 billion; the rest of the world will spend US$630 billion, although this will be the fastest growing segment.

Computer training and consulting will continue to gain market share within this expanding services sector, both in the United States and abroad. Growth rates in several foreign countries, especially Japan, are expected to exceed those in the US.

Increasing numbers of foreign firms' subsidiaries operating in the US create opportunities for US custom programming and design services, first in the US and eventually to enter foreign markets through those subsidiaries' foreign parents. Newly privatized corporations around the world are prime prospects for US providers of computer professional services because they need to automate their operations to be able to compete in free markets.

Consulting services are expected to become particularly important, as demand for complex solutions in vertical markets grow, and customers require innovative technologies to remain competitive. Systems integration is also likely to maintain good development rates, especially in view of the growing demand for telecom integration, the need for reorganization of complex information systems, and the wide adoption of client/server architectures.

The training and education segment, which experienced a slowdown in 1993, is also expected to recover, due to the need to prepare personnel to meet the challenge of new technologies. Facility management/outsourcing is the segment predicted to see the most rapid development in coming years. Several medium and large-sized end-users are considering the adoption of the outsourcing solution, mainly to reduce costs and to focus on their core businesses. It is expected that the annual growth rate in this segment may reach 15 percent in the next three years. Good prospects are also expected for value-added network services and disaster recovery services, while the growth of traditional data entry/data processing services is likely to be very limited.

Market Barriers

Government Barriers

Many countries have been placed on "watch lists," reflecting problems with protection of copyrights for computer software. Enactments of directives such as the EU software directive, making software copyright violations a criminal offense are major steps forward, but they have been few and far between. Many countries within the EC have been slow to increase enforcement actions against software pirates. Italy, for example, has made some moves forward, such as creating an Interministerial Anti-Piracy Committee, but software piracy is still a problem.

Because the computer services industry overlaps with other industries, barriers to entry can also overlap. The telecommunication systems in many countries, for example, are owned wholly by the government, and their strict regulations could affect firms providing Internet and telephony services as well.

Most countries have certain restrictions on work permits for aliens, i.e., the number of employees that can work there or the amount of time they can stay. Because computer services often include so much more than merely the installation of a system, employees often need to remain near the site to answer questions and solve problems.

Economic Barriers

A country's average turnaround time for paying invoices could be a problem for US companies. In Italy, for example, the turnaround time for paying invoices is never less than 90 days, and in many cases it may go up to 120-180 days. This often causes serious liquidity problems for the Italian importers/distributors from the US, as their terms of payment with the US are usually 30-60 days. The resulting mark-up imposed by local distributors/importers varies from 45 percent to 80 percent of the original selling price, depending on the type of products.

Before Entering a Market

The most common way for US firms to conduct business is by establishing a local presence directly in the country or through arrangements with other computer services firms in order to offer comprehensive services. Alternatively, US firms could form some type of partnership with US or other hardware or software firms already operating in the country. As part of their growth strategy, these firms continually seek to add to their wide network of strategic partners to provide technology solutions which are compatible with their existing products. Another option for small- and medium-size US companies is to offer niche expertise in large projects. In addition to these options, still another possibility for US firms to enter markets is to promote their solutions on their own to local firms, and to provide services by sending personnel from the US to the local country. This method is not as common as some of the other market entry options, due to the travel-related expense involved. Some key factors for a supplier's success include:

- solid financial and organizational structure

- a high degree of professionalism

- proven knowledge of innovative technologies

- availability of high quality solutions

- vertical market experience

- business reputation
- business references
- timely delivery

Extremely important factors for a new-to-market US firm are also the ability to understand the structure of the market and the users' culture, to constantly communicate with clients, to recognize their needs, and to adequately meet them.

Regional Opportunities

Note: These are only examples of regional opportunities and in no way constitute a complete list.

Canada

While good sales opportunities for a variety of computer services exist for large firms in large end-user organizations, there are also excellent sales opportunities for small- to medium-sized US firms as well, especially for niche oriented integration solutions such as networking and systems integration.

There are no tariff barriers to trade in computer hardware, accessories, software and services between Canada and the United States. Since the North American market for computer hardware, software, and services was relatively "open" prior to the enactment of the US-Canada Free Trade Agreement the effects of the agreement on the industry have been minimal.

The US-Canada Free Trade Agreement has increased sales across borders, but acquisitions of smaller Canadian firms by large US computer services companies, to take advantage of the market opening provisions, have been fewer than expected.

Since profit margins on hardware have dropped and margins on packaged software are in decline, there are good opportunities for companies providing general systems integration and outsourcing services, where margins are still high.

Market opportunities for US companies in the Canadian market can be found in the manufacturing, finance, banking, pharmaceutical, health care, and natural resources industries, as well as in the government. Small business is also an area of growing opportunity for system integration projects.

Canadian firms are receptive to services provided by US firms because these companies have a good reputation for providing leading edge technologies and proven solutions in the field.

Good sales prospects also exist for network training, network administration and client/server training, and for support on multi-vendor equipment and assistance in distributed systems management. Demand for software planning, implementation, and support is also growing at a significant rate. In the manufacturing sector, integration of manufacturing management systems will experience good growth, followed by supply chain systems.

Canadian customers seek service providers with the following qualities: expertise in both legacy and client/server systems, as well as the products that translate between them; the ability to provide consulting services that cover the complete customer cycle from business re-engineering to final design and deployment; technical and managerial skills, as well as familiarity with a client's business; vendor-independence and the freedom to recommend any vendor's products; competence; experience; local presence, or arrangements with other firms to provide comprehensive services; and, a willingness to accept some project risks.

Italy

After a period of very rapid growth throughout the 1980s, the computer services sector in Italy has entered a new phase of maturity, characterized by dynamic, although decreasing, growth rates in the range of 5 to 6 percent yearly. In 1994, the market for computer and data processing services was estimated at US$4.6 billion.

The heavy economic crisis of 1992/1993 created a strong need for cost-cutting measures. This contributed to the development of a new attitude towards outsourcing and increased acceptance as a tool to operate efficiently and cost effectively in times of recession. After a period of strong resistance to outsourcing, several large-sized and some medium-sized end-users have already adopted or are seriously considering the adoption of outsourcing solutions to maintain or increase their competitive edge.

Most multinational computer services companies have established a direct presence in Italy. In some cases, foreign computer services companies, usually specializing in vertical market niches, have reached cooperation agreements with well-established local companies or major end-users and have relocated personnel in Italy. US firms which decide not to have a direct presence in Italy should try to pursue the objective of teaming up with a carefully selected local company, which is well-established throughout the country, capable of offering good support services, experienced in the different market sectors, and with the ability to maintain person-to-person contact with customers.

US companies dominate the market. As US technological expertise is highly regarded and US superiority in the computer services sector is widely recognized, the US is forecast to increase its already excellent market position in the next three years. Good opportunities exist for new-to-market US companies offering highly specialized outsourcing services, which are willing to team up with well-established Italian firms for cooperation agreements.

In general, highly specialized companies with specific vertical market experience which are willing to team up with well-established Italian firms for cooperation agreements should find a good entry into Italy. The captive market is difficult to penetrate and generally not open to new suppliers in the short and medium term.

The Italian climate for cooperation agreements and investment is very favorable towards US companies. There are no trade barriers limiting the presence of foreign information technology companies in Italy. US firms supplied around 75 percent of the market for imports of computer software in 1994 and the US share is expected to grow in the near future. US strengths cited by Italian customers include high-quality solutions, vertical market experience, timely delivery, flexibility, and willingness to work with Italian joint venture partners. Most multinational computer services companies have established a direct presence in Italy.

Best Bet Opportunities

Note: These are only examples of industry opportunities and in no way constitute a complete list.

Custom Programming

The widespread availability of prepackaged software has led many providers of custom software to move from software development to software enhancements and modifications as their primary source of revenues, and to establish "help-desk" services. Reliance on documentation services—custom software manuals describing how to modify software—is also growing, as is the economic importance of network security services. These trends are expected to continue for at least five years.

Training Services

Consulting and training by US firms will continue to increase in the future. Revenue growth will continue to be constrained by the expansion rate of computer related training in secondary schools, colleges and universities, and by increases in software-based and video cassette tutorials available in retail stores.

Revenues from training services have been growing fastest in computer aided design/computer-aided manufacturing (CAD/CAM) and in computer-aided engineering (CAE), particularly for the use of graphics software in the automotive and aerospace sectors. The growth of revenues from training in word processing and data transaction systems has slowed, however, because the software has become easier to use.

The share of training provided by both interactive and digital video instruction is increasing sharply. System vendors are the leading suppliers of computer education and training for product related services, the largest market segment. One of the fastest growing revenue opportunities is telesupport (1-900 numbers) for technical support of information systems.

Systems Integration

Many firms are moving into systems integration through new or expanded operating units; others are acquiring existing providers of services, or merging to create new offerings.

The growth of this sector is difficult to assess on the basis of revenue data alone. Real growth rates over time were traditionally understated because the sector's rates included both a declining share of equipment costs and an increasing share of services costs. In addition, an increasing share of a firm's total revenue in this sector is derived from repair and maintenance services embedded in systems integration contracts.

The increasing use of single procurement contracts for integrated computer related services obscures trends in the revenues for any one component of those services. This use has changed competition patterns in the subsector. Only the largest companies can afford to prepare bids on the largest projects; medium and small firms must increasingly form strategic alliances to make such bids jointly.

Telephony Services

One growing area of opportunity is in the provision of telephony services. Computer telephony integration provides intelligent links between computer and telephone systems. This technology will be an integral part of future communications for businesses, and will be used by many to gain competitive advantage over companies that are slow to embrace it. Profit margins are excellent for these services.

Data Management Services

Data network management (including hardware maintenance, LAN management, network monitoring, and software distribution) represents one of the fastest growing market segments, as the network is becoming the core utility for most user organizations. In particular, the growth of data network management is being favored by the increasing importance of distributed environments and by the complexity of architectures, which make network administration more and more challenging for end-users. An important role will also be played by the increasing use of UNIX platforms to support "heavy" data processing tasks. Unlike standardized PC-based networks, UNIX-based networks require the management of a multiplicity of protocols and applications, thus making it increasingly difficult for the end-user to administer them directly. This trend is expected to accelerate in the next three years, also offering excellent opportunities to private outsourcing companies.

Sources of US Based Assistance

American Electronics Association
5201 Great American Parkway
P.O. Box 54990
Santa Clara, CA 95056-0990
Tel: (408) 987-4200
Fax: (408) 970-8565

Software Publishers Association
1730 M Street, NW
Suite 700
Washington, DC 20036
Tel: (202) 452-1600
Fax: (202) 223-8756

National Association of Computer Consultant Businesses
1250 Connecticut Avenue, NW
Suite 700
Washington, DC 20036
Tel: (202) 637-6483
Fax: (202) 637-9195

Association for Computing Machinery
1515 Broadway, 17th Floor
New York, NY 10036-5701
Tel: (212) 869-7440
Fax: (212) 944-1318

Publications

Computer and Computing Information Resources Directory
Gale Research Inc.
1-800-788-GALE
An international guide listing over 4,000 sources, such as associations and user groups; more than 1,500 periodicals, directories, and other printed materials and a wide range of trade shows and conventions serving the computer industry.

International Computer Law Adviser
Law & Technology Press
4 Arbolado Ct.
Manhattan Beach, CA 90266-4937
Tel: (310) 544-0272
Fax: (310) 544-4965

International Journal of Computer Research
Nova Science Publishers, Inc.
6080 Jericho Tpke., Ste. 207
Commack, NY 11725-2808
Tel: (516) 499-3103
Fax: (516) 499-3146
Email: novasci1@aol.com

Service & Support Management

Publications & Communications, Inc.
12416 Hymeadow
Austin, TX 78750-1896
Tel: (512) 250-9023
Fax: (512) 331-3900

Service Industry Newsletter
Ledgeway Publications
P.O. Box 5093
Westborough, MA 01581-5093
Tel: (508) 370-5555
Fax: (508) 370-6262

Service News (Yarmouth)
United Publications, Inc.
P.O. Box 995
Yarmouth, ME 04096
Tel: (207) 846-0600
Fax: (207) 846-0657

Education & Training

Defined

A broad definition of education is "the process through which people develop hard-won wisdom." Businesses around the world are beginning to realize that many of their employees must be re-educated and trained to adapt to a technological environment and an international marketplace.

Education and training services include not only public and private schools, colleges, and universities whose primary goal is education, but also expenditures by US employers to provide formal instruction and teach modern techniques in both manufacturing and services, and to retrain workers who lose their jobs due to automation and restructuring. Some services include:

- English and other languages
- personal development
- communication skills/literacy
- collaborative quality management
- preparation for multi-skilled and new technologies, particularly in the computerized workplace
- total quality management (TQM)
- report writing for the services sector
- speech and language consultants (all facets of communication as it applies to the work place, particularly cross-cultural communication)
- computer skills, especially word processing and spreadsheet
- sales skills/management training

Domestic Market Overview

Public and private expenditures for education and corporate training account for a huge portion of the GDP, second in size only to health and medical services. The education and training industry is labor intensive, employing an estimated 10 million workers in the private and public sectors.

The need for retraining employees has increased in recent years. Technological innovation has fostered considerable change in manufacturing processes relating to production quality and cost. The internationalization of production and markets has also intensified competition, resulting in significant automation and an increase in the use of computer-related technology. Technological growth has also raised the level of training required for the existing workforce and new entrants. Twenty-five to 50 percent of manufacturing industries, including fabricated metals, industrial machinery, electronic equipment and instruments and transportation equipment, now use computer-aided design and engineering in their overall operations. A slightly smaller percentage of these industries use computer-controlled technology directly on the factory floor. More than 30 percent of high school graduates and 60 percent of college graduates use computers in their jobs. The changes in the workplace have presented a challenge for secondary school teachers because only an estimated 25 percent are computer literate, according to Market Data Retrieval, a private research firm.

Workers once considered to have sufficient skills for lifetime employment now find they must learn new skills and processes to sustain their employment in an increasingly technological work environment. The growing importance of computer-aided design, computer-integrated manufacturing, total-quality management and just-in-time production requires a skilled workforce.

Besides work skills in manufacturing processes, employers and post-secondary institutions have found that a significant number of US high school graduates need remedial work in grammar, mathematics, and basic problem-solving skills before they are ready to take a job or college courses. A study found that of approximately 13 million college students in 1989, more than two million were enrolled in remedial courses in reading, writing, or math.

Educators and businesses have started cooperative ventures to address needs in education and skills development. Educators are also increasing remedial help and training for students and workers with insufficient knowledge and skills. Businesses have begun providing equipment to schools and colleges, and bringing teachers to their plants and factories to gain firsthand knowledge of the level of technical sophistication modern workers must have.

To provide additional skills, school systems in many states have introduced computer science, giving high school students hands-on experience in programming fairly complex problems. The average public school had one computer for every 92 students when the first data was collected in 1983, according to Market Data Retrieval. By 1990, however, there was one computer for every 21 students. In private elementary and secondary schools for the same period, the ratio of students to computers changed from approximately 56 students per computer in 1983 to 20 students in 1990.

To shorten the competitive cycle and to make incremental improvements in existing products, the US work force must have a broader and deeper understanding of the whole process involved in manufacturing a product, rather than the part for which each person is responsible. Because technology changes constantly, US workers must have continuous training to remain globally competitive.

International Market Overview

US educational organizations provide services overseas under contracts with foreign educational institutions and through contracts with development agencies such as US AID and the United Nations Development Program. A number of US companies have established language schools and trade schools abroad. Most US correspondence schools accept foreign students, and some have entered into licensing arrangements for correspondence course materials and administration. Factors that users consider important when selecting a course of training program are, in order of importance, expected results after training, experienced trainers, price, and credit.

Leading educators believe that better preparation, more training, and a greater commitment to professionalism are the keys to making businesses more competitive worldwide, as well as providing new career paths for those who leave school and for the victims of downsizing.

Many foreign industries want US firms to provide help in their language, especially when training blue collar workers. Having an office in the country, or a local partner or representative, could be the best way for a US company to enter the market. US multinational corporations are expected to increase the training they provide outside the US as they increase their investment in joint ventures abroad. Meanwhile, universities and colleges are reaching out to foreign markets to enhance the transfer of technology and training.

The labor ministries of several countries offer training programs, including training for unemployed persons, courses for persons to be hired by specific companies, and joint programs with public and private resources to improve the qualifications and productivity of employees of different industries. They also often have programs where the government may share up to 70 percent of the training costs for employed industrial workers, in order to improve competitiveness. Large companies have enough employees to justify their own training centers and instructors. They frequently hire foreign training or consultant firms to offer advanced technology courses to their employees.

Market Barriers

Government Barriers

International restrictions can include minimum requirements for employment of local nationals, local ownership requirements, limited local credits, and restrictions on repatriation of earnings.

US firms operating educational facilities overseas also face infringement of copyrights on curriculum, films, and correspondence course materials, and restrictions on remittance of profits. Some private sector organizations, seeking to expand their educational services internationally, have found a prejudice by some foreign governments against private industry expertise, in favor of non-profit educational institutions. Another problem involves misleading recruiting abroad by some US educational institutions, which has a serious negative impact on the attitudes of foreign students toward US education facilities.

Economic Barriers

Government rules that are meant to promote education and training are often ignored by businesses. Official statistics in Mexico, for example, show that only 36 percent of companies comply with employee training provisions, due to the problems that small businesses face to compete and survive. Large companies have enough employees to justify their own training centers and instructors. They also have strong finances to plan and organize training when they begin using new technologies.

Social and Cultural Barriers

American training services are respected but there is often a language barrier. Foreign training services are sometimes limited to training managerial staff or high executives, where translation services are commonly provided to those who do not speak English. Companies interested in penetrating this market should consider providing services in the native language. Language may be a decisive factor depending on the level of persons taking the course. When training is for managerial or trainer levels, simultaneous translation services are common. When training is for blue collar workers, using the local language is a requirement.

Market Channels

The private sector may be segmented into a number of main categories: privately-owned colleges offering a range of vocational/trade and training courses, mostly competing directly with the government programs offered at technical colleges or universities; private companies/consultancies (which may or may not be registered or accredited), with full-time trainers on staff, providing training courses to individuals as well as companies; and private trainers, providing consulting to individuals or companies, often not registered and usually not providing a certificate for services rendered. Larger training companies tend to stay in business longer because they have a stronger basis than the one-person ad hoc trainers who, often, do not have the necessary skills to diversify and adapt to the needs of businesses. Larger training companies often have a staff of 15-20 trainers working as consultants, each with his/her own individual area(s) of specialty.

The public training sector includes public companies, universities, technical colleges, state and federal government, and charitable organizations funded by the government. Governments often institute their own training programs, as well as establish organizations to regulate the private training companies by setting competency standards. The Australian federal government, for example, is spending around US$90 million (A$125 million) in research infrastructure, part of which includes funding universities to support and enhance further interaction with industry and its needs.

Regional Opportunities

Note: These are only examples of regional opportunities and in no way constitute a complete list.

Australia

US expertise in the training field is recognized in Australia and well-received, provided the training material/presentation is adapted to the Australian culture, including Australian language/spelling, weights/measures system, etc. The Australian government has embarked on a process of structural micro-economic reform including education and training to address technological and structural change. The goal is to develop a multi-skilled and efficient workforce, increasing the skills of those currently employed as well as training young people looking for employment and those people who want to return to the workforce. Approximately 75 percent of the existing workforce is expected to still be in the employment pool at the turn of the century. Only about 30 percent of the skills and knowledge they possess will be applicable in the year 2000, however.

Funding for up to 75 percent of English language and literacy training costs may be available under the Commonwealth government WELL program. WELL is also funding development training resources for the National Automotive Industry Training Board, the National Automotive Languages and Literacy Coordination Unit, and the National Food Industry Training Council.

Mexico

It is estimated that 70 percent of the value of training services in Mexico is provided by domestic companies. Imported services are gaining a bigger share, however, due to the high demand for advanced technologies and modern management systems. Now, imported training services are mainly used to train executives and advisors, which is normally the most expensive training. Imports of training services are still low, but with good potential, since Mexico has started programs to increase productivity and competitiveness which require new technologies and equipment to reach these objectives.

By law, all companies in Mexico must provide job training to their employees. It is estimated that only 36 percent of companies comply with this obligation, but with an employed labor force of over 30 million in 1995, there are still good opportunities for providers of training services.

The government hires foreign trainers for specific cases when needed. As part of a program to promote productivity and modernization of industries and services in Mexico, the National Development Bank (Nacional Financiera), using the resources of the World Bank, is financing projects, including training, for micro- and small-businesses.

Mexican industries like local service in Spanish, especially when training blue collar workers. Having an office in Mexico, a representative, or a Mexican partner could be the best way for an American company to enter the market.

France

Every company in France with over 10 employees is required by law to contribute 1.5 percent of its payroll to manpower training. Several US educational institutions have already established an "off-shore" campus in France to take advantage of this existing market.

Best Bet Opportunities

Note: These are only examples of industry opportunities and in no way constitute a complete list.

Communication

The need to meet international standards and implement new work practices has made many companies take a second look at their internal communication and operation. Companies are choosing to teach managers how to communicate effectively.

Language

Many markets recognize that English is a prerequisite for business and countries are racing to learn the language and compete in the international business market.

Computers

Computer training is in high demand world-wide. Many foreign firms can now afford modern computer systems and high technology equipment, but do not have the necessary skills to use them. US computer training firms are held in high regard internationally.

Other

Another area growing in many markets is tourism. In Australia, for example, an extra 250,000 workers will be needed in tourism and the hospitality industries by the year 2000, which translates into an increase in demand for training services—particularly in public relations, management, interpersonal skills, languages, and communication.

Sources of US Based Assistance

American Federation of Teachers
555 New Jersey Avenue, NW
Washington, DC 20001
Tel: (202) 879-4400
Fax: (202) 879-4556

Publications

AIPT Report
Association for International Practical Training
10400 Little Patuxent Pkwy
Ste. 250
Columbia, MD 21044-3510
Tel: (410) 997-2200
Fax: (410) 992-3924

Advising Quarterly
America-Mideast Educational & Training Services
1100 17th St. NW
Washington DC 20036
Tel: (202) 785-0022
Fax: (202) 822-6563
Telex: 440160
Email: 70523.3662@compuserve.com

International Journal of Vocational Education and Training
International Vocational Education and Training Association
676-B Enterprise Dr.
Lewis Center, OH 43035
Tel: (614) 847-9550
Fax: (614) 847-9844

News from Aprovecho
Aprovecho Institute
80574 Hazelton Rd.
Cottage Grove, OR 97424
Tel: (503) 942-8198

News from IES-IAS
Institute of European Studies - Institute of Asian Studies
223 W. Ohio St.
Chicago, IL 60610-4196
Tel: (312) 944-17500
Fax: (312) 944-1448

Perspective (New York)
Association of Teachers of Latin American Studies
Box 620754
Flushing, NY 11362-0754
Tel: (718) 428-1237

Vacation Study Abroad
Institute of International Education
809 United Nations Plaza
New York, NY 11017
Tel: (212) 984-5412
Fax: (212) 984-5385
Telex: TRT 175977

WCCI Forum
World Council for Curriculum and Instruction
c/o School of Education
Indiana University
Bloomington IN 47405
Tel: (812) 855-4702
Fax: (812) 855-3044

World Learning, Annual Report
1960 a. free.
World Learning
Kipling Rd., Box 676
Brattleboro, VT 05302-0676
Tel: (802) 257-7751

Internet Sites

Association for Experimental Education Home Page
http://www.princeton.edu/~rcurtis/aee.html

National Center for Research in Vocational Education
http://vocserve.berkeley.edu/

Entertainment

Defined

Although the term "entertainment" encompasses many different things—art forms, pastimes, and events to name a few—for purposes of this article it is limited to motion pictures, recorded music, videocassette programs, and television (including cable television).

This definition of the entertainment industry includes programs, but not equipment—motion pictures for example, but not the cameras and other gear involved in movie production. Revenues from programs recorded on tape and disc, as well as royalties for public performances, are included in the recorded music sector of the industry, but not the production or sales of the instruments and equipment used to record the music. Videocassette recordings and broadcast and cable television programming and transmission are included, but this definition does not address the actual making of the programs.

Domestic Market Overview

Revenues from all sectors of the entertainment industry have improved in the past few years, after falling significantly in the early 1990s. Movie admissions have steadily increased; sales of recorded music are strong; videocassette sales and rentals have grown each year and are expected to continue at a high rate of growth; and cable television providers seem to be taking advantage of technological developments to achieve impressive gains, despite the government's continued attempts to re-regulate the entire industry.

Technological advances continue to affect the future of the entertainment industry. Multimedia interactive entertainment—the use of digital technology to integrate audio, video, computers, and telecommunications media—has begun to attract investment from major movie companies and from firms in related industries. Some of the large studios are launching game versions of their movies, as well as an interactive video network for games.

The US entertainment industry is witnessing a mini-merger-mania as companies from different sectors form various partnerships in order to increase their ability to offer many forms of entertainment, including multimedia products.

The US motion picture industry is the largest in the world; US films (as well as videos and television tapes) are shown in over 100 foreign countries. A spurt in theater attendance has lifted box office receipts to record levels, and theater attendance is up again after dropping off precipitously upon the advent of video and cable television entertainment alternatives. Exhibitors operate well over 25,000 theater screens in the US; with the five largest exhibition companies owning about one-third of the screens. In addition to box office receipts, theater exhibitors earn revenues from concession sales, mostly food. While the exhibitor keeps 40 to 60 percent of ticket revenues—the rest going to the distributor—exhibitors retain all concession sales income, and this is an important contributor to total revenues; concessions generally account for 15 to 20 percent of an exhibitor's total revenues.

The past decade has witnessed a rise in the power of independent film makers and distributors; major studios saw their share of box office receipts decline from 95 percent in 1982 to about 70 percent today. Independent producers and distributors, unencumbered by large bureaucratic structures, seem to be in a particularly good position to take advantage of the rise in new entertainment media made possible by technological advances. Cable television and videocassette rentals and sales offer lower cost alternatives to providing consumers with viewing entertainment, and several independent film production companies produce for these markets exclusively.

The large studios have, however, begun to pick up on this action. The rights to videocassette versions of films are becoming a significant source of revenue for the studios. Although the studios get no share of the revenues from video rentals, consumers have proved exceptionally willing to purchase videos for their own libraries, and this has prompted major studios to set up their own subsidiaries to market video versions of their films. Studios are beginning to realize there is often a lucrative market in video sales and rentals for movies that flopped at the box office, and this has created a growing market for lower budget films made specifically for the direct-to-video market. This in turn has made it more difficult for the smaller independents to compete.

New film distributors receive only about one-half of their revenues from theatrical rentals (both domestic and foreign). Another 30 percent to 35 percent comes from home video, and 10 percent to 15 percent from television.

The studios have been making a major move to gain control of the various outlets for their products. Although possibly prohibited to some extent by antitrust laws, several major studios have taken advantage of the federal government's lack of interest in the matter to invest in theater companies. A couple of studios have purchased television stations, and many of them are becoming directly involved in cable program production.

Although US film companies retain their lock on the industry, while they have been busy repositioning and restructuring themselves, foreign film companies have been arriving in Hollywood in droves. Japanese companies aggressively bought large stakes in several studios during the 1980s, although they have of late seemed to shy off these investments.

Cable television programming and other forms of pay-TV have advanced rapidly over the past several years. The

US is almost fully wired for cable television—nearly 100 million homes have access to cable TV, and about 63 percent of these subscribe. The industry has, however, been in a near constant state of upheaval. The Federal Communications Commission (FCC) dithered over regulation—first failing to regulate at all, then over-regulating, then deregulating to the point of anarchy, and now beginning to re-regulate in a hopefully coherent manner. Indeed, it is difficult to control such a diverse and widely sought-after industry.

Cable television transmits via microwave or satellite, and companies sell their services through subscription. Satellite dishes are becoming increasingly common as their prices have fallen and consumers become more adept at picking up their desired programming free from the constraints of the providers. Although satellite dish owners are theoretically supposed to pay for the signals they receive, "signal piracy" is rampant due to the inability of providers to effectively police the air waves. The satellite television industry has used both criminal prosecutions and new technologies to try to foil the pirates, but only about one-third of the over four million dish owners are legitimate subscribers. There are numerous black market devices that unscramble signals and thus enable their users to avoid subscription fees.

Cable television includes any number of programming alternatives, including pay-per-view movies, sporting events, special niche programming, traditional advertiser sponsored broadcasts, and interactive programming. Cable operators are now forming alliances with telecommunications service providers to develop systems for providing wide-ranging TV and information services over fiber-optic phone lines. This might prove to be an especially profitable undertaking. Interactive television services, delivering not only a vast array of cable channels, but also video on demand, computer games, and information services, could prove to be the trunk of a vast electronic superhighway linking a majority of homes and businesses to an array of electronic media.

The videocassette industry has boomed in the past decade. Nearly as many American homes have VCRs as have televisions. Producers and studios are developing movies specifically for release to the direct-to-video industry, as both video rentals and sales continue to show large year on year increases.

Sales of special interest videos continue to be strong. Special interest video includes more than a dozen categories, such as children's (non-theatrical), music and dance, exercise (an especially profitable niche), corporate promotion, crafts and hobbies, health and medicine, instructional, and travel videos.

One significant pitfall in the videocassette business, however, has been piracy. Hollywood had long been plagued by the sale of unauthorized prints of feature films, but the problem was never a major one until the advent of videocassettes made illicit duplication much easier. Pirates can simply transfer film prints onto videocassettes, which are easily reproduced. Although Hollywood has desperately sought technical solutions to combat the problem, technology has proved inferior to pirates' ingenuity. Studios have taken great steps in obtaining greater control over distribution of their products, but there are still counterfeit copies of hundreds of films being produced in massive quantities around the world.

Sales of prerecorded music, encompassing all formats and including the new music videos, exceed one billion units annually, rising more than 10 percent a year over the past several years. Compact disc sales is the largest segment (constituting 63 percent of the dollar volume of prerecorded music and 49 percent of unit sales). As sales of CDs have grown, sales of music cassettes have slowed, both in dollars and in units. Buyers under 30 years old are the largest part of the customer base for prerecorded music, as they have been over the past couple of decades (purchasing approximately 55 percent of prerecorded music).

CD players are now in nearly half of all US households. This penetration, although well above the 30 percent usually considered the criterion for a mass market, is well below the 85 percent penetration of videocassette players and 98 percent penetration of television receivers.

Recorded music producers receive revenue both from direct sales of new recordings and from royalties paid for public performances of composers' music and writers' lyrics. In the US collection societies monitor the use of copyrighted music, collect royalties from users of music and lyrics by their members and, after paying expenses, distribute the royalties to members. Receipts of the largest of these (American Society of Composers, Authors, and Publishers (ASCAP)), have climbed to over $400 million each year. All but a tiny portion of this amount is license fees. Remittances to ASCAP from foreign licensing societies is generally about 25 percent of total receipts.

International Market Overview

In all segments of the entertainment industry, US producers and distributors are dominant players throughout the world. US products and services are considered superior to those of any other country, although some countries, such as Australia, New Zealand, France and China, have developed niche reputations as superior producers of specialty products.

US films continue to dominate the international motion picture industry, although growth in exporting has slowed significantly in recent years. Exports by independent film companies grew at a slightly faster rate than exports by the majors, but the rate of growth has diminished all the same. Revenues from international sales include box office, television viewings, videocassettes, and pay TV.

Foreign film rentals for theatrical exhibition total about $1.5 billion each year, and foreign affiliates play a crucial role in distributing US products abroad. Japan is the leading export market for films by the major studios, although growth rates have fallen considerably since 1990 (due in part to the exchange rate fluctuations). In the market for independent films, sales in Europe account for 59 percent of total foreign sales, the Far East for 21 percent. Germany and Austria, taken together, is the leading foreign market for independent film companies, generating nearly $200 million yearly in revenues.

US companies dominate international investment in cable

TV systems and sales of programming. But foreign competition is starting to emerge, in programming at least. Cable continues to develop worldwide, but the speed varies by country, as does the level of penetration. Outside of North America, Western Europe is the most mature cable market. Many small countries have higher penetration rates than large countries—Belgium, the Netherlands, and Switzerland are estimated at more than 80 percent penetration, whereas France and the UK are still only about 10 percent penetrated by cable TV.

Asia and Latin America offer potentially lucrative markets for investors, but growth has been slow due to underdeveloped infrastructures (which in many places are only now beginning to show rapid growth). Argentinean cable TV has the largest penetration in the region, with over seven percent. Brazil has only about 100,000 cable subscribers, and it seems primed for tremendous growth over the next several years.

In Japan, where only about 20 percent of households have cable TV, high fees for installation, competition from broadcasting, and negative lending practices have inhibited further growth in this segment. Although US companies have been successful in placing network programs on Japanese cable systems, the total market remains fairly small overall.

Several foreign countries match the US in VCR penetration of TV households. The leader is Japan with 82 percent penetration; Australia, Hong Kong and the UK have about 72 percent each, and 18 other countries have penetration rates higher than 50 percent. No developing country has reached the 50 percent penetration level yet, although Uruguay, with 39 percent and rising, is coming close. Uruguay has the highest penetration in Latin America, followed by Mexico with 34 percent; Argentina and Brazil both represent growing videocassette markets with still low levels of penetration.

Foreign video revenues are rising rapidly in many places. In Japan and the UK, where US films are especially popular, growth rates routinely average over 10 percent a year.

Piracy, however, remains a serious problem undermining the industry in many parts of the world. Pirated videocassettes make up a large part of some Latin American markets, and piracy is also a serious problem in East Asia, the Middle East, and Eastern Europe.

US music is popular worldwide, even in countries where English is not the native language, and US companies and musicians derive large revenues from foreign sales. Although trade statistics are impressive, they do not fully reflect the magnitude of foreign sales of US recorded music. A large percentage of music sold abroad is manufactured abroad by subsidiaries of US companies or under license agreements, and many imports to the US come from US companies' foreign manufacturing operations.

Worldwide sales of US recorded music are growing by about seven percent each year. US music accounts for about half of worldwide record sales of recorded music. Sales of CDs represent the largest category in nearly every country. CDs account for about 69 percent of unit sales of recorded music in Japan and almost 53 percent in France. In the US, by contrast, CD sales account for only about 49 percent of total unit sales. In developing countries the move to CDs has been slower than for other media, probably because CDs cost more than other media. In Brazil, for example, more the 29 million LPs are sold each year, compared with only 7.5 million CDs. In Mexico, cassette sales of 51.8 million far outstrip CD sales of under 10 million.

Before Entering a Market

Entering the electronic entertainment market is generally a fairly large undertaking. The industry is dominated by giants—even the independents have tremendous resources at their disposal. In addition, each market is distinct, and regional or national factors will have to be considered anywhere you go.

In addition to the common considerations of expanding internationally, the entertainment industry requires some unique and individualized research.

Copyright Issues

Review the procedures regarding utilizing copyrighted material and be certain about each country's rules and regulations. Determine how these laws will affect your operations, and what types of protection are available. How are fees collected and paid? Will you be competing with "pirates" who are not subject to licensing and use fees?

Revenue Sources

Primary revenues can come from sales of the material itself, licensing fees, royalties, or simply from advertising revenues. The source of revenue will have a tremendous impact on your operations and on the way you structure your business.

Penetration Levels

The entertainment industry is generally characterized by tremendously high growth rates in the beginning, with a tapering off as the market becomes more fully penetrated. Since establishing any type of entertainment enterprise usually depends on taking advantage of economies of scale, it is obviously far more profitable to enter the market early on, while penetration levels are still growing rapidly.

Language

Although recorded music is not terribly affected by language differences this is not so for the motion picture, cable TV or videocassette markets, which generally require language specific products—or at least subtitles or local language dubbing.

Market Barriers

Local government barriers can range from outright bans on imports of a product or service, to stringent regulation of content, distribution or standards. Typical barriers in the entertainment industry are quotas that limit television broadcast time, screen time in theaters, and imports of foreign films. Other barriers include taxes on box office receipts, with the proceeds often used for financing local productions; restrictions on remittances of funds abroad; and inadequate copyright protection. Many countries impose requirements that a certain percentage of local products or labor be included in foreign film or else heavy taxes or duties are imposed.

A major concern to the US motion picture industry is the television broadcast quota imposed by the European Union (EU), which requires that television programming in each member country contain at least 50 percent material of European origin "where practical," except for sports, news, advertising, game shows, and teletext. Negotiations between the US and the EU continue in an effort to liberalize application of this regulation.

Serious copyright violations threaten to undermine the US entertainment industry in many countries, particularly East Asia, the Middle East and Eastern Europe. Brazil, India, and Thailand are especially noteworthy violators of US intellectual property laws.

Regional Opportunities

Note: These are only examples of regional opportunities and in no way constitute a complete list.

The Netherlands

The market for home entertainment video films in the Netherlands—both for rentals and sales—has grown at close to 20 percent each year over the past few years. Local industry experts predict that the value of rentals of video films will grow by an annual average of 15 percent through 1999, while the value of purchases will increase by an annual average of 75 percent. Interestingly, the market share of the more expensive top titles has risen from 25 percent a few years ago to over 35 percent in 1995.

In the rental sector the most popular film genre is action/adventure (with a market share of 31.4 percent), followed by comedy (with a market share of 20.7 percent). In the video sales market, the most popular titles are children's films (94.5 percent market share) and cinema titles (21.6 percent market share). In the video film rental market, the major consumers are 20 to 29 year olds, followed by the 30 to 39 age group. In the video film sales market, however, those between 30 and 39 years old are the largest consumers.

With a market share of 75 percent, the US is the major supplier of home entertainment video films in the Netherlands. Since local production is negligible, the remaining 25 percent of the market is supplied by companies from European countries such as England, France and Germany, as well as companies from the Far East. The Dutch have a strong preference for American production in the video film sector, as they do for American television and cinema. The Dutch market is open and there are few regulations affecting the sales or rental of home entertainment video films.

A major factor playing a role in the Dutch home entertainment video film market, however, is unfair competition from video pirates and bootleggers. The Dutch government is taking action against piraters, and a special foundation has been set up as the industry's watchdog.

Japan

The Japanese government has begun to actively promote cable TV, and has taken steps to encourage US providers to develop a comprehensive cable TV system in the country. The total market is estimated to be worth over $1 trillion dollars by the year 2010—and only a fraction of the country is currently wired for cable.

The government has recently instituted significant deregulatory measures in this arena, which allow foreign cable TV operators to enter into communications services agreements and to form multiple system operations in Japan. The measures also raise the limits of foreign equity ownership in cable TV companies from 20 percent to 33 percent, paving the way for US firms to take advantage of larger ownership in joint ventures.

Japan also offers a potentially lucrative market for virtual reality in the entertainment industry. New technology has recently emerged which opens many interesting avenues in all forms of entertainment. Virtual reality theaters, and virtual reality game centers have already opened in Japan in the past few years. Several Japanese companies are actively seeking affiliations with US companies—they are looking for help with technology, programming, and distribution.

Turkey

During the past several years, the Turkish television and radio broadcasting industry has experienced explosive growth of local television and radio stations, many of them as yet unregulated. It has also experienced an increase in the types of broadcasting and programming offered.

The increase in the number of new television channels in urban areas is a reflection of the generally growing prosperity in Turkey. The stations are aggressive, western-oriented, and dominated by dubbed or subtitled US programs—as well as by many US-style quiz and talk shows. Original programming is limited. This is particularly so in news and current affairs, though on-site feature news stories are becoming more prevalent. Education programs and documentaries are still few, but children's programming is growing. Family films, action films, and comedies from the US enjoy a wide viewership, although many are pirated versions.

Local private television stations are established in almost every province. Broadcasting of major private television companies which transmit countrywide are under control to a certain extent, but local companies and stations are not at all regulated because of a lack of enforcement of the Turkish Broadcast Law. Approximately 200 local private TV stations and some 50 municipal TV stations broadcast films, most of them from the United States.

Mexico

The overall prospects for US services in Mexico are fair and getting better, but far from excellent. Amplifiers for TV signal transmitters, sound processing equipment, and signal compressing equipment seem to be the most promising markets for US providers.

The Mexican market and imports in this sector are both expected to increase by about ten percent each year over the next few years. New concessions for radio, television, and cable TV will sustain demand growth, and planned upgrades of television stations will further boost sales of programming, technology, and production equipment.

The government promotes expansion of coverage for television and also promotes use of education through satellite to provide elementary education in remote areas.

NAFTA eliminated import duties on US exports to Mexico of most entertainment-related products. This should give US producers a distinct advantage over third-country exporters in the long run.

Canada

The Broadcasting Act sets out Canada's broadcasting policy, and lists among its objectives, "to safeguard, enrich and strengthen the cultural, political, social and economic fabric of Canada." The federal broadcasting regulator, the Canadian Radio-Television and Telecommunications Commission (CRTC), is charged with implementing this policy. Under current CRTC policy, in cases where a Canadian service is licensed in a format competitive with that of an authorized non-Canadian service, the CRTC can drop the non-Canadian service, if the new Canadian service requests it to do so. This policy has already led to one "de-listing" and deterred potential new entrants from attempting to enter the Canadian market.

The CRTC has, however, recently announced that the regulation of foreign specialty broadcast services, including its de-listing policy, will be reviewed as part of a broader review underway of the convergence of the broadcasting and telecommunications industries.

Best Bet Opportunities

Note: These are only examples of industry opportunities and in no way constitute a complete list.

Virtual Reality

Virtual, or artificial, reality is one of the prime technologies for the future of multimedia. There is no clear definition of these new technologies yet, but there are a variety of applications which have already begun to show promise. Specially designed headsets, glasses, gloves, body suits, and/or other devices that input data for computer-designed imagery which create psychological and physical effects that cause a person to experience sensations which are not real are already the subject of much hype and some demand. Virtual reality theaters and virtual rooms for theme parks and large scale amusement facilities, as well as virtual reality games and home video games, are all viable technologies which are being sold to the entertainment industry.

Technical solutions to piracy

Piracy of videocassette movies has created major problems for US firms in many parts of the world. So far, no adequate technology has been developed to effectively combat the problem, but the movie industry is hopeful, and willing to spend large sums to develop an effective technology.

CableTV/Telecommunications Ventures

Alliances between the cable TV and telecommunications industries seem to be inevitable in the future as deregulation and new technologies increasingly blur the lines between these two industries. Accessing computer databases through cable TV and dialing up movies by phone have shown promise in market research tests and the industry is looking for ways to best utilize joint efforts between these two industries.

Movies

Film will continue to be a profitable sector of the entertainment industry—feature movies, made-for-video movies, and cable TV showings will all continue to show strong sales throughout the world. The best sales prospects in most every market continue to be:

* action/adventure films
* comedies
* films for children
* any feature length American-made movie for theater showings

Sources of US Based Assistance

Alliance of Motion Picture and Television Producers
14144 Ventura Blvd.
Sherman Oaks, CA 94123
Tel: (818) 995-3600

Directors Guild of America
7920 Sunset Blvd.
Hollywood, CA 90046
Tel: (213) 289-2000

International Alliance of Theatrical Stage Employees
1515 Broadway
New York, NY 10036
Tel: (212) 840-6161

Motion Picture Association of America
1133 Sixth Avenue
New York, NY 10036
Tel: (212) 840-6161

Writers Guild of America
8955 Beverly Blvd.
West Hollywood, CA 90048
Tel: (213) 550-1000

Association of Independent Television Stations
1200 18th Street NW
Washington, DC 20036
Tel: (202) 887-1970

National Cable Television Association
1724 Massachusetts Ave. NW
Washington, DC 20036
Tel: (202) 775-3550

Publications

Census of Service Industries
US Dept. of Commerce
Bureau of the Census
Washington, DC 20233
Tel: (301) 763-7039

Boxoffice
RLD Communications Inc.
1800 North Highland Ave.
Hollywood, CA 90028
Tel: (213) 465-1186

Encyclopedia of Exhibition
National Association of Theater Owners
4605 Lankershim Blvd., Ste. 340
North Hollywood, CA 91602
Tel: (818) 506-1778

Broadcasting & Cable Marketplace
Providence, N.J.: R.R. Bowker
A wide ranging compilation of data and listings

Television and Cable Factbook
Washington, DC: Warren Publishing
Annual directory of television and cable operators and programmers

International Motion Picture Almanac
New York: Quigley Publishing
Annual compilation of various data on the industry

Variety
154 West 46th Street
New York, NY 10036
Tel: (212) 779-1100

Internet Sites

American Film Marketing Association
http://www.afma.com/

Entertainment Through Technology Association
http://www.ibmpcug.co.uk/~ettc/

International Television Association
http://www.itva.org/

Environmental Technologies

Defined

The environmental equipment and services industry hopes to ease some of the environmental suffering that has gripped the world. In addition, environmental services also work to prevent environmental problems before they arise. This relatively young industry has evolved in response to the enactment and enforcement of pollution control legislation in the US, and growing concerns around the world about the risks and costs of pollution. Some examples of environmental services include:

- air pollution control equipment
- water and waste water systems
- solid waste recycling
- hazardous and toxic waste technologies
- the emerging pollution prevention industry

Domestic Market Overview

Because the environmental industry includes many diverse products, services, and technologies, it is extremely difficult to estimate market size or trade in environmental goods and services. The Organization for Economic Cooperation and Development (OECD) published a study in April 1992 estimating the global market for environmental technologies. This report, the only comprehensive study available, projected the global market in this sector would reach US$300 billion by the year 2000, possibly exceeding the size and importance of the aerospace industry in international trade.

The United States is the world's largest producer and consumer of environmental goods and services, accounting for about 40 percent—or US$80 billion—of the world market, according to the OECD. There are an estimated 7,000 to 10,000 US companies—consulting, engineering, designing, and manufacturing—involved in environmental markets, according to the US Department of Commerce.

Domestically, the environmental services industry is expected to continue to grow in response to the public's demand for a cleaner environment. The Clean Air Act Amendments of 1990 will continue to play a key role in business opportunities as major US industries invest in air pollution reduction and monitoring equipment required by the law. The shrinking number of municipal landfills will spur new technologies in waste treatment, recycling, and disposal.

The Clean Water Act, the Resource Conservation and Recovery Act, and the Comprehensive Environmental Response Compensation and Liability Act of 1980 (known as Superfund) and its subsequent amendments caused thousands of small and large companies to compete for work from increasingly sophisticated buyers of environmental products and services.

Government agencies aren't the only groups discovering the benefits of environmental services. Private industries are realizing that cleaner manufacturing processes not only mitigate waste but heighten cost savings and competitiveness, leading to adoption of more environmentally sound technologies on a voluntary basis. US industries, on their own initiative, have developed proactive responses to environmental concerns, examining their products and processes with the intent of creating new ones, or modifying existing ones to make them more environmentally acceptable.

DOE officials want to refocus the department's laboratories on transferring government-sponsored technology research to private business. Defense firms are also devoting resources to technology transfer, recognizing the potential for federal cleanup markets to offset losses from reduced government spending on military contracts.

The trend in US sanitary landfill practices is towards fewer but bigger solid waste sites. Landfill sites today require sophisticated design and construction procedures, quality assurance/control oversight and documentation, and rigid monitoring and reporting of site operations. Landfills in all states are now required to have liner systems. Similarly, final cover or cap designs involving multiple layers to minimize infiltration of surface water into the refuse mass, to promote bilateral movement of water over the retardation layer, and to support vegetation, are now required nationally. Monitoring of ground water and gas surrounding landfills is mandated nationwide.

Historically, domestic environmental laws and regulations have been primarily directed toward control or remediation of an environmental problem. Because of their mandatory requirements, such statutory language and regulatory instruments have driven the need to provide products, equipment, and services that address environmental concerns. In recent years, however, there has been a new emphasis on preventing pollution, rather than just controlling it.

While the environmental equipment and services sector will continue to grow, it probably will not experience the double digit growth rate of the last decade. The Clean Air Act Amendments of 1990, requiring industrial polluters to invest in air pollution monitoring and control equipment, will continue to drive the domestic market. In addition, the shrinking number of municipal landfills will most likely spur technology in the waste treatment, recycling, and disposal markets.

International Market Overview

A July 1993 EPA report on international trade in environmental protection equipment and services showed that the United States is a major exporter of environmental services, in general, and air pollution control equipment, in particular. Exports of US pollution abatement equipment and services are projected to increase over previous years. This estimate assumes US firms will be assisting the countries of the former Soviet Union to cleanup environmental degradation and that foreign government's standards are becoming more strict, forcing purchases of pollution control equipment to meet these new requirements.

Standards are needed to detail accepted methods for a range of environmental activities such as performance, audits, and assessments. The International Organization for Standardization (ISO) is working on uniform voluntary guidelines for the international marketplace.

The international environmental equipment market will continue to grow as more stringent anti-pollution regulations are enacted around the world and resources are committed to enforce them. Maturing markets overseas now offer US firms an unprecedented opportunity to meet the new and burgeoning needs of the international client. In addition, most multilateral lending and development institutions have made environmental controls a priority in projects subject to funding. For example, of the 222 World Bank projects receiving loans in fiscal year 1990, 48 percent of them included environmental components.

The environmental problems and regulations of other countries can influence or dictate the need and demand for import of environmental goods and services. An OECD report, *Trade Issues in the Transfer of Clean Technologies,* released in 1992, found that the existence and enforcement of environmental standards "help to create a demand for clean technologies." Regulatory activity and environmental problems in Eastern and Central Europe, Asia, and Latin American countries are driving US exports of environmental technologies, products, and services to those regions.

International environmental agreements (IEAs) can also create trade opportunities. For example, there is the expectation that the Interim Multilateral Fund of the Montreal Protocol to the Vienna Convention on Substances that Deplete the Ozone Layer could encourage trade in process technologies that are more environmentally acceptable than those using chloroflorocarbons (CFCs). Industrial development and technology transfer activities in response to the sustainable development mandate of the United Nations Conference on Environment and Development (UNCED) also present the potential for expanded environmental export opportunities.

The environment and trade policies of the future will be molded by two considerations: the interrelationship of trade and the environment and the commitment to environmentally and economically sustainable development. Some issues that countries consider when deciding on an environmental firm include:

Loans

Many water treatment companies make little profit and some even operate at a loss in many countries. Charging for domestic use of water is under discussion, but to date, there has been no plan to begin tapping this potential source of revenue. In many cases, the purchases of foreign equipment and services are primarily financed by foreign loans.

Price

The price factor is very important in the entry of foreign markets. High prices from US firms often push potential clients to use local products or to choose less expensive products among other foreign competitors.

Quality

Though a major factor, quality is not as important as price in many markets. In China, for example, quality is often not the only competitive edge to win an order, although that may not necessarily be true when the purchase is financed by multilateral lending organizations, when borrowers are encouraged to balance quality and price to find effective quality at a reasonable price.

Market Barriers

Government Barriers

The laws in many countries can be confusing for US firms. A confusing array of regulations apply to different industries and types of pollution sources. Some apply only to new plants, others to existing plants. Clean air regulations may differ by region, and may be overridden altogether by more stringent federal requirements. Standards are needed to detail accepted methods for a range of environmental activities such as performance, audits, and assessments. The ISO is working on uniform (voluntary) guidelines for the international marketplace.

Economic Barriers

Competition is a major problem when US firms try to break into international markets. Domestic environmental regulations may actually hurt US firms' chances, often increasing operating costs for US producers, putting them at a competitive disadvantage when compared to foreign firms that are subject to less stringent requirements. US firms are well respected for the quality of their work, but in many cases that factor is not as persuasive as price.

Social and Cultural Barriers

Environmentalism is a new idea in many countries, where factories have been producing goods for years with no thought to the effect they may have on the landscape. US firms may face some resistance to their ideas and technologies.

Regional Opportunities

Note: These are only examples of regional opportunities and in no way constitute a complete list.

Asia

Taiwan, Hong Kong, and Korea represent the best market opportunities in Asia for some US environmental companies. In Taiwan and Hong Kong, importing pollution control equipment is encouraged and is not subject to significant tariff and nontariff barriers. In both countries, the governments' commitment to environmental protection and restoration is strong. Korea has established a strong regulatory structure with stringent enforcement measures and a significant public investment in environmental remediation. US firms often face stiff competition from Japanese environmental companies who can often provide more attractive financing packages.

Another area in Asia that shows tremendous potential is the Association of Southeast Asian Nations (ASEAN) region. Sales of filtration and purification equipment for water and wastewater treatment alone will grow extremely rapidly—at rates of 30 to 40 percent over the next three years. The market for environmental instrumentation and monitoring equipment is expected to expand at an annual rate of 20 percent over the next several years, in part as a response to Development Bank demands for strong environmental controls on the projects they finance.

Opportunities are available in China, although financing may be a problem. The US has no aid program in China, and is restricted from tendering soft loans. Other countries, notably European companies and Japan, enjoy a competitive advantage over American countries due to their ability to tender soft-loans. USAID is barred by law from operations in China. The US Export-Import bank does have a soft-loan matching program where, with evidence, they will match a soft loan. American products have a high reputation for their quality.

Although import tariffs in China are relatively high, preferential treatment has been given for equipment imports in the water supply sector. Such treatment is not automatic and should be worked out in advance. Nevertheless, importation of equipment can be extremely difficult and time consuming.

Eastern Europe

Perhaps the most dramatic change in demand for environmental accountability is found in the emerging democracies of Eastern Europe. Because of budget restraints, the near-term market opportunities for environmental technologies, equipment, and services are limited. But the prospects for long-term market growth are strong. The US is expected to capture about a 10 to 15 percent share of all environmental technology imports in the region, but competition from Western European countries presents a strong challenge.

Latin America

In Latin America, Mexico represents the largest market for environmental technologies, equipment and services. Competition in this market from Japan, Germany, France, and Switzerland is strong.

Best Bet Opportunities

Note: These are only examples of industry opportunities and in no way constitute a complete list.

Air Quality Control

Air quality control removes pollutants from a gaseous stream or converts pollutants to non- or less-polluting forms before discharge into the atmosphere. Equipment to control particulates include fabric filters, electrostatic precipitators,

and mechanical collectors. Acid emissions may be controlled by scrubbers, catalytic reduction, and electron beam methods. The US leads the world in air quality control equipment and services, and there are a number of opportunities for firms.

Environmental technology expert Robert W. McIlvaine of the McIlvaine Co. of Northbrook, Illinois forecasts that utilities worldwide will spend more than US$800 billion in the next 10 years for fossil-fuel fired power generation equipment and related air pollution control systems. Asia will be the largest purchaser of this equipment, followed by the Americas and Western Europe.

Water Pollution Prevention and Cleanup

As the largest segment of the environmental industry worldwide, water pollution abatement focuses on purification of groundwater/wastewater and reclamation. Filters and clarifiers remove solid particles, biological treatment and chlorination remove bacteria, and reverse osmosis/chemical recovery systems remove chemical or metal compounds. The OECD estimated worldwide sales of water treatment equipment at about US$60 billion in 1990 and projected the market would increase to about US$83 billion by the year 2000.

Waste Management

Waste management encompasses products for collecting and transporting solid waste, landfill policies, treatment and disposal of toxic wastes, and recycling. Not all solid waste ends up in landfills. Waste-to-energy plants can recycle materials into valuable products. Using pyrolysis (controlled burning at high temperatures), waste can be converted into valuable commodities. Hazardous waste presents another set of problems—with potential solutions. The hazardous waste management industry involves a wide variety of services which are purchased by industry and government to address hazardous waste problems. New techniques and technologies for treating and disposing of waste are in the testing stage and could ultimately reshape this critical industry. Some of the high-technology treatment methods involve putting wastes through high-temperature electric arcs, ionizing remediation, and pyrolysis.

Sources of US Based Assistance

US Department of Commerce

The US Department of Commerce, as chair of the Trade Promotion Coordinating Committee, and its environmental trade working group are spearheading interagency efforts to boost the export of environmental goods, services and technologies. This is a cooperative effort among the Departments of Commerce and Energy, the US Agency for International Development, Small Business Administration, Trade Development Agency, Overseas Private Investment Corporation, and the Export-Import Bank. The private sector also is enlisted for its expertise, creativity and financial resources.

Environmental Protection Agency

The EPA helps promote the adoption and sale of US environmental technologies and services abroad. It fosters the creation of environmental protection regimes and provides technical assistance–especially to developing countries–to help solve environmental problems. The EPA also works to harmonize international environmental standards, to ensure that US industry does not suffer a competitive disadvantage. For more information, contact: US Environmental Protection Agency, 401 M Street, SW, A-149-C, Washington, DC 20460; telephone (202) 260-2087; fax (202) 260-4470.

Committee on Renewable Energy, Commerce and Trade, US Department of Energy

Established in 1983, CORECT coordinates federal programs to assist export efforts of renewable energy and energy efficiency industries. CORECT assistance to industry deals primarily with issues related to technical competitiveness, market development, and federal financing. For more information, telephone (202) 586-8302; fax (202) 586-1605.

United States-Asia Environmental Partnership (US-AEP)

The US-AEP program is a coalition of public, private and non-governmental organizations which promote environmental protection and sustainable development in 34 nations in the Asia/Pacific region. The partnership also mobilizes US environmental technology, expertise and financial resources, and links businesses, communities and governments across the Pacific in public and private sector partnerships. The Trade Information Center (800-USA-TRADE) has an environmental business specialist on hand to answer US environmental companies' exporting questions and to provide information on various programs and services of the US-AEP; federal export promotion programs for environmental technologies, products and services; international environmental/energy trade shows and events and market research, financing sources and promotional forums. For more information contact the US-AEP, 1720 I Street, Suite 700, Washington, DC 20006; telephone (202) 835-0333; fax (202) 835-0366.

Environmental Technology Network for Asia (ETNA), US-Asia Environmental Partnership

Operated by Saudis Center for Trade and Investment Services, ETNA matches environmental trade leads sent from US-AEP technology representatives, located in nine Asian countries with appropriate US environmental firms and trade associations that are registered with ETNA's environmental trade opportunity database. US environmental firms receive trade leads via a broadcast fax system within 48 hours of leads being identified and entered electronically from Asia. For more information: telephone (202) 663-2674; fax (202) 663-2760.

Coal and Technology Export Program, US Department of Energy

This program promotes the export of US clean coal equipment and services by acting as an information source on coal and coal technologies. For more information telephone (301) 903-2657; fax (301) 903-2406.

National Association of Environmental Professionals
5165 MacArthur Blvd. N.W.
Washington, DC 20016
Tel: (202) 966-1500
Fax: (212) 966-1977

American Academy of Environmental Engineers (AAEE)
130 Holiday Courts, Suite 100
Annapolis, MD 21401
Tel: (410) 266-3311
Fax: (410) 266-7653

National Association of Energy Service Companies
1440 New York Avenue
Washington, DC 20005
Tel: (202) 371-7812
Fax: (202) 393-5760

Publications

Environmental Pollution
Elsevier Science
650 White Plains Rd.
Tarrytown, NY 10591-5153
Tel: (914) 524-9200
Fax: (914) 333-2444
An international journal concerned with the biological, chemical, and physical aspects of environmental pollution and pollution control. Publishes research and review articles on the distribution and ecological effects of environment pollutants and on new techniques for their study and measurement.

International Environmental Technology
160 Charlemont St.
Newton, MA 02161-9887
Tel: (617) 527-9874
Fax: (617) 965-5812
Introduces new equipment and services for pollution monitoring and control; also covers water analysis and testing, safety, and waste.

Water, Air, and Soil Pollution
Box 358, Accord Station
Hingham, MA 02018-0358
Tel: (617) 871-6600
Fax: (617) 871-6528
Publishes interdisciplinary work on all the physical and biological processes affecting flora, air, water, and solid earth in relation to environmental pollution.

Water Environment Research
Water Environment Federation
601 Wythe St.
Alexandria VA 22314-1994
Tel: (703) 684-2400
Fax: (703) 684-2492
Discusses pollution control and effects of water pollution, as well as general water-quality issues.

Water Pollution Control
The Bureau of National Affairs, Inc.
1231 25th St. N.W.
Washington DC 20037
Tel: (202) 452-4200
Fax: (202) 822-8092
Telex: 285656 BNAI WSH
Reference and advisory service on the control of water pollu-tion. Designed to meet the information needs of individuals responsible for complying with agency, federal and state water pollution control regulations.

Internet Sites

The National Association of Environmental Professionals
http://www.enfo.com/NAEP/

Export Intermediaries

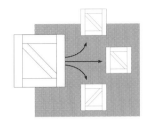

Defined

Export Management Companies (EMCs) and Export Trading Companies (ETCs) are indirect sellers and international marketers of products and services for various types of clients. They offer a multitude of services, such as performing market research, appointing overseas distributors or commission representatives, exhibiting a client's products at international trade shows, advertising, shipping and arranging documentation.

There are more than 2,000 EMCs and ETCs in the United States. Their client rosters typically consist of non-competing firms. Companies and individual business people primarily seek out export intermediaries to do the legwork necessary to successfully penetrate a foreign market(s) and gain an edge over competitors. Export intermediaries will rarely take on accounts that could create a conflict of interest for their marketing teams.

The best export intermediaries operate with an aggressive, entrepreneurial style and strive to become experts in niche markets. For example, an export intermediary may decide to represent a US meat processor looking to market its prepared food products to Japan. The same export intermediary might also be simultaneously assisting a US timber company to sell its products in Japan and Hong Kong. The products being marketed and their ultimate consumers are completely different from one another, but the geographic area serves as the common denominator for the export intermediary.

EMCs are driven by supply. They solicit and transact business in the names of the clients they represent, usually on an exclusive basis. EMC staff members are compensated for their work through a commission, salary, or retainer coupled with a commission. EMCs work to maintain close contact with manufacturers, but generally keep loose ties with overseas distributors. Relaxed relationships with foreign distributors allow EMCs to negotiate unbiasedly for the best prices on exporting arrangements.

Washington, DC-based International Trade and Marketing Corp. (ITM) is an example of an EMC. ITM maintains exclusive agreements with ten US suppliers of orthopedic equipment and supplies. The EMC promotes its clients' products worldwide, but focuses primarily on markets in developed countries. ITM takes title to 90% of the goods it handles. It makes a profit by marking these products up for resale.

ETCs are demand-driven and transaction-oriented. These export intermediaries can exist in many forms. An ETC can be a trade intermediary, devoted to providing export services to producers. An ETC can also be an organization created by the producers themselves. ETCs offer services very similar to their EMC counterparts. However, EMCs do not usually take title to goods they are responsible for exporting. These organizations tend to focus on providing export facilitation services only. This gives EMCs the reputation of being somewhat less profit-oriented and more client-friendly than their ETC counterparts.

One major advantage for manufacturers working with a large, established ETC is that intermediary's ability to purchase goods for export on site. This usually eliminates the need for clients to secure financing for exporting. Many larger ETCs are also willing to provide short-term financing to their clients. More importantly, ETCs' links with foreign contacts make it easier for their exporter clients to obtain credit and credit insurance to operate abroad. ETCs are also in a better position than ETCs to work countertrade (barter) deals with foreign countries because they act like trade organizations.

Domestic Market Overview

The majority of US-based export intermediaries are smaller than their European and Japanese counterparts, which typically have very large staffs. A recent survey by the US Department of Commerce revealed that the staffs of US trading companies averaged two to 50 people. More than 60 percent of respondents to the survey stated that they employ six or fewer persons. Approximately 15% of the trading companies polled by the US Department of Commerce employed 21 or more persons.

Since they are limited by their staff size, US-based EMCs and ETCs usually specialize their field of expertise by type of product, foreign market, or a combination of both. As a result, the top EMCs and ETCs have well-established networks of foreign distributors and commission agents. Commission agents locate foreign firms that want to purchase US products. They bargain for the lowest price on these products or services and are paid a commission by their foreign clients. Foreign government agencies often act as commission agents.

The biggest obstacle export intermediaries face to attracting new clients is their controlling nature. Manufacturers often lose control of the foreign sales of their products once they strike a deal with an EMC or ETC. Export intermediaries have a reputation for taking the ball from a client and running with it. Most clients using the services of export intermediaries for the first time become frustrated by the lack of information coming to them on a regular basis. Companies more experienced with these arrangements will be up front about how much control and communication they want in an exporting deal. Not all EMCs and ETCs will be flexible on these matters because they consider themselves experts and prefer their clients to take a laissez-faire stance. But most intermediaries are willing to negotiate with clients to secure the account.

International Market Overview

Annual revenues have been on the rise during this decade for the majority of US export intermediaries. Recent and rapid advancements in technology and communications have caused international trade to skyrocket. Export intermediaries which keep on top of these trends are proving to be of great value to their clients. They usually are able to enter into and maneuver around foreign markets more easily than a company attempting to do its own direct international marketing. More importantly, they are able to maintain their presence in various foreign markets because their staffs are completely devoted to the effort.

More companies than ever before are hiring export intermediaries to handle their global marketing. The arrangements save many US manufacturers a great deal of money that would otherwise be spent trying to establish a productive relationship with a foreign representative. Time saved is also an attractive bonus. Export intermediaries can make available marketing resources that could take years for an inexperienced client to develop. As a result, the export intermediary industry is becoming increasingly profitable for its members.

Approximately one-third of the export intermediaries surveyed by the US Department of Commerce reported annual earnings between $1 million and $5 million. More than 10 percent of export intermediaries surveyed reported annual revenues between $10 million and $50 million. A handful of well established firms bring in revenues annually of as much as $500M. In contrast, the remaining percentage of export intermediaries average less than $1M in revenues per year.

According to the US Department of Commerce, approximately 25 percent of US export intermediaries maintain at least one overseas office. This easy access to foreign markets is the primary reason US companies choose to pursue indirect product marketing through an export trading company. It allows companies to enter the international marketplace without getting caught up in the red tape and risks of exporting.

Export intermediaries are increasingly willing to take big risks to secure the best deals. More firms are comfortable demanding to take title to goods, sharing in a greater portion of total profit. They are also working with banks, credit risk insurance firms and various government agencies in order to provide the capability required to carry foreign receivables. As a result, export intermediaries have become increasingly reliant on federal and state government export finance programs. This financial support has been essential to the growth and success of the export intermediary industry.

Market Opportunities

It is impossible to list the number of international business opportunities available to export intermediaries. The industry is relatively easy to enter because it is entrepreneurial in nature. Becoming established, however, is more difficult. Those looking to enter the field should focus on what existing skills and international links they have before jumping into the arena. It must be stressed again that success in

the export intermediary industry is tied directly to the ability to operate in a niche market(s). Novice export intermediaries may want to consider joining forces with other companies or individuals to pool resources, instead of trying to go it alone.

Market research is also essential. The Office of Export Trading Company Affairs (OETCA) has established the Contact Facilitation Service (CFS) as an information databank for manufacturers of US goods and services, as well as for organizations that provide trade facilitation services. The CFS directory is updated and published annually. It provides users with the names and addresses of banks, export trading companies, manufacturing firms and services organizations. More importantly, it lists the export products and related services that these companies supply. The CFS directory is a solid research source for anyone looking to enter the export intermediary industry.

It should be noted that countertrade is a rapidly growing niche for export intermediaries. This barter-type system requires an exporter to accept goods in exchange for products as a condition of the sale. EMCs and ETCs are actively working to establish a worldwide network through which countertrade goods can be converted to hard currency.

Market Channels

The Export Trading Act of 1982 virtually guarantees EMCs and ETCs access to foreign markets. It is—in a way—an export intermediary's license to operate. Also known as Title III, the Export Trading Act was created to stimulate US exports by the following methods:

- promotion and encouragement of the formation of export trading companies;

- expansion of the options available for export financing by permitting bank holding companies to invest in export trading companies and reducing restrictions on trade finance provided by financial institutions; and

- reduction of uncertainty regarding the application of US antitrust law to export applications.

Title III gives special priority to export-oriented companies. Its enactment resulted in the adoption of regulatory changes in the antitrust and banking spheres to encourage greater use of export intermediaries. It allows banks to make equity investments in commercial ventures that qualify as export trading companies. In addition, it permits the Exim Bank to make working capital guarantees to US exporters.

Market Barriers

The only significant market barrier for export intermediaries exists in the same measure that gives them international access. The Export Trading Company Act specifically excludes US trading firms from antitrust prosecution. However, this exemption is subject to two very definite qualifications: 1) collaboration in export markets will not affect competition within the US, and 2) in business practices abroad, American firms must follow the same standard of behavior that is required in the United States.

The US Department of Commerce, through OETCA, promotes the formation of export trading companies, administers the antitrust certification process, and issues certificates of review. Certificates of review are granted by the Secretary of Commerce with approval from the Department of Justice. Any US corporation, partnership, resident individual, and state or local entity may apply for a certificate of review.

The Certificate of Review program provides exporters with anti-trust "insurance." It promotes joint venture activities where economies of scale and risk diversification can be achieved. Certificates of Review will be issued to applicant only if it is determined that the proposed export trade activities and methods of operation will not result in a substantial lessening of domestic competition or restraint of trade in the United States.

Sources of US Based Assistance

American Association of Exporters and Importers
11 West 42nd Street
30th Floor
New York, NY 10036
Tel: (212) 944-2230
Fax: (212) 382-2606

American Association of Port Authorities
1010 Duke Street
Alexandria, VA 22314
Tel: (703) 684-5700
Fax: (212) 684-6321

Export Managers Association of California
110 East Ninth Street
Suite A669
Los Angeles, CA 90079
Tel: (213) 892-0087

National Customs Brokers and Forwarders Association
1 World Trade Center
Suite 1153
New York, NY 10048
Tel: (212) 432-0050
Fax: (212) 432-5709

Office of Export Trading Company Affairs (OETCA)
US Department of Commerce
Company Affairs
Fourteenth & Constitution
Room 1800
Washington, DC 20230
Tel: (202) 482-5131
Fax: (202) 482-1790

Small Business Administration (SBA)
Office of International Trade
409 Third St., SW
Suite 8500
Mail Code: 7550
Washington, DC 20416
Tel: (202) 205-6720

Publications

The Export Yellow Pages
The Office of Export Trading produces this publication for both the public and private sector through the US Department of Commerce. The directory contains more than 12,000 active ETCs and EMCs, as well as manufacturers, producers, banks, and service organizations. Companies or individuals can obtain copies of the *Export Yellow Pages* by contacting any local Department of Commerce District Office. The directory is distributed free of charge and is updated annually.

Export Trading Company Guidebook
This guidebook is designed to assist companies and individuals looking to expand their exporting activity through an ETC. This publication was created as a result of the 1982 Export Trading Company Act. The Export Trading Company Guidebook will be particularly helpful to those who are relatively new to exporting. This publication is available through the US Government Printing Office, stock number: 003-009-00523-0.

Internet Resources

American Material Resources, Inc.
http://www.commerce.com/placette
Active export trading company

Assist International
http://www.assist-intl.com
Comprehensive export information

IBEX Yellow Pages
http://www.cba.uh.edu/ylowpges/yi.html
Listing of exporting companies

Small Business Administration (SBA)
http://www.sbaonline.sba.gov
Information on financial sources for small exporters

Franchising

Defined

The word "franchise" can be defined as a right or privilege granted to an individual or group. Acquiring a business franchise means obtaining the right to use a particular trademark or system of operation owned by a company. The corporation selling the franchise is a "franchisor," and an individual, group, or company purchasing a franchise is a "franchisee." Franchisees typically pay a franchise fee and royalties to franchisors for the right to do business.

The most publicized franchises are restaurants, especially fast food operations such as McDonalds, Burger King, Pizza Hut, and Kentucky Fried Chicken. There are, however, many other types of businesses which are increasingly being franchised around the world. A representative sampling includes:

- gas stations
- printing and copy shops
- theme parks
- motion picture theaters
- photo service stores
- real estate agencies
- temporary personnel agencies
- convenience stores
- dry cleaning shops
- hotels
- travel agencies

Franchises are often retail outlets, but dental and optometry clinics, emergency medical organizations, and legal service firms have also been successfully franchised.

Domestic Market Overview

Business franchises have become an economic juggernaut in the US market. They account for more than 40 percent of all US retail sales—more than US$800 billion annually. Between 1970 and 1995, the number of restaurant franchises alone more than tripled, and it is estimated that a new franchise outlet opens somewhere in the US every eight minutes. More than eight million members of the US work force are employed in over 500,000 franchise units. According to the US Department of Commerce, buying a franchise is the average person's most viable avenue to owning a business.

Many consider franchising the closest thing to a win-win situation in today's unpredictable business market. It is safer for the franchisee because they are going into business using a name consumers identify with, standardized designs for buildings and furnishings, financial assistance, and other business aids. It is often successful for the franchisor because they get a percentage of the franchise's revenue, generally three to five percent of the franchise's sales. Franchisors also can expand their name recognition without bearing the full cost of acquiring land and equipment. One disadvantage for franchisees is the lack of freedom to do what they want. In fast food, for example, the franchisor decides what to put on the menu and what to charge.

International Market Overview

The international market contains a great deal of potential for franchisors, with consumers who are not only willing but in many cases eager to buy US products and services. In 1971, there were 156 franchising companies operating 3,565 outlets in foreign countries. Today, there are more than 400 companies with over 40,000 foreign outlets. Some markets are already saturated with franchises, particularly fast food restaurants, so be sure yours has realistic potential before going international.

Although laws and regulations may be similar on paper from region to region within a country, their implementation and practice could be very different. In Latin America, for example, a particular country's customs laws may be enforced differently from port to port.

Cultural differences within a country create market challenges as well. This is obvious when comparing urban and rural areas, but differences can also be seen between different cities, just as Boston is a much different market than Houston or Phoenix.

In many markets, where you sell is almost as important as what you sell. Pick your real estate carefully, and determine costs and finance ahead of time. Also be sure to hire a local lawyer and accountant for their knowledge of the business environment in that country.

As markets continue to open, some side effects have been created—some good, some surprisingly bad. Foreign consumers used to buy products merely because they were imported from the US, regardless of the quality. Now many think before buying, compare prices, and are generally more selective.

Businesses may have to regionalize products so they are accepted by the market. When franchising into Argentina, for example, Donut Inn introduced "Choco Baires" and "Buenos Aires" cookies featuring dulce de leche, an ingredient similar to caramel that is very popular in Argentina. Donut Inn also reduced the size of its donuts by 10 percent to adapt to the size of the common Argentine pastry. The 66 varieties of donuts offered in the US were reduced to 24 in Argentina. These changes were well-received by the public, and Donut Inn became very popular within the country.

Before Entering a Market

Establishing and working an international franchise is not a venture to be taken lightly. As with any business venture in the US, you can expect to invest resources before seeing any profits. Be committed to staying in the market and doing everything necessary to seeing the international franchise succeed. Unfortunately for many businesses, studies and research are not made until after a deal has been reached. This could lead to some disastrous results: discovering that the mark to be licensed is already owned by another party, finding that the local withholding taxes severely cut into the expected return on royalties, and discovering that trade secrets will become the property of the franchisee at the end of the relationship. Some common steps before expanding internationally include:

Review the business structure

Will it work in a foreign market? Assess whether an alternative organizational structure is needed and determine the short- and long-term costs of the transaction to the franchisor.

Intellectual property issues

Review the steps to getting your trademark registered, and establish a plan for obtaining protection in countries where trademark registration is difficult. Determine how local trade secret, copyright, and patent laws could affect your franchise. What protection is there after termination of an international franchise agreement? What protection is there if registration or other protective measures are not undertaken? Always check for prior registration of your trademark by third parties.

Collecting money

Are there any restrictions imposed by the target foreign country on the amount that can be charged for royalties?

Taxes

Determine the existence and impact of any withholding tax, value added tax, income tax, stamp tax, and financial operations tax. Franchisors should also determine what fees are subject to the tax (franchise, royalty, management, consulting, etc.) and who is liable for them.

Hidden costs

Additional costs always seem to come up. Franchisors should consider costs for translators, on-site inspections and obtaining and shipping products, ingredients, equipment, and other miscellaneous costs.

Initial costs

Consider a letter of intent or memorandum of understanding requiring payment by prospective franchisees to cover any up front costs just in case the transaction is not completed.

Just in case

Evaluate the business implications of a failed franchise. Can the franchisor realistically re-market the franchise or carry on with the business?

Market Barriers

Government Barriers

Local government barriers can range from an outright ban of a product or service to intense regulation. Franchises may be forced to use local products. Taxes can also be levied on franchises or on the products that need to be imported for the franchise to operate.

Franchising is a relatively new concept on a global scale, and some countries do not have legislation that specifically covers franchising. Many of the laws concerning franchising agreements are found in the civil and commercial codes and rules applicable to commercial contracts. Local legislation may cover ethical rules, prohibiting the franchisor from omitting any relevant information concerning the parent company to the potential franchisee during the negotiation process. Some countries have strict rules on franchise terms to protect franchisees.

Cultural Barriers

Investigate who the market to your franchise will be. McDonalds is an upper middle class gathering place in some Latin American countries. Some US consumer patterns just don't work elsewhere.

Market Channels

There are a number of ways US franchisors can expand into foreign markets:

Master Franchise Agreements

The most frequently used arrangement is the master franchise agreement, where the franchisor grants a sub-franchisor the right to develop a foreign territory. The sub-franchisor only owns some retail units and franchises others to third parties.

Area Development Agreement

An area development agreement lets the franchisor grant a developer exclusive rights to develop a foreign territory and own all the retail units that sprout up inside of it.

Joint Venture Agreement

In a joint venture arrangement, the franchisor finds a local partner who will share an equity investment in the market.

Wholly-Owned Subsidiary

In a wholly-owned subsidiary, the franchisor agrees to own a subsidiary in a host country.

The process of picking a franchising partner is tricky, but the correct partner can mean the difference between success and failure. The typical arrangement has the franchisee paying a start-up fee and ongoing royalties that provide training, research, development, and support for the system.

Regional Opportunities

Note: These are only examples of regional opportunities and in no way constitute a complete list.

Franchise markets vary widely depending on the type of franchise. Almost 40 countries now have regional offices in their country that promote franchising to US businesses. Although when thinking of exporting, the buzz word these days is the North American Free Trade Agreement, NAFTA did very little to open doors to franchisors because both Canada and Mexico had very little franchise regulation before the agreement.

Mexico

Mexican companies and citizens are very familiar with US products and services, and like the quality offered by franchises. Many sectors are saturated, but professional service franchises are entering the market and becoming very popular here.

Brazil

US franchises have a high level of receptivity in this market. It is the most industrialized and populous country in Latin America with over 150 million people (72 percent of them living in or near urban areas). The estimated population of real consumers is around 30 million.

Indonesia

US franchises have a definite advantage in this market, although many sectors may become saturated in the near future. Six US companies chose to franchise there in 1991, but that number blossomed to 66 by 1995. The growing middle class and a trend toward using foreign brand services and products will help this market grow even further.

Thailand

Although a small market, Thailand is an example of a country primed for US franchises. Except for fast food, franchises are almost non-existent, which means this is an unexploited market. The improving economy has transformed Thailand into one of the more advanced developing countries in Asia. Demographic considerations have made Thailand very attractive to potential franchises, with a growing middle class.

Best Bet Opportunities

Note: These are only examples of industry opportunities and in no way constitute a complete list.

Fast Food

Far and away the most popular franchise sector. Some markets may be saturated with fast food restaurants, so intense research should be made before jumping in.

Printing

Many local companies are now joining together with chains to operate under a more prestigious and recognized brand name.

Maintenance and Repair

Professional service and guarantees are new concepts in many parts of the world, and US companies that can offer them are being well rewarded.

Sources of US Based Assistance

International Franchise Association
1350 New York Avenue, N. W., Suite 900
Washington, DC 20005-4709
Tel: (202) 628-8000
Fax: (202) 628-0812

The International Franchise Association (IFA) enhances and safeguards the business environment for franchising worldwide. It serves as the national agency for franchising in the US and is increasingly becoming a major presence in the international arena.

International Franchise Research Centre
University of Westminister
35 Marylebone Road
London. NW1 5LS
UK
Tel: +44 (0)171 911 5000 x 3025
Fax: +44 (0)171 911 5059
Email: purdy@westminister.ac.uk or 100041.475@compuserve.com

Publications

Franchising World
International Franchise Association
1350 New York Ave. N.W., Ste. 900
Washington DC 20005
Tel: (202) 628-8000
Fax: (202) 628-0812
Telex: 323175

Franchise International
Franchise Development Services Ltd.
Castle House, Castle Meadow
Norwich, Norfolk NR2 1PJ
UK
Tel: 01603-62301
Fax: 01603-630174

Franchise Update
Box 20547
San Jose, CA 95160-0547
Tel: (408) 997-7795

Internet Sites

International Franchise Association
http://www.entremkt.com/ifa/

Health and Medical

Defined

Health and medical services see to the care and well-being of people. Some healthcare professionals include:

- doctors
- dentists
- pharmacists
- hospital Information Managers
- veterinary surgeons
- non-academic medical practitioners
- masseurs and physiotherapists
- nurses and midwives
- assistant nursing staff
- hospital administrators
- assistant dieticians, techno-pharmaceutical assistants
- doctor's assistants and receptionists
- health insurance providers
- medical laboratory assistants
- HMO managers

A major issue with health care is paying for the services. In many countries, particularly developing ones, the payment system is unreliable and, as a result, care services are weak. Managed care consists of prepaid plans such as health maintenance organizations (HMOs), preferred provider organizations (PPOs) and independent practice associations (IPAs).

Domestic Market Overview

The nation's health care services industry includes thousands of independent medical practices and partnerships, as well as public and non profit institutions, and major private corporations. America's complex health care system is a leader in the use of sophisticated and expensive technology.

In regards to costs, the health care market is unique among industries. For most products and services, the purchaser knows the price, quantity, and quality of goods before consumption. In the health care industry, however, price information is not generally available. To further complicate the cost issue, the health care industry is dominated by third party providers in the form of private insurers and publicly funded Medicare and Medicaid systems that insulate patients from assessing price. The consistent rise in health care costs discourage worker liability, particularly among older workers who are concerned about losing insurance coverage. Approxi-

mately half the estimated 37 million uninsured Americans are in the 16- to 34-year age group that is entering the workforce or who are undergoing the most frequent job changes. Increasing health care costs have put pressures on the budgets of federal, state, and local governments. Workers and governments have less to spend on other priorities.

Managed health care, a system of prepaid plans providing comprehensive coverage to voluntarily enrolled members, continues as the growth leader in the health care industry. Providers of managed care include health maintenance organizations and preferred provider organizations, as well as traditional indemnity insurance companies. Prepaid managed care is designed to control the use of health care services so that these services are provided cost effectively. Because traditional indemnity plans or programs do not control health care costs effectively, employers, including the US government, are offering their employees the opportunity to join HMOs and PPOs. Currently, HMOs and PPOs service more than 25 percent of the US population, up from 3 percent in the 1970s.

Survey and certification state agencies, usually state health departments, with which the Department of Health and Human Services enters into agreements, are responsible for conducting various survey and certification activities on the part of the federal government. These activities ensure that facilities receiving payment under Medicare and Medicaid meet certain conditions of participation established by regulation. The state agency of the Health Care Financing Administration (HCFA) regional office "certifies" the conditions of participation, thus allowing providers to participate in the Medicare and Medicaid programs. The Secretary of Health and Human Services agrees to provide funds to the states for a portion of the costs of performing these functions.

The economic drain on US society represented by higher and rising health care costs threatens to jeopardize the United States' competitive position in international trade. Although the United States spends more on health care than any other industrialized nation, a lower proportion of US citizens have health insurance coverage and a typical insurance policy provides less coverage than in any other industrialized nation.

Over the past 20 years, the wages of US workers have fallen in real terms while health care costs have climbed 10 to 15 percent each year. For small businesses, premiums have risen by as much as 50 percent annually. Skyrocketing health care costs make it harder for US companies to compete in the global marketplace. Health care costs add more than US$1,000 to the price of every car manufactured in the United States—Japan spends half of this amount. In 1990, General Motors spent US$3.2 billion in medical coverage for its 1.9 million for employees and retirees. That is more than the company spent on steel.

International Market Overview

The business climate in many countries appears favorable for US business expansion in health care services. In some foreign markets, US firms face trade and regulatory barriers. This is very visible in Japan, for example, where foreign ownership of health care firms is prohibited. The best opportunities for US health care providers are in the areas of primary care, home care, and nursing home care services. In addition, opportunities exist in hospital management, ancillary services, private health insurance and drug rehabilitation programs.

Governments of many nations have made health care a centerpiece of their social policy and are providing steady annual budget increases for health care. The World Bank's annual *World Development Report* calls for US$2 billion of increased official development assistance for health care to developing countries. The World Bank, in particular, will contribute the most–US$1 billion annually. Other development banks are expected to follow the World Bank's lead, with increased expenditures. Rising health care budgets could present significant commercial opportunities to US providers.

This sector is unique among other service industries because of its ethical component. Health care firms must make human needs an important part of its reputation. US firms who want to merely make money and pull out can damage not only their own image, but those of other US firms.

Treatment of foreign visitors in the United States is probably the most familiar form of healthcare service export, but the management or operation of hospitals and clinics is the most common operation abroad. Hospital construction and architectural services are also becoming more prevalent. Clinic construction is expected to expand in many countries, primarily because of the trend toward decentralized systems and the need to relieve pressure on overburdened hospitals. Foreign healthcare decisionmakers are also growing increasingly aware of the importance of organizing how services are delivered as well as purchasing the optimal hardware.

Managed care is another alternative to alleviate dwindling central budgets and pressures to reduce costs. In countries such as India, Mexico, and Central and Eastern Europe, US providers should find success, but they will involve explaining to a local partner how to construct a managed care system and several related issues (the financial relationship between insurers, providers, and patients, for example) before adapting a system in the target country.

In Eastern Europe, Russia, and other successor states to the former Soviet Union, the painful adjustments accompanying the transition to market-oriented economies have not prevented the establishment of medical service operations by foreign providers. This development has been encouraged by the generally poor treatment provided, the breakdown of state-run distribution and supply channels, and the worsening environmental conditions in these states. Hungary, Poland, and the Czech Republic have offered the most numerous opportunities thus far in Eastern Europe, in line with these

countries' earlier steps to attract foreign investment and, particularly in Poland, to decentralize budgetary allocations for health care. Foreign and US health care providers have capitalized primarily on small-scale undertakings, such as medical clinics and HMOs. Private and supplementary health insurance represents another area of opportunity, due to a greater stabilization of inflation rates.

Over the past 40 years much progress has been made in improving health conditions in many areas of the world. Life expectancy overseas has improved from 40 years in 1950 to 65 years in 1990, for example, and vaccines have drastically reduced the incidence of killer diseases such as yellow fever, measles, and smallpox. Yet in spite of the remarkable strides made worldwide, several countries are still confronted with a number of health problems caused by prevailing environmental and economic conditions. If not resolved, these problems will continue to hamper the development process in many countries. Infant mortality in sub-Saharan Africa (countries south of the Sahara Desert), for example, ranges from 100 to 170 deaths for every 1,000 live births. Malnutrition and childhood diseases like tetanus, measles, pertussis, pneumonia, and polio are rampant and remain an underlying cause of mortality among children.

This situation is exacerbated by the fact that most governments still devote less than the World Health Organization-recommended 10 percent of their budgets to directly meeting the basic health needs of their people. Furthermore, governments have not been known to be good health planners. Many health care delivery systems are poor with emphasis placed on expensive urban-oriented curative care in modern hospitals, rather than cost-effective preventive community-based care.

Market Barriers

Government Barriers

Ownership restrictions are a problem for companies operating in Latin America, Australia, and Canada. Although foreign ownership of hospitals is prohibited in most of the Middle Eastern countries and Japan, US firms have profitable operations there through management contracts.

Other problems faced by US health service firms include import restrictions and excessive import duties on medical equipment, difficulty in getting approval for projects, and labor restrictions on US personnel.

Economic Barriers

Restrictions on repatriation of profits are a problem in Latin America and in parts of Asia and Africa. US health service companies have not encountered restrictions on establishment and repatriation of funds in most of the European countries.

Competition from European government-sponsored financial consortia has also been cited as a problem by US health service firms. German, British, and Swiss hospital firms are conspicuous on vying for contracts abroad. Firms from these countries can call on government-backed lines of credit unavailable in the United States. They may also have an advantage due to geographical proximity and shared ethnicity.

Social and Cultural Barriers

Many countries already have a primary country they do health care business with, and it may be difficult for US firms to break through. The markets in many African countries, for example, are defined along ex-colonial and linguistic lines. English-speaking countries like Kenya or Ghana tend to prefer to buy from the United Kingdom (UK) while French-speaking countries like Cote d'Ivoire or Senegal typically buy from France, and Portuguese-speaking countries from Portugal. All of these considerations should be taken into account by US exporters developing a marketing strategy for the region.

Market Channels

US companies have several alternatives to enter foreign health care markets and they should decide how to market their services before entering. They can:

- sell the same pre-paid health care services they sell inside the US to the upper-income level persons who can pay for them, including the possibility of receiving medical attention either in the US or in their home country.

- offer pre-paid health care services to be provided in a country where most medical expenses are lower.

- provide a mix of the two previous alternatives.

- create a joint venture with an already existing local pre-paid health care company, insurance company, or large hospital.

Regional Opportunities

Note: These are only examples of regional opportunities and in no way constitute a complete list.

Russia

As the most populous of the Soviet successor states, Russia and the Ukraine present the most promising long-term markets for US health care providers, despite the present shortage of hard currency and persisting inflationary pressures. Immediate prospects are proving most favorable in regions rich in oil or other marketable raw materials, such as Russia's Ural Mountain region and Tatarstan, where health care facilities are being constructed for workers and some hard currency exists. The reduction of central government authority in Russia and increasing regional access to financial resources have resulted in opportunities for services firms seeking to open and manage diagnostic clinics, private physician practices, and mini-hospitals. Maternity care and home health care represent two secondary areas for health care providers in these states.

South Africa

Health care services that enhance the ability of the government to deliver the promise of health care, particularly in the rural areas, could prove the most lucrative. The growth of informal towns around the major cities of South Africa as well as the existing "townships," which have better infrastructures with water and sewage, could also command the attention of health care services, but possibly with different delivery systems. "Township" residents also have the advantage of generating income because they are closer to employment opportunities.

The major thrust is to provide equal health care services to all patients equally by the state health care delivery system, with a primary health care focus, for the disadvantaged mainly black urban and rural population.

This will require low technology, high training approaches to qualify relatively unskilled health care professionals, mainly nursing staff, to establish or re-establish the primary contact with patients so that confidence in the new approach to health care will be developed. Impartial and dispassionate consulting and training in the methods to be applied to make the new system efficient and effective in South Africa could be both welcome and lucrative for the service provider.

Germany

Like much of western Europe, Germany has an efficient health care system, and opportunities for US firms, while available, are few. Almost 90 percent of the population are insured through a statutory health insurance fund. In addition, a number of non-profit organizations are involved in health care, including, in particular, voluntary welfare organizations such as the Arbeiterwohlfahrt (Workers' Welfare Organization), the Caritas, and the Deutscher Paritaetischer Wohlfahrtsverband (German Parity Welfare Association). Germany also claims one of the highest doctors per capita ratio worldwide averaging one doctor per 340 persons.

The Health Care Structural Reform Act of 1993 may have created some opportunities in Germany's health care industry. Public-owned hospitals formally became stand-alone, non-profit businesses, most commonly in the form of limited partnerships, although local authorities do retain some influence on hospital decisions. Outpatient services are also being promoted to increase the efficiency of bed utilization. A number of services are being outsourced, including kitchen, cleaning, laundry, and technical support. This will mean the personnel expenditures will be used for more qualified staff.

Best Bet Opportunities

Note: These are only examples of industry opportunities and in no way constitute a complete list.

Health Services Management and Training

Most health administrations lack the capability to plan and manage cost-effective health programs. US consultants in health should be aware of the lack of health planning in most countries, and therefore the need for consultants to undertake, health sector studies involving analysis of more cost-effective health programs.

Health Manpower Training

Existing training programs in many countries are poorly planned. Priority is rarely given to training community health workers, for example, in spite of the fact that these are the people who are in the most regular contact with the citizens.

Procurement and Distribution of Essential Drugs

The lack of appropriate procedures for obtaining and distributing drugs and other pharmaceuticals, as well as the inability of many economies to generate enough foreign exchange to import them, also compounds health problems worldwide. Some plans include supporting projects and programs aimed at improving the procurement and distribution of essential drugs, focusing particularly on storage, distribution, and local manufacture.

Nutrition and Population

Malnutrition and nutritional stunting are severe problems in many parts of the world, primarily due to drought and civil disturbances. Projects in this field call for nutrition experts who can provide training to health staff and parents. Family planning is expected to be an integral part of health services and programs, particularly in connection with maternal and child health care.

Functional Restructuring

Outpatient services are being promoted to increase the efficiency of bed utilization. Pre- and post-operation treatment are measures that can reduce a hospital's costs significantly. Specific functions may be shared between hospitals, such as pharmacies that supply member hospitals upon request. A number of hospitals have already outsourced services which can be provided more effectively by independent suppliers, e.g., kitchen, cleaning, laundry, technical support. The personnel expenditures saved are used for the employment of more qualified staff, an added value to the hospital's services.

Emergency/Evacuation Services

This is a particularly viable service where there are colonies of Western business professionals, embassy officials, and representatives of international organizations in countries lacking highly developed delivery systems. Evacuation of well-to-do Latin Americans to parts of the southern United States is one such example, but this service is also seeing its application in the ex-Communist world.

Home Healthcare

Home healthcare is one of the fastest growing sub-sectors in the United States, will also be an area of notable growth in foreign markets. It costs less than inpatient treatment and is more desired by the elderly than hospitals care has created its expansion, although it is necessary to adapt this service to meet local conditions.

Sources of Assistance

World Health Organization
2 United Nations Plaza
DC 2 Room 973
New York, NY 10017
Tel: (212) 963-4388
Fax: (212) 223-2920

American Medical Association
515 N. State Street
Chicago IL 60610-4377
Tel: (312) 464-5000
Fax: (312) 464-4184

The Health Care Forum
425 Market Street, 16th Floor
San Francisco, CA 94105
Tel: (415) 356-4300
Fax: (415) 356-9365

Healthcare Marketing Division of AMA
250 South Wacker Drive, Suite 200
Chicago, IL 60606
Tel: (312) 648-0536
Fax: (312) 993-7542

Health Industry Manufacturers Association
1200 G Street, NW, Suite 400
Washington, DC 20005
Tel: (202) 783-8700
Fax: (202) 783-8750

Publications

International Journal for Quality in Health Care
Elsevier Science
660 White Plains Rd.
Tarrytown, NY 10591-5153
Tel: (914) 524-9200
Fax: (914) 333-2444
Seeks to make more widely available the results of quality assessment studies and quality assurance activities.

International Journal of Clinical and Laboratory Research
Springer-Verlag New York Inc.
44 Hartz Way
Secaucus, NJ 07096-2491
Tel: (201) 348-4033
Fax: (201) 348-4505

International Journal of Medical and Biological Frontiers
Nova Science Publishers, Inc.
6080 Jericho Tpke, Ste. 207
Commack, NY 11725-2808
Tel: (516) 499-3103

International Rehabilitation Review
Rehabilitation International
25 E. 21 St., 4th Floor
New York, NY 10010
Tel: (212) 420-1500
Fax: (212) 505-0871
*Issues and developments in disability prevention and reha-
bilitation worldwide.*

International Review of Experimental Pathology
Academic Press, Inc.
525 B St., Ste. 1900
San Diego, CA 92101-4495
Tel: (619) 231-0926
Fax: (619) 699-6715

Medical Industry Executive
Medical Industry Publications, Inc.
1130 Hightower Trail
Atlanta, GA 30350-2910
Tel: (404) 998-9797
Fax: (404) 594-6998
*Focuses on reports and analyses of market trends, business
issues, regulatory requirements, product development and
technology research for executives in the medical equipment
device and supply manufacturing industry.*

Internet Sites

Aerobics and Fitness Association of America
http://wwwcybercise.com/affa.html

Healthcare Information and Management Systems Society
http://www.himss.org/

International Federation of Health Funds
http://www.fhf.com/
*The FHF is a worldwide association of companies engaged
in the financing and delivery of independent health care.
Altogether, members of the International Federation of
Health Funds provide health care protection for some 120
million people in over 20 countries.*

National Federation of Professional Trainers
http://www.nfpt.com/nfpt/

Information Technology and Networking

Defined

Information technology (IT) and networking firms perform much of the behind the scenes work necessary for a business to operate and succeed. Some information technology services include: credit card authorization and billing, data entry, medical claims processing, payroll processing, and data center management. Networking services firms install and maintain computer networking systems providing services such as electronic data interchange, delivery of electronic mail, electronic file transfer, and accessing of databases, software programs, and bulletin boards. An activity with enormous potential in the networking services industry is electronic data interchange (EDI), the electronic exchange of business documents such as invoices and purchase orders. It is gaining popularity among suppliers and purchasers because it reduces transaction costs, time, and errors. Other examples of information technology and networking services include:

- hardware peripherals for multimedia systems
- telecommunications hook up and maintenance
- executive information services
- hook-up and maintenance of on-line services
- CD-ROM database maintenance
- training and education
- creating systems for businesses who wish to be autonomous
- transaction processing services for data input and transaction
- contingency firms for any networking emergencies

Domestic Market Overview

The increasing use of information services has contributed significantly to productivity, efficiency, competitiveness, and employment in the United States. More than one million persons are employed domestically at more than 25,000 information service establishments.

Electronic information services grew 16 percent in 1993 to an estimated US$13.6 billion, slightly faster than the previous year's 15 percent increase. The industry continues to attract new suppliers and customers. Keen interest is shown by the increasing attendance at the Information Industry Association's annual investor conference. In 1992 there were 150 attendees while in 1993 there were 600.

Most of the industry's revenues come from business users of information for financial management, research, marketing, purchasing, and general business administration. Consumers' and small businesses' use of on-line services for news, information, transactions and bulletin boards account for an increasing share of the industry's growth, according to a survey by Digital Information Group, a marketing research company.

Additional opportunities should come from the "National Information Superhighway." This project's goal is to connect US homes, businesses, government agencies, universities, and medical facilities to a broadband communications network capable of offering video, voice, and data. This project has important implications for the industry because it will encourage the use of information services, create new businesses, supply new and improved devices, and reduce the cost of information services.

Another measure of the industry's growth is the amount of information available in the electronic format. According to Gale Research, publisher of the Directory of Databases, 221 companies produced 300 databases worldwide in 1979; by 1993, however, a total of 2,221 companies produced 5,210 databases. On-line services increased explosively from 59 to 824. In addition to the on-line format, 3,200 databases are available on CD-ROM, diskette and magnetic tape.

Most segments of electronic information services are dominated by two or three companies although the industry is highly competitive. New competition is emerging as companies in other sectors of the information industry, such as Microsoft and AT&T, begin to move into electronic information services.

The commercialization of the Internet, a global computer networking system originally used by the education and research communities, has enhanced awareness of electronic research communities and electronic information services and has encouraged the development of new services. Interactive multimedia, a new technology combining computer, telephone, and television services, could attract more at-home users to information services. Personal communications networks will serve as additional means of delivering information.

The growth of electronic information services should remain strong, with revenues continuing to rise. Principal drivers of growth will be new service offerings and new customers in the US and abroad. Prices are expected to decline with increasing competition. Restructuring in industry and government should increase demand for electronic information services. The long-term outlook is for annual growth above 15 percent for the next five years as companies continue to deliver valuable services at a reasonable cost on systems that are "user friendly."

International Market Overview

The US information services industry derives about 35 percent of its revenue from foreign customers. Nearly all major US suppliers of electronic information services are established overseas. The European Union (EU) and Japan are the largest overseas markets.

By establishing working relationships with counterparts overseas, US-based trade associations contribute to the globalization of the information services industry. The Information Technology Association of America, the Information Industry Association, the Software Publishers Association and the Electronic Data Interchange Association are especially active abroad.

Many countries, including Canada and members of the European Union, have planned to develop national networks similar to the one underway in the United States.

US companies are strong overseas because they provide some of the most advanced and diversified services. Additional reasons include the widespread use of the English language and the thirst for information about the United States. Overseas sales come in many ways: direct sales, typically CD-ROM products; remote access, using global networks; US subsidiaries, licensing, and distribution agreements.

Best sales prospects for new-to-market US suppliers lie in new, more high-technology products that can command a price premium. These include networking software and hardware accessories, hardware peripherals for multimedia systems, telecommunication products, and other data communication-related products. There is a growing market for US companies that provide systems solutions that are very technical and the skills required to implement advanced networking systems.

Many large distributors have regionalized their operations, usually by establishing their own or joint venture offices in one or more countries in the region. In countries where offices have not been set up, companies frequently work through associated distributors or dealers. Smaller distributors tend to perform fewer logistical, marketing, and technical servicing functions. Marketing and servicing is carried out from the country or through associated distributors/dealers in the region.

Many regions have a springboard country, one where companies can easily export their services through. The country is usually centrally located in the region, has an advanced, modern infrastructure (compared to the other countries in its region), and relatively light import duties. When dealing with countries of the Pacific Rim, for example, many companies will move their services through Singapore. It is centrally located in the heart of Southeast Asia and its infrastructure is superior to many other countries in the region.

Make sure to visit the country you wish to enter, even if no business is transacted or distributors are selected initially. Some time should be spent studying the market to assess the competition, the service needs of customers, potential distributors, the infrastructure, the prices and margins, and other factors of importance. Initial visits may also include discussions with information technology hardware and software manufacturers, who can recommend distributors. It is important to obtain visibility in the market, especially since many are small and work closely together. Thus, "word of mouth" can play an important role in finding a distributor or dealer.

Participation in trade shows and trade missions sponsored by the US Department of Commerce are recommended to begin to gather market and contact information.

For certain types of products (e.g. networking software), it may be more appropriate to initially work with a system integrator/reseller to introduce your service to the market. These companies are actively seeking new methods that provide unique solutions to their customers. Major distributors may also require a certain sales volume before they will handle a new service. This can best be achieved by attempting to "pull" the service through the marketing channel.

The introduction of service should be backed by strong marketing support to distributors to attract a significant number of dealers, retailers, and traders. Brand name and the image of reliability are extremely important in the market.

A growing area of opportunity is for specialty on-line services. Even in developed countries, where most of the well-known, on-line databases are being used, there is a growing demand for smaller, professionally-specialized services, particularly those dealing with medicine and a variety of technical specialties.

Price is still the leading factor affecting choice of service, although it is not as important a factor when compared to just a couple of years ago. Buyers now weigh other factors when making purchases, such as efficiency, reliability, and servicing.

Market Barriers

Government Barriers

The policies and regulations of several countries have failed to keep pace with the technological advances in services. For example, technology for securing information is advancing so rapidly that law enforcement and national security agencies fear that their monitoring activities could be impeded. The industry is also concerned about policies regarding access to government information, competition between government and industry, and the cost of government information and services.

Another problem that affects information technology services, as well as most computer industry services, is intellectual property protection. Many countries have been placed on "watch lists," primarily reflecting problems with protection of copyrights for computer software.

Because the information services industry overlaps with other industries, the barriers can also overlap. The telecommunication systems in many countries, for example, are owned wholly by the government, and their strict regulations could affect firms providing Internet and telephony services as well.

A country may have certain restrictions on the number of employees that can work there or the amount of time they can stay. Because information services often include so much more than merely the installation of a system, employees often need to remain near the site to answer questions and solve problems.

Social and Cultural Barriers

Language can be a problem. Training should be in the

country's native language, and system programmers will probably have to have some knowledge of the country's language and culture to make any progress. Language can also be a problem with labelling and shipping. Canada, for example, requires bilingual labelling in its official languages—English and French—for most products. Labels should include a product identity, net quantity, and dealer's name and principal place of business in both languages. Pre-packaged products manufactured for resale should include a name and address sufficient for postal delivery.

Market Channels

The distribution channel for information technology services is very fragmented. It is difficult to define clearly the scope of each company involved in the industry. Companies handle a variety of products and may perform different functions for each. Consequently, it is often difficult to classify a firm as a distributor, dealer, producer, systems integrator, or trader. Virtually all groups overlap in terms of their scope of practice, customer, and vendor base.

The first distribution tier consists of end users of services. These include local and multinational corporations, small and medium enterprises, home users, and customers in the export market.

Dealers comprise the second tier. The term "dealers" encompasses system integrators/resellers, who only sell information technology products, traders, and retail outlets. System integrators/resellers offer system development and integration services and may also serve as distributors for relatively small volume hardware and software product lines. A large volume of products is reported to be moved through "traders," whose business focuses on trading software and hardware products to ASEAN and other destinations.

Markups by the second tier of sellers to end users range in the neighborhood of 10-15 percent for many hardware and software products. Additional fees are usually charged for value-added services rendered by system integrators/resellers for system design, support and implementation.

For more complex software packages and information technology systems, however, suppliers sell their product directly to and through dealers, rather than authorized distributors. This is due to the fact that such products require technical support, which can be provided more quickly and effectively through shorter channels.

Regional Opportunities

Note: These are only examples of regional opportunities and in no way constitute a complete list.

Singapore

Singapore serves as a regional hub for the distribution of information technology services in the ASEAN Region. Many of the companies in the industry in Singapore export a significant share of their products to the other countries: Malaysia, Indonesia, Thailand and Philippines. A large num-

ber of these firms have also established marketing networks in the region and are likely to perform some degree of logistical, warehousing, technical servicing, administrative, sales and marketing, and training support to these networks.

Among the factors that have contributed to Singapore's good trading status is a strategic geographic location, free ports, established financial and telecommunications infrastructure, and an efficient work force. The small size of the market, which has a population of three million, and its maturity for a large number of product lines has encouraged Singapore companies to regionalize their operations.

The Singapore market is small and appears to be maturing for many product lines. Competition is extremely keen and margins have generally been declining in recent years. Of all of the markets in the region, Singapore is the most sophisticated in terms of its computer infrastructure and technology knowledge and servicing capability. For example, a 1992 survey by the National Computer Board revealed that 84 percent of Singapore companies that employ ten or more employees were computerized and 63 percent were networked.

Growth in the Singapore market is forecast at 10-20 percent per year for the next five years. More sophisticated products, such as networking software, information technology services, and portable computers, are expected to have the best sales prospects.

Canada

US firms currently dominate the information technology market in Canada. Emerging niche markets and the upgrading of existing EDI systems are two areas of growth with a high degree of penetration.

It is believed the Canadian market will respond very favorably to information technology products and services from US-owned companies. The reasons for this include: the existing high penetration rate of US-owned EDI software companies, the well-established reputation of US software producers, the local presence of close proximity of the US companies to Canada, allowing for improved servicing and monitoring of the market for changes or developments, and the existing trade relationships between companies in the United States and Canada.

China

Many experts believe that China holds significant potential for information technology exporters. The larger companies are positioning themselves to take advantage of this opportunity by setting up offices or developing relationships with associated distributors/dealers in Hong Kong. Mainframes, software, desktop microcomputers, and other peripherals were the most popular computer-related export items, while radio-telephonic and telegraphic receivers, parts of TVs, etc. and transmitters and receivers accounted for the largest telecommunication shipments. Due to its large size and unique requirements, a large number of information technology suppliers are planning manufacturing facilities in China or will attempt to service this market from Hong Kong and Taiwan.

The ASEAN Countries

The economies of this region are among the fastest growing in the world and industrial systems and infrastructures are developing rapidly.

There is a possibility that more products will move direct from foreign suppliers to ASEAN countries and some evidence suggests that this is already happening in networking and technical software, where small direct shipments are more economical and local technical servicing is required. Other software distributors indicated that margins on some software products have fallen to the point where shipments need to move direct to be competitive in ASEAN markets, particularly with the recent imposition of a 3 percent general services tax on shipments through Singapore.

Nevertheless, several observations concerning future developments are possible. The first is that a larger share of information technology revenues will stem from sales in other ASEAN markets. As a result, more distributors, manufacturers, and systems integrators will open offices in the region. The local offices of these companies will assume responsibility for marketing and sales, systems integration, and technical servicing. In contrast, the Singapore head office will provide greater marketing, training, and technical backup.

Israel

Commercial firms, government entities, the academic/research community, and individuals are all users of electronic information services in Israel. The major end user (45 percent) is the Israeli business community which has a high demand for economic and financial data, market research, data on companies, and business intelligence. US databases are considered the best. An additional factor to be taken into account is the local positive approach to US products.

The total market demand for electronic information systems in Israel is estimated at US$22.5 million for 1994. Electronic information is provided in Israel by government entities, information service specialists, public organizations, and research institutes both through on-line databases and CD-ROMs. Domestic sources of information tend to produce general information and information on business opportunities.

The competition in the Israeli information market is primarily between US and European companies. So far, there is little competition from Far Eastern information services. Although US services are well-entrenched in the market, European companies are becoming increasingly active in reaching out to Israeli business both independently and through their central EU databases.

Both the US and the EU have free trade agreements with Israel, and therefore compete under the same set of rules in this sector. As competition grows, US firms will have to become more aggressive reaching out to the Israeli business information suppliers to compete effectively with those from the European Union.

Belgium

The total Belgian market for software and services is estimated at US$2.7 billion. Due to the current recession in Belgium and in other European economies, the anticipated increase of the market has slowed, but is still expected to amount to 5 to 10 percent for the current and coming years. Significant trends

for the information technology business throughout the industrialized world and in Belgium are toward:

- smaller systems—"downsizing"—with the use of intelligent workstations;

- networking, which allows different types and brands of computers to work together; and

- the consolidation of mainframes where they remain more economical.

Corporations and organizations with operations in Belgium face mounting competitive and economic pressures. Just-in-time inventory, factory automation, and other accelerated business operations and practices have created the need for fast, reliable, intuitive information for executives and managers. Belgian executives realize that they need to be able to quickly find out how their company is performing in all departments. Senior managers need regular updates on key financial indicators, profit margins of a new product, cash flow trends, personnel turnover, and quality control. The information they need exists on computer systems throughout the company but they cannot get to it fast enough and cannot obtain it in the most appropriate form.

Venezuela

Venezuela is a good example of a country just beginning to open its doors to networking services. The television and telecommunication networking were recently opened to privatization, and a private cellular system was authorized. Rapidly, concessions were granted for digital data transmission, including voice and video, trunking, alphanumeric paging, various value-added services and numerous private networking. This opened the way to foreign and local companies to install subscriber services for corporate clients, mainly in the data transmission field where the greatest need existed, as well as to a considerable number of intra-corporate systems.

Best Bet Opportunities

Note: These are only examples of industry opportunities and in no way constitute a complete list.

On-line Services

Popular, well-known on-line services are in demand in developing countries (although the country's poor infrastructure may impede the services from reaching throughout the countries). Smaller, sophisticated, professionally-specialized databases are in demand in developed countries, particularly those dealing with medicine and a variety of technical specialties. Services will be needed to install the services, teach people how to use them, and for maintenance and troubleshooting.

Executive Information Systems (EIS)

Executive Information Systems (EIS) are sophisticated data processing systems that collect and convert massive amounts of data from many different sources into usable information for management. EIS companies, such as SAS

Institute and COMSHARE, which are currently selling on the Belgian market, are informing and educating Belgian executives on the advantages of the implementation of an EIS solution. The most popular EIS packages currently sold in the Belgian market allow information to be presented in an attractive way making use of color and graphics. This makes it easy for executives by using touch screens and mice to avoid any necessity for touching a keyboard.

Several large companies are already equipped with an EIS system. The market demand is driven by large companies, multinational headquarter operations, and governmental organizations. For most of these companies, it is a question of when to install an EIS, rather than whether to do so. The others, representing 85 percent of Belgian companies, currently do not use EIS. Some 60 percent of these companies believe that an EIS system might help solve poor management and communications. However, many companies still must be convinced that the benefits of an EIS solution exceed the costs.

Best sales prospects for new-to-market US suppliers lie in new, more high-technology products that can command a price premium. These include networking software and hardware accessories, hardware peripherals for multimedia systems, telecommunication products, and other data communication-related products. There is a growing market for US companies that provide systems solutions that are very technical and the skills required to implement advanced networking systems.

CD-ROM Databases

Many consider CD-ROM databases inexpensive, user-friendly, and able to be updated at set intervals. Databases, offering a wide range of technical and general information, as well as large directories, are popular in several countries.

Internet and Intranet Opportunities

The Internet and company wide Intranet opportunities will be a very fast worldwide market opportunity. The demand to communicate and transact business electronically from the desktop will be the major business driver for the next five years. Software, hardware, and service firms who assist in helping people and companies communicate across this medium will succeed with the right kind of niche marketing. Training services will also be in great demand on a worldwide basis.

Networking Setup and Service Providers

Setting up networking within a company is becoming more popular. US services are often the first business looked to for servicing. Employees will probably need to stay in the home country for an extended period of time, because setting up the networking includes training the local employees, answering any questions, and being available for help in case of an emergency.

Networking Training and Assistance

Inter-office networking is a new idea to much of the world, and employees will probably have to be trained to use them. In addition, after setting up networks, users will still have a number of questions. These services will undoubtedly require having local workers stay in the area.

Bar Code Installation and Assistance

Bar codes, specific networking where sales data is immediately transferred to a central computer, is particularly important in supermarkets, drugstores, and other retail outlets. This not only allows sales to be processed much faster, but also helps store employees maintain better stock control through data transmission. Although this technology has been available in advanced countries for years, many developing countries are just beginning to realize how bar codes can help their businesses.

Sources of US Based Assistance

Information Access Institution
10927 Pecan Dr.
LaPorte, TX 77571
Tel: (713) 471-2965

Information Council of the Americas
931 Canal St.
Room 800
New Orleans, LA 70112
Tel: (504) 523-3614

Information Industry Association
555 New Jersey Ave. NW
Ste. 800
Washington, DC 20001
Tel: (202) 434-8826

Information Systems Association
c/o New Horizons
920 S. Waukegan Rd.
Lake Forest, IL 60045
Tel: (708) 253-1545

Information Technology Association of America
1616 N. Fort Myer Dr., Ste. 1300
Arlington, VA 22209
Tel: (703) 522-5055

Information Technology Industry Council
1250 Eye St. NW, Ste. 200
Washington, DC 20005
Tel: (202) 737-8888

Publications

Information Industry Association
555 New Jersey Ave. NW, Ste. 800
Washington DC 20001
Tel: (202) 639-8262
Fax: (202) 638-4403
Annual directory of the members of the Information Industry Association, profiles of key executives, company descriptions, key products and services.

International Computer Law Adviser
Law & Technology Press
4 Arbolado Ct.
Manhattan Beach, CA 90266-4937
Tel: (310) 544-0272
Fax: (310) 544-4965

International Journal of Computer Research
Nova Science Publishers, Inc.
6080 Jericho Turnpike., Ste. 207
Commack, NY 11725-2808
Tel: (516) 499-3103
Fax: (516) 499-3146
Email: novasci1@aol.com

Internet Sites

International Federation for Information Processing
http://www.ifip.or.at/

Society for Information Management
http://www.simnet.org/

Insurance

Defined

Insurance is the transfer of risk (chance of loss) from one party (the insured) to another party (the insurer). The arrangement, which is typically specified in a written contract, calls for the insurer to pay the insured (or others on the insured's behalf) an amount of money, services or both, for economic losses sustained from an unexpected event. Examples include accidental death, auto collisions, fire or theft of property. The insured makes payments (premiums) to the insurer over an agreed period of time to guarantee compensation for losses suffered from such an event.

Reinsurance is the most global and corporate-oriented segment of insurance industry—and the least regulated. Reinsurers insure insurers. Retrocessionaires reinsure reinsurers. In both cases, these firms assume part of the risk and premium originally taken on by the primary company (insurer). Some of the largest and most influential players in the reinsurance industry are European and Asian firms, such as Munich Re, Caisse Centrale or Korean Re. Top American firms with interests abroad include General Re in Connecticut and Kansas-based Employers Re.

The two basic categories of reinsurance are treaty and facultative. Under treaty, a reinsurer accepts specific percentages of entire classes of an insurer's business, such as auto or fire, up to pre-agreed limits. Facultative reinsurance generally involves the more unusual risks of conducting business internationally. This risk area includes coverage of loss from unexpected events for items as large as offshore oil drilling platforms or airplanes. Acts of terrorism on individuals and property in foreign countries also fall under this category.

Items and areas covered by insurers and reinsurers include:

- marine
- health
- dental
- auto
- earthquake
- property/casualty
- life
- workers compensation
- environmental
- professional liability

Domestic Market Overview

The US insurance industry was started with global intentions. American insurers first offered coverage to merchant ships carrying cargo abroad. World War II also spurred growth of the US insurance industry as the demand for international coverage skyrocketed. But the growth of domestic wealth within the United States following WWII caught the full attention of insurers, who in turn focused their efforts on providing coverage to American businesses and individuals. As domestic insurance operations grew, the time and effort required to enter and survive in foreign markets was labeled too costly. As a result, international insurance became and remained a specialized field for decades.

In 1991, the US was rated as the largest insurance market in the world, with about 34 percent of the US$1.41 trillion in premiums worldwide. The US was also the global leader that year in the non-life insurance sector with 42.3 percent of world premiums. The size of the US non-life market is due mainly to health and casualty insurance programs. Private insurers provide most of the health insurance in the US, instead of the public sector. The US tort-liability system also leans strongly toward fully indemnifying people harmed as the result of the action of products or others. This results in higher US premiums for liability insurance in comparison to other countries.

Despite this obvious strength on the home front, US insurers are feeling threatened by the growing presence of foreign-owned insurers operating in the US These insurers had sales of US$72.9 billion in 1991, up sharply from US$62.6 billion in 1990, due to major foreign acquisitions. Foreign-owned insurers, primarily from Europe, Japan and Canada, captured more than 11 percent of the US premium market in 1991. The non-life insurance sector and other providers sold policies worth more than US$39 billion in the US in 1991. Foreign-owned life insurers in the US recorded US$33.7 billion in sales that same year.

International Market Overview

Technological advancements, especially in communication, make the world a smaller place every day. Government deregulation of industry, the growth of multinational companies, easement of trade barriers, and the rise in market-based economies are also factors which have made conducting business around the world unavoidable. This dramatic and fairly recent globalization has resulted in demand from the business world for the availability of international insurance services.

There is no shortage of opportunity for US insurers looking to penetrate global markets. The rise in personal income, wealth and savings in countries such as Thailand, South Korea and Brazil, give US insurers, especially life insurance companies, a reason to seek premiums and place investments globally. To date, most foreign sales by US insurers have been from non-life operations. But US life insurers are becoming increasingly aggressive in foreign markets as competition from Canadian and European insurance firms continues to rise. Diminished returns on life insurance in the US has already prompted some life insurance companies to search abroad for new investment opportunities.

US-owned insurers operating in foreign countries had sales (premium income plus investment income plus other income) of US$36.2 billion in 1991. This was the time when Canada, Europe and Japan represented key markets for US insurers. Although these markets are still strong, the untapped potential for new insurance policies and programs in industrializing nations far exceeds the growth potential of underwriting in mature markets.

Cross-border trade is a small but important segment of the US insurance market. US-based insurers received more than US$5.5 billion of premiums from overseas exports in 1992. Premiums of US$11.9 billion went to foreign-based insurers (imports) to cover risks in the United States. Most premiums sent abroad went to Europe or off-shore centers, such as Bermuda, for reinsurance. Reinsurance premiums sent abroad represent about one-third of the reinsurance market in the US This area includes marine insurance.

International Competition

The integration of the financial services industry is a key issue affecting competition among insurers. For years, the banking industry has argued that its presence in the insurance and securities industries will increase competition in financial services, create stability for the financial marketplace, improve economic and capital market efficiencies, and provide greater conveniences for consumers.

International regulatory and market developments, especially in Europe, do point to a competitive need to integrate US financial service markets. Some opponents have argued that current restrictions are necessary to protect consumers from unfair practices and to insure the soundness of financial institutions. Opponents of financial integration emphasize, for example, that banks are in a strong position to unduly tie insurance sales to loans.

Banks may eventually be authorized to sell and underwrite insurance. Banks, mutual funds and other financial institutions will offer investment and savings products that compete directly with insurance and annuities products. This increase in competition will also allow foreign insurers to expand into largely restricted markets, including the United States.

International Market Barriers

Government Barriers

US insurers and other foreign insurers share a common bond when it comes to attempting to penetrate a new international market: the waiting process. Local, state and federal governments of any given country greet US-based and other foreign insurers with varying degrees of warmth—if any.

Foreign governments are reluctant to open their markets to outside insurance sources for two primary reasons. First, most governments and their officials are interested in keeping as much business as possible in the hands of existing domestic insurers. This applies especially to life insurance and other personal lines providers. The North American Free Trade Agreement, for example, was supposed to break down trade barriers between the US and Mexico. US insurers anxiously awaited NAFTA's ratification and the day they could operate equally with Mexican insurers. But little has changed for US insurers in the few years that NAFTA has been in place. US insurers must still joint venture with Mexico-based insurers and take a minority stake in the operation in order to do business in that country.

The second reason foreign governments give US insurers the cold shoulder is their inability to see how foreign insurance operations immediately benefit their economies or their people. This is especially true in countries like China, which almost completely refuse to even consider granting licenses to US or other foreign insurers. Again, it is the area of personal lines that is met with the most barriers. Commercial lines operations have been so long established in most countries that their necessity is not questioned. Foreign governments and businesses also prefer to rely on single sources for all of their insurance needs. Therefore, if the insurers already operating in a particular country are doing a sufficient coverage job, licenses for new providers will be difficult to secure.

Once a US insurer does manage to enter a new foreign market, they will be labeled as an "admitted" or "non-admitted" insurer. Admitted signifies that an insurance company is permitted to conduct insurance business in a particular country. Admitted insurers must adhere by law to a country's specific policy wording requirements and usually must allow local insurers to do the underwriting for designated classes of businesses.

Non-admitted insurers are prohibited by law to operate in several countries, such as Nigeria or Egypt. Some countries do allow "non-admitted" companies to sell coverage that's unavailable from licensed companies within their borders. This kind of coverage is called "excess and surplus lines insurance." Coverage needs vary by country and can include the policies used by entertainment and promotions companies to cover music concerts, or corporate pollution liability insurance.

It should also be noted that some countries, such as the United Kingdom and Saudi Arabia, do permit foreign insurance companies to operate simultaneously within their borders on both an admitted and non-admitted basis.

Social and Cultural Barriers

US insurers must understand the characteristics and values of families and individuals living in foreign countries, as well as the legal systems they adhere to, when participating in international claim handling. These "legal families" observed by the international insurance industry are outlined in *Introduction to Comparative Law* by Konrad Zweigert and Hein Kotz. The book contains general groupings of legal families that serve as models for insurers working in global markets. Legal family models include Romanistic, Germanic, Islamic, Hindu, Far Eastern, Nordic, Common Law, and Socialist. Insurers looking to enter new global markets should familiarize themselves with the applicable models to avoid cultural misunderstandings.

Market Channels

Brokers/Brokerage Networks

International insurance programs are administratively intense, and the need for insurers entering foreign markets to adhere to the laws and customs of a particular country is absolutely essential. International brokers are used to identify client needs, gather operational and financial information and conduct risk analysis. A broker hired by a company (controlling broker), will contact a brokerage network familiar with the desired foreign market. The controlling broker then issues an account brief stating the specifics of a client's background and intentions. These transactions are normally conducted in English.

Brokers are essential for helping insurers set up the right programs in the right markets. They specialize in risk management, which can include political risks, export credit risks and employers' liability. Other special risks include acts of terrorism, product tampering or kidnap/ransom situations. Brokers can also familiarize clients with specific cultural barriers and attitudes that could easily kill any business deal if they are not understood and observed.

Generally, foreign insurance companies will work to establish permanent alliances with certain international brokers and/or agents. Insurers, and the insured, both rely on the resources and expertise of brokers when involved with international claims handling. Broker "intermediaries" act as conduits of information between the insurer, the insured, claims adjusters and other significant parties.

Joint Ventures (JVs)

JV arrangements basically boil down to shared ownership in an insurance operation. US insurers can fully expect their foreign partner to take a majority ownership stake in the business. This could be as much as 70 percent. In most countries, JVs are considered a temporary business arrangement, and US insurers are expected to gradually "sell down" their 30 percent interest in a partnership by a certain amount of time. The upside to this arrangement is instant penetration of a new foreign market, as well as affiliation with an established national insurer.

Foreign Contractual Relationships

Contractual relationships within the insurance industry are, in a nutshell, licenses to operate. Licensing is the permission an agency or government gives to another party for the right to manufacture or distribute its product. Licensing can also take the form of fees or taxes paid by the insurer to the grantee. For the US insurance industry, licensing is a frustrating but necessary aspect to doing business abroad. Countries such as China, Japan, Brazil and Argentina have been less than generous about granting licenses to US insurers, primarily because they do not want their local operators to lose any business to foreign firms.

Formation of a Foreign Subsidiary

Subsidiaries are business entities owned or controlled by another company. Many foreign subsidiaries are actually joint venture partnerships with local businesses. The difference is that subsidiaries issue stock and the controlling company must hold at least 50 percent of the shares in order to be considered a subsidiary. This rule bends, however, in countries like Mexico where at least 51 percent local ownership is required. Therefore, a US-owned company can still be considered a foreign subsidiary in Mexico because it is required by law to adhere to the local ownership rule.

Regional Opportunities

Note: These are only examples of regional opportunities and in no way constitute a complete list.

Mexico and Latin America

According to information gathered by the International Insurance Council in Washington, DC, Argentina, Chile and Brazil are emerging as the three top markets for entry by foreign life insurance providers. Employment is stable and industry is growing rapidly in all countries. This has resulted in increased personal wealth for Argentineans, Chileans and Brazilians and a growing need for life insurance with retirement or similar savings plans. Personal and commercial lines for property/casualty coverage are also in great demand. As these and other Latin American countries continue to liberalize and deregulate their insurance markets, entry into these markets will become quite easy for US insurers. Many Latin American countries have made great strides recently to privatize government-owned insurers and allow foreign investment.

Mexico is still a strong market for cross-border insurance, such as reinsurance and marine insurance. But other types of underwriting, especially personal lines, look as though they will remain under the control of domestic providers. Most US insurers will need to enter joint venture agreements with Mexican insurers if they want to gain a foothold in the market.

Asia

Industrializing nations such as Thailand, Vietnam, South Korea, Taiwan, the Philippines, India and Indonesia have been attracting droves of US insurers for several years now. Most US insurers have had a relatively smooth entry into several of these markets, especially commercial lines underwriters and reinsurers. It is the personal lines market that remains largely untapped in most of these countries. US insurers have had a hard time going up against domestic life insurance providers. They have also had difficulty convincing consumers that they need to protect via an insurance/savings program. Citizens of countries like Vietnam and South Korea have only recently experienced increased personal incomes and are still investigating ways to protect that wealth. It will take US life insurers a good deal of time, effort and patience to successfully penetrate these markets.

Japan is not welcoming many foreign insurers these days because it wants underwriting operations to stay within domestic hands. Japan has recently become quite stingy in granting licenses to foreign insurers, which is causing anger and frustration for insurance companies around the globe. China stands as the most tempting—and most impenetrable— foreign insurance market. However, this country lacks the infrastructure needed for advanced insurance policies. China is considered to be an embryonic insurance market and looks to remain that way for years to come.

Best Bet Opportunities

Note: These are only examples of industry opportunities and in no way constitute a complete list.

Life Insurance and Pension Plans

An increasing number of individuals in Asia and Latin America are growing their personal wealth as more people invest in their countries and stimulate their economies. These individuals want and need to protect their wealth. Cash value insurance combines financial protection against premature death with a savings or investment feature, such as pension plans.

Commercial and Personal Lines (Property/Casualty)

The demand for personal lines in foreign countries, such as auto or home insurance, will grow almost simultaneously with the underwriting of new life insurance policies. US insurers have an advantage in this arena because they are well-versed with underwriting such specialized, multi-peril policies for their clients at home.

The need for comprehensive and diversified commercial lines programs will also become an unavoidable investment for any business looking to be successful abroad. Companies involved in subsidiary and joint venture agreements with foreign investors look for financial protection from losses suffered from countless potential events, including: systems/ equipment breakdown; destruction of property from natural disasters; workers compensation, libel and malpractice suits; and crime and vandalism. Multiple commercial lines policies are already gaining popularity abroad, as more businesses set up shop in countries like the Philippines, where the labor is talented and inexpensive, but the government is far from stable.

Pollution/Pollution Risk Insurance

Interest in pollution coverage for businesses is on the rise, especially in rapidly industrializing countries. Pollution insurance specifically covers losses and liabilities arising from damages caused by pollution. This applies only to sites that have been inspected and found uncontaminated prior to damage. Policies are written on a claims-made basis. This means the insurer will only pay for claims presented during the term of the policy or within a specified amount of time thereafter.

Incidental International Exposures

This area focuses primarily on potential loss scenarios arising from activities conducted outside of the US, but can apply to foreigners doing business within the US as well. These "scenarios" include overseas travel by company representatives; sales conducted in foreign nations via direct action or a distributor; participation in foreign trade shows/exhibitions; products or services imported from foreign countries; and the establishment of international sales offices.

Sources of US Based Assistance

International Insurance Council
1212 New York Avenue, N.W., Suite 250
Washington, DC 20005
Tel: (202) 682-2345
Fax: (202) 682-4187

Insurance Information Institute
110 William Street
New York, NY 10034
Tel: (212) 669-9200
Fax: (212) 791-1807

Insurance Library Association of Boston
156 State Street
Boston, MA
(617) 227-2087

Reinsurance Association of America
1301 Pennsylvania, N.W., Suite 900
Washington, DC 20004
Tel: (202) 638-3690
Fax: (202) 638-0936

Publications

Insuranceweek
I.W. Publications, Inc.
1001 Fourth Ave. Plaza, Ste. 3029
Seattle, WA 98154
Tel: (206) 624-6965
Fax: (206) 624-5021

International Insurance Monitor
Box 9001
Mt. Vernon, NY 10552
Tel: (914) 699-2020

Internet Sites

American Insurance Association
http://www.aiadc.org/

Legal

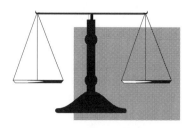

Defined

The legal services industry is a broad grouping of various services performed by legal professionals. In the US, legal services are provided by licensed attorneys or in a limited capacity by lawyers with a professional law degree. Attorneys perform a wide range of duties, not all of them related to business. In addition to business attorneys there are family and probate attorneys, personal injury attorneys, criminal attorneys, and government attorneys. Each of these is a specialty, and many attorneys limit their practice to one or a few specialties. Others, however, maintain general practices, where they take on a variety of cases in several different fields.

The scope of the legal profession has grown considerably in the past 25 years, as business becomes increasingly complex, and geographic markets extend beyond one's own familiar backyard. Attorneys are called upon to provide a wider range of services, to become involved in a company's business earlier and to a greater extent, and to provide advice ranging well beyond traditional legal counsel.

Attorneys have become an integral part of many companies and are intimately involved in all aspects of the company's operations.

Attorneys who limit their practice to business matters will often specialize in a particular area of business. There are attorneys that specialize in corporate, tax, real estate, antitrust, environmental, labor, insurance, bankruptcy, or contract matters, to name a few. There are also in-house corporate attorneys who are employed by a company to handle all of the company's legal transactions.

In short, the legal services profession in the US is loosely defined in terms of duties and responsibilities, but it is very rigidly limited to those with a professional law degree.

In other countries, however, there are various levels of legal professionals, and the duties they perform vary widely. Some countries maintain two or more categories of legal professionals, depending on education or licensing. Each category operates in a different field or undertakes different duties within each field. While in the US these different categories might be referred to as paralegal, licensed advisor, or even legal secretary, in some countries these duties and responsibilities might actually be considered a part of the legal profession.

Domestic Market Overview

The US legal profession has, over the past 40 years, grown at a yearly rate much faster than population growth in general. There are over a million lawyers in the US, one for every 315 people. In some cities, such as San Francisco, there is one attorney for every 66 people. About 37,000 new lawyers join the profession each year, and women make up about 40 percent of the yearly total. The percentage of women actively practicing law, however, remains at about 25 to 30 percent.

Approximately 63 percent of attorneys go to work in private practice, and this percentage seems to be growing (in 1974 only about 53 percent went into private practice). Another 28 percent go to work for government agencies or public interest law firms, or they accept judicial clerkships.

Most attorneys practice as sole practitioners or in small partnerships. Most single practitioners and small law firms deal with everyday legal problems like wills and trusts, small real estate deals, divorce and child custody, criminal matters, and incorporations.

In large urban areas, however, there will be several big law firms, with many attorneys. These firms as a whole will provide comprehensive legal services—from probate to bankruptcy—for their clients, but each attorney or group of attorneys in the firm will specialize only in a particular field of law. Thus, any one client will probably deal with several different attorneys during the course of the business relationship, depending on the particular matter at hand.

Competition in the legal services sector forced firms to perform more like a business and to use corporate management techniques such as identifying profitable niche markets, packaging firms' services to address target markets, and advertising these services to specific markets. Thus, during the 1980s law firms grew rapidly, from individual or small entrepreneurial professional enterprises, into larger, more corporate-like (some say bureaucratic) business structures. The past decade has, however, witnessed a definite trend toward a reduction in the number of attorneys at any single firm—over half of the biggest law firms in the US have significantly reduced the number of attorneys they employ. Interestingly, the number of partners in large firms has actually increased, indicating that many firms are restructuring back toward a more entrepreneurial approach to the practice of law.

There are also small, high quality "boutique" law firms, in which a limited number of attorneys specialize in one field of law exclusively. These are generally the highest priced attorneys, and they often practice throughout the US, associating with one or more local attorneys to avoid the proscriptions of state bar requirements.

In the US, attorneys' salaries vary widely, depending on geographic area of practice, size of firm, and areas of specialization. Private firms tend to pay more than corporations or government agencies, and attorneys in boutique firms generally charge the highest fees and earn the highest incomes. The most lucrative specialties are labor law, insurance law, taxation, negligence (defense), real property, and corporate and business. The least lucrative areas of specialization are estates and probate, domestic relations, criminal law, and banking.

Each state in the US operates its own legal system and imposes individual requirements and professional standards on the attorneys who practice therein. Most states require graduation from a recognized law school and a satisfactory score on a grueling examination prior to issuing a license to practice law within state borders. The requirements and a large portion of the examination are different in each state, and very few states have reciprocity agreements with one another. Bar exams (as the tests are generally called) are offered only twice a year in most states and require several weeks of study time. As such, most attorneys are licensed in only one or a couple of states and they may not practice before the courts of any other. This, obviously, limits the mobility of professional attorneys. The geographic areas in which attorneys can generally expect to find the highest salaries are Boston, New York (especially at the large Wall Street firms), Washington, DC, Chicago, Atlanta, Houston, and Los Angeles.

Corporate law departments have shown tremendous growth in the past decade, spurred by complex litigation (especially antitrust, racketeering, or mass tort suits), high outside legal fees, and new government regulations. The largest corporate legal departments have several hundred attorneys (American Telephone and Telegraph has over 900), and many companies employ well over one hundred attorneys on a full time basis. Corporate lawyers often specialize within their companies in such areas as energy, antitrust, environmental law, employment discrimination, product liability or pension funds. The rate of pay for corporate counsel varies greatly with the type of work performed and the nature of the company.

International Market Overview

It is difficult to present an overview of the international market for legal services because the practice of law does not lend itself to globalization. Nations operate under vastly different legal systems and structures, and even similar government systems maintain diverse legal structures.

In addition, most countries regulate the legal industry, requiring rigid licensing procedures or onerous testing and professional qualifications. Even within the US, where the laws do not vary greatly from state to state and it is thus possible to comply with individual states' licensing requirements and procedures, it is a large undertaking to obtain a professional in more than one state and few attorneys do so. When dealing between more than one country, the endeavor takes on new proportions, and obtaining a license to practice law in a foreign country is more often than not virtually impossible. Not only do countries impose educational requirements which are quite difficult for foreigners to meet, it is not uncommon to restrict the practice of law to legal residents or citizens. Therefore, in many countries it is rare to find a fully licensed foreign attorney, able to carry on a complete legal practice.

The ways and means around such obstacles, however, are limited only by the ingenuity of those in the profession.

Since the practice of law involves many intangibles rather than any specific skill set, there are any number of ways to describe the services being offered. Many countries allow foreigners to operate general "consulting" services, and in such places there will likely be some specialists in contracts, taxes, etc., who hold law degrees from foreign universities.

US attorneys may also associate with a local practitioner and, although prohibited from actually practicing law, may "assist" the local practitioner in his or her legal practice. US attorneys can also be found all over the world in the legal departments of multinational corporations. Since much of their daily work involves corporate transactional matters, and there is virtually no professional contact with outside clients, attorneys in corporate legal departments are for the most part free to fulfill their duties and responsibilities within the foreign country.

None of these options will work, of course, for US attorneys intent on active litigation outside the United States. Despite the vast globalization of many businesses, the legal profession in most parts of the world remains highly nationalistic and restricted to outsiders.

Despite the difficulties, foreign operations of US firms have increased faster than their domestic operations due to the general expansion in the international marketplace. The new markets in Eastern Europe and the countries of the former Soviet Union have created an extremely competitive environment for the multinational law firms. In fact, the trade surplus for legal services is nearly $1 billion. Payments for providing legal services to foreigners is nearly $1.5 billion annually, while payments for legal services prohibited by foreign law firms are less than $500 million.

Notwithstanding its successes, the US legal profession still faces a somewhat negative image in many places. Foreign companies not accustomed to the litigious nature of US businesses, have been less than enthusiastic when approached by a new executive accompanied by a large delegation of legal counselors. This has tended to be greeted negatively—with antipathy and even hostility—and has more than once led to failure of the deal. US attorneys must realize that the role of lawyers in nearly every other country (even England and Australia, which operate very similar legal systems as the US) remains much more limited than it does in the US. Most countries do not rely on lawyers for business planning and implementation, relying instead on accountants or financial managers for these tasks, and they simply do not understand the leading role US lawyers take in a company's operations.

Market Channels

Private partnerships and sole-proprietor law offices are the principal organizations in the legal services sector, accounting for about 65 percent of all practicing attorneys. About 30 percent of all lawyers practice law outside the legal services sector—in banks, corporations, government agencies or trade associations, or legal aid societies. While many lawyers remain general practitioners, the trend is toward specialization in one or a couple of fields. There are five types of professional legal service establishments:

Business Specialist

Elite, business law firm that does premium billing work for major domestic and international corporations and financial institutions.

Boutique

Relatively small, boutique firm that charges premium rates for its specialty services.

Regional

Regional powerhouse firm that provides routine legal services to large local corporations and smaller corporations that lack sufficient in-house counsel.

National

National specialty firm that concentrates on a particular industry and serves national or international clients.

General

Low-cost providers of routine legal services, generally handling matters such as family law, criminal, and personal injury cases.

Before Entering a Market

There are many important considerations to address before entering an international market for legal services. Legal matters are complicated for international traders by virtue of the fact that they are operating simultaneously under two or more legal systems—their own and that of the country or countries with which they are trading. As such, it is imperative that legal counsel be well-schooled in all matters relating to the transaction as it pertains to his or her particular country. This is often best undertaken by local legal counsel, familiar with the ins and outs of the local business environment. US attorneys offering advice in another country must be certain they have an excellent understanding of the matter on which they are advising.

Relationships

The exact nature of the business relationship between individuals will differ by country—in some places it might be considered an agency, for example, in others an employment relationship. Further, agency relationships carry with them different rights and obligations in different countries, as do employment relationships, and these differences can spell the difference between success and failure—both of the business and the relationship—in the long run.

Regulations

There are a host of legal requirements that must be complied with or avoided when trading in or with foreign countries, and these are often fully understood only by local counsel, or those with close local ties to the business or government community.

Intellectual property

Protection of intellectual property rights has proved a nightmare for many US businesses; at a minimum it is sure to be a quagmire. Different countries maintain various procedures and paperwork requirements to effectively protect these rights, and failure to comply to the letter in some places results in complete loss of protection.

Language

The legal profession is one of words, and legal disputes often turn on language. Therefore, it is essential that a foreign practitioner have more than an adequate grasp of the local language, including nuances and idioms, before undertaking to hang a shingle in a foreign market.

Culture

Attorneys in most countries do not play such a large role in business as they do in the United States. As such, they are generally not compensated to quite the same extent as are attorneys in the United States. Neither do they have the same prestige as they are accorded in the United States. Be prepared, therefore, to accept a lesser role in your client's affairs than you might have expected.

Market Barriers

The legal profession throughout the world is heavily regulated. In many places, the US included, there are educational requirements, testing requirements, licensing fees and professional association requirements that can effectively impose barriers to the practice of law.

Some countries simply prohibit outright foreigners from engaging in legal practice therein; others impose stringent limitations on the duties and responsibilities foreign attorneys may undertake. Many countries allow foreign lawyers to practice only in association with or in a limited capacity with local firms.

Other barriers include requiring specific prior governmental approval before establishing a legal practice, or restrictions on the number of offices or attorneys who may practice within a specific region. Limitations on capital investment or repatriation of earnings are other means employed to restrict the practice of foreign lawyers.

Regional Opportunities

Note: These are only examples of regional opportunities and in no way constitute a complete list.

Quite simply, the US is probably the best place for a US attorney to practice law. For those determined to go elsewhere, however, a few regions are undergoing economic growth and development and at the same time liberalizing their foreign trade regimes, and these would tend to offer the most opportunities for US attorneys. The new markets in Eastern Europe and the countries of the former Soviet Union have already created an extremely competitive environment for the multinational law firms. The People's Republic of China, Hong Kong, and Taiwan, appear to be the next major markets of opportunity.

China

Foreign lawyers have operated in China for over 15 years with the tacit but unofficial approval of the Chinese government. American law firms were the earliest to enter the China market and are among the most active of the increasing ranks of foreign law firms pursuing China business today. Nonetheless, the Chinese government has made it clear that it still regards allowing foreign law firms to operate in China as an experiment. It is trying to strengthen its domestic legal profession.

China in fact operates a somewhat schizophrenic policy toward foreign attorneys. In December 1994 it required two large US firms with official offices in Beijing to close down their Shanghai law practices as being in contravention of the country's policy restricting foreign law firms to registration in only one city. Shortly thereafter, the Chinese government announced approval of 16 more foreign law firm offices, five of them in Shanghai, bringing the total of foreign law firms operating in the country to 57. It appears that while the government has no solid objection to foreign lawyers practicing within its borders, it does insist on maintaining tight control over their operations.

Hong Kong

As the hub of Asia/Pacific trade, Hong Kong offers substantial opportunity for foreign attorneys. The British legal system is dominant (at least until the transfer of power in 1997), and US lawyers are able to practice relatively free of restrictions for the time being. US law firms are well represented in the country, and many multinational corporations maintain large legal staffs in Hong Kong.

Japan

Although Japan has loosened its restrictions on foreign lawyers, there are still many obstacles to practicing law in the country. Not least of considerations is the fact that Japan in one of the least litigious societies in the world, and lawyers are used sparingly if at all in most business matters.

Foreign lawyers are prohibited from operating full service law offices, but they may work in Japanese law firms as legal consultants. Some of the larger US firms do maintain actual offices, staffed by attorneys, to perform contract and consulting services, and to maintain their American clients' business interests in Japan.

Mexico

A remarkable transformation of the role of legal counsel in Mexican business transactions is underway. Although a large number of attorneys were in practice prior to the 1980s, few firms handled commercial transactions. During the past two decades, attorneys have played an increasingly significant role in Mexico's business community. Today, commercial companies usually seek legal counsel in the early stages of a transaction, not just for opinions and advice, but for assistance in actually structuring, negotiating, and consummating the deal. The role of legal counsel has rapidly expanded as Mexican industries are privatized and deregulated, and opportunities for US attorneys have grown immeasurably since implementation of NAFTA. Specifically, NAFTA reduced restrictions on US

service firms, mandated the creation of a dispute arbitration system, and increased protections for intellectual and industrial property rights. All of these things have proved a boon to US attorneys operating in Mexico.

Many foreign companies operating in Mexico use both foreign and Mexican attorneys. Foreign attorneys are permitted to act as consultants in Mexico, but they may not practice law there; the practice of Mexican law is restricted to attorneys licensed in Mexico.

A growing number of foreign law firms are establishing local offices in Mexico, some as consulting firms with branch offices, others as correspondents or joint ventures with Mexican law firms. These firms typically have alliance, referral, or other arrangements with Mexican law firms for work that requires local expertise and licenses.

Australia

A foreign attorney with appropriate qualifications can be admitted to unrestricted practice in Australia. In the absence of authority to practice in the country, a foreign attorney can practice Australian law as an employee of a firm, or can practice foreign law.

Attorneys in Australia are known as solicitors, and they are regularly consulted by Australian and foreign parties that plan to transact business in the country. Legal services commonly rendered include assistance and advice in determining the legal requirements for a particular business activity; negotiation, preparation, and review of contracts; preparation and execution of legal instruments; and response to a business dispute that moves beyond amicable resolution. Solicitors can also suggest alternative means for structuring transactions so as to account for differences in the laws of the parties' respective countries.

Australian businesses routinely consult solicitors whenever they enter contracts or transactions involving significant funds or obligations, and Australian citizens generally trust and esteem solicitors.

The Philippines

Only Philippine lawyers—who must be Philippine citizens, must complete a bachelor's degree in law, and must pass a bar examination—can practice before Philippine courts. Foreign attorneys can appear before the BPTT, not as legal counsel, but in their individual capacity, or as a member of a firm, or as an officer or authorized representative of a corporation or association. Non-Philippine lawyers cannot form partnerships with Philippine lawyers. Thus, foreign businesses must retain Philippine lawyers to deal with most matters related to Philippine law. A non-Philippine attorney may render advice on the international aspects of commercial transactions and investments, and foreign attorneys can usually refer their clients to Philippines lawyers as needed.

Argentina

As Argentina has undergone waves of foreign investment and privatizations involving foreign capital, the role of Argentine attorneys in (and their familiarity with) international transactions has expanded. Many Argentine attorneys have not only Argentine but foreign law degrees, are multi-lingual, and are at least as experienced in international business law as lawyers elsewhere in the world.

Argentine lawyers must graduate from public or private accredited universities in Argentina. Foreign lawyers can practice in Argentina if they pass national licensing examinations. This procedure is sometimes simplified for attorneys from other Latin American countries. Generally, foreign businesses must retain Argentine lawyers to deal with matters related to Argentine law. Foreign attorneys are, however, used extensively by foreign businesses for advice on the international aspects of commercial transactions and investments, and foreign attorneys can usually refer their clients to Argentine lawyers as needed. Some foreign law firms have formed official alliances with Argentine firms for this purpose.

Best Bet Opportunities

Note: These are only examples of industry opportunities and in no way constitute a complete list.

Alternative Dispute Resolution

As businesses throughout the world increasingly turn to alternative dispute resolution, there are many opportunities available in mediation, arbitration, democratic solutions, and negotiation.

Environmental Law

Under increasing pressure from the US and Europe, many countries have implemented environmental laws and regulations with which companies must now comply or face heavy penalties. The US has already developed a thriving legal market for environmental lawyers—not necessarily to protect the environment or enforce environmental regulations—but to analyze environmental rules and regulations and determine how to challenge them or comply in the least expensive and intrusive manner. Businesses pay exorbitant sums to for these services, and companies in many other countries will soon do the same. The Philippines, for example, has recently implemented new environmental regulations, as have Australia and Malaysia.

Contracts

Bilateral or multinational contracts are becoming more familiar to the business community, and these bring with them a host of legal problems in addition to domestic contract issues. For example, which country's laws will govern the contract terms, and will that country even recognize international contracts? Is there an international law which applies to the contract, or a treaty between any of the countries involved? Are each country's laws regarding terms of payment and delivery adequately addressed in the agreement, and is enforceable provision made for any dispute relating thereto? These and other questions require legal counsel, and many attorneys are finding a market for contract specialists in the growing economies of Asia and the Pacific Rim.

Asian Legal Framework Development

The Asian Development Bank intends to expand its activities in setting up appropriate legal frameworks in key sectors of several Asian economies. The bank will provide assistance such as expert legal advice and training to promote private sector investments, privatization and capital market development, protecting the environment, improving the status of women, reforming the public sector, and strengthening public administration.

Special attention will be given to transitional economies undergoing systematic legal reforms; industry-specific regulatory frameworks (such as electricity, telecommunications, and transport); capital market development and build-operate-transfer projects; security and credit; and legal training. Skilled attorneys from the US can provide assistance in these endeavors, as well as in the training of government lawyers.

Sources of US Based Assistance

American Bar Association
750 N. Lake Shore Dr.
Chicago, IL 60611
Tel: (312) 988-5000

American Arbitration Association
140 West 51st St.
New York, NY 10020
Tel: (212) 484-4000

International Academy of Trial Lawyers
210 South First Street, Suite 206
San Jose, CA 95113
Tel: (408) 275-6767

International Anti-Counterfeiting Coalition
818 Connecticut Avenue, NW, 12th Floor
Washington, DC 20006

Tel: (202) 223-5728

International Association for Insurance Law
c/o Life Office Management Association
5770 Powers Ferry Road
Atlanta, GA 30327
Tel: (404) 951-1770

International Association for Philosophy of Law and Social Philosophy
c/o Robert Moffat
College of Law
University of Florida
Gainesville, FL 32611
Tel: (904) 392-2211

Publications

Employee Relations Law Journal
John Wiley & Sons, Inc.
Journals
605 Third Ave.
New York, NY 10158
Tel: (212) 850-6645
Fax: (212) 850-6021
Designed to make employer and personnel manager proficient in handling E.E.O., occupational health and safety, labor-management relations, employee benefits and compensation problems.

International Journal of Law and Information Technology
Oxford University Press Inc.
2001 Evans Rd.
Cary, NC 27513
Tel: (919) 677-0977
Fax: (919) 677-1714
Provides information about all aspects of the use of information technology in legal practice and of the legal implications of developments in information technology.

International Journal of the Legal Profession
Carfax Publishing Co.
875-81 Massachusetts Ave.
Cambridge, MA 02139

International Labour Law Reports
Kluwer Academic Publishers Group
P.O. Box 358
Accord Station
Hingham, MA 02018-0358
Tel: (617) 871-6600
Fax: (617) 871-6528

Management and Public Relations

Defined

International managers and public relations representatives act as consultants for clients who need their expertise to enter into and manuever within foreign markets. The industries operate on a contractual basis, with clients usually hiring consultants for a certain period of time to achieve a particular goal. For example, a US-based construction equipment manufacturer—Company X—is looking to market more of its products abroad. The company has already done enough research to determine that the Philippines is its primary target country for export. Company X executives estimate that the total market demand for excavating, extracting and earth-moving equipment increased by close to 65% from 1991 to 1996. The manufacturer has sold its equipment to various US construction companies working on infrastructure projects in the Philippines. But it does not have any perceivable market share with Philippine-based firms or other foreign construction companies operating in the country.

Company X does not want to rely on its export intermediary contacts alone to increase its market share in the Philippines. The company already has established product channels into the country and plans on using its export intermediary to sell mass quantities of its products to clients once demand for Company X's particular brands increases. It does not want to employ an advertising company in the Philippines because it has a tight budget, and advertising services do not come cheap anywhere in the world. Company X's executives decide instead to hire an individual public relations consultant with construction industry experience who lives in the US, but specializes in exposing the Philippines market to various products made by US manufacturers.

The public relations consultant then sets forth to get the word out about Company X's products. His or her marketing methods are often more subtle than the route taken by an advertising agency. Instead of relying on television, radio or print media, Company X's new consultant writes news releases and sends these along with product photos to Philippine-based construction companies, as well as select firms in Japan, Germany, the United Kingdom and the United States The consultant also secures and/or mans booths at international and domestic trade shows, and promotes the name and products of its client through local advertising and community exposure (i.e., supporting local community projects, donating to causes).

Once Company X has established a strong reputation for its products in the Philippines and throughout other parts of the world, the contract with the public relations representative may be allowed to expire. In most cases, if the consultant has done a good job, a company will retain his or her services for an indefinite period of time or will agree to call upon them again when needed.

International management consultants play a more internal role for operating abroad by offering reengineering, design and human resources services. They are called upon to restructure organizations, retrain personnel, increase productivity, secure financing, evaluate investment risks and control pollution. The field of international management consulting is incredibly diversified. Contracts in this area can be even more short-term in nature than public relations because firms are called upon to complete such specific tasks. However, for expert consultants, short term contracts still bring in very large paychecks.

The US Department of Commerce has broken down the management and public relation services industries into five main categories. These are as follows:

- management, which includes business and construction management

- management consulting (marketing, personnel and administrative consulting)

- public relations (including lobbyists)

- facilities support (base maintenance, jail and prison management)

- other niche and/or specialized consulting services

Domestic Market Overview

The US management and public relations services industries have both experienced explosive growth during the past two decades. The number of consultants increased during the 1980s and early 1990s at a double-digit rate. This outstanding period of growth is attributed primarily to industry market trends originating in the mid 1980s. The 1980s was a decade of huge business growth across the board. In order to stay competitive, many firms created satellite entities to specialize on particular areas of expertise. Many individuals followed the trend set by their employers, broke out of the corporate structure, and put their expertise for sale on the market. Hence, the modern US consulting industry was born.

Receipts for management and public relations establishments with payrolls reached an estimated $72 billion in 1993, which was an increase of nearly 6% from the previous year. Receipts are expected to reach close to $100 billion by the end of this decade. The payrolls of US management and public relations companies consisted of nearly 700,000 consultants in 1993. This figure represents an increase of 3.8% from the previous year. It is estimated that by the year 2000 the management and public relations sector will encompass more than 1,000,000 personnel in the US alone. This sector is staffed primarily by accountants, economists, engineers, designers, and public relations specialists.

International Market Overview

Competition is fierce among management and public relations firms in the US, and as a result, international operations of companies in this sector has grown more rapidly than US activity domestic activity. US firms are being forced to look to foreign markets for business in order to stay on top of the game. The most recent data, which was gathered by the US Department of Commerce in 1992, indicates that trade surplus for management and public relations services reached $491 million in that year alone. Receipts for the provision of management and public relations services to foreign individuals or organizations were $170 million that same year. The top 10 management and public relation service providers in the US recorded gross revenues of $10.6 billion in 1992.

The top consulting firms operating worldwide are Andersen Consulting, McKinsey & Co., and Coopers & Lybrand. Andersen Consulting also leads the pack in the United States. Other top companies include Ernst & Young, Towers Perrin, Price Waterhouse and Deloitte & Touche. These firms are multi-task companies. Towers Perrin, for example, provides an array of services to insurance companies worldwide and counsels a wide variety of organizations on evaluating and controlling risk. The company currently provide communications consultation services for AT&T and British Telecommunications; manufacturing management services for Caterpillar, Inc., Ford Motor Company and Hewlett Packard Company. Towers Perrin has office around the globe, from Denver, Colo., to Caracas, Venezuela.

The accounting firm Arthur Andersen, through its affiliate Andersen Consulting, dominates as an international management and public relations consulting firm. The company has grabbed onto a large portion of global market share by managing to operate adeptly in specialized areas. Arthur Andersen is a leader in information consulting technology. Within the last decade, the firm created a new entity under its corporate umbrella solely devoted to information technology consulting. International Business Machines (IBM), although not among the world's top ten management consulting firms, has also carved a niche for itself in the global marketplace by the diversifying into the realm of information consulting technology.

Outsourcing complements specialization in areas such as information consulting technology, human resources, or accounting. It is not a new concept or trend, but more international and domestic firms than ever before are employing the practice. Companies choose to focus on their principal activity and hire external specialists to perform ancilliary business activities. Outsourcing can include information technology, telecommunications and accounting services. Here, facilities management activity has seen an evolution where contracts are based less on price than on the intangible benefits resulting from a strong relationship between the client and contractor. Sometimes, the out-sourcing users also transfer assets and staff to the service company, which then manages the operation for a fee, and operates much like a business partner.

Market Barriers

US public relations and management consultants face stiff competition from indigenous companies and individuals well established in foreign markets. In Taiwan alone, there are hundreds of domestic organizations providing a large array of business training programs. These providers include university extension centers, semi-official organizations and private training companies. Government-backed cooperative educational centers and university training centers dominate the market in China.

As with any firm or individual trying to operate abroad, obtaining work permits presents a major headache. Mandatory work permits often require lengthy paperwork and a significant investment of time and money. Advance scheduling for obtaining work permits is also usually required. Some countries even prohibit the use of foreign consultants if domestic companies can provide the same service.

How To Enter a Market

Follow clients abroad or pursue joint ventures with local partners

These are two of the easiest roads into foreign markets. Large and mid-sized management and pubic relations firms rely on their clients to penetrate international markets. Smaller firms can usually do the same, but may have more success operating on a one-on-one basis with an established domestic provider. Overall, the relationship with a client can be the strongest selling point for any consulting firm.

Specialize in niche areas

The boutique marketing approach is alive and well and quite essential to international profitability. This method of doing business has flourished especially throughout the accounting industry in recent years. US consulting firms should examine their existing domestic client base to determine what markets and regions are best suited for their services. Foreign firms will pay consultants both big and small a good deal of money for their expertise and reputation.

Use trade shows

These are an excellent source of exposure for both consultants and their clients. Marketing consulting services as a tangible product at conventions and trade fairs provide consultants with the personal contact needed to make a good and lasting impression on a potential foreign client. It also shows that a consultant or consulting firm is successful and solid, if either is able to spend the money to attend and network at a trade show.

Use the media

Consultants should use publications such as trade magazines, major metropolitan newspapers and business magazines to advertise their services. The Internet also provides invaluable, international exposure source for countless public relations and management consultants. These globally-minded entrepreneurs must be able to sell themselves to their domestic clients before they can take on accounts in foreign markets. The international marketplace, although growing smaller in scope each day, remains an uncharted frontier for most companies in the US and abroad. More US companies are turning to Internet resources, hoping to find answers, information, and contacts necessary to make a break into foreign markets. Consultants should use the Internet as a yellow pages and advertise.

Be advertising savvy

It is essential for public relations consultants to easily tap into media resources abroad, such as radio, television and print media. Many smaller clients will typically forego this type of media exposure in the beginning, but will most likely request exposure in newspapers, trade publications or radio over time. This depends, of course, on what type of products or services are being offered by the firms. But it is a safe bet that exposure in at least one form of the aforementioned media sources will become necessary at some point during a client's contract. This is especially true for highly-specialized services products that often require advertising in the classified advertisements or suppliers supplements found in most trade magazines and newsletters.

Know the language and the culture of a target foreign market

In short, the number one stepping stone toward failure for an global consultant is cultural ignorance. This is absolutely true for any type of international consultant or consulting firm. The quickest road to "bad PR" for any client attempting to break into markets abroad is failure by its consultant(s) to deliver international expertise. Language and culture barriers not only stand in the way of good business, but also serve as huge roadblocks toward earning registration or certification to operate in a foreign market.

Top Country Opportunities

Taiwan

Instruction in the English language, information technology consultation and international sales top the demand list. Taiwan's business training sector is expected to grow steadily as its economy continues to develop and the country becomes more globally competitive in business and industry. Factors contributing to the increasing demand for business training in this country include state policy, private initiative and individual need. The private sector in particular has recognized the growing importance of manpower and is willing to invest in staff to increase productivity and improve workforce skills to stay ahead

of stiff competition in the region. In 1993, private companies spent more than 2 percent of their payroll on training, compared to only 1.6 percent in 1990. Employer-financed training amounts roughly to 35 percent of Taiwan's training industry. Taiwan's authorities have also provided financial incentives to encourage even greater investments in staff training, as well as establishing and funding semi-public training organizations.

Vietnam and South Korea

These countries have similar business training demands as Taiwan. The Japanese are already infiltrating these markets with their own consulting services. Their presence is strong in major cities and metropolitan areas throughout Vietnam and South Korea. However, secondary cities and rural areas host a large amount of industry and are generally underserved by the business consulting industry right now. China, an emerging market with seemingly endless potential, shows little sign of opening its arms any wider to foreign firms in any type of business. It will be some time into the next decade before China proves to be a lucrative and safe investment for most any international investor or business.

Korea is one of the fastest developing markets for service industries centered on public relations. Most Korean organizations are still not putting importance on the role of public relations. Technically, Korea's public relations market is less than 10 years old. Still, the US Department of Commerce predicts annual growth of 20 to 30 percent for Korea's service industries market. Major national events such as the 1988 Seoul Olympics and the 1993 Taejon Expo have given Korea a better understanding of the role of public relations. Top business conglomerates such as Samsung and Daewoo employ public relations firms for both domestic and international activities. However, another decade may pass before small businesses jump on the public relations bandwagon.

Mexico

The Mexican market for management consulting services was US$968.6 million in 1992, US$1.259.3 billion in 1993, and was reached roughly $1.422 million in 1994. According to the US Department of Commerce, the management consulting market is expected to continue growing at an average annual rate of 12 percent into the year 2000. More than 80 percent of large groups or multinational firms use consulting services. There are more than 1,500 consulting firms operating in Mexico. Ten of these companies dominate as the largest suppliers of consulting services for Mexico. They are US subsidiaries and account for approximately 80 percent of the market. The implementation of NAFTA, and the recent privatization of banks in Mexico, have opened the doors for foreign consulting firms to set up shop.

Hot demand areas for consulting services in Mexico include the following: administration, financial, technical support, re-engineering, planning and design, and environmental. The market distribution for consulting services in management administration is more than 20 percent. This entails insurance, accounting, marketing and public relations services. Urban and architectural services, which includes planning, design and development of urban and regional centers; and environmental impact services, which focuses on pollution risk and control, each have a 14 percent share of Mexico's market distribution.

US management and public relations consultants looking to tap into the Mexican market should either 1) work in the country through their US clients; or 2) form a strategic alliance or joint venture with a Mexican company. These routes provide the least amount of red tape and strengthen the position of foreign consultants looking to compete with domestic consulting firms. US consultants are able to forego joint ventures now that Mexico's Foreign Investment Law is in place. The measure allows foreign consulting firms to have 100 percent ownership in their Mexico operations. Joint ventures in Mexico, which are almost unavoidable for US accountants and insurance providers, require a 70 percent ownership stake by the domestic firm. The foreign operator is also required to sell off its 30 percent interest within a pre-agreed period of time in order to insure market dominance by domestic firms.

Sources of US-Based Assistance

American Management Association
International Department
135 West 50th Street
New York, NY 10020-1201
Tel: (212) 903-7928
Fax: (212) 903-8175

American Marketing Association
250 South Wacker
Suite 200
Chicago, IL 60606-5819
Tel: (312) 648-0536
Fax: (312) 648-0536
Internet Address: http://www.ama.org/hmpage.htm

Council of Consulting Organizations
(Includes ACME, Inc., and the Institute of Management Consultants)
521 Fifth Avenue
New York, NY 10175
Tel: (212) 455-8200
Fax: (212) 949-6571

Institutional of Management Consultants
521 Fifth Avenue, 35th Floor
New York, NY 10175-3598
Tel: (212) 697-8262
Fax: (212) 949-6571

International Management Council (IMC)
430 South 20th Street
Suite 3
Omaha, NE 68102-2506
Tel: (402) 345-1904
Fax: (402) 345-4480

Public Relations Society of America

33 Irving Plaza
Third Floor
New York, NY 10022
Tel: (212) 995-2230
Fax: (212) 995-0757

The Society for Marketing Professional Services
99 Canal Center Plaza
Suite 250
Alexandria, VA 22314
Tel: (703) 549-6117
Fax: (703) 549-2498

Towers Perrin
333 Bush Street
Suite 1600
San Francisco, CA 94104-2836
Tel: (415) 955-5200

Publications

Inside Public Relations
Editorial Media and Marketing International, Inc.
235 W. 48th St.
New York, NY 10036
Tel: (212) 245-8680
Fax: (212) 245-8699

Journal of Management Consulting
858 Longview Rd.
Burlingame, CA 94010-6974
Tel: (415) 342-1954
Fax: (415) 344-5005
Covers all aspects of management consulting, including issues and trends, the consulting process, practice development and management, professional ethics, and more.

Public Relations News
Phillips Business Information, Inc.
1201 Seven Locks Rd.
Potomac, MD 20854
Tel: (301) 424-3338
Fax: (301) 309-3847
Geared to public relations, public affairs, and communications executives. Reports public relations techniques and trends, case studies of programs, and news of the industry.

Internet Sites

Public Relations Society of America
http://www.prsa.org/

Society for Human Resources Management
http://www.shrm.org/

Retailing

Defined

Retailers sell an ever-changing combination of merchandise directly to the public. The goods are classified as either durable, items that are expected to last a long time like furniture and major household appliances, or nondurable, items that are perishable or not expected to last, like food and paper products.

The Census Bureau classifies a retail establishment that derives at least half of its revenue from food as a food retail store, despite the fact that it also receives part of its revenue from the sale of paper products, soaps, housewares and services, such as renting rug cleaners or arranging flowers. Some examples of retail outlets include:

- hardware dealers
- garden supply stores
- mobile home dealers
- general merchandise stores
- food stores
- automobile dealers
- gasoline service stations
- apparel and accessory stores
- home furniture, furnishings, and equipment stores
- eating and drinking places
- miscellaneous retail stores

The Census Bureau's practice of reporting the total sales revenue of a retailer by the principal merchandise line makes it difficult to accurately interpret trends in retail sales of individual merchandise items, as retailers constantly alter their mix of products to adjust to changing consumer demands. The Census Bureau reported all of K-Mart's sales as nondurable sales, for example, because their principal merchandise lines are nondurable. All durable merchandise K-Mart sells is grouped together as nondurable.

Domestic Market Overview

The retail trade sector is one of the major sources of jobs in the US economy, consistently accounting for about 21 percent of all non-farm jobs in the private sector. Retail establishments are primarily engaged in selling merchandise for personal or household consumption.

According to *Chain Store Age Executive* magazine, discount stores and warehouse clubs achieved their current market position mainly by underpricing department stores, variety stores, and drug stores. Supermarkets also increased their market share at the expense of drug stores, and specialty apparel stores captured markets formerly claimed by department stores. A new category of retailer— "G" stores, operated by the major gasoline companies—encroached on the market share of traditional convenience stores.

Retailers of nondurable merchandise face a dual challenge of a slow-growing market and changes in demographics and consumer buying habits that have spawned structural changes within the industry. The retailers that adjust their competitive strategies to these new realities, and take advantage of the new marketing techniques such as electronic retailing, catalog marketing, smaller stores, and improved customer service, should succeed in improving their market position in the changing retailing era of the 1990s.

To keep up with the increased competition, retailers are exercising a full array of strategies, including downsizing and restructuring, changing their merchandise mix, adding services, and adapting the "quick response system" for controlling inventory management costs. Over the past decade, these strategies, singly or in combination, helped retailers faced with declining market shares and falling profit margins to prevent further erosion of their market positions and improve their overall revenues. These competitive strategies may not be enough for the 1990s, however, because customer service may reign as the most important factor in a retail outlet's success. P.R. Trimmer, in his book, *Powerful Ideas You Can Use to Keep Your Customer*, called customer service "the competitive battleground for the 1990s." The retail customer of the 1990s is significantly different from those of a decade ago and strategies need to be reassessed in view of the changing demographics and new buying patterns.

The most significant demographic change is in the declining importance of households composed of married couples. At the same time, the number of people living alone increased, influencing consumer buying habits and forcing retailers to respond with appropriate packaging and marketing, as evidenced by the increase in "single serving" products.

Many married couples consisting of maturing baby boomers have changed their priorities to emphasize more leisure time. Increasingly they have rejected the day long shopping trips of the past in favor of quick "buy and go" patterns. These changing attitudes toward shopping appear to have had an effect on the retailing scene. Sales at super regional malls—those with at least three anchor stores—dropped by as much as 7.3 percent in recent years. During the same period, retail sales at smaller community shopping centers increased 15 percent and sales at neighborhood strip centers increased nearly 7 percent. Consequently, superstores are being downsized to attract the 1990s consumer. In the 1980s, the superstores had

220,000-260,000 square feet. In the 1990s, the superstores will cover 116,000-188,000 square feet.

Department store sales increased in recent years, highlighted by a five-year increase of nearly 20 percent, according to Census Bureau data. Despite the growth in sales volume, department stores lost market share to discount stores, warehouse clubs, and specialty apparel shops. To adjust to the competitive pressures from other types of retailers, several department stores, including R.H. Macy and Federated Stores, filed chapter 11 bankruptcy actions while they downsized and restructured their operations. Other department stores have changed their merchandise mix to de-emphasize their durable lines, and highlight their fashion apparel, gifts, and designer household items.

During the last several years, supermarkets lost sales to drugstores, discount stores, and warehouse clubs. To meet these competitive challenges, supermarkets changed their merchandise mix by dropping duplicated product lines and allocating more shelf space to fast-moving, non-food items and promotional items. Some supermarkets also have revised their marketing strategy, shifting some of their advertising dollars from weekly newspaper inserts to direct main circulars.

The number of warehouse clubs has decreased since the early 1990s, and warehouse club sales and earnings have declined. Part of this deterioration in sales and earnings is due to competitive challenges from other types of retailers such as supermarkets. In response, warehouse clubs are downsizing and restructuring, changing their mix of merchandise, adding more services, and opening new markets.

Discount stores' sales have begun to slow, increasing only about 10 percent in the past few years. As a result, several stores have implemented strategies to maintain their market standing, including downsizing and restructuring, changing their merchandise mix, adding services, and intensifying the use of their quick response systems.

In terms of market position, apparel and accessory stores have maintained a fairly stable 8 percent of total sales of all retailers of nondurable merchandise. Apparel and accessory stores have been effective in maintaining their market position by emphasizing fashion and value, thereby capturing consumer clothing sales previously claimed by department stores.

Convenience stores are losing sales to "G" stores, convenience-like stores owned and operated by the major gasoline companies—including BP, Shell, Texaco, and Hess—in conjunction with their gasoline sales. "G" Stores tend to offer a greater merchandise mix than convenience stores, including fresh fruits and vegetables, salads, and sandwiches. Convenience stores have not undertaken the full range of strategies adopted by others to meet the competition; they rarely enter into strategic alliances since they seldom employ bar coding or other essentials of a quick response system.

In response to competition from supermarkets and discount stores, traditional and chain drug stores have changed their merchandise mix to include many food and convenience items and downsized their hardware and related departments. Some have expanded their services to include free delivery of medicines and drugs, a valuable service to the elderly and mothers of young children. Others have made shopping easier by relocating in strip malls and other easy in and out locations, rather than in large shopping malls.

Restaurant sales have increased during the past few years, however, as *Nation's Restaurant News* magazine points out, the number of restaurants is constantly changing: the new entrants come and go and chains expand into new areas. Dinner houses posted the fastest growth rates, both in terms of sales and the number of outlets opened. Family restaurants were a close second. Sandwich shops lost sales to dinner houses and family restaurants during that period.

International Market Overview

Until recently, few retailers attempted to expand into foreign markets. But the easing of investment restrictions in some foreign countries and the emerging trend of establishing affiliated firms abroad has launched a new era in retailing.

The precise volume of exports and imports attributed to retailers is not known because merchandise trade flows are identified by type of product (e.g., manufactured, agricultural, metals, minerals, etc.), rather than type of organization. The only export data identified by type of organization are listed in *US Direct Investment Abroad* (DIA) reports. The latest shows that 50 US retailers, with 211 foreign affiliates, exported merchandise valued at US$200 million to foreign markets. They included retailers of general merchandise, food, clothing, autos, garden supplies, hardware as well as sales from discount stores and catalog retailers. In addition, US retailers reported US$500 million in direct sales to foreign customers.

Major stores with at least one affiliate in a foreign market included Sears, J.C. Penney, Woolworth's and Carter-Hawley. The foreign affiliates of these retail parent firms were either wholly-owned or majority-owned by a US firm. Since then, several other major US retailers have established affiliates in foreign countries, including Toys-R-Us, Sam's Club, K-Mart, Price Club, Blockbuster, Dillard's and others.

A major objective of the Uruguay Round of multilateral trade negotiations, as well as separate bilateral consultations, is to reduce or eliminate restrictions on investment. If the negotiations are successful, more US retailers will be encouraged to expand to new foreign markets. For example, bilateral consultations with Japan have resulted in an easing of restrictions on the size of foreign retail stores, prompting Toys-R-Us and Blockbuster Video to establish affiliated firms there. Additional US investment in retail affiliates abroad may increase the demand for American exports from US parent retail firms to their foreign affiliates.

Catalog retailers are maintaining their competitive edge in part by expanding into foreign markets. For example, L.L. Bean has formed four joint ventures in Japan; Land's End is developing the British market and plans to test the market in France; and J. Crew recently hired a vice president for international development to guide their expansion into foreign markets.

Marketing tools for US companies wishing to export and establishing a presence in a foreign market could include:

- participating in trade shows

- preparing brochures and promotional materials in the country's language

- contacting companies directly with sales agents who speak the country's language

- using local associations and chambers as multipliers

- preparing technical seminars to inform manufacturers about new technologies and innovations

- setting up representative offices

- establishing joint ventures, benefiting from the market knowledge of established companies

Potential local sales representatives, distributors and agents may be identified through the United States & Foreign Commercial Service (US&FCS) Agent/Distributor Service (ADS). Also, US firms interested in obtaining specific market information on their products may order a Customized Sales Survey, a market research study providing data on issues such as market potential, distribution channels, competition, prices, and duties. These services may be requested from the District Offices of the US Department of Commerce in the United States.

Market Barriers

Government Barriers

Foreign governments often impose restrictions on how or where foreign firms may operate or limit foreign investment to certain sectors or organizational arrangements. These constraints discourage US retailers from expanding into new markets through affiliates in foreign countries.

Ventures may have to be licensed by proper authorities. It is often not clear, however, who has the authority to provide a license. Sometimes, licenses issued by local or provincial authorities seem to contradict regulations of the central government.

Shipments often must be labelled in a certain language prior to import. Importers and customs agents will usually provide information on current and proposed labelling requirements.

Governments often regulate all media advertising. They may set rates for television, radio, billboard and printed media advertising. At the same time, foreign companies may be ordered to pay for advertising in hard currency. This cost and currency burden puts foreign advertisers at a huge disadvantage relative to their local competition.

Retailers may also face currency issues, poor legal infrastructure, fierce competition in the more attractive geographic areas and tortuous distribution networks. The infrastructure in many countries is poorly equipped to handle a national market, as roads and the rail system are overburdened.

The metric system of units is, by law, the official standard of weights and measures in many countries, and importers will usually require metric labelling for packaged goods.

Dual labelling is often acceptable. Imported products should be labelled in the country's language containing the following information: name of product, trade name and address of the manufacturer, net contents, serial number of equipment, date of manufacture, electrical specifications, precautionary information on dangerous products, instructions for use, handling and/or product conservation, and mandatory standards.

Trade mark violations are a major problem for foreign retailers and manufacturers. In some countries, street sellers on every block offer everything from fake copies of name brand clothes to copies of computer software. Many countries have agreed to adhere to international intellectual property rights standards, yet enforcement remains a problem. IPR remains an important issue for foreign companies that offer brand-name goods.

Economic Barriers

Fluctuation in exchange rates can also pose a problem. In China, for example, the exchange rate dipped 20 percent in five months in 1993, from RMB10.5 to the dollar in the summer of 1993 to RMB8.5 to the dollar in November. This instability has created significant foreign exchange risks for foreign companies, especially those who import goods.

Land issues can be a major problem. Most of the land in China, for example, is owned and managed by municipal government agencies, which demand high rents from foreign clients. In addition, foreign retailers who have run profitable operations have complained about landlords demanding excessive rent increases, even though contracts had already been signed. Due to lack of suitable retail locations, the future development of the retail industry is closely associated with expansion of the real estate industry. Foreign retail firms will often find newly-built office or residential developments to be the best available location. Outlets in these developments can be ordered in advance and can be constructed with world-class materials.

Social and Cultural Barriers

Matching a product to the market's tastes can be a problem. Often, goods will have to be adjusted somewhat to be popular. Remember, just because a product is successful in the US doesn't mean it will be so elsewhere.

Regional Opportunities

Note: These are only examples of regional opportunities and in no way constitute a complete list.

Mexico

Mexico's young population, industrial base, and commercial infrastructure have helped the country develop a strong retail sector, not only in the three largest cities (Mexico City, Guadalajara, and Monterrey) but also in 33 other important cities that have a population of more than 300,000 people.

An increase in trade as a result of NAFTA will include retail merchandising equipment and services. US firms which offer competitive products, and are not presently doing business in Mexico, should take advantage of this opportunity and consider entering this market. Similarly, suppliers who are currently operating in Mexico should capitalize on their position, and continue to improve their market presence. American products are considered of the highest quality and have good sales potential in Mexico.

The proximity between Mexico and the US is a decisive factor. This translates into shorter delivery periods, relatively less expensive transportation costs, and in general a better communication between buyer and supplier. Price plays an important role in purchasing decisions, and buyers will always look closely for the best price. Quality is also an important element for buyers.

The general import climate in Mexico is very favorable. In an effort to revitalize and open the economy, the government of Mexico has implemented a series of structural changes. The most important was the accession to the General Agreement on Tariff and Trade (GATT) in August of 1986. The maximum import duty was reduced from 100 percent to 20 percent. With the ratification of the NAFTA, trade with Mexico is increasing. The establishment of a general framework of trade will facilitate US export sales into Mexico. Additional sales opportunities for US suppliers to Mexican businesses will certainly develop.

Distribution practices are similar to those in the US, although on a smaller scale. Imports of retail merchandising equipment and products are promoted and sold through sales representatives and distributors operating on a commission basis. After sales service, fast delivery times, geographical proximity, price, and financing are extremely important. Trained personnel are required to operate and repair the more sophisticated equipment. Local distributors are important factors in penetrating the Mexican market. Usual credit terms are 30 days (considered as cash) and 60-90 days (considered as cash by government agencies).

China

China is a good example of a country just beginning to open up to US retailers. China's retail market remains under developed, but its economy has slowly opened up, and the market is expanding rapidly. US and other foreign companies have started to open stores and sell goods. Foreign retailers are lured by a rapidly expanding class of urban residents with middle class income and values.

China has at least five urban markets with a total of about 50 to 60 million people, and an average annual income of US$1,000 per person. These statistics indicate the growing consumer power of China's densely populated urban areas. The average figures, however, hide a great disparity in actual spending, even in the urban areas. For example, one market research firm calculated average annual family income at US$3,240 in Shenzhen compared to approximately US$1,260 in Shanghai or Beijing.

Many families that before could only afford food, clothing, housing and other basic necessities, leaving little to spare, can now consider buying what used to be seen as luxury items: color TVs, fashionable clothes, multi-speed bicycles or a trip to the local fast food outlet. Washing machines are owned by the majority of Chinese urban households. Similarly, more than 50 percent of Chinese urban residences have refrigerators.

These improvements have also begun to change the spending habits of Chinese consumers. Displaying wealth in communist China has become fashionable, particularly among younger Chinese who did not experience the Mao Era or Cultural Revolution. Consumers seek goods such as flashy suits and brand name clothing as symbols of success. This new class of consumers has displayed a strong preference for imported goods.

Despite China's attempts at liberalization, the Chinese government still dominates the retail sector. Though most of the nation's 8.7 million retail enterprises are privately owned, the state still runs the largest operations. The government also maintains considerable control over the production and distribution of goods. Every product sold by retail enterprises must be approved by state commercial bureaus and other administrative departments, which categorize all products according to industry, manufacturing process, and nature of product—an incredibly time consuming process for retailers who wish to sell a wide array of items.

Japan

Conventional pricing in Japan was set by manufacturers. With the new open pricing system, however, both wholesalers and retailers decide what margin they will place on the cost of the goods they sell. Under this system, which allows retailers to set their own prices, stores can differentiate themselves. The consumer electronics market in Japan has adopted this system, and large discrepancies between the manufacturers' suggested retail prices and the store prices are common. The influence that retailers have with manufacturers is directly proportional to the retailer's buying power. This suggests that the open pricing system will flourish.

Best Bet Opportunities

Note: These are only examples of industry opportunities and in no way constitute a complete list.

Department Stores

Foreign invested stores can import directly from overseas and bypass import and wholesale agencies. This allows them to respond to the changing needs of consumers rapidly and cost effectively. In contrast, state owned retailers must absorb the costs of Chinese importers who serve as middlemen, as well as government taxes on these intermediaries.

Foreign department stores have reported problems with their preliminary marketing strategies. Customers are often far more discriminating and sophisticated than anticipated. While they clearly preferred western goods, they would not simply buy "anything western." Rather, they looked for quality at a good price.

Boutiques

There are a small, yet rapidly growing, number of foreign boutiques worldwide. A number of European brands are extensively sold through this channel, including Pierre Cardin. Several US companies have also started boutique-like businesses. These include: Nike, Concord, Playboy, and

American Place (owned and operating by the former chairman of Macy's, Mr. Edward Finkelstein). Each of these companies run independent retail outlets.

American companies often choose to rent counter space on a long-term basis. They usually pay rent and a percentage of sales to the store owner. They generally sell a combination of imported and domestically produced branded merchandise.

Due to high import duties and the foreign exchange problems mentioned above, retailers are often forced to limit the amount of imported merchandise. Products are sold in local currency only for a high premium, between 50 and 70 percent above the domestic retail price. This premium allows boutique retailers to pay for the hard currency costs associated with imports. Many consumers are willing to pay this premium, however, for the prestige of owning foreign merchandise.

Franchises

Despite the obvious potential of franchising, there remain many serious obstacles. Foremost is the currency. Franchisors also must be very cautious about their intellectual property. Many countries lack a trade secrets law and trade mark protection is not assured. Quality control is very uncertain. Given difficulties in finding local suppliers, it is difficult to guarantee that customers receive the same array and quality of goods at different operations.

As a result of the above barriers, most foreign franchise operators have chosen the joint venture model over the standard franchise relationship. A joint venture requires a much higher degree of foreign personnel, capital and management commitment than the traditional franchise model.

Sources of US Based Assistance

International Mass Retail Association
1901 Pennsylvania Avenue, N.W.
10th Floor
Washington, DC 20006
Tel: (202) 861-0774
Fax: (202) 785-4588

National Retail Federation
325 7th Street, N.W.
Suite 1000
Washington, DC 20004
Tel: (202) 783-7971
Fax: (202) 737-2849

Publications

Retail & Consumer Products Retail Trade Review
Economist Intelligence Unit
111 W. 57th St.
New York, NY 10019
Tel: (800) 938-4685
Fax: (800) 586-1182
Telex: 175567

Retail Business: Market Reports
Economist Intelligence Unit
111 W. 57th St.
New York, NY 10019
Tel: (800) 938-4685
Fax: (212) 586-1182
Telex: 175567
Contains market surveys, consumer spending forecasts, a technology review and a sector overview.

Retail Business Review
National Retail Federation
Retail Services Division
325 7th St. NW, Ste. 1000
Washington DC 20004-2802

Retail Monitor International
Euromonitor
60-61 Britton St.
London EC1M 5NA
UK
Tel: (0171) 251-8024
Fax: (0171) 608-3149

Retail Trade
Euromonitor International
122 S. Michigan Ave., Ste. 1200
Chicago, IL 60603
Tel: (312) 922-1115
Fax: (312) 922-1157
Contains statistical analysis examining trends in retailing and the distribution of consumer goods in 70 countries throughout the world with time series data from 1985-1990.

The Retailer
Holco Communications Inc.
Box 80727
Conyers, GA 30208-0727
Tel: (404) 483-4860
Fax: (404) 483-2447
Contains wholesale and manufacturing news and local distributor news.

Retailing Today
Robert Kahn and Associates
Box 249
Lafayette CA 94549
Tel: (510) 254-4434
Fax: (510) 284-5612
For CEOs in retailing. Commentary on current trends, with emphasis on ethical business practices.

Telecommunications

Defined

In addition to voice, data is transmitted by means of telecommunications, from simple facsimiles to on-line computer messages, to massive information downloads of medical, financial or scientific data.

The telecommunications industry is divided into local and long-distance telephone service providers, competitive access providers (CAPs), wireless communications services, cable television operators, and value-added services including a variety of specialized offerings that can be accessed over the regular telephone network or via special carrier networks.

Although there is no industry agreement on definitions for value-added network services, several service categories are generally recognized. Traditional value-added network services include packet transmission and protocol conversion. Newer information services include on-line databases and electronic yellow pages. There are messaging and conferencing services such as voice messaging, electronic mail, specialized fax services, audioconferencing, and specialized data services such as frame relay, new services being introduced over ISDN, and transaction processing services such as electronic data interchange (EDI). All of these methods of electronic communication can be carried over several lines, including telephone, cable, and wireless.

There are also advanced PBX systems designed to handle voice communications and faxes, and in some cases data transfers between computer modems are an important segment of the telecommunications industry. Offices with as few as two or as many as several hundred computers may be networked so that each of these computers can communicate with any of the others. PBX systems support local area computer networks (LANs), and are designed to handle computerized communication functions such as electronic mail and shared databases.

Pagers are radio receivers that are programmed to display simple messages, such as the telephone number of someone trying to reach them. Cellular phones are actual telephones, connected to the network not by wires, but by a radio signal. Each cellular phone operates off a host antenna located nearest to it. As the caller moves from one area to another (called "cells") the system hands the call over to another antenna in an adjacent cell. This allows the caller to roam anywhere within a service area without losing the connection.

Telecommunications is a business tool, every bit as essential to an enterprise as personnel, capital, and marketing. To a manager, telecommunications is synonymous with access—access to capital, access to markets, access to information—and it becomes increasingly important as time becomes a greater competitive factor.

The proliferation of ever more efficient networks, banded together to form one gigantic network, provide users as well as service providers with tremendous economies of scale. The result is a business resource that can establish agreements and contracts, maintain good relationships, and even provide products. As a result, good management of the telecommunications system is essential. As a result, the telecommunications services industry is growing rapidly.

Domestic Market Overview

Although traditionally highly regulated, over the past decade, the US telecommunications industry has been characterized by continued deregulation, increasing competition, an emphasis on data communication and digital technology, and globalization. In addition, traditional distinctions between different communication and transmission industries have become blurred. Telecommunications companies are increasingly branching out into cable television, cellular telephone, and satellite communications, as well as an array of other communication services. Cable television and other electronic media providers are moving into telecommunications. Fundamental to modern business, the telecommunications industry is likely to continue to undergo steady overall expansion over the next several years, as well as continued mergers into comprehensive communications services providers.

The telecommunications industry serves 100 percent of American businesses and 95 percent of American households, resulting in more than one telephone line for every two citizens—the highest concentration in world.

The US telecommunications industry is broadly divided into providers serving the communications markets for local exchange, long distance, international, cellular and mobile radio, satellite, and data communications. The industry is comprised of both regulated common carriers and unregulated network providers. The Federal Communications Commission regulates interstate common carrier communications, while individual state public utility commissions regulate communications within their jurisdictions.

Local service providers operate separately and under separate regulations from long distance providers; there are over 1300 local telephone companies in the United States. Until recently, each local carrier had a monopoly in its area, and all calls between the business and other parties on network were switched through this local exchange carrier (LEC). Businesses were served by this single local carrier that was authorized by the federal government to provide service in a given area. Local telephone services have, however, recently been opened to competition, and it is anticipated that local providers will soon be operating much like, or in conjunction with, the long distance providers. Already, many local service providers have begun restructuring operations and promoting service plans designed to more effectively compete in the new, free market.

Many cellular and personal communications service providers are eagerly positioning themselves to capture a significant share of the local access market for traditional voice and low rate data transmission. Cable TV companies are also eager to compete in the local telecommunications market. New digital and fiber optic technologies allow them to provide telephone services over their networks—something cable operators are already doing in other countries. There are no regulations prohibiting cable companies from offering these services, but approval from the PUC is probably required in order to provide any intrastate telecommunications services.

Cable companies are best poised to provide competition in the consumer markets. They already have hundreds of miles of cable running through neighborhoods, are connected to millions to households and have armies of repair and installation workers. More importantly, their wiring consists of coaxial cable, which can provide high-speed data and computer networking as well as television programs and telephone calls.

Unlike the local market, the long distance telecommunications market has long allowed competition, and fierce competitive wars characterized its development over the past decade. Over the next several years, however, long distance carriers will likely become increasingly involved in the local loop through wireless technology. The major long distance carriers will continue to focus on the global marketplace, in part because of prospects for rapid growth in telecommunications in many foreign markets, although much will depend on the degree to which liberalization spreads among the world's major telecommunications markets.

The domestic telecommunications industry should continue to grow at an average pace of about five percent per year through the end of the century. The areas of fastest growth will be international long distance and CAP services, both of which should continue to realize double-digit growth. The market for data communications will also grow rapidly, prodding wireline servicers to convert their systems to digital technology and to increase their installation of fiber-optic lines.

New technology and more competitive markets will foster a proliferation of new services for both residential and business customers, including caller identification (which, with the purchase of special equipment, tells a customer who is calling); call blocking (which allows people to restrict access to their line); video-conferencing; three-way calling; and portable 1-800 numbers (which allow the same 1-800 number phone number to be switched to a different carrier).

The distinction between long distance carriers, local carriers, cellular service companies, satellite services, cable television providers, and other communications and electronics industries will become increasingly blurred as companies in different industries merge or form partnerships, resulting

in one-stop comprehensive communication services that handle voice, data, and video. Wireless technology has the potential to become a dominant industry force, obliterating the current structure and methods of the industry.

International Market Overview

International telecommunications is in a state of rapid change characterized by the development of new technologies and new services, new business alliances, and legal and regulatory changes affecting the structure of, and rules for, participation in telecommunications markets. The desire on the part of developing countries to modernize their communications infrastructure has led to deregulation and liberalization with the result that European and American telecom players are competing to provide and build new services. Traditionally, separate national networks have been connected internationally in accordance with service agreements between national telecommunications carriers, most often owned or controlled by the government. However, the emergence of new firms and service offerings—some of which provide alternatives to international voice service from foreign points, others which use private networks to bypass public switched network facilities—as well as liberalization of data services in some countries, are working to force a large scale restructuring of these long-standing arrangements for international telecommunications services. Many countries are coming to realize that a modern telecommunications infrastructure and the availability of high quality voice and date services are essential ingredients for economic growth and social well-being. Wireless growth in particular has been astronomical in China, Asia, Latin America, and the former Soviet bloc over the past 10 years.

US telecommunications service providers are among the most competitive in the world. Their technological experience, sophisticated marketing techniques, and the loosely regulated domestic environment enable them to enter foreign markets which allow international competition. The US has invested heavily in wireless telecommunications (which could eventually dominate long distance services), and its aggressive marketing and bold attempts to enter foreign markets have ensured its place as an industry leader at least for the next few years.

Both local and long distance carriers are actively seeking to expand overseas. Many are doing so through mergers and acquisitions, while others prefer partnerships or joint venture arrangements. The overall strength of the industry places it in an excellent position to take advantage of overseas opportunities as they arise. The knowledge, skills and advanced services possessed by US firms are assets that can help boost US exports to overseas markets as those telecommunications sectors open up to foreign investment and participation.

In the past few years, a global telecommunications market has developed, in part due to the increased importance of international trade and investment in the world economy, and spurred by the liberalization of telecommunications sectors in many countries. Facilities-based competition, permitting domestic and foreign companies to build networks to compete with the established government monopoly supplier, will become a reality in many countries. Also, 1-800 international and detailed billing services, made possible by advances in software and intelligent switching, will spread to new markets, as will electronic data communications services.

In addition to global ventures by US competitors, a growing number of foreign companies have begun to enter the US market since the reclassification by the FCC of carriers operating the US which reduced the regulatory control of foreign enterprises that invest in telecommunication services. Often the carriers in national markets lack the resources to compete. The solution has been to create alliances, mergers, and partnerships with some of the largest US and European carriers. These companies serve primarily smaller niche markets, but they are working to position themselves for the coming integration and globalization of telecommunications services.

Market Barriers

The telecommunications industry has traditionally been heavily regulated by government. The US has long been one of the more loosely regulated markets in the world, although for some time regulations and restrictions have been falling. Many countries are opening their wireless and value-added markets to foreign competition—often in partnership with a local provider. Opportunities in traditional wireline service remained more limited to outsiders, but this too is changing. Even in countries where legal or regulatory changes have been made to permit some competition in telecommunications services, such as in Australia, the Philippines, or the UK, the former monopoly provider has retained its dominant position.

Legal prohibitions, regulatory delay and policy uncertainty in many underdeveloped countries can complicate the business of telecommunications. Restrictions on the resale of leased circuit capacity, the connection of leased lines to the public network, and restriction on data service providers continue to impede access to many markets.

Market Channels

Due to the large economies of scale in the telecommunications industry, and the massive investment in infrastructure often required, many companies operate as consortiums or joint ventures. In many countries, the government (or one of its agencies) will be a key partner in any undertaking in this industry.

Licensing arrangements are another popular method of doing business abroad, especially in this time of rapid change and liberalization throughout the industry. Companies like Motorola in Argentina, for example, which initially entered the market through licensing agreements (in order to comply with then restrictive regulations), are finding themselves now in a dominant market position and able to go it alone as the government has loosened its restrictions on foreign investment.

In the wireless communications sector cellular licensing is a growing trend.

Before Entering a Market

Technology

Technology development is perhaps the most important factor to consider before entering a foreign market. Technological standards differ around the world—for instance, much of Europe and Australia employ identical standards, which are presently incompatible with those utilized in the US—and thus the equipment and services you intend to offer must be compatible with those standards.

Infrastructure

Infrastructure is another important consideration. Many countries simply do not have adequate or up-to-date telephone lines to serve the population. While this may in and of itself present opportunities for export, it is more likely to be somewhat inhibiting in providing telecommunications services abroad. Telecommunications often operates on huge economies of scale (which explains its long tradition of governmental regulation) and these are hard to achieve in places like the Philippines, for example, which has only about seven telephone lines per 100 inhabitants, most of which are located in central Manila!

Regional Opportunities

Note: These are only examples of regional opportunities and in no way constitute a complete list.

Mexico

The North American Free Trade Agreement significantly liberalized the provision of enhanced telecommunications services in Mexico. As the Mexican economy expands and the modernization of the country's telecommunications network continues, a growing market for value-added services will emerge. Since US service providers have expertise in software development and customer support series, they will be able to take advantage of emerging opportunities in Mexico's information services market.

NAFTA guarantees US telecommunications companies access to and use of the Mexican public telecommunications network for their own international communications networks. US companies are now able to operate their corporate communications networks across the border without a local partner. Other NAFTA provisions require that telecommunications service tariffs reflect the economic cost of providing the service and establish safeguards that constrain anti-competitive behavior by monopoly telephone companies.

Mexico's telecommunications sector is one of its most promising areas of opportunity. Improvements are being made to the system and private companies are now allowed to invest in this sector. Concessions have been granted to companies offering advanced services, including satellite pagers, trucking radio services, and radiotelephones. Cellular phone service is available in the largest business centers.

Australia

Australia's telecommunications system incorporates the

very latest technology, providing simple operations and rapid access for businesses through telephone calls, facsimile and data transfers. A modern communications system, supported by satellite, microwave, optical fiber and radio technology, makes voice, video and data contact with international networks instantly possible from even the most remote parts of the country. In 1990, the government introduced across the board competition in the delivery of telecommunications services, and loosened restrictions on foreign participation in the industry.

Australia's telecommunications market is expanding as the country eagerly embraces the superhighway concept of international communications. Demand for comprehensive and sophisticated telecommunications services is especially high throughout rural Australia, where a surprising number of businesses are found. Technologies are being implemented that will see a host of digital services being provided to homes even in the most remote locations. The mobile-phone sector has grown tremendously and is now worth A$1.5 billion a year; the number of subscribers has surpassed one million, and is expected to keep growing. The industry is preparing for further expansion, both to keep up with the competition and to benefit from the rapid advance in telecommunications technology.

Asia

The Asian markets in value-added services, which are growing at a phenomenal rate. Liberalization of international value-added network service regulations and market access is taking hold in places such as the Philippines, Taiwan, Thailand and Singapore. The cable and satellite industries all across Asia have experienced explosive growth over the past years, and this trend is expected to continue with the economic development of the region.

There are many opportunities to be found. Unlike many western markets, which are reaching saturation point for many traditional telecommunications services, many Asian nations are only now wiring homes for electronic communications. While they are not always ready for the latest technologies and gadgets, they are rapidly developing markets for more traditional services, which will continue to grow as expansion continues. Foreign firms who establish themselves early in these economies which thrive on long-term business relationships will be well placed to grow with the technology and to be at the forefront as demand for newer and better equipment and services continues to grow.

Japan

Japan's telecommunications industry has been largely deregulated, although entry and participation therein is still quite complex and cumbersome. The market for mobile communications is expanding rapidly, and is far from saturated. Digital cordless telephone equipment and services represent lucrative opportunities, as do on-line databases and electronic messaging. It should be noted, however, that foreign firms need to establish nationwide distribution channels in order to compete against Japanese vendors, so strategic alliances with Japanese manufacturers or trading firms may be the best way to go.

Best Bet Opportunities

Note: These are only examples of industry opportunities and in no way constitute a complete list.

International Value-Added Network Services (IVANS)

Unlike basic voice and data telecommunications services that are still reserved for the dominant telecommunications operator in most countries, foreign firms are allowed to offer IVANS (although still under many restrictions in most countries) in most of the major world telecommunications markets. Information services, including on-line databases and electronic yellow pages, continue to grow faster than voice services, and are expected to grow from 13 to 15 percent yearly over the next several years.

Electronic mail services are growing especially fast. Enhanced fax services, transactional-related services such as electronic data interchange (whose usage internationally will markedly increase over the next few years) and public data services will offer the best potential for investors.

There is no reliable number for fax transmission services because faxes appear on the network as regular telephone calls, but it is estimated that over 40 percent of all international calls between the US and Japan, for example, are fax messages.

Although the domestic on-line database market is a more mature market, increased access to US-based databases by overseas customers is a potentially lucrative niche.

Call-Back

High prices for calling the US from abroad have provided opportunities for US telecommunications firms to offer international discounted telephone services. The firms resell US carriers' international 800 services or international switched voice or private line services and operate only from foreign soil. In some cases, and what seems to represent a growing niche, users can also access enhanced services such as voice mail and fax broadcasting on a global basis and receive multi-currency billing and worldwide system access through a calling card.

A call-back arrangement allows a subscriber abroad to dial a particular US telephone number, let it ring, and then hang up. A computer attached to the line calls the subscriber back at his number abroad and provides a dial tone. The subscriber then can dial any number in the US or worldwide and be billed at US rates.

Although call-back services have so far captured only a tiny share of the US inward bound telephone traffic it is a competitive alternative to the foreign monopoly carrier for making international calls. Revenues for firms providing this service are expected to double each year over the next few years.

Multimedia/Interactive Services

Technology and applications that could deliver telecommunications and computer services (including voice, data and video services) as well as pay-per-view movies, interactive shopping, and an enormous number of TV channels into the home are being created from the convergence of communications technology, computers, consumer electronics, and entertainment. Interactive services accessed through the telephone line offer the best potential for simple and convenient operation of these services. Local telephone companies are looking to invest in or work with other industries in an effort to fully develop this technology.

Travel Calling Cards

An increasingly popular means of international calling makes use of prepaid travel telephone cards issued by individual carriers. Many travel cards are now marketed to residents in foreign countries and many foreign carriers are now beginning to offer similar travel cards for international calling. Forth foreign carriers now offer their country direct services from the US through use of travel telephone cards.

Cellular

This sector is expected to register phenomenal growth through the year 2000 and beyond. Largely driven by declining equipment costs, the cellular industry has begun to attract users from the consumer market at a higher rate than business users. Although this trend is bringing down average revenues per subscriber, industry revenues should continue to increase as new service offerings, such as messaging, become available during the next few years.

Many local carriers have already made hefty investments in cellular systems, and are already looking for new and improved technology in order to expand on this tremendous market.

Paging

The paging industry has also shown remarkable growth during the last few years. Despite being one of the oldest wireless telecommunications technologies, paging continues to see record growth in both subscribers and revenues, driven by lower costs of both service and subscriber equipment, as well as the increasing availability of advanced services.

The most significant trend for the future of the industry is the increasing number of non-business users. The mass consumer market is a new one for paging, and carriers will pursue it aggressively through retail marketing and special promotions. This tremendous growth has been fueled in part by the increased use of pagers as screening devices by cellular users. Because it is much less expensive to receive a page than an incoming cellular call, cellular users find it more economical to give out their pager number and return only the most urgent cellular calls. It is estimated that over 20 percent of all cellular subscribers employ paging in this manner.

Paging is well positioned to capture part of the potentially huge wireless data market, especially with the increased use of alphanumeric pagers.

Competitive Access Providers (CAPS)

CAPS are the fastest growing segment of the telecommunications industry, growing between 15 and 20 percent each year over the past few years. CAPS offer local telephone services to businesses by furnishing dedicated fiber-optic telephone lines that connect the customer to a long distance carrier, thus allowing the customer to bypass the high business rates charged by local carriers. CAPS are not subject to government regulation so they are able to deliver service to high-volume corporate customers at reduced rates.

Sources of US Assistance

American Public Communications Council
10306 Eaton Pl., Ste. 520
Fairfax, VA 22030
Tel: (703) 385-5300
Represents manufacturers, suppliers, distributors, and operators involved in the sale, lease, installation, and maintenance of pay telephone equipment.

Association of Telemessaging Services International
1150 S. Washington St., Ste. 150
Alexandria, VA 22314
Tel: (703) 684-0016
Seeks to foster growth in the industry; represent members interests before Congress and regulatory agencies.

Carrier Liaison Committee
1200 G St. NW, Ste. 500
Washington, DC 20005
Tel: (202) 434-8824
Works to resolve issues associated with exchange access service industry.

Cellular Telecommunications Industry Association
1250 Connecticut Ave. NW, Ste. 200
Washington, DC 20036
Tel: (202) 785-0081
Fax: (202) 785-0721
Represents enterprises actively engaged in cellular radio-telephone communications industry.

Inter-American Telecommunications Conference
c/o OAS
1889 F. St. NW
Washington, DC 20006
Tel: (202) 458-3004
Fax: (202) 245-6854
Represents countries organized to facilitate the advancement of telecommunications industries in the Americas. Studies and educates regarding government regulations affecting the industry.

International Communications Association
12750 Merit Dr., Ste. 710-LB-89
Dallas, TX 75251
Tel: (214) 233-3889
Fax: (214) 233-2813

International Telecommunications Society
University of Colorado Campus
Box 530
Boulder, CO 80309
Tel: (303) 492-8717

Fax: (303) 492-1112
*Concerned with telecommunications planning, policy forma-
tion, and economic analysis.*

National Association of Cellular Agents
6128 Snowden
Mesa, AZ 85215
Tel: (713) 522-0528
Fax: (713) 820-228
*Works to foster members' financial and professional success
in the cellular industry.*

Publications

**US Telecommunications in a Global Economy: Competi-
tiveness at a Crossroads**
US Dept. of Commerce
Washington DC 20230
Tel: (202) 783-3238

International Communications Traffic Data Report
Federal Communications Commission
1250 23rd St. NW
Plaza Level
Washington, DC 20254
Tel: (202) 632-0745

**Reference Book: Rates, Price Indexes, and Household
Expenditures for Telephone Service Federal Communica-
tions Commission**
1250 23rd St. NW
Plaza Level
Washington, DC 20254
Tel: (202) 632-0745

Communications Week International
CMP Publications, Inc.
600 Community Dr.
Manhasset, NY 11030
Tel: (516) 562-5882

**Telecommunications Market Review and Forecast:
Annual Report of the Telecommunications Industry**
North American Telecommunications Association
2000 M St. NW
Washington, DC 20036
Tel: (202) 296-9800

Travel and Tourism

Defined

The travel industry is really a conglomeration of different and often interrelated sectors, many of which are themselves made up of several sub-sectors. Transportation, lodging, eating and drinking establishments, entertainment, consumer goods, and travel agency services are some of the primary sectors that together make up the travel industry.

The transportation sector includes travel by air, train, boat, automobile, bus, taxicab, and recreational vehicle. It also includes automobile rentals, gasoline service stations and other related services which are necessary to support travel by any of the above means.

The lodging sector is made up of hotels and motels, campgrounds and trailor parks, and private residence rentals. Food service is often connected to lodging, and it is certainly interrelated, but it makes up its own sector of the travel industry. Restaurants, bars and other food and beverage establishments, as well as grocery stores, are included in this category.

Travel entertainment and consumer goods enterprises are generally limited to those directly associated with or connected to another travel-related sector, although many local entertainment and retail establishments cater to and are influenced by the local tourist market as well. In general, travel entertainment and consumer goods enterprises are connected to or associated with a hotel or a transportation enterprise. Their revenues are generated directly by the primary enterprise and they receive little outside business.

Travel agency services are an important engine for the travel industry. Although travelers are increasingly taking advantage of on-line technology that allows them to research and book their own travel itineraries, travel agency services continue to be a driving force in the industry, especially in the international travel market.

Together these sectors make up the travel industry, which can then be further divided into domestic and international, business and tourism. While domestic travel clearly involves travel within a nation's own borders and international travel involves a crossing of national borders, there is no set definition to distinguish business travel from tourism. Nor is there an established set of circumstances under which one can be said to travel as a tourist or on business; in fact, more often than not, travel for many people involves an element of both. In general, however, tourism is overnight travel for pleasure, family reasons, health, to meetings, or in a representative capacity of any kind, as opposed to overnight travel for the purpose of obtaining pay from products sold or services performed at the destination.

Domestic Market Overview

The travel industry has always been a large and growing sector of the US economy. Although domestic travel far exceeds international travel (almost 90 percent of overnight trips are to destinations within the US), international travel is growing more rapidly—the rate of increase in international travel expenditures was nearly twice that of domestic travel expenditures from 1994 to 1995. The domestic industry, however, is not suffering. Total travel spending in the US, by both US and foreign travelers, grew by nearly six percent in 1994.

The US travel industry is made up a wide variety of business organizations and individual service providers. Most travel agencies and restaurants, for example, are small businesses, while the airline and lodging sectors are dominated by a few large, multinational organizations.

The domestic travel market has changed radically over the past decade as internationalization in business has given rise both to increased international travel for business purposes and to larger numbers of affluent consumers in the developing countries, many of whom travel to the US for pleasure. In addition, increased competition from many newly developed or developing countries as travel destinations, as well as competition from foreign service providers, has given rise to a trend in US travel toward price-shopping for travel and travel-related services. There has also been a clear trend toward travel to all-inclusive destination resorts which offer a variety of goods and services for one price, environmental travel tours which specialize in educational sight-seeing excursions, and guided adventure tours. This has hurt the travel industry in many large US cities which traditionally played host to domestic visitors.

Another trend which has become more and more noticeable over the past decade is the shift toward shorter, weekend or extended weekend vacations instead of the traditional two-week vacation favored in the past. Weekend trips accounted for over 55 percent of total domestic tourist travel in 1993. Domestic business travel, on the other hand, has remained fairly stable over the past several years, both in terms of length of time and expenditures made for such travel.

Domestic travel has grown by between 2 and 5 percent each year over the past five years. The Southeast region of the country is the most popular destination, followed by the West and the Midwest. The US accounts for approximately eight percent of world tourist arrivals and just over 10 percent of world tourism receipts.

By far the most popular mode of domestic travel is by private automobile. Despite vigorous price wars between the airlines and the trend toward shorter trips, nearly 80 percent of all trips taken within the US are by automobile. The relatively cheap price of gasoline in the US makes travel by auto quite inexpensive, and this is expected to continue in the near term despite the increase in the federal gasoline tax.

US commercial airliners carry approximately 500 million passengers each year, with domestic traffic accounting for more than 91 percent of the total passenger emplanements. The US airline industry is expected to continue the consolidation of the large airlines which service longer routes, and an increase in discount commuter airlines which offer skimmed-back services and easy access for short-haul flights.

Cruise lines have shown increased passenger volumes and a wider variety of routes in the past five years, and this sector is expected to continue to grow rapidly as higher visibility and discounted fares, coupled with strong travel agent support, lure a broader range of traveler.

Travel lodging and food and beverage establishments are beginning to recover from the slowdown which occurred as a result of changes in US tax law which limited the availability of business expense deduction for such expenditures. This sector grew by five percent in 1995 and is expected to show similar growth patterns in the near term.

Within the US travel industry, eating and drinking establishments, individualized transportation services (including taxicabs), and specialized local travel support services offer the best opportunities for entrepreneurs to successfully become involved in this lucrative and growing market.

International Market Overview

.US airlines, hotel firms, and travel agencies are preeminent throughout many parts of the world. Along with some large European and Japanese companies, US firms enjoy a tremendous competitive advantage over many local enterprises in foreign countries because of their ready access to their own affluent domestic markets and their ability to make use of economies of scale in purchasing and service provider arrangements. Often, several US travel service providers will work together to provide a broad range of travel services from one central, and hopefully convenient, clearing organization. In this way, they are able to bind together air and ground transportation, lodging, entertainment, and, in some cases meals, in one purchase.

There are two primary reasons why US firms should be able not only to continue to enjoy widespread acceptance worldwide, but also to increase the range and depth of services they provide to travelers in many parts of the world. First, US firms from all sectors of the travel industry have traditionally been leaders in opening and promoting both tourist and business travel areas. As such, they enjoy widespread and positive name recognition, as well as a reputation for reliability, comfort and quality in the goods and services they provide. This is further enhanced by the sheer numbers of US travelers to be found all over the world (surpassed only by the Japanese). The number of US travelers traveling internationally has been called a "mini-mass-market," both in terms of absolute size (nearly 50 million in 1995) and in the relatively small proportion of US travelers it represents overall. Only about 10 percent of tourist travel taken by US residents is outside the country, providing huge potential for growth in this area.

Travelers will generally favor a domestic provider over an unfamiliar local one, and US firms have been quick and efficient in meeting this need. From air travel to fast food, US firms have made tremendous inroads wherever travelers are found. And this process perpetuates itself: more US travelers become willing to travel abroad as more familiar goods and services become available in foreign locations.

Most US travelers who travel outside the country continue to visit Canada (about one-third) and Mexico (about one-third and growing rapidly). Travel to Mexico has shown the greatest increase in recent years—increasing by between three and seven percent each year over the past few years. Over 50 million Americans visit Mexico each year, and the number is expected to continue to grow with the implementation of the North American Free Trade Agreement. Travel to Canada, while continuing to make a very strong showing, has increased only slightly over the past few years.

NAFTA, which substantially liberalizes cross-border trade in travel and travel-related services, has been a boon to the travel industry in these three countries. US firms from all sectors of the travel industry are well represented in both Canada and Mexico, and there is still room for more.

Another 17 percent of US international travelers go to Europe. The most popular European destinations for US travelers are the United Kingdom, Germany, France, Switzerland, and Italy. Over 70 percent of US travelers to Europe visit only one country; only about 12 percent visit three or more countries. Although US travel to Europe increased remarkably between 1970 and 1985, it has since leveled out, and absolute numbers have remained fairly flat over the past few years. In the future, it is likely that European integration will increase business travel from the United States.

Before Entering a Market

Although the travel industry is made up of numerous segments, offering a variety of goods and services, entry into this market is not always simple. While some services, such as eating and drinking, entertainment, and taxicabs, offer opportunities for individual entrepreneurs or small businesses, many others, such as long-range transportation and lodging, are and will probably continue to be dominated by large, multinational organizations.

There are several considerations which must be addressed before entering this diverse and complex market:

Define the market

Whether you intend to commence operations in the US or in a foreign country you must decide whether you will be catering primarily to domestic travelers or to foreign travelers, or to both. Pricing, the type and quality of services offered, presentation, and adaptability are all factors which must be considered and modified in accordance with who you think your customer is.

Will the location support your product?

You must have the organizational capability to adapt products to coincide with the infrastructure within which you must work. This includes having access to suppliers who produce a wide variety of good and services (or at least all necessary goods and services) that are required for the operation of your business. You must also be able to employ qualified personnel at all levels at reasonable wages.

Will the population support your good or service?

Other things being equal, regions and countries with large populations generate larger volumes of travelers. This is not true in places such as India and China where a huge proportion of the population lives in poverty, but generally countries with a large middle class have a larger number of people with the money to travel. In countries such as India and China which are in the process of significant economic reforms, the growing middle classes will likely produce a substantial increase in the number of people willing and able to travel and thus demanding travel services. These countries provide the greatest potential for long-term growth.

Does a country or region mandate generous annual leave entitlements?

A major contributor to the amount of travel time people have is the amount of paid time-off available to them. In some countries, especially many European ones, the minimum annual leave entitlement is five weeks; in Australia it is four, in New Zealand and Canada three. In general, the more time available, the more time they will spend and the farther people will travel. This will impact both the type and quantity of goods and services demanded.

Are exchange rates volatile or stable?

Relative exchange rates can have a tremendous impact on the number of travelers entering and leaving a country. A country whose currency is relatively weak will likely see an increase in both foreign and domestic visitors as its attractions become inexpensive in comparison with those available elsewhere. A country with a strong currency, on the other hand, will probably see a decline in the overall number of visitors as domestic travelers choose to visit a relatively less expensive country, and foreign visitors are unable to afford local attractions. In general, the fortunes of the travel industry will rise and fall inversely to currency fluctuations.

Market Barriers

Government Barriers

Although the near-universal trend is towards liberalizing trade regulations, many governments continue to throw up stringent barriers against the entry of foreign providers into their markets. Developing countries, especially, fear that their own infant service industries will be driven out of business by entering transnationals which are often bigger, stronger, and far more experienced than the struggling local industry. There are virtually unlimited ways in which a government can impose barriers against the entry of foreign firms, but some of the more common ones include: regulations forbidding foreign participation or requiring local participation in business concerns, heavy taxation of foreign firms, cumbersome licensing or regulatory requirements, laws against foreign ownership of property, and restrictions on capital and repatriation of earnings.

A special barrier found in the US is the Americans with Disabilities Act, which has required all sectors of the travel industry to make structural adjustments to their properties and to augment their staffing to accommodate travelers with wheel chairs, oxygen tanks, and a plethora of other special needs.

Economic Barriers

Economic barriers, including lack of adequate financing options, lack of available capital, the price of input factors and supplies, the cost of labor, and the time required to get an enterprise up and running, can be significant barriers to operating a travel or travel-related service abroad. Many countries maintain heavy and comprehensive tax structures, which can quickly wipe out would-be profits. In all cases, even if financial implications look all right on paper, a visit to the country and a meeting with a local accountant should always be undertaken before the go-ahead is given to locate abroad.

Social and Cultural Barriers

Perhaps the most significant potential barrier for travel and travel-related service providers is the vast social and cultural differences they are likely to encounter in their clientele. Many societies are voluminous meat eaters and would not consider traveling where none is available; others are quite offended by the practice of eating meat and are equally loathe to travel to a place where this is done openly. Some cultures are open and liberal about physical appearances and their dress reflects what to other cultures seems a despicable lack of morals. Some cultures favor loud and raucous behavior, others abhor it. In short, it is very difficult to adapt your service or product to appeal perfectly to the wide variety of cultural traditions and beliefs found around the world.

A knowledgeable and well thought out decision must be made as to an appropriate level of adaptability, and you must then tailor your goods or services accordingly and market your product appropriately. Unfortunately, there is rarely, if ever, a formula that will apply to make this decision easier; more often than not it is a difficult process of trial and error.

Market Channels

There are nearly as many ways to do business in the travel industry as there are goods and services to sell. Individual entrepreneurs or small businesses are often found in the eating and drinking, entertainment, and taxicab sectors, while large, well-known, multinational corporations dominate the air travel, cruise, lodging, and car rental businesses. Many train services are operated by government, or quasi-government organizations, and private ownership is rare.

A recent trend in many areas has been to utilize cooperative or joint efforts of several sectors to "bundle" travel services into one or a few packages. This can be done within a geographic region, such as where service providers across several sectors bundle a comprehensive package for a complete travel itinerary. It is also done within a sector by joining with providers in other geographic areas to create a comprehensive network to provide a single product or service. Many airlines operate joint agreements with foreign or commuter carriers, each one specializing in its own routes, and moving passengers beyond these routes through joint reservation, ticketing, and baggage services.

Cross-sector or cross-region bundling is likely to become more popular as travel and travel-related service providers realize the tremendous benefits and increased markets they can attain through such arrangements.

Regional Opportunities

Note: These are only examples of regional opportunities and in no way constitute a complete list.

The vast majority of travel occurs in developed countries, although developing countries contribute significantly to the numbers traveling in developed countries as their growing middle classes increase their travel abroad. Europe receives over 65 percent of all international arrivals and approximately 60 percent of all travel receipts. The US receives nearly 13 percent of all international arrivals and over 20 percent of all receipts. East Asia and the Pacific, which account for 10 percent of arrivals, are the regions showing the most growth. Estimates by the travel industry indicate that between 1990 and 2000 the number of international trips will more than double for Germany, Denmark, and Norway; almost triple for the UK, Spain, and Japan; and more than quadruple for Sweden. The number of international trips taken by US residents, however, is forecast to decline by 17 percent.

The two leading generators of international tourism expenditures are the US and West Germany, followed by the UK, Japan, France, Canada, and the Netherlands.

The vast majority of international travel occur between neighboring countries, and this is true in the US, where the majority of visitors arrive from Canada and Mexico. However, travel and tourism between the US and more distant countries should grow as a result of US bilateral and multilateral trade, investment, and tourism agreement—including those with Poland, Hungary, Argentina, and Venezuela.

Asia/Pacific Rim

Rapidly growing economies of this region present almost unlimited opportunities for US travel and travel-related service providers. Many governments, including the Philippines, Australia, New Zealand, Taiwan, and Korea, are actively liberalizing restrictions on foreign participation in many industries - especially travel. In addition, the numbers of tourists arriving in the US from these countries is growing at a phenomenal rate. Visits from Taiwan residents alone increased by over 25 percent from 1991 to 1992; although the rate of increase has slowed somewhat, it is still expected to show strong growth over the medium term. The increasing affluence of people from this region means they are more willing to spend money on luxury tours or on trips to unique destinations. Tours with special themes are popular: golf tours, wildlife tours, intensive English language training tours, and tours specially designed for parents and kids have shown remarkable growth over the past few years.

Taiwan provides perhaps the most intriguing opportunities, as its government is rapidly eliminating restrictions on all sectors of the economy, and is actively seeking to build the country into the premier gateway to Asia. This emphasis on travel will create demand for a wide variety of goods and services, and the government seems to recognize that many of these will be provided by foreigners.

Thailand is another rapidly growing market. Thai travelers, coming from one of the fastest growing economies in the world, have shifted away from nearby destinations in Thailand and surrounding countries to more distant destinations, including the US. Thai travel to the US has grown by approximately 10 percent each year over the past few years. The influence of American culture on Thai society is evident throughout the country. With this constant exposure to Americana, the US is a dreamed of destination for many Thai tourists, and the opportunities for travel and travel-related service providers are many.

Latin America

Travel to the US from Latin America, led by Mexico, has shown and will continue to show rapid growth. The business opportunities presented by NAFTA have generated a huge demand for travel-related services between the two countries, and liberalized regulations have created many opportunities for providers of those services. Business travel to fairs and exhibitions has increased exponentially, and travel to pleasure resorts, national parks and theme attractions has shown steady growth as Latin America's fortunes grow. The US could increase the number of Latin American travellers by effective promotion of non-traditional destinations, by promoting trade fairs and exhibitions together with attractive tourist packages, and by widely publicizing special cultural and sport events which are popular with Latin Americans.

American companies that wish to penetrate the Latin American markets can best do so through a local representative. Many US hotels, car rentals, cruise lines, attractions and other tourism related companies that are represented in Latin America have increased considerably their sales volume by having a representative with well-established relations with the local tourism industry and especially with the local travel agencies.

Europe

Two-way travel between Europe and the US has always been popular, although the past decade has seen a significant decrease in the rate of growth as travel across the Pacific has grown in popularity. Implementation of the European Community (EC) should provide opportunities for US travel providers as they will no longer have to comply with the various rules and regulations in the different countries. The single community will also create economies of scale in production, advertising and sales.

The relatively generous annual leave entitlements found in many European countries allow Europeans to take longer and more diverse vacations, and they are generally familiar with and interested in US destinations. However, current trends and the sophistication of the market dictate special needs in generating future demand for travel to the US; these include the need to increase individual travel, improve the quality level, target groups with a higher education level, and exploit the increasing interest for long-haul destinations.

Saudi Arabia

Special mention must be made of the opportunities to exploit the tremendous increase in travel and trade between the US and Saudi Arabia over the past couple of years. Both Saudi and non-Saudi citizens living and working in the Kingdom travel to the US principally for tourism, business, education and medical treatment. Saudi-originated travel to the US grew by seven percent between 1993 and 1995, and the figures look likely to grow further over the next few years. Most tourists from Saudi Arabia do not use a travel agent or buy a tour, but the things they do and places they go suggests that they are a lucrative potential market for more organized tourist services. There is a significant percentage of group travellers among Saudi-origin tourists, many of whom enter the US in cities that lend themselves to organized tourism services. Further, in traditional Islamic societies such as Saudi Arabia, larger families are the norm; organized tourist travel to amusement and theme parks as well as other family oriented destinations with attractions featured in international print and electronic media have strong sales potential. Organized tour packages that include family-oriented destinations in Florida, California, Hawaii, New York, Texas, Colorado and Washington, DC would be the strongest performers. The provision of Arabic-speaking guides by travel agencies in key entry points would also be a strong selling point.

Saudi residents, and local tour operators and travel agents, look for good service, good prices, and reliability. Reputation is most important and name recognition of a tourist destination of US travel agent weighs very heavily in the tourist travel decisions of Saudi residents.

Best Bet Opportunities

Note: These are only examples of industry opportunities and in no way constitute a complete list.

Eating and Drinking

Food and beverage services are predominantly run by individual entrepreneurs or small businesses. Except for a few nationally recognized chains and franchises which will draw a certain proportion of travelers, local eating and drinking establishments have fared well with visitors to most areas. Appearance, price and service are the most important factors in drawing visitors, and locating near to hotels or other travel attractions is almost a necessity.

Local Ground Transportation

There is much demand for taxicab and other local transportation services in larger cities as many travelers (especially foreign ones) are hesitant to drive in unfamiliar locales. Also, local tour service providers can become quite successful, especially if they link up or somehow otherwise generate sales through hotels or other lodging organizations.

Travel Agents

There is increasing demand for travel agents to put together comprehensive or all-inclusive tour packages for travelers arriving from abroad. Family oriented tours and destinations are especially popular, as are specialized wildlife or environmental tours.

Sources of US Based Assistance

US Department of Commerce
International Trade Administration/Tourism Industries
Washington, DC 20230
Tel: (202) 482-0140
Fax: (202) 482-2887

Office of Technology Assessment
Congress of the United States
US Travel Data Center
1133 21st Street., NW
Washington, DC 20036
Tel: (202) 293-1040

Air Transport Association of America
1300 Pennsylvania Avenue, NW
Suite 1100
Washington, DC 20004
Tel: (202) 626-4000

The Travel Industry Association of America
2 Lafayette Center
1133 21st St., NW
Washington, DC 20036
Tel: (202) 293-1433

Publications

Analysis: The Potential of International Pleasure Travel Markets to the USA
US Dept. of Commerce
International Trade Administration
Washington, DC 20230
Tel: (202) 482-0140
Fax: (202) 482-2887

Travel Market Report
US Travel Data Center
1133 21st St., NW
Washington, DC 20036
Tel: (202) 293-1040

Survey of Business Travelers
US Travel Data Center
1133 21st St., NW
Washington, DC 20036
Tel: (202) 293-1040

Economic Review of Travel in America
US Travel Data Center
1133 21st St., NW
Washington, DC 20036
Tel: (202) 293-1040

Summary and Analysis of International Travel to the United States
US Dept. of Commerce
International Trade Administration
Washington, DC 20230
Tel: (202) 482-0140
Fax: (202) 482-2887

Internet Sites

American Society of Travel Agents (ASTA)
http://www.astanet.com/

Association of Corporate Travel Executives
http://www.acte.org/

National Business Travel Association
http://www.nbta.org/

Tourism Industries (ITA-DOC)
http://tinet.ita.doc.gov

Wholesaling

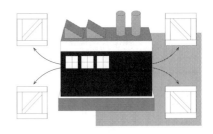

Defined

Wholesalers and distributors buy products from manufacturers, then sort, assemble, grade, and store them so they will be resold to retailers and commercial, agricultural, governmental, and industrial users.

Some products wholesaling companies distribute include:

- apparel and clothing
- beer, wine, and distilled alcoholic beverages
- durable and nondurable goods
- pharmaceutical products
- electrical goods
- farm products
- furniture and home furnishings
- groceries and related products
- hardware
- lumber and other construction materials
- machinery, equipment, and supplies
- metals and minerals
- motor vehicle parts, and supplies
- paper and paper products
- petroleum and petroleum products
- plumbing and heating equipment
- professional and commercial equipment and supplies

The wholesaling industry has three categories: merchant wholesalers, manufacturers' sales branches and offices, and commission merchants. Merchant wholesalers account for about 60 percent of all wholesale sales, and at least a majority of all sales in each major product line except motor vehicles and parts. Merchant wholesalers are distinguished from other types of wholesalers in that they actually take title to the goods. They may also sort, assemble, grade, and store them. Some also provide certain "value-added" services, such as packaging and labeling—a business strategy that is becoming increasingly important as thousands of wholesalers, selling products that are similar in quality and design, compete for customers.

Other wholesale transactions involve agents or brokers, who sell supplier-owned products primarily to retailers and other wholesalers for a commission or fee, and manufacturers' sales branches and offices, which sell the parent manufacturer's products mainly to retailers and industrial users.

Domestic Market Overview

The wholesaling industry, a large and diverse sector of the US economy, employs approximately six million people and sells an estimated US$3.2 trillion in raw materials and manufactured products. The industry is highly fragmented, consisting of a few large companies and many small firms. The number of wholesalers has dropped from 364,000 firms counted by the Census Bureau in 1987 to approximately 280,000 companies in 1993, and has continued to fall due to mergers, acquisitions and business failures.

Merchant wholesalers have been challenged recently, primarily by so-called "alternative" channels of distribution. The most popular alternative channels of wholesale distribution are direct manufacturer-to-retail arrangements, usually made under strategic alliances with major retail chain stores, warehouse clubs, discount stores, and home center stores.

Merchant wholesalers have also been challenged by the changing mix of products they have carried over the past decade. They are becoming more dependent on product lines, such as consumer goods, that are increasingly being distributed through alternative channels and therefore represent a shrinking market for wholesalers.

The market for bulk commodities is a mature one, with little or no growth. For example, sales of farm raw materials, a major bulk commodity line, dropped more than 12 percent from 1988 to 1994. Metals and minerals also showed a drop in sales over the period. The other bulk commodity lines showed minor growth during the same period.

The consumer product group is of increasing importance for merchant wholesalers, now accounting for nearly 54 percent of all sales revenue for merchant wholesalers, up from 52 percent in 1988. The major product lines within this group, in terms of sales volume, are: groceries; durables not elsewhere classified, such as sporting goods, toys, and jewelry; and motor vehicles and parts. Nearly all consumer products handled by merchant wholesalers are also distributed through alternative channels. The increasing dependence of merchant wholesalers on consumer product lines challenges merchant wholesalers to make viable competitive adjustments in a structurally changing market.

Alternative channels of distribution also adversely affect the sales of another category of wholesalers—agents and brokers. According to industry estimates, agents' and brokers' share of the total wholesale market has fallen, dropping from 11 percent in 1987 to nearly 7 percent in 1992. Although these losses were not across the board, some agents, particularly those selling groceries, apparel, and miscellaneous nondurable consumer products were hit hard.

The structural changes that continue to take place in distribution channels are forcing wholesalers to re-examine and readjust their strategies to maintain a competitive edge, including reorienting their services and product mix. Historically, wholesalers were known for the products and brands they carried and the basic services they provided. This traditional competitive edge has been blunted, however, by a similarity of quality among brands and the tendency of wholesalers to expand geographically and by product line until the market is saturated, creating a surplus of intermediary firms that tend to look alike.

In addition, the basic services traditionally offered by wholesalers—in-stock inventory, small order handling, credit terms, and product training for their employees and customers—are no longer sufficient. In response to these changes, wholesalers are offering more value-added services such as free delivery, relabeling, repackaging, and applying bar codes—in short, whatever it takes to keep the customer satisfied.

The National Association of Wholesalers says the best way to reverse, or at least reduce, the surge toward alternative distribution channels is to "become invaluable to your customer and establish closer partner-arrangements with your manufacturing supplier." In other words, adopt an aggressive program to improve and expand value-added services by anticipating the needs of the customer, and utilizing the technologies now available to improve productivity, reliability, and service quality. Much of this can be done by implementing bar coding and a system of electronic data interaction to assure next-day delivery, product-lot tracking, and comprehensive inventory controls. Other competitive strategies recommended for the near future include developing markets for manufacturers and servicing manufacturers' warranties.

Alternative channels of distribution will continue to siphon off sales of particular wholesale product lines. The pace will be slower, however, because the sales trends of discount stores, warehouse clubs, and other major retailers, now heavily involved in strategic alliances and other methods of implementing alternative channels of distribution, are showing signs of weakening.

The number of wholesalers, already down 25 percent since 1987, will continue to decline as firms merge in order to expand geographically, and to diversify product lines. By some estimates, the number of merchant wholesalers will decrease an additional 15 percent by the year 2000.

Competitive wholesalers will have the opportunity to increase their market share, however. Investing in the newer technologies, adding services, and opening export markets in foreign countries will provide them with alternative sources of market strength and raise the capital needed to improve productivity and institute the additional value-added services now being demanded by wholesalers' customers.

Competitive wholesalers will have the opportunity to increase their market share in the future. Investing in new technologies and adding services will provide them with alternative sources of market strength and allow them to raise the capital needed to improve productivity. The opening export markets in Mexico, China, and the EU also create opportunities for wholesalers.

International Market Overview

Wholesalers demonstrate their international competitiveness by establishing and maintaining a position in foreign markets and by delivering the products and services where needed, at the right time, and at a reasonable price. To maintain a competitive position in a foreign market, however, a wholesaler must continually adjust to the ever-increasing demands of the foreign customer for value-added services. Some are able to do this simply by exporting. Others establish affiliates in foreign markets to be close to the customer.

A Department of Commerce study on the importance of wholesalers as exporters revealed that 43,616 independent wholesale firms filled at least one export order from a foreign buyer in 1987—the latest year for which figures were available—with a total value of US$68.5 billion. The majority of the exports were manufactured goods.

More than 75 percent of these exporting wholesalers were small firms, employing fewer than 20 employees. They accounted for 25 percent of all exports of manufactured products from wholesalers, with a total value of US$13.6 billion in 1987. However, the export market was dominated by fewer than 300 large wholesalers. Although they represent less than one percent of the total number of wholesaling firms, they accounted for more than half of all exports of manufactured products in 1987.

Another measure of the international competitiveness of US wholesalers is the number of affiliates they have established in foreign markets. In 1989, for example, 178 US wholesaling firms established a total of 645 affiliates in one or more foreign markets.

Wholesalers of raw farm materials appear to be very competitive in international markets. The Commerce Department's 1989 benchmark survey of US Direct Investment Abroad showed that 10 US wholesalers of raw farm materials have 138 affiliates located in several different foreign markets. In contrast, only three US wholesalers of lumber and construction materials established a total of four affiliates abroad. Other US wholesalers with a large number of foreign affiliates include those handling consumer electronics, electrical appliances, professional equipment, groceries and machinery equipment.

Of the US$3 billion in exports shipped from US parent firms to their affiliate wholesale firms, about 60 percent were ready for immediate resale. The rest needed additional value-added services incorporated, such as repackaging or labeling, before they were ready for resale in the foreign market.

Despite strong evidence that the competitiveness of wholesalers is best exercised through foreign affiliates, there are few or no wholesaling affiliates in certain countries, such as China, because of investment restraints. Multilateral trade negotiations, under the auspices of GATT and NAFTA, also are expected to result in fewer restrictions on conducting business in several countries.

Market Barriers

Government Barriers

Market barriers imposed by governments include limitations on the right of foreign companies to directly access a country's wholesale and retail markets through local offices or directly hired sales forces; foreign exchange controls; product standards and quality control requirements; and continued lack of transparency in the trading system. Restricted access for foreign services continues to be a problem. Many goods need to be repackaged or relabelled to meet a country's standards.

Economic Barriers

The retail system can cause several barriers for US wholesalers. Many goods are pirated and while governments have sworn to protect intellectual properties, laws are rarely enforced in developing countries. Other economic barriers that could inflict US wholesalers include inefficient banking systems, difficulty in repatriating currency, and an inadequate system for dispute resolution.

Cultural and Social Barriers

Wholesalers' sales can sometimes be hurt by limitations such as restricted business hours or prohibition of sales on Sundays. Importers will usually require metric labelling for packaged goods. Dual labelling is often acceptable. Imported products should be labelled in the country's language containing the following information: name of product, trade name and address of the manufacturer, net contents, serial number of equipment, date of manufacture, electrical specifications, precautionary information on dangerous products, instructions for use, handling and/or product conservation, and mandatory standards.

Market Channels

The traditional channel for wholesalers is buying products from manufacturers and selling them directly to retailers. "Alternative" channels of distribution are being used by manufacturers and retailers now, however, cutting into a wholesaler's profits. Direct manufacturer-to-retail arrangements have proven the most popular alternative distribution, but others include mail order, catalog sales, and direct sales from manufacturer to industrial user or from retailer to industrial user.

The value of products distributed through these alternative channels are lost sales as far as most wholesalers are concerned. The size of the current and potential market for wholesalers is diminished by the volume of products distributed through alternative channels. These structural changes in distribution channels are forcing wholesalers to re-examine and readjust their strategies for maintaining a competitive edge, including reorienting their services and product mix.

Foreign markets often utilize another market channel, one that creates a problem for US wholesalers. Many large retail outlets in foreign countries compete with small street vendors who often get products from underground sources and cut into the wholesaler's profit. While governments have criticized vendors selling goods that have been pirated or stolen, enforcement has been lax. That is beginning to change, however, and many governments are cracking down on piracy. This will force vendors to use legitimate wholesalers, as well as drive more consumers into department stores and other large retail outlets.

Regional Opportunities

Note: These are only examples of regional opportunities and in no way constitute a complete list.

Germany

Germany is a good market for wholesalers, with an affluent population that is used to the quality US products bring. The eastern part of Germany is still trying to climb from the depression of recent years, but is an open market for US firms. While piracy has been a problem here, new regulations seem to be working and legitimate wholesalers will be more in demand.

Korea

Distribution in Korea has been one of the fastest developing industries in the past few years. The distribution market has opened gradually in three stages: in 1989, the Korean government opened the wholesale and distribution technology industry; in 1991, the retail industry was opened with a maximum of 10 outlets per company and 1,000 square meters of floor space per outlet; and the third stage occurred in 1993, when the limit of outlets per company was increased to 20 and 2,000 square meters for each outlet was allowed. As of 1996, the Korean distribution industry will be fully liberalized with no limit on the number of outlets nor any limit on the size of the outlet.

Stimulated by deregulation, new-to-market distribution channels are rapidly developing. These new distribution channels include discount stores, membership wholesale clubs, general merchandising stores, category killers (or specialty discount stores), convenience stores and door-to-door sales. Catalog sales are included in communication sales or home shopping under door-to-door sales. In Korea, new distribution technologies and membership wholesale clubs imported from the US already have been successful.

New types of distribution channels have been established including discount stores, membership warehouse wholesale stores, general merchandising stores, and convenience stores (including 7-11).

Japan

New regulations and laws help wholesaling firms in general, and US firms in particular. It is an unfair trading practice and a violation of the Anti-Monopoly Act for manufacturers to manipulate wholesale prices as part of their product marketing strategy. Certain products such as books, CDs, newspapers, as well as items (currently 14 types of cosmetics and 14 types of medicines) designated by the Japan Fair Trade Commission to prevent bait and switch selling tactics, are not subject to the act. Since economic and social circumstances change with time, regulations are periodically reviewed and revised in order to promote free competition and to protect consumer interests.

Manufacturers controlled and set wholesale and retail prices under the traditional Japanese system. Under a new pricing system, however, wholesalers and retailers decide what margin they will place on the cost of the goods they sell. This new system will undoubtedly lead to more control for wholesale firms.

Russia

The Russian government has sponsored a wholesale food market chain, to begin in 1996. This project is to support the existing and projected food distribution channels in Moscow and the region. Its purpose is to supply various foodstuffs to the Russian capital from domestic and foreign sources. Representatives in charge of the project will be highly interested in establishing business contacts with US food producers, and distributors and operators of large wholesale facilities to provide goods and food market equipment and management services, food processing equipment and technologies. The project has called for the construction of four food wholesaling outlets with a total area of 40,000 square meters in the vicinities of Moscow, purchase or rental of a haulage fleet for goods delivery, the establishment support centers for local agribusinesses participating in the project and supplying foods for the wholesale markets.

US participation in this project is preferred, both in terms of funding and technical assistance, food shipments and management training, warehousing technologies and equipment for food outlets and processing plants. Implementation of this project could serve as an example for the rest of Russia.

China

China has historically been a tough market for US wholesalers to break into. This may be changing, however. The Ministry of Overseas Trade has invited several leading US wholesalers and retailers to a symposium in late 1996, in an attempt to open up the market.

Best Bet Opportunities

Note: These are only examples of industry opportunities and in no way constitute a complete list.

Food

Supermarkets and other food retail outlets are becoming very popular in foreign markets, and US wholesalers have found a great deal of success dealing with them. Food is a good wholesaling product because there is such a need for it. There are many restrictions when exporting food, such as certain goods not accepted in other countries due to phytosanitary laws.

Manufactured Goods

Manufactured products are among the most popular wholesaling exports. As developing countries grow more affluent, wholesalers of manufactured goods will find more markets to sell their goods in. Manufactured goods are by far more popular in developed countries, however, simply because consumers there have more money to spend. This category has proven especially profitable for smaller companies. Those with fewer than 20 employees account for a substantial amount of all exports. As with other sectors, piracy, particularly of computer hardware and software, is a recurring problem.

Sources of US Based Assistance

Bureau of Wholesale Sales Representatives
1801 Peachtree Road, N.E.
Suite 200
Atlanta, GA 30309-1854
Tel: (404) 351-7355
Fax: (404) 352-5298

National Association of Wholesaler-Distributors
1725 K Street, N.W., 3rd Floor
Washington, DC 20006
Tel: (202) 872-0885
Fax: (202) 785-0586

Publications

Wholesale-By-Mail Catalog
St. Martin's Press
175 Fifth Ave.
New York NY 10010
Tel: (212) 674-5151

World Retail Directory and Sourcebook
Gale Research Inc.
(800) 877-GALE
Provides 3,500 addresses of retailers and retail-related information sources, libraries, conferences and trade fairs around the world. Each directory entry includes: company name, head office address, telephone, telex and fax number of outlets; type of business and much more. Also contains complete marketing information such as profiles of the top 250 world retailers with sales over US$1 billion, key data on over 2,000 other world retailers and national and international legislation affecting retail trade.

WSA Digest
Wholesale Stationers' Association
1034 Lela Ct.
Schaumburg, IL 60193-1337

APPENDICES

Appendix 1:
Service Industry-Related Associations

Each country has its own associations which may be of help to you; these are a few that are particularly involved in service industries. If the country you are interested in is not listed here, check the *Europa World Year Book* or the *Encyclopedia of Associations: International Organizations* in your library. The US Embassy in that country may also be a good source of information for professional associations that can assist you.

United States

Coalition of Service Industries, Inc.
805 15th St. NW, Suite 110
Washington, DC 20005
Tel: (202) 289-7460
Fax: (202) 775-1726
The Coalition of Service Industries (CSI) was established in 1982 to represent the interests of the largest segment of the US economy—the service sector. Since its founding, CSI has directed its efforts towards increasing public awareness of the major role services play in our national economy, and to shaping domestic and foreign policy that affect the interests of that sector.

Small Business Foundation of America
722 12th St. NW
Washington, DC 20005
Export Opportunity Hotline: (800) 243-7232
Tel: (202) 628-8389
Fax: (202) 628-8392
The staff at the Export Opportunity Hotline answers questions about getting started in exporting. Advice on product distribution; documentation; licensing and insurance; export financing; analyzing distribution options, export management firms; customs; currency exchange systems and travel requirements.

Argentina

The Union Argentina de Entidades de Servicios (UADES)
Viamonte 352, Piso 2
1053 Buenos Aires, Argentina
Phone/Fax: [54] (1) 312-4771, 312-0928

Australia

Australian Coalition of Service Industries
CEDA Building, 1st Floor
123 Lonsdale Street
Melbourne 3000, Australia
Tel: [61] (3) 9663-2996
Fax: [61] (3) 9663-3507

Belgium

European Services Industries Forum
't Hooghuys
B-2590 Beraar, Belgium
Tel: [32] (3) 482-4791
Fax: [32] (3) 482-2755

Canada

Service Exporters Committee of the Canadian Exporters Association
411 Roosevelt Avenue, Suite 310
Ottawa, ON K2A 3X9
Tel: (613) 722-8853
Fax: (613) 722-5082

Finland

Employers' Confederation of Service Industries (Liiketyonantajain Keskuslitto)
Etelaranta 10
SF-00130 Helsinki 13, Finland
Tel: [358] (0) 172831
Fax: [358] (0) 655588

Hong Kong

Hong Kong Coalition of Service Industries
c/o Hong Kong General Chamber of Commerce
22/F United Centre
95 Queensway
GPO Box 852
Hong Kong
Tel: [852] 2529-9229
Fax: [852] 2527-9843

India

South Asian Service Industries Forum
1113 New Delhi House
27 Barakhamba Road
New Delhi 110001, India
Tel: [91] (11) 331-3016
Fax: [91] (11) 331-0457

Ireland

Irish Coalition of Service Industries
Holbrook House
Holles Street
Dublin 2, Ireland
Tel: [353] (1) 661-2128
Fax: [353] (1) 661-2315

Japan
Keidanren
9-4, Otemachi 1-chome
Chiyoda-ku, Tokyo 100, Japan
Tel: [81] (3) 3279-1411
Fax.: [81] (3) 5255-6250

New Zealand
New Zealand Coalition of Service Industries
P.O. Box 3029, Level 3
Eagle Technology House
150-154 Willis Street
Wellington, New Zealand
Tel: [64] (4) 385-2145
Fax: [64] (4) 385-3510

Norway
Confederation of Norwegian Business and Industry, NHO
Postboks 5250
Majorstua
0303 Oslo 3, Norway
Tel: [47] 22-33-40-41
Fax: [47] 22-42-00-19

Sweden
Tjansteforbundet
(Swedish Coalition of Service Industries)
Mastet Samuelsgatan 51
S-111 56 Stockholm, Sweden
Tel: [46] (8) 21-0700
Fax: [46] (8) 791-7601

United Kingdom
Liberalization of Trade in Services (LOTIS)
Committee of British Invisibles
6th Floor, Windsor House
39 King Street
London WC2V 8DQ, England
Tel: [44] (171) 600-1198
Fax: [44] (171) 606-4248

Appendix 2:
US Government Contacts

US Department of Commerce Domestic Offices

The staff of the Commercial Service Domestic Offices can sit down and personally help export-ready companies conduct business in foreign markets around the world and helps resolve trade complaints against foreign companies. Normally, the Domestic Office is your personal link to the Commercial Service Overseas Offices and is the one-stop-shop for trade information and exporter services.

US Export Assistance Centers (USEACs) are co-located with domestic offices and offer a full range of federal export programs and services under one roof. Clients receive assistance by professionals from the SBA, the Department of Commerce, the Export-Import Bank, and other public and private organizations. It's a partnership that makes it easier for you to get the help you need to compete and succeed in the global marketplace. Each USEAC is ready to meet your business needs with export marketing and trade finance assistance at convenient one-stop locations; customized counseling that best suits your company's experience and commitment to exporting; and customer service that uses the latest technology to bring export assistance to your doorstep.

US DOC Regional Offices

Eastern Region
World Trade Center, Suite 2432
401 East Pratt Street
Baltimore, MD 21202
Tel: (410) 962-4539
Fax: (410) 962-4529

Mid-Eastern Region
Federal Building, Room 9504
550 Main Street
Cincinnati, OH 45202
Tel: (513) 684-2947
Fax: (513) 684-3200

Mid-Western Region
8182 Maryland Avenue, Suite 1011
St. Louis, MO 63105
Tel: (314) 425-3300
Fax: (314) 425-3375

Western Region
250 Montgomery Street, 14th Fl.
San Francisco, CA 94104
Tel: (415) 705-2310
Fax: (415) 705-2299

District & Branch Offices

Alabama
Medical Forum Bldg., 7th Floor
950 22nd Street North
Birmingham, AL 35203
Tel: (205) 731-1331
Fax: (205) 731-0076
Email: obirming@doc.gov

Alaska
World Trade Center
421 West First Street
Anchorage, AK 99501
Tel: (907) 271-6237
Fax: (907) 271-6242
Email: oanchora@doc.gov

Arizona
Phoenix Plaza
Tower One, Suite 970
2901 North Central Avenue
Phoenix, AZ 85012
Tel: (602) 640-2513
Fax: (602) 640-2518
Email: ophoenix@doc.gov

Arkansas
TCBY Tower Bldg, Suite 700
425 West Capitol Avenue, 7th Floor
Little Rock, AR 72201
Tel: (501) 324-5794
Fax: (501) 324-7380
Email: olittler@doc.gov

California
One World Trade Center, Suite 1670
Long Beach, CA 90831
Tel: (310) 980-4551
Fax: (310) 980-4561
Email: OLongBea@doc.gov
(A US Export Assistance Center)

101 Park Center Plaza, Ste. 1001
San Jose, CA 95113
Tel: (408) 271-7300
Fax: (408) 271-7307
(A US Export Assistance Center)

411 Pacific St., Ste. 200
Monterey, CA 93940
Tel: (408) 641-9850
Fax: (408) 641-9839

330 Ignacio Blvd., Ste. 102
Novato, CA 94949
Tel: (415) 883-1966
Fax: (415) 883-2711

530 Water St., Ste. 740
Oakland, CA 94607
Tel: (510) 273-7350
Fax: (510) 273-7352

917 7th St.
Sacramento, CA 95814
Tel: (916) 498-5155
Fax: (916) 498-5923

11000 Wilshire Blvd., Room 9200
Los Angeles, CA 90024
Tel: (310) 235-7104
Fax: (310) 235-7220
Email: olosange@doc.gov

6363 Greenwich Drive, Suite 230
San Diego, CA 92122
Tel: (619) 557-5395
Fax: (619) 557-6176
Email: osandieg@doc.gov

250 Montgomery Street, 14th Floor
San Francisco, CA 94104
Tel: (415) 705-2300
Fax: (415) 705-2297
Email: osanfran@doc.gov

345 California St., 7th Floor
San Francisco, CA 94104
Tel: (415) 705-1053
Fax: (415) 705-1054

3300 Irvine Avenue, Suite 305
Newport Beach, CA 92660-3198
Tel: (714) 660-1688
Fax: (714) 660-8039
Email: onewport@doc.gov
(Branch office with a trade specialist)

5201 Great American Parkway, Suite 456
Santa Clara, CA 95054-1127
Tel: (408) 970-4610
Fax: (408) 970-4618
Email: osantacl@doc.gov
(Branch office with a trade specialist)

Colorado
1625 Broadway, Suite 680
Denver, CO 80202
Tel: (303) 844-6622
Fax: (303) 844-5651

Email: odenver@doc.gov
(A US Export Assistance Center)

Connecticut
Federal Bldg., Room 610-B
450 Main Street
Hartford, CT 06103
Tel: (203) 240-3530
Fax: (203) 240-3473
Email: ohartfor@doc.gov

Delaware
Serviced by Philadelphia, Pennsylvania Office

District of Columbia
Serviced by Baltimore, Maryland Office

Florida
5600 N.W. 36th Street, Suite 617
Miami, FL 33166
Tel: (305) 526-7425
Fax: (305) 526-7434
Email: omiami@doc.gov
(A US Export Assistance Center)

128 North Osceola Avenue
Clearwater, FL 34615
Tel: (813) 461-0011
Fax: (813) 449-2889
Email: oclearwa@doc.gov
(Branch office with a trade specialist)

Eola Park Centre, Suite 1270
200 E. Robinson Street
Orlando, FL 32801
Tel: (407) 648-6235
Fax: (407) 648-5756
Email: oorlando@doc.gov
(Branch office with a trade specialist)

Collins Bldg., Room 366G
107 West Gaines Street
Tallahassee, FL 32399-2000
Tel: (904) 488-6469
Fax: (904) 487-1407
Email: otallaha@doc.gov
(Branch office with a trade specialist)

Georgia
285 Peachtree Center Ave. NE, Suite 200
Atlanta, GA 30303-1229
Tel: (404) 657-1900
Fax: (404) 657-1970
Email: oatlanta@doc.gov
(A US Export Assistance Center)

120 Barnard Street, A-107
Savannah, GA 31401
Tel: (912) 652-4204
Fax: (912) 652-4241
Email: osavanna@doc.gov

Hawaii
P.O. Box 50026
300 Ala Moana Blvd., Room 4106
Honolulu, HI 96850
Tel: (808) 541-1782
Fax: (808) 541-3435
Email: ohonolul@doc.gov

Idaho
Joe R. Williams Bldg., 2nd Floor
700 West State Street
Boise, ID 83720
Tel: (208) 334-3857
Fax: (208) 334-2783
Email: oboise@doc.gov
(Branch office with a trade specialist)

Illinois
55 West Monroe Street, Room 2440
Chicago, IL 60603
Tel: (312) 353-8040
Fax: (312) 353-8098
Email: ochicago@doc.gov
(A US Export Assistance Center)

P.O. Box 1747
515 North Court Street
Rockford, IL 61110-0247
Tel: (815) 987-8123
Fax: (815) 963-7943
Email: orockfor@doc.gov
(Branch office with a trade specialist)

Illinois Institute of Technology
201 E. Loop Road
Wheaton, IL 60187
Tel: (312) 353-4332
Fax: (312) 353-4336
Email: owheaton@doc.gov
(Branch office with a trade specialist)

Indiana
Penwood One, Suite 106
11405 North Pennsylvania Street
Carmel, IN 46032
Tel: (317) 582-2300
Fax: (317) 582-2301
Email: oindiana@doc.gov

Iowa
Federal Bldg., Room 817
210 Walnut Street
Des Moines, IA 50309
Tel: (515) 284-4222
Fax: (515) 284-4021
Email: odesmoin@doc.gov

Kansas
151 North Volutsia
Wichita, KS 67214-4695
Tel: (316) 269-6160
Fax: (316) 683-7326
Email: owichita@doc.gov
(Branch office with a trade specialist)

Kentucky
601 West Broadway, Room 634B
Louisville, KY 40202
Tel: (502) 582-5066
Fax: (502) 582-6573
Email: olouisvi@doc.gov

Louisiana
365 Canal Street, Suite 2150
New Orleans, LA 70130
Tel: (504) 589-6546
Fax: (504) 589-2337
Email: oneworle@doc.gov
(A US Export Assistance Center)

Maine
145 Middle Street
P.O. Box 8119
Portland, ME 04104
Tel: (207) 772-2811
Fax: (207) 772-1179

Maryland
World Trade Center, Ste. 2432
401 E. Pratt Street
Baltimore, MD 21202
Tel: (410) 962-4539
Fax: (410) 962-4529
Email: obaltimo@doc.gov
(A US Export Assistance Center)

Massachusetts
World Trade Center, Suite 307
Boston, MA 02210
Tel: (617) 424-5990
Fax: (617) 424-5992
Email: oboston@doc.gov

Michigan
McNamara Bldg., Room 1140
477 Michigan Avenue
Detroit, MI 48226
Tel: (313) 226-3650
Fax: (313) 226-3657
Email: odetroit@doc.gov
(A US Export Assistance Center)

301 West Fulton Street, Suite 718-S
Grand Rapids, MI 49503-6495
Tel: (616) 458-3564
Fax: (616) 458-3872
Email: ograndra@doc.gov
(Branch office with a trade specialist)

Minnesota
Federal Bldg., Room 108
110 South Fourth Street
Minneapolis, MN 55401
Tel: (612) 348-1638
Fax: (612) 348-1650
Email: ominneap@doc.gov

Mississippi
201 West Capitol Street, Suite 310
Jackson, MS 39201-2005
Tel: (601) 965-4388
Fax: (601) 965-5386
Email: ojackson@doc.gov

Missouri
8182 Maryland Avenue, Suite 303
St. Louis, MO 63105
Tel: (314) 425-3302
Fax: (314) 425-3381
Email: ostlouis@doc.gov
(A US Export Assistance Center)

601 E. 12th Street, Room 635
Kansas City, MO 64106
Tel: (816) 426-3141
Fax: (816) 426-3140

Montana
Served by the Boise, Idaho Branch Office

Nebraska
11135 "O" Street
Omaha, NB 68137
Tel: (402) 221-3664
Fax: (402) 221-3668
Email: oomaha@doc.gov
(Branch office with a trade specialist)

Nevada
1755 East Plumb Lane, Suite 152
Reno, NV 89502
Tel: (702) 784-5203
Fax: (702) 784-5343
Email: oreno@doc.gov

New Hampshire
601 Spaulding Turnpike, Suite 29
Portsmouth, NH 03801
Tel: (603) 334-6074
Fax: (603) 334-6110
Email: oportsmo@doc.gov
(Branch office with a trade specialist)

New Jersey
3131 Princeton Pike
Bldg. 6, Suite 100
Trenton, NJ 08648
Tel: (609) 989-2100
Fax: (609) 989-2395
Email: otrenton@doc.gov

New Mexico
c/o New Mexico Dept. of Economic Development
1100 St. Francis Drive
Santa Fe, NM 87503
Tel: (505) 827-0350
Fax: (505) 827-0263
Email: osantafe@doc.gov
(Branch office with a trade specialist)

New York
6 World Trade Center, Room 635
New York, NY 10048
Tel: (212) 264-0635
Fax: (212) 264-1356
Email: onewyork@doc.gov
(A US Export Assistance Center)

Federal Bldg., Room 1304
111 West Huron Street
Buffalo, NY 14202
Tel: (716) 846-4191
Fax: (716) 846-5290
Email: obuffalo@doc.gov

111 East Avenue, Suite 220
Rochester, NY 14604
Tel: (716) 263-6480
Fax: (716) 325-6505
Email: orochest@doc.gov
(Branch office with a trade specialist)

163 West 125th Street, Suite 1301
New York, NY 10027
Tel: (212) 860-6200
Fax: (212) 860-6203
(Branch office with a trade specialist)

North Carolina
400 West Market Street, Suite 400
Greensboro, NC 27401
Tel: (910) 333-5345
Fax: (910) 333-5158
Email: ogreensb@doc.gov

North Dakota
Serviced by Minneapolis, Minnesota District Office

Ohio
Federal Bldg., Room 9504
550 Main Street
Cincinnati, OH 45202
Tel: (513) 684-2944
Fax: (513) 684-3200
Email: ocincinn@doc.gov

600 Superior Ave. East, Suite 700
Cleveland, OH 44114
Tel: (216) 522-4750
Fax: (216) 522-2235
Email: oclevela@doc.gov

Oklahoma
6601 Broadway Extension, Rm 200
Oklahoma City, OK 73116
Tel: (405) 231-5302
Fax: (405) 231-4211
Email: ooklahom@doc.gov

440 S. Houston Street, Rm 506
Tulsa, OK 74127
Tel: (918) 581-7650
Fax: (918) 581-2844
Email: otulsa@doc.gov
(Branch office with a trade specialist)

Oregon
One World Trade Center, Suite 242
121 S.West Salmon Street
Portland, OR 97204
Tel: (503) 326-3001
Fax: (503) 326-6351
Email: oportlan@doc.gov

Pennsylvania
615 Chestnut Street, Suite 1501
Philadelphia, PA 19106
Tel: (215) 597-6101
Fax: (215) 597-6123
Email: ophilade@doc.gov
(A US Export Assistance Center)

Federal Bldg., Room 2002
1000 Liberty Avenue
Pittsburgh, PA 15222
Tel: (412) 644-2850
Fax: (412) 644-4875
Email: opittsbu@doc.gov

Puerto Rico
Federal Bldg., Room G-55
Chardon Avenue, PR 00918
Tel: (809) 766-5555
Fax: (809) 766-5692

Rhode Island
7 Jackson Walkway
Providence, RI 02903
Tel: (401) 528-5104
Fax: (401) 528-5067
Email: oproide@doc.gov
(Branch office with a trade specialist)

South Carolina
Federal Bldg., Suite 172
1835 Assembly Street
Columbia, SC 29201
Tel: (803) 765-5345
Fax: (803) 253-3614
Email: ocolumbi@doc.gov

81 Mary Street
Charleston, SC 29403
Tel: (803) 727-4051
Fax: (803) 727-4052
Email: ocharles@doc.gov
(Branch office with a trade specialist)

South Dakota
200 North Phillips Ave., Suite 302
Commerce Center
Sioux Falls, SD 57102
Tel: (605) 330-4264
Fax: (605) 330-4266
Email: osiouxfa@doc.gov
(Branch office with a trade specialist)

Tennessee
Parkway Towers, Suite 114
404 James Robertson Parkway
Nashville, TN 37219-1505
Tel: (615) 736-5161
Fax: (615) 736-2454
Email: onashvil@doc.gov

301 East Church Avenue
Knoxville, TN 37915
Tel: (615) 545-4637
Fax: (615) 545-4435
Email: oknoxvil@doc.gov
(Branch office with a trade specialist)

22 North Front Street, Ste 200
Memphis, TN 38103
Tel: (901) 544-4137
Fax: (901) 575-3510
Email: omemphis@doc.gov
(Branch office with a trade specialist)

Texas
World Trade Center
2050 North Stemmons Freeway, Suite 170
Dallas, TX 75258
Tel: (214) 767-0542
Fax: (214) 767-8240
Email: odallas@doc.gov
(A US Export Assistance Center)

#1 Allen Center
500 Dallas, Suite 1160
Houston, TX 77002
Tel: (713) 229-2578
Fax: (713) 229-2203
Email: ohouston@doc.gov

P.O. Box 12728
1700 Congress, 2nd Floor
Austin, TX 78701
Tel: (512) 912-5939
Fax: (512) 916-5940
Email: oaustin@doc.gov
(Branch office with a trade specialist)

Utah
324 South State Street, Suite 105
Salt Lake City, UT 84111
Tel: (801) 524-5116
Fax: (801) 524-5886
Email: osaltlak@doc.gov

Vermont
c/o Vermont Dept. of Economic Development
109 State Street, 4th Floor
Montpelier, VT 05609
Tel: (802) 828-4508
Fax: (802) 828-3258
Email: omontpel@doc.gov
(Branch office with a trade specialist)

Virginia
700 Centre
704 East Franklin Street, Suite 550
Richmond, VA 23219
Tel: (804) 771-2246
Fax: (804) 771-2390
Email: orichmon@doc.gov

Washington
2001 Sixth Avenue, Suite 650
Seattle, WA 98121
Tel: (206) 553-5615
Fax: (206) 553-7253

320 North Johnson Street, Suite 350
Kennewick, WA 99336
Tel: (509) 735-2751
Fax: (509) 783-9385
Email: otriciti@doc.gov
(Branch office with a trade specialist)

West Virginia
405 Capitol Street, Suite 807
Charleston, WV 25301
Tel: (304) 347-5123
Fax: (304) 347-5408
Email: ocharle1@doc.gov

Wisconsin
517 E. Wisconsin Avenue, Room 596
Milwaukee, WI 53202
Tel: (414) 297-3473
Fax: (414) 297-3470
Email: omilwauk@doc.gov

Wyoming
Served by the Denver, Colorado Office

US Government Offices in Washington, DC

Bureau of Export Administration
Dept. of Commerce
Washington, DC 20230
Tel: (202) 482-2721
Fax: (202) 482-2387
Web site: www.bxa.doc.gov

Environmental Protection Agency (EPA)
Office of International Activities
Tel: (202) 260-0424
Fax (202) 260-4470

Export Import Bank of the United States
811 Vermont Ave. NW
Washington, DC 20571
Tel: (800) 563-3946, (202) 565-3900
Fax: (202) 565-3380
Web site: www.exim.gov

International Trade Administration
Department of Commerce
Washington, DC 20230
Tel: (800) USA-TRADE (800-872-8723)
Fax: (202) 482-5487
Web site: www.ita.doc.gov

Office of the US Trade Representative
600 17th St. NW
Washington, DC 20508
Office of Investment, Tel: (202) 395-4510
Office of Intellectual Property, Tel: (202) 395-6864
Office of Services, Tel: (202) 395-7271; Fax: (202) 395-3891
Web Site: www.ustr.gov

Small Business Administration
409 Third St. SW
8th Fl.
Washington DC 20416
SBA Answer Desk: (800) 8-ASK-SBA (800-827-5722)
International Trade: (202) 205-6720; Fax: (202) 205-7272
Web site: www.sbaonline.sba.gov

State Department, Trade Policy & Programs
Main State Bldg.
EB/TPP
Rm. 3831A
Washington DC 20520.
Tel: (202) 647-3784
Fax: (202) 647-1537

US & Foreign Commercial Service
US & FCS
International Trade Administration
Dept. of Commerce
Washington DC 20230
Tel: (202) 482-5777
Fax: (202) 482-5013
TDD: (202) 482-1669

Telephone Hotlines
These are telephone hotlines that are generally staffed during business hours (eastern time).

US Department of Commerce

Trade Information Center
US Department of Commerce
1401 Constitution Avenue
N.W., Room 7424
Washington, DC 20230
Tel: (800) USA-TRADE (800-872-8723)
TDD line: 800-TDD-TRADE (1-800-833-8723)
Web site: www.ita.doc.gov/how_to_export/
The Trade Information Center provides personalized export counseling and a wealth of information, including the publication, *A Business Guide of Federal Export Assistance Programs*. The TIC is staffed Mon-Fri from 8:30am to 5:30pm, eastern time.

US Small Business Administration Answer Desk

Tel: (800) 8-ASK-SBA (800-827-5722)

US Agency for International Development, Center for Trade and Investment Services (CTIS)

Tel: (202) 663-2660
Fax: (202) 663-2670
Provides tailored country-specific information. 9:00am–5:30 EST Monday through Friday.

Regional Trade Information Offices

Asia Business Center, ITA

Room 2327
US Dept. of Commerce
Washington, DC 20230
Tel: (202) 482-2522
Fax: (202) 482-4453
Global Export Market Information Service fax retrieval: (800) USA-TRADE (1-800-872-8723)
The Asia Business Center provides information and assistance in the following areas of economic and commercial assessments for Asian/Pacific countries; Asia/Pacific trade and investment regulations; Asia/Pacific tariff and import tax rates; best prospects in Asia/Pacific for US manufacturers and service providers; trade promotion events in Asia and the Pacific; Asia/Pacific organizations and other contacts for additional information and assistance; help to resolve commercial difficulties encountered in doing business in Asia/Pacific; and participation in seminars on doing business in Asia and the Pacific.

Business Information Service for the Newly Independent States (BISNIS)

Tel: (202) 482-4655
Global Export Market Information Service fax retrieval: (800) USA-TRADE (1-800-872-8723)
Email: bisnis@usita.gov;
Web site: www.itaiep.doc.gov/bisnis/bisnis.html
BISNIS provides its clients with trade leads; current market information; data on commercial law, transportation, financing, and logistics; and one-on-one counseling. Innovative BISNIS publications and services include *BISNIS Bulletin,* a monthly newsletter covering major business issues and regions, as well as the latest on US government trade promotion programs and activities; *BISNIS On-Line,* an Internet home page, which makes hundreds of documents and publications on business in the NIS

available electronically around the clock; the BISNIS fax retrieval service; specialized Email groups for the most time-sensitive trade leads in specific sectors; Search for Partners, which identifies NIS enterprises looking for US partners in a variety of business endeavors; and *Commercial Opportunities,* which publicizes NIS sales opportunities.

Central and Eastern Europe Business Information Center (CEEBIC)

Tel: (202) 482-2645
Fax: (202) 482-4473
Small Business Support Facility
Tel: (202) 482-3462
Bosnia/Balkan Reconstruction Hotline
Tel: (202) 482-5418
Fax: (202) 482-4473
Global Export Market Information Service fax retrieval
(800) USA-TRADE (1-800-872-8723)

CEEBIC offers a wide array of services, business counseling, and information products designed to help US companies expand into the Central and East European markets. CEEBIC publishes a monthly newsletter, *the Central and Eastern Europe Commercial Update,* that highlights current economic, financial and commercial trends, marketing, partnership opportunities, and regulatory changes. In addition, CEEBIC recently opened a new small business support facility that provides additional hands-on assistance to small firms providing step-by-step support through the exporting process.

Japan Export Information Center (JEIC)

Room 2320
US Dept. of Commerce
Washington, DC 20230
Tel: (202) 482-2425
Fax: (202) 482-0469
Global Export Market Information Service fax retrieval: (800) USA-TRADE (1-800-872-8723)
The JEIC assists US companies interested in developing business to Japan by providing them with business counseling services; complete, current information on exporting to Japan; Japanese business customs and practices; market entry alternatives; economic conditions; available market information and research; standards and product testing procedures; and tariffs and nontariff barriers. The JEIC also informs US companies of the types of assistance available through the Japanese government's import promotion programs and works with the Japanese government to better adapt these programs to the needs of US exporters.

Office of the Near East and North Africa (ONENA)

Tel: (202) 482-1860
Fax: (202) 482-0878
FlashFax retrieval system: (202) 482-1064
The Office of the Near East and North Africa assists US companies interested in developing export business to the region by providing them with business counseling services; complete, current information on exporting to the Near East and North Africa; business customs and practices; market entry alternatives; economic conditions; available market

information and research; standards and product testing procedures; and tariffs and nontariff barriers.

Office of NAFTA (North American Free Trade Agreement)

Tel: (202) 482-0305
Fax: (202) 482-5865
Global Export Market Information Service fax retrieval: (800) USA-TRADE (1-800-872-8723) or (202) 482-4464
The Office of NAFTA assists US exporters take advantage of opportunities in Canadian and Mexican markets within the framework of the North American Free Trade Agreement (NAFTA). Trade specialists provide business counseling on Mexico and Canada, NAFTA regulations, investment opportunities, and in-country contact information.

Through the NAFTA Fax System, exporters can obtain tariff rates, information on the NAFTA Certificate of Origin, rules of origin by product, industry specific business opportunities and updates, financing information, and other helpful "How To" guides on exporting to Canada and Mexico.

International Economic Policy Country Desk Officers

For a list of IEP country desk officers, call (800) USA-TRADE (1-800-872-8723).
The International Trade Administration's IEP desk officers provide information on trade potential for US products in specific countries. Individual IEP country desk officers, plus several regional business centers, highlight new opportunities for trade and investment. These specialists look at the needs of an individual firm wishing to sell in a particular country in the full context of that country's economy, trade policies, and political situation. Desk officers collect information on their assigned country's regulations, tariffs, business practices, economic and political developments, trade data, and market size and growth, keeping a current pulse on the potential markets for US products, services, and investments. IEP desk officers are organized into regional areas.

US Department of State, Region Bureaus

US Department of State
Main State Bldg.
Washington DC 20520
Bureau of African Affairs
Tel: (202) 647-2530
Fax: (202) 647-6301
Bureau of East Asian and Pacific Affairs
Tel: (202) 647-9596
Fax: (202) 647-7350
Bureau of European and Canadian Affairs
Tel: (202) 647-9626
Fax: (202) 647-0967
Bureau of Inter-American Affairs
Tel: (202) 647-5780
Fax: (202) 647-0791
Bureau of South Asian Affairs
Tel: (202) 736-4255
Fax: (202) 736-4459
Bureau of Arabian Peninsula Affairs

Tel: (202) 647-6184
Fax: (202) 736-4459
Ambassadors-at-Large for the Newly Independent States
Tel: (202) 647-3112
Fax: (202) 647-2699

Automated Fax Retrieval Services

You may access these services 24 hours a day and 7 days a week if you have a telephone and a fax machine. In most cases, you should dial the number from your telephone, follow the instructions given by the voice prompts, and the requested information will automatically be faxed to you. In a few cases you may be told to call from the handset on your fax machine instead of from your telephone.

Global Export Market Information Center (International Trade Administration)

Tel: (800) USA-TRADE (800-872-8723)
TDD line: 800-TDD-TRADE (1-800-833-8723)
This is the main fax retrieval system of the International Trade Administration. There are separate document lists available for information on:

- Federal and state export information

- Central and Eastern Europe

- Russia and the Newly Independent States

- NAFTA, Canada, Mexico, the Caribbean, and Latin America

- Japan

- Asia (excluding Japan), Australia and New Zealand

- Northern Ireland and the border counties of the Republic of Ireland

- Trade Compliance Center, Uruguay Round, GATT/WTO

Office of the Near East and North Africa (ONENA)

FlashFax retrieval system: (202) 482-1064
At press time, the information from this office was available only through this separate line and not through the toll-free number for the Global Export Market Information Center described above. However, this may change in coming months.

Export Hotline

Tel: (800) USA-XPORT (800-872-9767)
Presented by AT&T and the Hotline Referral Network in cooperation with the US Department of Commerce. The Export Hotline is a corporate sponsored, nationwide fax retrieval system providing international trade information for US business. Its purpose is to help find new markets for US products and services.

STAT-USA/Fax

Tel: (202) 482-0005
You must call from the handset on your fax machine. Press "2" for guest access. You may then either press "800" for a list of available information, titles, and codes or "801" for a schedule of release dates and times. Provides fax copies of the most popular files found on the Economic Bulletin Board. Access costs are $29.95 per quarter or $100 per year. Limited guest access is available. For more information, con-

tact: STAT-USA HelpLine, (202) 482-1986 or 800-STAT-USA (800-782-8872), fax (202) 482-2164.

On-line and Electronic Sources

National Trade Data Bank (NTDB)
Tel: (202) 482-1986 or (800) STAT-USA (800-782-8872)
Fax (202) 482-2164
Updated each month and released on two CD-ROM discs, the NTDB enables a user with an Internet account or with an IBM-compatible personal computer equipped with a CD-ROM reader to access over 200,000 trade-related documents. The NTDB contains the latest Census data on US imports and exports by commodity and country; the complete set of Country Commercial Guides; current market research reports compiled by the Commercial Service; the complete Commercial Service International Contacts (CSIS), which contains over 80,000 names and addresses of individuals and firms abroad interested in importing US products; State Department country reports on economic policy and trade practices; the publications *Export Yellow Pages, A Basic Guide to Exporting, and the National Trade Estimates Report on Foreign Trade Barriers;* the Export Promotion Calendar; and many other data series.

The NTDB can be purchased in the form of CD-ROM discs for $59 per monthly issue or $575 for a 12-month subscription. Non-US shipments will be charged $75 monthly or $775 for an annual subscription. It is also available on the Internet through STAT-USA (see below).

The NTDB is also available at over 1,100 federal depository libraries nationwide. Call 1-800-USA-TRADE for a list of these libraries.

Economic Bulletin Board (EBB)
Modem: (202) 482-3870 (300/1200/2400 bps)
Modem: (202) 482-2584 (9600 bps)
Modem: (202) 482-2167 (14.4 kbps)
Internet access by telnetting to ebb.stat-usa.gov. Set your communications software to no parity, 8 data bits, and 1 stop bit. The EBB is an on-line and fax-accessible information system that offers daily trade leads and the latest statistical releases, and is divided into two separate components: State of the Nation and GLOBUS. The EBB collects information from many federal agencies including the Federal Reserve Board, the Bureau of Economic Analysis, the Bureau of the Census and the Department of the Treasury. Internet connection charges are $50 per quarter ($150 per year) for unlimited access to the STAT-USA site (NTDB and EBB).

A free limited-access service is available to those who would like to get acquainted with the EBB before subscribing. Call the EBB (see access numbers below) and type GUEST when prompted for a User ID. GUEST users have access to bulletins, some sample and special files, and can access a complete list of files on the EBB.

STAT-USA/Internet
Web site: www.stat-usa.gov
Tel: (202) 482-1986 or 800-STAT-USA (800-782-8872)
Fax: (202) 482-2164

The site contains the National Trade Data Bank CD-ROM and the best of the Economic Bulletin Board. Subscriptions are $50/quarter or $150/year for unlimited access.

International Data Base (IDB)
Tel: (301) 457-1403 (Information Resources Branch)
Fax: (301) 457-1539
Email: peterj@census.gov
From the Bureau of the Census, US Department of Commerce. The International Programs Center compiles and maintains up-to-date global demographic and social information for all countries in its International Data Base (IDB), which is available to US companies seeking to identify potential markets overseas. Information about the IDB, including on-line access and free download, is on-line. Also available are printed tables on selected subjects for selected countries with a minimum charge of $5. The IDB is available on diskette for $40.

SBA On-line, Small Business Administration
Modem: (800) 697-4636
This line provides SBA and other government agency information and some downloadable text files.
Modem: (900) 463-4636 or (202) 401-9600
This number allows you to access, for $.04 a minute, SBA and other government information, a wide range of downloadable files, including application and software files, the gateway, mail, interact mail, and news groups and on-line searchable data banks.

Technical Support Tel: (202) 205-6400
Technical Support TDD line: (202) 205-7333
An electronic bulletin board developed to expedite dissemination of information on starting, expanding, and financing a business to the small business community. The system operates 23 hours a day and 365 days a year. All you need is a computer, modem, phone line, and communications software. Data parameters are 14.4, N, 8, 1.

SBA Internet Home Page, Small Business Administration
Web site: www.sbaonline.sba.gov/
Help Desk telephone: (202) 205-6400
Provides SBA services, plus services from agency resource partners, links to other federal and state governments, and direct connections to additional outside resources. Special areas of interest focus on assistance for individual groups, such as those starting out, ready to finance, looking to expand, as well as help for minorities, women, and those interested in international trade. Large libraries of business-focused shareware, downloadable SBA loan forms, and huge volumes of agency publications are also available. A wide variety of services listed by state are provided, including calendars of local training courses sponsored by SBA. On-line workshops are offered for individuals to work through self-paced activities that help them start and expand their business. In addition, the home page links directly to the White House home page and the US Business Advisor, which houses a large volume of regulatory information for small businesses. SBA provides full text search capabilities as well as an area for user comments and suggestions.

US & Foreign Commercial Service Overseas Posts

Albania
American Embassy
PSC 59
Box 100 (A)
APO AE 09624
Tel: [355] (42) 32875, 33520
Fax: [355] (42) 32222

Algeria
American Embassy
B.P. Box 549
Alger-Gare 16000, Algeria
Tel: [213] (2) 69-23-17
Fax: [213] (2) 69-18-63

Angola
American Embassy
Caixa Postal 6484
Luanda, Angola
Tel: [244] (2) 346-418, 345-481
Fax: [244] (2) 346-924;

Argentina
American Embassy
4300 Colombia
1425 Buenos Aires, Argentina
US mailing address: Unit 4334, APO AA 34034
Tel: [54] (1) 777-4533, 777-4534
Fax: [54] (1) 777-0673

Armenia
American Embassy
18 Gen Bagramian, Yerevan
Tel: [374] 215-1144, 252-4661
Fax: [374] 215-1138

Australia
American Consulate General, Sydney
59th Fl., MLC Centre
19-29 Martin Place
Sydney NSW 2000, Australia
US mailing address: PSC 280, Unit 11026
APO AP 96554-0002
Tel: [61] (2) 9221-0574, 9373-9200
Fax: [61] (2) 9221-0573
Note: Commercial Office of American Embassy (Canberra) is in Sydney

American Consulate General, Perth
13th Fl., 16 St. George's Terr.
Perth, WA 6000, Australia
US mailing address: APO AP 96530
Tel: [61] (9) 231-9410
Fax: [61] (9) 231-9444

American Consulate, Brisbane
4th Fl., 383 Wickham Terr., Brisbane, QLD 4000, Australia
US mailing address: APO AP 96529
Tel: [61] (7) 3831-1345
Fax: [61] (7) 3832-6247

Austria
American Embassy
Boltzmanngasse 16, A-1091 Vienna, Austria
Tel: [43] (1) 313-39
Fax: [43] (1) 310-6917

Azerbaijan
American Embassy
Azadliq Prospekti 83, Baku, Azerbaijan
Tel: [994] (12) 98-03-36, 98-03-37, 96-00-19, 93-64-80
Fax: [994] (12) 98-37-55
Telex 142110 AMEMB SU

The Bahamas
American Embassy
P.O. Box N-8197, Nassau, The Bahamas
US mailing address: Amembassy Nassau, P.O. Box 9009, Miami, FL 3315
Tel: (242) 322-1181
Fax: (242) 328-3495

Barbados
American Embassy
P.O. Box 302, Bridgetown, Barbados
US mailing address: FPO AA 34055
Tel: (246)436-4950
Fax: (246) 429-5246

Bahrain
American Embassy
Box 26431
Manama, Bahrain
US mailing address: FPO AE 09834-5100
Tel: [973] 273-300
Fax: [973] 256-717

Bangladesh
American Embassy
GPO Box 323, Dhaka 1000
Tel: [880] (2) 884700-22
Fax: [880] (2) 883-744

Belgium
American Embassy
27 Boulevard du Regent, B-1000 Brussels, Belgium
US mailing address: PSC 82, Box 002, APO AE 09724
Tel: [32] (2) 508-2111
Fax: [32] (2) 512-6653

US Mission to the European Union
40 Blvd. du Regent, B-1000 Brussels, Belgium
US mailing address: APO AE 09724
Tel: [32] (2) 508-2746
Fax: [32] (2) 513-1228

Belize
American Embassy
Gabourel Lane and Hutson St., Belize City, Belize
US mailing address: P.O. Box 286, Unit 7401, APO AA
34025
Tel: [501] (2) 77161/3
Fax: [501] (2) 30802

Bolivia
American Embassy
P.O. Box 425, La Paz, Bolivia
Tel: [591] (2) 430251
Fax: [591] (2) 433900
US mailing address: APO AA 34032

Botswana
American Embassy
P.O. Box 90, Gaborone, Botswana
Tel: [267] 353-982
Fax: [267] 356-947

Brazil
American Embassy
Avenida das Nacoes, Lote 3, Brasilia, Brazil
US mailing address: Unit 3500, APO AA 34030
Tel: [55] (61) 321-7272
Fax: [55] (61) 225-9136
Web site (Commercial Service): www.ita.doc.gov/csbrazil/

American Consulate General, Rio de Janiero
Avenida Presidente Wilson, 147 Castelo, Rio de Janeiro-RJ
20030-020, Brazil
US mailing address: Unit 3501, APO AA 34030
Tel: [55] (21) 292-7117
Fax: [55] (21) 240-0439

American Commercial Office, Belem Para
Rua Osvaldo Cruz 165, 66017-090 Belem Para, Brazil
Tel: [55] (91) 223-0800, 223-0613
Fax: [55] (91) 223-0413

American Commercial Office, Belo Horizonte
Av Alvares Cabral, 1600 Andar, Belo Horizonte
MG CEP 30170, Brazil
Tel: [55] (31) 335-3250
Fax: [55] (31) 335-3054

American Commercial Office (US Trade Center), Sao Paulo
Rua Estados Unidos, 1812, Sao Paulo
S.P. 01427-002, Brazil
Tel: [55] (11) 853-2011, 853-2411, 853-2778
Fax: [55] (11) 853-2744

Bulgaria
American Embassy
1 Saborna St., Sofia, Bulgaria
US mailing address: Unit 1335, APO AE 09213-1335
Tel: [359] (2) 88-48-01/5
Fax: [359] (2) 80-38-50

Burkina Faso
American Embassy
01 B.P. 35, Ouagadougou, Burkina Faso
Tel: [226] 30-67-23/5
Fax: [226] 30-38-90

Burma (Myanmar)
American Embassy
GPO 521, Rangoon, Burma (Myanmar)
US mailing address: Box B, APO AP 96546
Tel: [95] (1) 82055, 82182
Fax: [95] (1) 80409

Burundi
American Embassy
B.P. 1720, Avenue des Etats-Unis, Bujumbura, Burundi
Tel: [257] 22-34-54
Fax: [257] 22-29-26

Cambodia (Kampuchea)
American Embassy
27 EO Street 240, Phnom Penh, Cambodia (Kampuchea)
US mailing address: Box P, APO AP 96546
Tel: [855] (23) 426-436, 426-438
Fax: [855] (23) 234-26437

Cameroon
American Embassy
Rue Nachtigal, B.P. 817, Yaounde, Cameroon
Tel: [237] 23-40-14, 23-05-12
Fax: [237] 23-07-53

Canada
American Embassy
100 Wellington St., Ottawa ON, K1P 5T1, Canada
US mailing address: P.O. Box 5000
Ogdensburg, NY 13669-0430
Tel: (613) 238-5335, 238-4470
Fax: (613) 233-8511
Web site (Commercial Service): www.ita.doc.gov/cscanada/

American Consulate General, Calgary
1050, 615 Macleod Trail SE, Calgary
AB T2G 4T8, Canada
Tel: (403) 266-8962
Fax: (403) 264-6630

American Consulate General, Halifax
Suite 910, Cogswell Tower, Scotia Sq., Halifax, NS B3J
3K1, Canada
Tel: (902) 429-2480
Fax: (902) 423-6861

American Consulate General, Montreal
P.O. Box 65, Postal Station Desjardins
Montreal, PQ H5B 1G1
US mailing address: P.O. Box 847
Champlain, NY 12919-0847
Tel: (514) 398-9695
Fax: (514) 398-0711, 398-0973

American Consulate General, Toronto
360 University Ave., Toronto, ON M5G 1S4, Canada
US mailing address: P.O. Box 135
Lewiston, NY 14092-0135
Tel: (416) 595-1700
Fax: (416) 595-0051

America Consulate General, Vancouver
1095 West Pender St., Vancouver, BC V6E 2M6
US mailing address: P.O. Box 5002
Point Roberts, WA 98281-5002
Tel: (604) 685-4311
Fax: (604) 687-6095

Chile
American Embassy
Av. Andres Bello 2800, Santiago, Chile
Tel: [56] (2) 232-2600
Fax: [56] (2) 330-3172

China
American Embassy
Xiu Shui Bei Jie 3, Beijing 100600, P.R. China
US mailing address: PSC 461, Box 50, FPO AP 96521-0002
Tel: [86] (10) 532-6924, 532-6927
Fax: [86] (10) 532-3297

American Consulate General, Guangzhou
No. 1 Shamian Street South, Guangzhou 510133, P.R. China
US mailing address: PSC 461
Box 100, FPO AP 96521-0002
Tel: [86] (20) 667-4011
Fax: [86] (20) 666-6409

American Consulate General, Shanghai
1469 Huai Hai Middle Road, Shanghai 200031, P.R. China
US mailing address: PSC 461
Box 200, FPO AP 96521-0002
Tel: [86] (21) 6433-6880
Fax: [86] (21) 6433-1576

American Consulate General, Shenyang
52, 14th Wei Road, Heping District, Shenyang 110003
US mailing address: PSC 461, Box 45, FPO AP 96521-0002
Tel: [86] (24) 282-0068
Fax: [86] (24) 282-0074

Colombia
American Embassy
Calle 22D-BIS, No. 47-51, AA 3831, Bogota, Colombia
US mailing address: APO AA 34038
Tel: [57] (1) 315-0811
Fax: [57] (1) 285-7945

Costa Rica
American Embassy
Pavas, San Jose, Costa Rica
US mailing address: APO AA 34020
Tel: [506] 220-3939
Fax: [506] 231-4783

Côte d'Ivoire
American Embassy
5 Rue Jesse Owens, 01 B.P. 1712, Abidjan, Côte d'Ivoire
Tel : [225] 21-09-79
Fax: [225] 22-32-59

Croatia
American Embassy
Andrije Hebranga 2, Zagreb, Croatia
Tel: [385] (1) 455-5500
Fax: [38] (1) 455-3126
US mailing address: Unit 1345, APO AE 09213-1345

Cyprus
American Embassy
Metochiou and Ploutarchou Streets, Engomi, Nicosia, Cyprus
US mailing address: P.O. Box 4536, FPO AE 09836
Tel: [357] (2) 476100
Fax: [357] (2) 465944

Czech Republic
America Embassy, Commercial Office
Hybernska 7A, 117 16 Prague 1, Czech Republic
US mailing address: Unit 1330, APO AE 09213-1330
Tel: [42] (2) 2421-9844, 2421-9846/7
Fax: [42] (2) 2421-9965

Denmark
American Embassy
Dag Hammarskjolds Alle 24, 2100 Copenhagen
US mailing address: PSC 73, APO AE 09716
Tel: [45] 31-42-31-44
Fax: [45] 31-42-01-75

Dominican Republic
American Embassy
Calle Cesar Nicolas Penson y Calle Leopoldo Navarro, Santo Domingo, Dominican Republic
US mailing address: Unit 5500, APO AA 34041
Tel: (809) 221-2171
Fax: (809) 688-4838

Ecuador
American Embassy
Avenida 12 de Octubre y Avenida Patria, Quito, Ecuador
US mailing address: APO AA 34039
Tel: [593] (2) 562-890
Fax: [593] (2) 504-550

American Consulate General, Guyaquil
9 de Octubre y Garcia Moreno, Guayaquil, Ecuador
Tel: [593] (4) 323-570
Fax: [593] (4) 324-558
US mailing address: APO AA 34039

Egypt
American Embassy
8, Kamal El-Din Salah St., Garden City, Cairo, Egypt
US mailing address: Unit 64900, APO AE 09839-4900
Tel: [20] (2) 355-7371
Fax: [20] (2) 355-8368

American Embassy, Branch Office
3 El Faraana Street, Alexandria, Egypt
US mailing address: Unit 64900
Box 24, APO AE 09839-4900
Tel: [20] (3) 482-5607, 483-6330
Fax: [20] (3) 482-9199

El Salvador
American Embassy
Final Blvd. Santa Elena, Antiguo Cuscatlan
San Salvador, El Salvador
US mailing address: Unit 3116, APO AA 34023
Tel: [503] 278-4444
Fax: [503] 298-2336

Estonia
American Embassy
Kentmanni 20, EE 0001 Tallinn, Estonia
Tel: [372] (6) 312-021, Cellular Tel (5)244-091
Fax: [372] (6) 312-025

Ethiopia
American Embassy
P.O. Box 1014, Addis Ababa, Ethiopia
Tel: [251] (1) 550-666
Fax: [251] (1) 552-191

Finland
American Embassy
Itainen Puistotie 14A, FIN-00140 Helsinki, Finland
US mailing address: APO AE 09723
Tel: [358] (0) 171-931
Fax: [358] (0) 635-332

France
American Embassy
2 Avenue Gabriel, 75382 Paris Cedex 08, France
US mailing address: PSC 116, APO AE 09777
Tel: [33] 1-43-12-23-83
Fax: [33] 1-42-66-48-27

US Mission to the OECD
19 Rue de Franqueville, 75016 Paris, France
US mailing address: PSC 116 (USOECD), APO AE 09777
Tel: [33] 1-45-24-74-77
Fax: [33] 1-45-24-74-10

US Commercial Office, Lyon
45, Rue de la Bourse, Lyon
US mailing address: PSC 116, APO AE 09777
Tel: [33] 4-72-40-59-20
Fax: [33] 4-78-39-14-09

American Consulate General, Marseille
12 Boulevard Paul Peytral, 13286 Marseille Cedex 6, France
US mailing address: Paris Embassy (MAR)—PSC 116, APO
AE 09777
Tel: [33] 4-91-54-92-00
Fax: [33] 4-91-55-09-47

US Commercial Office, Nice
Rue du Marechal Joffre, 06000 Nice, France
US mailing address: PSC 116, APO AE 09777
Tel: [33] (16) 4-93-88-89-55
Fax: [33] (16) 4-93-87-07-38

American Consulate General, Strasbourg
15 Ave. D'Alsace, 67082 Strasbourg Cedex, France
US mailing address: PSC 116, APO AE 09777
Tel: [33] 4-88-35-31-04
Fax: [33] 4-88-24-06-95

Gabon
American Embassy
B.P. 4000, Libreville, Gabon
Tel: [241] 762-003/4, 743-492
Fax: [241] 745-507

Germany
American Embassy
Deichmanns Aue 29, 53170 Bonn, Germany
US mailing address: PSC 117, APO AE 09080
Tel: [49] (228) 339-1
Fax: [49] (228) 334-649
Web site (USIA): www.usia.gov/posts/bonn.html

American Embassy, Branch Office
Neustaedtische Kirchstrasse 4-5, 10117 Berlin, Germany
US mailing address: PSC 120, Box 1000, APO AE 09265
Tel: [49] (30) 238-5174
Fax: [49] (30) 251-0246

US Consulate General, Dusseldorf
Kennedydamm 15-17, 40476 Dusseldorf, Germany
Tel: [49] (211) 4706-1
Fax: [49] (211) 43-14-31

American Consulate General, Frankfurt am Main
Siesmayerstrasse 21, 60323 Frankfurt a.M., Germany
US mailing address: PSC 115, APO AE 09213-0115
Tel: [49] (69) 7535-0
Fax: [49] (69) 748-204

American Consulate General, Hamburg
Alsterufer 27/28, 20354 Hamburg, Germany
Tel: [49] (40) 41171-351
Fax: [49] (40) 410-6589

American Consulate General, Leipzig
Wilhelm-Seyfferth-Strasse 4, 04107 Leipzig, Germany
US mailing address: PSC 120, Box 1000, APO AE 09265
Tel: [37] (41) 213-8440
Fax: [37] (41) 213-8441

American Consulate General, Munich
Koeniginstrasse 5, 80539 Munich, Germany
US mailing address: Unit 24718, APO AE 09178
Tel: [49] (89) 2888-735
Fax: [49] (89) 285-261

American Consulate General, Stuttgart
Urbanstrasse 7, 70182 Stuttgart, Germany
US mailing address: Unit 30607, APO AE 09154-0001
Tel: [49] (711) 21008-0
Fax: [49] (711) 21008-20

Ghana
American Embassy
P.O. Box 194, Accra, Ghana
Tel: [233] (21) 775348, 776601
Fax: [233] (21) 775747

Greece
American Embassy
91 Vasilissis Sophias Blvd., 10160 Athens, Greece
Tel: [30] (1) 721-2951, 721-8401
Fax: [30] (1) 721-8660
US mailing address: PSC 108, APO AE 09842

Guatemala
American Embassy
7-01 Av. de la Reforma, Zone 10, Guatemala City, Guatemala
US mailing address: APO AA 34024
Tel: [502] (2) 311-541
Fax: [502] (2) 317-373

Guyana
American Embassy
P.O. Box 10507, Georgetown, Guyana
Tel: [592] (2) 54900-9, 57960-9
Fax: [592] (2) 58497

Haiti
American Embassy
P.O. Box 1761, Port-au-Prince
Tel: [509] 22-0354, 22-0368, 22-0200, 22-0612
Fax: [509] 23-1641

Honduras
American Embassy
Avenida La Paz, Apdo. Postal 3453, Tegucigalpa, Honduras
US mailing address: APO AA 34022
Tel: [504] 36-9320, 38-5114
Fax: [504] 38-2888

Hong Kong
American Trade Office
26 Garden Rd., Hong Kong
US mailing address: PSC 464, Box 30, FPO AP 96522-0002
Tel: [852] 2841-2350
Fax: [852] 2845-0943

Hungary
American Embassy
V. Szabadsag Ter 1, Budapest
US mailing address: Unit 1320, APO AE 09213-1320
Tel: [36] (1) 122-8600, 122-1217
Fax: [36] (1) 342-2529

India
American Embassy
Shanti Path, Chanakyapuri, New Delhi 110-021, India
Tel: [91] (11) 600-651
Fax: [91] (11) 687-2391

US Commercial Office, Bangalore
W-202, II Fl., West Wing "Sunrise Chambers," 22 Ulsoor
Rd., Bangalore 560-042, India
Tel: [91] (80) 558-1452
Fax: [91] (80) 558-3630

American Consulate General, Mumbai (Bombay)
Lincoln House, 78 Bhulabhai Desai Rd.
Mumbai 400-026, India
Tel: [91] (22) 363-3611
Fax: [91] (22) 262-3850

American Consulate General, Calcutta
5/1 Ho Chi Minh Sarani, Calcutta 700-071, India
Tel: [91] (33) 242-3611
Fax: [91] (33) 242-2335

American Consulate General, Madras
220 Mount Rd., Madras 600-006
Tel: [91] (44) 827-3040, 827-7542
Fax: [91] (44) 825-0240

Indonesia
American Embassy
Medan Merdeka Selatan 5, Jakarta, Indoneisa
US mailing address: Box 1, APO AP 96520
Tel: [62] (21) 360-360
Fax: [62] (21) 385-1632

American Consulate General, Medan
Jalan Imam Bonjol 13, Medan, Indonesia
US mailing address: APO AP 96520
Tel: [62] (61) 519-590
Fax: [62] (61) 518-711

American Consulate General, Surabaya
Jalan Raya Dr. Sutomo 33, Surabaya, Indonesia
US mailing address: Am Con Gen Box 1, Unit 8131, APO
AP 96520-0002
Tel: [62] (31-582-287
Fax: [62-31-574-492

Ireland
American Embassy
42 Elgin Rd., Ballsbridge, Dublin, Ireland
Tel: [353] (1) 660-3208, 668-8777
Fax: [353] (1) 688-2840

Israel
American Embassy
71 Hayarkon St., Tel Aviv, Israel
US mailing address: PSC 98, Box 100, APO AE 09830
Tel: [972] (3) 517-6161
Fax: [972] (3) 510-7215

Italy
American Embassy
Via Veneto 119/A, 00187 Rome, Italy
US mailing address: PSC 59, Box 100, APO AE 09624
Tel: [39] (6) 4674-1, 4674-2202
Fax: [39] (6) 4674-2113

American Consulate General, Florence
Lungarno Amerigo Vespucci, 38, 50123 Florence, Italy
US mailing address: APO AE 09613
Tel: [39] (55) 211-676
Fax: [39] (55) 283-780

American Consulate General, Genoa
Via Dante 2/43 (Palazzo Borsa), 16121 Genoa, Italy
Tel: [39] (10) 247-1412
Fax: [39] (10) 290-027

American Consulate General, Milan
Via Principe Amedeo, 2, 20121 Milan, Italy
US mailing address: PSC 59, Box 60 (M), APO AE 09624
Tel: [39] (2) 2900-1165, 659-2260
Fax: [39] (2) 659-6561

American Consulate General, Naples
Piazza della Repubblica 80122 Naples, Italy
US mailing address: Box 18, PSC 810, FPO AE 09619-0002
Tel: [39] (81) 761-1592
Fax: [39] (81) 761-1869

Jamaica
American Embassy
2 Oxford Rd., 3rd Fl., Kingston, Jamaica
Tel: (809) 929-4850
Fax: (809) 929-4850 x1042

Japan
American Embassy
10-5, Akasaka 1-chome, Minato-ku, Tokyo 107, Japan
US mailing address: Unit 45004
Box 258, APO AP 96337-0001
Tel: [81] (3) 3224-5000, 3224-5060
Fax: [81] (3) 3589-4235
Web site (Commercial Service): www.spinnet.or.jp/usa/

US Trade Center, Tokyo
7th fl., World Import Mart, 1-3 Higashi Ikebukuro 3-chome, Toshima-ku, Tokyo 170, Japan
Tel: [81] (3) 3987-2441
Fax: [81] (3) 3987-2447, 3987-2447 (Commercial Office)

American Consulate General, Osaka
11-5, Nishitenma 2-chome, Kita-Ku, Osaka 530, Japan
US mailing address: Unit 45004
Box 239, APO AP 96337-5004
Tel: [81] (6) 315-5900
Fax: [81] (6) 361-5978

American Consulate General, Sapporo
Kita 1-Jo Nishi 28-chome, Chuo-ku, Sapporo 064, Japan
US mailing address: Unit 45004
Box 276, APO AP 96337-0003
Tel: [81] (11) 641-1115, 641-1117
Fax: [81] (11) 643-0911

American Consulate, Fukuoka
5-26 Ohori 2-chome, Chuo-ku, Fukuoka 810, Japan
US mailing address: Unit 45004
Box 242, APO AP 96337-0001
Tel: [81] (92) 751-9331
Fax: [81] (92) 713-9222

American Consulate, Nagoya
Nishiki SIS Building, 6F, 10-33 Nishiki 3-chome, Naka-ku, Nagoya 460, Japan
US mailing address: c/o AMEMB Tokyo, Unit 45004, Box 280, APO AP 96337-0001
Tel: [81] (52) 203-4277
Fax: [81] (52) 201-4612

Jordan
American Embassy
P.O. Box 354, Amman 11118, Jordan
US mailing address: APO AE 09892-0200
Tel: [962] (6) 820-101
Fax: [962] (6) 820-146

Kazakhstan
American Embassy
99/97 Furmanova St., Almaty, Rep. of Kazakstan 480012
Tel: [7] (3272) 63-39-05, 63-13-75, 63-24-26
Fax: [7] (3272) 63-38-83

Kenya American Embassy
P.O. Box 30137, Nairobi, Kenya
US mailing address: Unit 64100, APO AE 09831
Tel: [254] (2) 334-141
Fax: [254] (2) 216-648

Korea (South)
American Embassy
82 Sejong-Ro, Chongro-ku, Seoul, Rep. of Korea
US mailing address: Unit 15550, APO AP 96205-0001
Tel: [82] (2) 732-4114
Fax: [82] (2) 739-8845, 739-1628

US Export Development Office
US Commercial Center, c/o US Embassy 82 Sejong-Ro, Chongro-ku, Seoul, Rep. of Korea
US mailing address: Unit 15550, APO AP 96205-0001
Tel: [82] (2) 397-4212
Fax: [82] (2) 739-1628

Kuwait
American Embassy
P.O. Box 77, Safat 13001, Kuwait
US mailing address: Unit 69000, APO AE 09880-9000
Tel: [965] 242-4151
Fax: [965] 244-7692

Laos

American Embassy
Rue Bartholonie, B.P. 114, Vientiane, Laos
US mailing address: Box V, APO AP 96546
Tel: [856] (21) 212581, 212582, 212585
Fax: [856] (21) 212584

Latvia

American Embassy
Raina Boulevard 7, LV-1510, Riga, Latvia
US mailing address: PSC 78, Box R, APO AE 09723
Tel: [371] (2) 210-005, IDD 782-0046
Fax: [371] (2) 226-530

Lebanon

American Embassy
P.O. Box 70-840, Beirut, Antelias, Lebanon
US mailing address: PSC 815, Box 2, FPO AE 09836-0002
Tel: [961] (1) 402-200, 403-300, 406-650, 406-651
Fax: [961] (1) 407-112

Lithuania

American Embassy
Akmenu 6, 2600 Vilnius, Lithuania
US mailing address: PSC 78, Box V, APO AE 09723
Tel: [370] (2) 227-224
Fax: [370] (2) 670-6084

Luxembourg

American Embassy
22 Blvd. Emmanuel-Servais, 2535 Luxembourg
US mailing address: PSC 9, Box 9500
APO AE 09123
Tel: [352] 460123
Fax: [352] 461401

Macedonia (The Former Yugoslav Republic of)

American Embassy
ul. 27 Mart No. 5, 9100 Skopje, FYR of Macedonia
Tel: [389] (91) 116-180
Fax: [389] (91) 117-103

Madagasgar

14-16 Rue Rainitovo, Antsahavola, B.P. 620
Antananarivo, Madagascar
Tel: [261] (2) 212-57, 200-89, 207-18
Fax: [261] (2) 234-539

Malawi

American Embassy
P.O. Box 30016, Lilongwe 3, Malawi
Tel: [265] 783-166
Fax: [265] 780-471, access code 835

Malaysia

American Embassy
P.O. Box No. 10035, 50700 Kuala Lumpur, Malaysia
Tel: [60] (3) 248-9011
Fax: [60] (3) 242-1866
US mailing address: APO AP 96535-8152

Malta

American Embassy
P.O. Box 535, Valletta, Malta
Tel: [356] 235-960
Fax: [356] 243-229

Mauritania

American Embassy
B.P. 222, Nouakchott, Mauritania
Tel: [222] (2) 526-60, 526-63
Fax: [222] (2) 515-92

Mauritius

American Embassy
P.O. Box 544, Port Louis, Mauritius
Tel: [230] 208-2347, 208-2354, 208-9763/7
Fax: [230] 208-9534

Mexico

American Embassy
Paseo de la Reforma 305, 06500 Mexico City, D.F., Mexico
US mailing address: P.O. Box 3087, Laredo, TX 78044-3087
Tel: [52] (5) 211-0042
Fax: [52] (5) 208-3373, 511-9980
Web site (Commercial Service): uscommerce.org.mx/

US Export Development Office
Liverpool 31, 06600 Mexico City, D.F., Mexico
Tel: [52] (5) 591-0155
Fax: [52] (5) 566-1115

US Travel and Tourism Office
Plaza Comermex, M. Avila Camacho 1-402, 11560 Mexico
City, D.F., Mexico
Tel: [52] (5) 520-2101
Fax: [52] (5) 202-9231

American Consulate General, Ciudad Juarez
Chihuahua, Avenue Lopez Mateos 924 Norte
32000 Ciudad Juarez, Chihuahua, Mexico
US mailing address: P.O. Box 10545
El Paso, TX 79995-0545
Tel: [52] (16) 113000
Fax: [52] (16) 169056

American Consulate General, Guadalajara
Progreso 175, 44100 Guadalajara, Jal., Mexico
US mailing address: Box 3088, Laredo, TX 78044-3088
Tel: [52] (3) 825-2998, 825-2700
Fax: [52] (3) 826-6549

American Consulate General, Monterrey
Ave. Constitucion 411 Poniente, 64000 Monterrey, N.L.,
Mexico
US mailing address: P.O. Box 3098, Laredo, TX 78044-3098
Tel: [52-8) 345-2120

American Consulate General, Tijuana
Tapachula 96, 22420 Tijuana, B.C.N., Mexico
US mailing address: P.O. Box 439039
San Diego, CA 92143-9039
Tel: [52] (66) 81-7400

Morocco
American Consulate General
8 Blvd. Moulay Youssef, Casablanca, Morocco
US mailing address: PSC 74, Box 24, APO AE 09718 (CAS)
Tel: [212] (2) 264-550
Fax: [212] (2) 220-259

American Embassy
2 Ave. de Marrakech, Rabat, Morocco
US mailing address: PSC 74, Box 003, APO AE 09718
Tel: [212] (7) 762-265
Fax: [212] (7) 765-661

Mozambique
American Embassy
P.O. Box 783, Maputo, Mozambique
Tel: [258] (1) 49-27-97
Fax: [258] (1) 49-01-14

Namibia
American Embassy
Private Bag 12029, Ausspannplatz, Windhoek, Namibia
Tel: [264] (61) 221-601
Fax: [264] (61) 229-792

Netherlands
American Embassy
Lange Voorhout 102, 2514 EJ The Hague, Netherlands
US mailing address: PSC 71, Box 1000, APO AE 09715
Tel: [31] (20) 310-9209
Fax: [31] (20) 363-2985
Web site (Commercial Service): www.luna.nl/~attic/

American Consulate General, Amsterdam
Museumplein 19, 1071 DJ Amsterdam, Netherlands
US mailing address: PSC 71, Box 1000, APO AE 09715
Tel: [31] (20) 575-5351, 575-5309
Fax: [31] (20) 575-5350

Netherlands Antilles
American Consulate General
P.O. Box 158, Willemstad, Curacao, Netherlands Antillies
Tel: [599] (9) 613066
Fax: [599] (9) 616489

New Zealand
American Embassy
P.O. Box 1190, Wellington, New Zealand
Tel: [64] (4) 472-2068
Fax: [64] (4) 478-1701
US mailing address: PSC 467, Box 1, FPO AP 96531-1001

American Consulate General
Private Bag 92022, Auckland, New Zealand
US mailing address: PSC 467, Box 99, FPO AP 96531-1099
Tel: [64] (9) 303-2724
Fax: [64] (9) 302-3156, 366-0870

Nicaragua
American Embassy
Km. 41/2 Carretera Sur., Managua, Nicaragua
US mailing address: APO AA 34021
Tel: [505] (2) 666010, 666013, 666015/8, 666026/7
Fax: [505] (2) 669056

Niger
American Embassy
Rue Des Ambassades, B.P. 11201, Niamey, Niger
Tel: [227] 72-26-61/4
Fax: [227] 73-31-67

Nigeria
American Embassy
P.O. Box 554, Lagos, Nigeria
Tel: [234] (1) 261-0097
Fax: [234] (1) 261-9856

Norway
American Embassy
Drammensveien 18, 0244 Oslo, Norway
US mailing address: PSC 69, Box 1000
APO AE 09707
Tel: [47] 22-44-85-50
Fax: [47] 22-55-88-03

Pakistan
American Embassy
Diplomatic Enclave, Ramna 5, Islamabad, Pakistan
US mailing address: P.O. Box 1048, Unit 62200
APO AE 09812-2200
Tel [92] (51) 826161 thru 790
Fax: [92] (51) 214222

American Consulate General, Karachi
8 Abdullah Haroon Rd., Karachi, Pakistan
US mailing address: Unit 62400, APO AE 09814-2400
Tel [92] (21) 568-5170 thru 79
Fax [92] (21) 568-1381, 568-0496

American Consulate General
50 Shahrah-E-Bin Badees, Lahore, Pakistan
US mailing address: Unit 62216, APO AE 09812-2216
Tel: [92] (42) 636-5530
Fax: [92] (42) 636-5177

Panama
American Embassy
Apartado 6959, Panama 5, Rep. de Panama
US mailing address: Unit 0945, APO AA 34002
Tel: [507] 227-1777
Fax: [507] 227-1964

Papua New Guinea
American Embassy
P. O. Box 1492, Port Moresby, Papua New Guinea
Tel: [675] 321-1455
Fax: [675] 321-3423

Paraguay
American Embassy
1776 Mariscal Lopez Ave., Casilla Postal 402
Asuncion, Paraguay
US mailing address: Unit 4711, APO AA 34036-0001
Tel: [595] (21) 213-715
Fax: [595] (21) 213-728

Peru
American Embassy, Commercial Office
P.O. Box 1995, Lima 1
US mailing address: APO AA 34031
Tel: [51] (14) 33-0555
Fax: [51] (14) 33-4687

Philippines
American Embassy, Commercial Office
395 Senator Gil J. Puyat Ave., Makati, M.M., Philippines
US mailing address: APO AP 96440
Tel: [63] (2) 890-9717
Fax: [63] (2) 895-3028

Poland
American Embassy
Aleje Ujazdowskie 29/31, Warsaw, Poland
US mailing address: Unit 1340, APO AE 09213-1340
Tel: [48] (2) 628-3041, 621-4516
Fax: [48] (2) 628-8298, 621-6327

US Trade Center, Warsaw
Aleje Jerozolimskie 56C, IKEA Building, 2d floor, 00-803
Warsaw, Poland
US mailing address: Unit 1340, APO AE 09213-1340
Tel: [48] (2) 621-4515, 621-4216, 625-4300
Fax: [48] (2) 621-6327

Portugal
American Embassy
Avenida das Forcas Armadas, 1600 Lisbon, Portugal
US mailing address: PSC 83, APO AE 09726
Tel: [351] (1) 726-6600, 726-5086
Fax: [351] (1) 726-8914

American Business Center, Porto
Praca Conde de Samodaes, 65, 4100 Porto, Portugal
US mailing address: APO AE 09726
Tel: [351] (2) 606-3094, 606-3095
Fax: [351] (2) 600-2737

Qatar
American Embassy
P.O. Box 2399, Doha, Qatar
Tel: [974] 867460
Fax: [974] 861669

Romania
American Embassy
Strada Tudor Arghezi 7-9, Bucharest, Romania
US mailing address: Unit 1315, APO AE 09213-1315
Tel: [40] (1) 210-4042
Fax: [40] (1) 210-0690, 210-0395

Russia
American Embassy, US & Foreign Commercial Service
Novinskiy Bul'var 15, Moscow, Russia
US mailing address: APO AE 09721
Tel: [7] (502) 224-1105, (095) 956-4255, 255-4848
Fax: [7] (502) 230-2101, 224-1106

American Consulate General, St. Petersburg
US & Foreign Commercial Service
Bolshaya Morskaya Ulitsa 57, 190000 St. Petersburg, Russia
US mailing address: PSC 78, Box L, APO AE 09723
Tel: [7] (812) 110-6656, 110-6727
Fax: [7] (812) 110-6479

American Consulate General, Vladivostok
Ulitsa Pushkinskaya 32, 690000 Vladivostok, Russia
Tel: [7] (501) 300-093
Fax: [7] (501) 300-092

Consulate General, Yekaterinburg
P.O. Box 400, 620151 Yekaterinburg, Russia
Tel: [7] (3432) 564-619, 564-691
Fax [7] (3432) 564-736, 564-515

Saudi Arabia
American Embassy
P.O. Box 94309, Riyadh 11693, Saudi Arabia
US mailing address: Unit 61307, APO AE 09803-1307
Tel: [966] (1) 488-3800
Fax: [966] (1) 488-3237

American Consulate General, Dhahran
P.O. Box 81, Dhahran Airport 31932, Saudi Arabia
US mailing address: Unit 66803, APO AE 09858-6803
Tel: [966] (3) 891-3200
Fax: [966] (3) 891-8332

American Consulate General, Jeddah
P.O. Box 149, Jeddah 21411, Saudi Arabia
US mailing address: Unit 62112, APO AE 09811
Tel: [966] (2) 667-0040
Fax: [966] (2) 665-8106

Singapore
American Embassy, Commercial Services Office
1 Colombo Court, Unit #05-16 Colombo Ct. Building
North Bridge Road, Singapore 0617
US mailing address: FPO AP 96534
Tel: [65] 338-9722
Fax: [65] 338-5010

Slovakia
American Embassy
Hviezdoslavovo Namestie 4, 81102 Bratislava, Slovakia
Tel: [42] (7) 5330861
Fax: [42] (7) 5335-096, 533-5439

Slovenia
American Embassy
Box 254, Prazakova 4, 61000 Ljubljana, Slovenia
Tel: [386] (61) 301-427, 301-472, 301-485
Fax: [386] (61) 301-401

South Africa
American Consulate General
P.O. Box 2155, Johannesburg, Rep. of South Africa
Tel: [27] (11) 331-3937
Fax: [27] (11) 331-6178

American Consulate General, Cape Town
Broadway Industries Centre, Heerengracht, Foreshore
Cape Town, Rep. of South Africa
Tel: [27] (21) 214-280
Fax: [27] (21) 254-151

Spain
American Embassy
Serrano 75, 28006 Madrid, Spain
US mailing address: APO AE 09642
Tel: [34] (1) 577-4000, 577-2301
Fax: [34] (1) 575-8655

American Consulate General, Barcelona
Reina Elisenda 23, 08034 Barcelona
US mailing address: PSC 61, Box 0005, APO AE 09642
Tel: [34] (3) 280-2227
Fax: [34] (3) 205-7705

Sri Lanka
American Embassy
P.O. Box 106, Colombo, Sri Lanka
Tel: [94] (1) 448007
Fax: [94] (1) 437345, 446013

Sweden
American Embassy
Strandvagen 101, S-115 89 Stockholm, Sweden
Tel: [46] (8) 783-5346, 783-5300
Fax: [46] (8) 660-9181

Switzerland
American Embassy
Jubilaeumstrasse 93, 3005 Bern, Switzerland
Tel: [41] (31) 357-7011
Fax: [41] (31) 357-7336

US Trade Representative (USTR)
Botanic Bldg., 1-3 Avenue de la Paix
1202 Geneva, Switzerland
Tel: [41] (22) 749-4111
Fax: [41] (22) 749-5308

American Consulate General, Zurich
Zollikerstrasse 141, 8008 Zurich
Tel: [41] (1) 422-23-72
Fax: [41] (1) 382-26-55

Syria
American Embassy
P.O. Box 29, Damascus, Syria
Tel: [963] (11) 333-2814, 333-0788, 332-0783
Fax: [963] (11) 224-7938

Tanzania
American Embassy
P.O. Box 9123, Dar Es Salaam, Tanzania
Tel: [255] (51) 66010/5
Fax: [225] (51) 66701

Taiwan
Note: There is no US Embassy in Taiwan
American Trade Center
Room 3207, International Trade Building, Taipei World
Trade Center, 333 Keelung Road Section 1
Taipei 10548, Taiwan
Tel: [886] (2) 720-1550
Fax: [886] (2) 757-7162

American Institute in Taiwan, Taipei
#7 Lane 134, Hsin Yi Road Section 3 Taipei, Taiwan
Tel: [886] (2) 709-2000
Fax: [886] (2) 702-7675

American Institute in Taiwan, Kaohsiung
5th fl., #2 Chung Cheng 3d Rd. Kaohsiung, Taiwan
Tel: [886] (7) 224-0154
Fax: [886] (7) 223-8237

Thailand
American Embassy, Commercial Office
3d fl., Diethelm Towers Bldg., Tower A, 93/1 Wireless Rd.,
Bangkok 10330
US mailing address: APO AP 96546
Tel: [66] (2) 255-4365
Fax: [66] (2) 255-2915

Togo
American Embassy
Rue Pelletier Caventou & Rue Vauban, B.P. 852, Lome, Togo
Tel: [228] 21-77-17, 21-29-91/4
Fax: [228] 21-79-52

Trinidad and Tobago
American Embassy
P.O. Box 752, Port-of-Spain, Trinidad & Tobago
Tel: (809) 622-6372
Fax: (809) 622-2444

Tunisia
American Embassy
144 Ave. de la Liberte, 1002 Tunis-Belvedere, Tunisia
Tel: [216] (1) 782-566
Fax: [216] (1) 789-719

Turkey
American Embassy
110 Ataturk Blvd., Ankara, Turkey
US mailing address: PSC 93, Box 5000, APO AE 09823
Tel: [90] (312) 467-0949, 468-6110
Fax: [90] (312) 467-1366

American Consulate General, Istanbul
104-108 Mesrutiyet Caddesi, Tepebasi, Istanbul, Turkey
US mailing address: PSC 97, Box 0002
APO AE 09827-0002
Tel: [90] (212) 251-3602
Fax: [90] (212) 252-7851

Uganda
American Embassy
P.O. Box 7007, Kampala, Uganda
Tel: [256] (41) 259792/5
Fax: [256] (41) 259794

Ukraine
American Embassy
10 Yuria Kotsubynskoho, 254053 Kiev 53, Ukraine
Tel: [380] (44) 417-1413
Fax.: [380] (44) 417-1419

United Arab Emirates
American Embassy, Commercial Office
P.O. Box 4009, Abu Dhabi, UAE
Tel: [971] (2) 345-545
Fax: [971] (2) 331-374

American Consulate General, Dubai
P.O. Box 9343, Dubai, UAE
Tel: [971] (4) 313-584
Fax: [971] (4) 313-121

United Kingdom
American Embassy
24/31 Grosvenor Sq., W. 1A 1AE, London, U.K.
US mailing address: PSC 801, Box 40; FPO AE 09498-4040
Tel: [44] (171) 499-9000
Fax: [44] (171) 408-8020

American Consulate General, Belfast
Queen's House, 14 Queen St., Belfast, BT1 6EQ, U.K.
US mailing address: PSC 801, Box 40, APO AE 09498-4040
Tel: [44] (1232) 328-239
Fax: [44] (1232) 248-482

American Consulate General, Edinburgh
3 Regent Ter. Edinburgh EH7 5BW, U.K.
US mailing address: PSC 801, Box 40, FPO AE 09498-4040
Tel: [44] (131) 556-8315
Fax: [44] (131) 557-6023

Uzbekistan
American Embassy
82 Chilanzarskaya, Tashkent, Uzbekistan
Tel: [7] (3712) 771-407
Fax: [7] (3712) 891-335

Venezuela
American Embassy
P.O. Box 62291, Caracas 1060-A, Venezuela
US mailing address: APO AA 34037
Tel: [58] (2) 977-2011
Fax: [58] (2) 977-0843

Vietnam
American Embassy
7 Lang Ha Road, Ba Dinh District, Hanoi, Vietnam
US mailing address: PSC 461, Box 400
FPO AP 96521-0002
Tel: [84] (4) 431500
Fax: [84] (4) 350484

Yemen
American Embassy
P.O. Box 22347, Sanaa, Republic of Yemen
Tel: [967] (1) 238-843/52
Fax: [967] (1) 251-563

Yugoslavia
American Embassy, Belgrade
(No local street address is currently available)
US mailing address: Unit 1310, APO AE 09213-1310
Tel: [381] (1) 645-655
Fax: [381] (1) 645-096

Zaire
American Embassy
310 Avenue des Aviateurs, Kinshasa, Zaire
US mailing address: Unit 31550, APO 09828
Tel: [243] (12) 21533/5, Cellular Tel: [243] (88) 43608
Fax: [243] (88) 43467, 43805 ext. 2308

Zambia
American Embassy
P.O. Box 31617, Lusaka, Zambia
Tel: [260] (1) 250-955, 252-230
Fax: [260] (1) 252-225

Zimbabwe
American Embassy
P.O. Box 3340, Harare, Zimbabwe
Tel: [263] (4) 728-957
Fax: [263] (4) 796-488

NATIONAL CENTER FOR STANDARDS & CERTIFICATION INFORMATION (NCSCI)

The National Center for Standards and Certification Information, established in 1965, provides information on US, foreign, and international voluntary standards; government regulations; and rules of conformity assessment for non-agricultural products. The Center serves as a referral service and focal point in the United States for information about standards and standards-related information.

The Center is located in the Office of Standards Services. It contributes to the Institute's goals of improving US competitiveness in domestic and world markets and strengthening and advancing the development and use of the nation's science and technology by providing up-to-date information on standards, technical regulations, and conformity assessment programs.

NCSCI staff respond to inquiries, maintain a reference collection of standards and standards-related documents, and serve as the US inquiry point for information to and from foreign countries.

General Information Services

Center staff respond to written, telephone and walk-in requests for information by identifying relevant standards and/or regulations. Searches are made with the aid of various indexes, by contacting professional and standards-developing organizations, and through communicating directly with foreign standards bodies. The requester is referred to the appropriate standards-developing organization for additional (technical) information and/or copies of the document. NCSCI does not provide copies of standards.

The NCSCI reference collection of standards and standards-related documents includes:

- microfilm files of military and federal specifications, US industry and national standards, and international and selected foreign national standards;

- reference books, including directories, technical and scientific dictionaries, encyclopedias and handbooks;

- articles, pamphlets, reports and handbooks on standardization and conformity assessment; and

- standards-related periodicals and newsletters.

These documents are available in the Center for review only. NCSCI does not provide copies of its reference documents.

The Center is open to visitors Monday through Friday, 8:30 a.m. to 5:00 p.m. It is located about 25 miles (40 km) northwest of Washington, DC.

WTO/GATT, NAFTA and ISONET Information

GATT (WTO) Hotline: (301) 975-4041

NCSCI serves as the US inquiry point in response to obligations resulting from the World Trade Organization (formerly the General Agreement on Tariffs and Trade, the Agreement on Technical Barriers to Trade, the North American Free Trade Agreement, and the International Organization for Standardization Information Network). NCSCI, with other national inquiry points, form networks—for WTO and ISO—that regularly exchange standards-related information. These networks also provide NCSCI with access to foreign trade-related technical standards, regulations and conformity assessment procedures. In some instances, the requester may be referred to the appropriate foreign inquiry point directly to obtain information.

Signatories to the WTO TBT Agreement are required to notify proposed governmental and state regulations which may significantly affect trade. NCSCI maintains information on notifications of proposed foreign regulations issued through the WTO Secretariat and disseminates them to interested parties in the United States for their review and comment. NCSCI

staff are responsible for notifying the WTO Secretariat of proposed US technical regulations which may affect trade.

A TBT/GATT Hotline, updated weekly, provides information on notifications of proposed foreign regulations received by NCSCI.

European Union Information

EU Hotline: (301) 921-4164

NCSCI recognizes the importance of the European Union (EU) market to US exporters. Center staff utilize the following documents, which are available in the reference collection, to assist US exporters in identifying product standards and regulations:

- standards catalogs for most of the EU members;

- official Journal of the European Communities, which contains proposed and final directives;

- catalogs and mementos of the European Committee for Standardization (CEN) and European Committee for Electrotechnical Standardization (CENELEC); and

- copies of relevant documents related to the harmonized standards and legislation for the single European market and EU directives.

An EU hotline provides information on draft standards of CEN, CENELEC and the European Telecommunications standards Institute (ETSI).

For Further Information

National Center for Standards and Certification Information (NCSCI)
National Institute of Standards and Technology (NIST)
TRF Building, Room A163
Gaithersburg, MD 20899
Tel: (301) 975-4040, 975-4038, 975-4036, 975-5155
Fax: (301) 926-1559

Call the above numbers for information on existing US, foreign, and international standards, as well as information on foreign regulations and conformity assessment procedures and information on the TBT Agreement and notifications of proposed foreign regulations.

Call (301) 975-4033 for technical assistance concerning standards-related issues.

ISO Quality Management Standardization (ISO 9000 Series)

The OSS Technical Office, established in response to the Trade Agreements Act of 1979, provides technical assistance to US industry for standards-related trade problems, provides analyses of standards issues; prepares and publishes indexes and directories of specialized standards information, and arranges for translations of foreign standards (for which there is a charge).

The Office of Standards Services (OSS) has published two booklets and several other documents with basic information on the ISO 9000 Standard Series and related issues. Tens of thousands of copies of these documents have been distributed. In addition, OSS responds to requests for information on this topic from government and the private sector.

OSS has also assisted several government agencies in their efforts to use the ISO 9000 standards within the scope of their regulatory and procurement programs, and OSS staff have given presentations at many domestic and international training seminars and related meetings to educate private sector and government participants about ISO 9000 Standard Series and its usage. OSS is represented on the Technical Advisory Group to the International Organization for Standardization Technical Committee 176, the committee responsible for the development of the ISO 9000 and 10000 standard series.

For further information contact:
Maureen Breitenberg
NIST Bldg. 820, Room 282
Gaithersburg, MD 20899
Tel: (301) 975-4031
Fax: (301) 963-2871
Email: mbreitenberg@nist.gov

Conformity Assessment Systems Evaluation (The NVCASE Program)

The National Institute of Standards and Technology, through its Office of Standards Services, offers on a fee for service basis, a voluntary program to evaluate and recognize organizations which support conformity assessment activities.

The National Voluntary Conformity Assessment Systems Evaluation (NVCASE) Program includes activities related to laboratory testing, product certification, and quality system registration. After NVCASE evaluation, NIST provides recognition to qualified US organizations that effectively demonstrate conformance with established criteria. The ultimate goal is to help US manufacturers satisfy applicable product requirements mandated by other countries through conformity assessment procedures conducted in this country prior to export.

NVCASE recognition (1) provides other governments with a basis for having confidence that qualifying US conformity assessment bodies are competent, and (2) facilitates the acceptance of US products in foreign regulated markets based on US conformity assessment results.

NVCASE does not unilaterally establish program areas. Operational areas are established only after a formal request from a conformity assessment body and concurrence of need from the affected industry sector. If another US government agency has domestic regulatory responsibility for a sector, that agency will be consulted prior to any program action by NIST.

Conformity assessment activities may be considered to be conducted on three levels: the conformity level (e.g., product testing, product certification and quality system registration); the accreditation level (e.g., the actions of accreditors of bodies operating at the conformity level); and the recognition of accreditors. NVCASE recognition may be sought by a body that accredits other bodies, (i.e., an accreditor of laboratories, certifiers or registrars). If acceptable accreditation is not available elsewhere, a body may be accredited directly by NVCASE to perform a function (i.e., to certify specific products).

In the NVCASE evaluation process, an applicant provides NIST with sufficient information to allow thorough assessment. The applicant's management system is thoroughly reviewed based on established internationally accepted criteria, such as ISO/IEC 9000 series. The criteria for technical operation are based on internationally accepted criteria such as ISO/IEC Guide 25 for laboratories and ISO/IEC Guide 58 for their accreditors, ISO/IEC Guide 61 for accreditors of registrars, and ISO/IEC Guide 62 for registrars.

Each participant must undergo an initial on-site assessment by peer assessors prior to obtaining recognition. All elements of non-conformance must be resolved before recognition will be granted. Once recognized, follow-up assessments are conducted on a regular two-year cycle, with periodic surveillance visits both announced and unannounced. NVCASE recognition is effective until either voluntary or involuntary termination.

NVCASE maintains listings of all recognized bodies, including the name, address, pertinent contacts and the scope of recognition. NVCASE also maintains listings of bodies which have been accredited or otherwise approved by a NVCASE recognized accreditor (only within the scope and period of recognition of the accreditor), indicating they are traceable to NIST via the NVCASE recognized body. All listings are freely disseminated to the public through various media.

Negotiations with the EU

The US has been actively negotiating with the EU to develop an mutual recognition agreement concerning the acceptance of each others conformity assessment results. The US has proposed that NVCASE recognition be one means of acceptance by the EU of US bodies as equivalent to EU notified bodies to approve products for entry to the EU marketplace.

At the time of publication these talks are active and it is hoped that an agreement will be forthcoming in 1996. Names of all bodies considered competent to perform conformity assessment actions and acceptable to each side will be part of the agreement.

For further information contact:
Robert L. Gladhill, Program Manager
NIST Bldg 820, Room 282
Gaithersburg, MD 20899
Tel: (301) 975-4273
Fax: (301) 963-2871
Email: robert.gladhill@nist.gov

Appendix 3:
Services Trade Statistics

A Brief Tutorial on Service Trade Statistics

Understanding the way statistics are compiled is important to the service provider since it can affect market research interpretations and conclusions. Tracking international services data is difficult due to their "invisible" nature. Unlike manufactured products which are registered at the border, services do not have any formal international registration method, making reliable measurement of international patterns in services trade difficult. In addition, trade data fails to capture the fact that services generally facilitate the sale of goods.

US services companies do not always have access to the kind of data available to goods exporters, such as long-term market trends, which can help to plan export strategy. Services statistics often lack timeliness, specificity, and comparability among differing service industries. (Data for services are available for 31 broad categories of activity, in comparison to the 15,400 categories available for goods. Since this data is so aggregated, it is difficult to distinguish international transactions for specific industries and markets.)

Although services trade statistics can reveal the relative magnitude of broad service industries and their exports, they cannot necessarily be construed as numerically accurate. Underreporting of actual services trade flow has been estimated to be as high as one-third. The intangibility of services output makes it impractical to physically measure services output in the same way as goods. Moreover, trade in goods and services is measured using gross receipts, which does not take into account the difference in the price of services due to quality changes, vs. other changes (increases in demand). The difficulty in measuring services "output" can be illustrated in estimating the output of education. The output--human capital created—related to educating one individual can vary immensely depending on the person, and on the inputs used (class size, etc.)

Data Collection for Services

The Bureau of the Census maintains statistics on all US product exports. The Census takes raw data from a shipper's export declaration, which must be filed on all export shipments valued at $1,000 or more. In general, the value of services is equated to the value of sales receipts in the services provided. Export statistics are then categorized by product sales, in quantity and dollar value, to countries of destination in the Census FT 410 series, published monthly.

Service export figures, however, are only estimates and are based on data collected by individual business establishments and their corresponding Standard Industrialization Classification (SIC), identifying their principal business activity. SIC categories are then tabulated and prepared by the Bureau of Economic Analysis of the US Department of Commerce. All data is self-reported, which is harder to enforce than the mandatory Shipper's Export Declaration for shipments abroad.

For example, when a lawyer or engineer visits a foreign country on business, chances are that his or her movement will be picked up in the passenger and travel service statistics, but the value of the legal or engineering services provided in the foreign country frequently will not be recorded in either country's trade statistics. Similarly, if these legal or engineering services were instead provided via an international telecommunications link, the communications charges might be picked up by the government's statisticians, but the value of the legal or engineering services that were exported almost certainly would not. Due to the difficulty in quantifying services trade, data on services, is generally considered to be very conservative.

A 1989 article published by the Organization of Economic Cooperation and Development, entitled "Services in the Domestic and Global Economy," identified five main reasons for this "downward bias" in services trade statistics:

1. With the exception of Hong Kong and Taiwan, comparable data on trade in services is not publicly available for certain important non-members of the International Monetary Fund.

2. Some countries do not report statistics on specific service items. Examples include Greece and Indonesia for maritime transport of freight.

3. Many service transactions simply are not registered. In the case of surveys, the coverage of trading establishments is often incomplete. A particularly serious problem is that services transmitted electronically are frequently unregistered, especially when the transactions are between affiliates and parent multinational firms.

4. Statistics may be reported on a net (exports minus imports) rather than gross basis.

5. A final source of downward bias is the misclassification of transactions. Transactions may be registered as factor income, remittances (transfers), or trade in merchandise, rather than trade in services. For example, legal services are recorded as services only when they are purchased from an independent firm. But if a goods-producing firm has a legal department, the output of its lawyers is recorded in the statistics for goods production.

Another reason for the downward bias in trade statistics, not discussed in the OECD article, is that some countries do not acknowledge certain services as "economic activities," such as wholesaling, legal services and several social and recreational services.

Sources for Service Trade Statistics

The US Standard Industrial Classification code is the classification standard underlying all establishment-based US economic statistics, classified by industry. The SIC identifies industries within the United States and classifies them under a seven-digit number. SIC codes can be found in the Standard Industrial Classification Manual at most public libraries. The SIC manual can also be purchased through the Government Printing Office (GPO), Stock Number: 041-001-00214-2.

Bureau of Economic Analysis

The most detailed data source for service sector exports is the *Survey of Current Business,* published by the Bureau of Economic Analysis of the US Department of Commerce. Data includes in-depth exports and import figures by type of service, historical data, sales of MOFAS (majority-owned foreign affiliates of US companies), and MOUSAS (majority-owned US affiliates of foreign companies), and also sales of services by region and major country, current and historical. Many of these statistics are also available on the National Trade Data Bank as well.

For further information on direct investment and international services, write: International Investment Division, BE-50, Bureau of Economic Analysis, US Department of Commerce, Mailstop BE-50, 1441 L Street, NW, Washington, DC 20230; telephone (202) 606-9805; fax (202) 606-5318. For specific questions, contact:

International Services: (202) 606-9804

Operations of US Companies and their Foreign Affiliates: (202) 606-9867

Operations of US Affiliates of Foreign Companies: (202) 606-9893

US Direct Investment Abroad: (202) 606-9867

User's Guide to Bureau of Economic Analysis (BEA)

This guide contains descriptions and entries for specific products. Statistics available from BEA cover four areas: national economics, regional economics, international economics' and other tools for economic analysis. The annual publication describes individual statistical products available from the bureau, in what form and how to obtain them. Selected bureau data series are available through an on-line data system called CENDATA, which also is described in the guide. To order or for general information, call the BEA's public information office at (202) 606-9900.

Direct Investment and International Services

BEA conducts quarterly, annual and benchmark surveys of US direct investment abroad and foreign direct investment in the United States. The information collected relates to the direct investment position and flows of capital, income, royalties and license fees, and other service charges between parent companies and affiliates; capital expenditures by majority-owned foreign affiliates of US companies; the financial structure and operations of US parent companies and their foreign affiliates; the financial structure and operations of US affiliates of foreign companies; and US business enterprises acquired or established by foreign direct investors. Summary information on the quarterly and annual surveys for US direct investment abroad usually appears in the *Survey of Current Business* on the following schedule: the position and balance of payments flows (June with additional detail in August), operations of US parent companies and their foreign affiliates (June) and capital expenditures by majority-owned foreign affiliates of US companies (March and September).

The Balance of Payments of the United States: Concepts, Data Sources, and Estimating Procedures

This publication describes in detail the methodology used in constructing the balance of payments estimates for the United States. It explains underlying principles and describes the presentation of the estimates. It also includes a comprehensive list of data sources. Available from the GPO: Stock No. 003-010-00204-2.

Status Report on Statistical and Methodological Improvements in the US Balance of Payments Statistics

This publication reviews major problems, such as timing and coverage, in balance of payments accounts; describes statistical and methodological improvements BEA has undertaken to resolve some of these problems; and discusses projects for future improvements. Available from the BEA: Accession No. 53-88-10-002.

Bureau of Labor Statistics, US Department of Labor

Employment and earnings data for services workers, average hourly and weekly earnings.

US Industrial Outlook, International Trade Administration, US Department of Commerce

A yearly compilation of historical and forecast data by SIC. Shipments (current and constant dollars), employees, imports, exports, capital expenditures, and miscellaneous data.

Value Line Investment Survey Ratings and Reports

Historical and forecast industry-specific financial data. Contact: Value Line, 711 Third Ave., New York City, NY 10017.

Standard and Poors Industry Reviews

Detailed analyses of various services industries, primarily covering the domestic market. Sales figures, profit ratios, investment market performance. Contact: Standard and Poors Co., 300 W. Chestnut, Ephrata, PA 17522.

Export and Import Trade Data, Bureau of the Census

The Bureau of the Census maintains worldwide export and import statistics tracked by mode of transportation and port of entry or exit. Various levels of classification are available including: the harmonized system of commodity classification, standard international trade classification, standard industrial classification-based codes and end-use classification. Customized tabulations and reports can be prepared to user specifications. Prices begin at $25 and vary depending upon user requirements and job size. For more information, telephone Trade Data Services, telephone (301) 457-7754; fax (301) 457-4615.

CENDATA

This tool is a menu-driven, on-line database of statistical data from the census and surveys conducted by the US Census Bureau. It contains several hundred thousand regularly updated records. CENDATA offers text and tabular data on a wide range of topics, including: census data, foreign trade data, agricultural data, wholesale and retail trade, and service industries. CENDATA is available through CompuServe (800) 848-8199 and Dialog (800) 334-2564.

Service Industries USA

This publication is a comprehensive resource on more than 150 US service industries along with information on more than 4,000 leading public and private corporations and non-profit institutions active in those industries. It lists services by SIC code and provides industry data for the US and individual states, using various federal statistics for service industries. It also contains metro area statistics, including industry descriptions, general statistics, indices of change, selected ratios, statistical analyses by state and region, occupations employed, leading companies and employment. Service Industries USA also includes tables on numbers of establishments, total employment, revenues and ownership patterns for each service industry in the United States. For more information, contact Gale Research Inc. at 1-800-877-GALE.

Worldcasts

This eight-volume annual series presents 60,000 abstracted forecasts for products and markets outside the United States (150 countries). Forecasts are arranged by modified SIC codes and are typically one-line entries providing short- and long-range projections for consumption, employment, production, and capacity. The complete annual set of four product volumes and four regional volumes costs $1,375; the product set and regional set are $950 each; single volumes are $450 each. Contact: Information Access Company, 362 Lakeside Drive, Foster City, CA 94404; telephone (415) 378-5200 or (800) 227-8431.

World Bank Atlas

This publication provides demographics, gross domestic product, and average growth rates for every country. Contact World Bank Publications, P.O. Box 7247-8619, Philadelphia, PA 19170-8619; telephone (202) 473-1155; fax (202) 676-0581.

World Population

The US Bureau of Census collects and analyzes worldwide demographic data that can help exporters identify potential markets for their products. Information on each country includes total population, fertility, mortality, urban population, growth rate and life expectancy, and is updated every two years. It also contains detailed demographic profiles of individual countries, including analyses of labor force structure and infant mortality. Contact the Superintendent of Documents, US GPO, Washington, DC 20402; telephone (202) 512-1800; fax (202) 512-2250.

International Financial Statistics

This book is published by the International Monetary Fund and presents statistics on exchange rates, money and banking, production, government finance, interest rates, and other subjects. It is available by monthly subscription for $188 yearly; single copies are $20. Contact: Publication Service, International Financial Statistics, Room 10-540, 700 19th Street, N.W., Washington DC 20431; telephone (202) 623-7430; fax (202) 623-7201.

UN Statistical Yearbook

Published by the United Nations (UN), this yearbook is one of the most complete statistical reference books available. It provides international trade information on products, including information on importing countries useful in assessing import competition. The yearbook contains data for 220 countries and territories on economic and social subjects including population, agriculture, manufacturing, commodities, and export-import trade. Contact United Nations Publications, 2 UN Plaza, Room DC2-0853, New York, NY 10017; telephone (212) 963-8302; fax (212) 963-3489.

Census Catalog and Guide

How to find census reports, statistics, maps, computer tapes, and disks is the focus of this catalog. Complete indexes and subject guides simplify research. Detailed listings connect users with more than 1,400 State and Business Data Centers and 1,500 depository libraries throughout the US Published by the Bureau of the Census. Stock Number: 003-024.

Appendix 4:
Bibliography

US Government Printing Office

The US Government collects and disseminates information pertaining to general business activity, national demographics, and the economy. Government-published books noted with a stock number, can be ordered through the Superintendent of Documents or purchased at your closest US Government Bookstore. Government bookstores are located in several metropolitan areas, and local numbers are listed under Federal Government in your telephone directory.

To get a complete listing of bibliographies available from the Government Printing Office, write and ask for the Subject Bibliography Index at:

US Government Printing Office
Superintendent of Documents, Stop: SM
Washington DC 20401

You may order GPO publications by writing or calling:

Superintendent of Documents
US Government Printing Office
P.O. Box 371954, Pittsburgh, PA 15250-7954
Tel: (202) 512-1800; Fax: (202) 512-2250
Web site: www.gpo.gov

When ordering books, provide the list stock number (S/N) which is provided at the end of each book entry.

Andean and Caribbean Basin Financing Guide (1992)
S/N 003-009-00617-1. $9.50

Business America: The Magazine of International Trade (Monthly periodical)
Dept. of Commerce international trade publication. Each monthly issue includes discussions of US trade policies, news of government actions affecting trade, and a calendar of upcoming trade shows, exhibitions, fairs, and seminars.
S/N 703-011-00000-4-W. $43.00/year (domestic), $53.75/year (foreign)

CIA World Factbook (Annual)
Produced by Central Intelligence Agency, this book gives geographic and demographic information about each country around the globe.
Updated annually in July. $23.00

Development Assistance, Export Promotion, and Environmental Technology: Background Paper (1993)
Discusses environmental problems in developing countries; and markets for environmental technologies and services
S/N 052-003-01332-1. $6.50

Exporter's Guide to Federal Resources for Small Business (1992)
Describes the major Federal programs designed to assist small business owners in exporting their goods and services. Also identifies individuals in various government agencies who are able to provide technical assistance and support to small business owners interested in international trade.
By the Small Business Administration.
S/N 045-000-00263-2, ISBN 0-16-030231-5. $4.75

Final Act Embodying the Results of the Uruguay Round of Multilateral Trade Negotiations (1993)
Includes the texts of the December 15, 1993 Final Act. This Final Act relates to the General Agreement on Tariffs and Trade.
S/N 041-001-00422-0, ISBN 0-16-043037-2. $30.00

Foreign Labor Trends
Dept. of Labor
A series of reports, issued annually, that describes and analyzes labor trends in some 75 foreign countries. The reports cover labor-management relations, labor and government, international labor activities, and other significant developments. A list of key labor indicators is also included. The US Department of Labor's Office of Foreign Relations will publish additional reports on four foreign countries each year, beginning in 1996.
Contact: Sudha Haley, Office of Foreign Relations, (202) 219-6234, fax (202) 219-5613

General Agreement on Trade in Services: Examination of Major Trading Partners' Schedules of Commitments - Canada, European Union, Japan and Mexico
By the US International Trade Commission (USITC)
USITC Publication 2940, Washington, DC, December 1995.

Global Trade and Economic Outlook (1995)
S/N 003-009-00650-3. $8.00

International Business Practices (1993)
Covers business organizations; exporting; commercial policies; foreign investment; intellectual property rights; taxation; regulatory agencies; and useful contacts in countries worldwide.
S/N 003-009-00622-8, ISBN 0-16-042256-6. $18.00

Key Officers of Foreign Service Posts: Guide for Business Representatives (semi-annual periodical)
Lists key officers at Foreign Service posts—the Chiefs and Deputy Chiefs of Missions, the senior officers of the political, economical, commercial, and consular sections of the post, and the agricultural attache. It also lists all embassies, legations, and consulates general.
S/N 744-006-00000-7. LIST ID KOFS. $5.00/year, or $3.75/single copy (domestic), $6.25/year or $4.69/single copy (foreign).

National Trade Estimate Report on Foreign Trade Barriers, 1994 (1996)
By the Office of the US Trade Representative. Surveys significant foreign barriers to United States exports. When feasible, provides quantitative estimates of the impact of these foreign practices upon the value of United States exports. ISBN 0-16-043149-2, S/N 041-001-00473-4. $23.00

North American Free Trade Agreement Between the Government of the United States of America, the Government of Canada, and the Government of the United Mexican States (1993)
Also known as the legal text of the NAFTA. 2 volumes.
S/N 041-001-00407-6, ISBN 0-16-041960-3. $40.00

Results of the Uruguay Round Market Access Negotiations, GATT Schedule 20, United States of America: Volume 4, Services, Schedule of Commitments, and List of MFN (Most Favored Nation) Exemptions (1994)
S/N 041-001-00441-6, ISBN 0-16-045038-1. $8.50

US Industrial Outlook, 1995-2000
Focuses on seven export growth sectors, including medical equipment, computer software and information services, whose exports are projected to grow at double digit rates between 1995 and 2000. The Global Outlook also assesses US export prospects in 18 key markets among the industrialized nations: the big emerging markets of Asia, Africa and Latin America, and the economies in transition of Russia and Eastern Europe.
S/N: 003-009-00650-3. CD-ROM version also available.

United States Industrial Outlook, 1994: Forecasts for Selected Manufacturing and Service Industries (1993)
Industry reviews and forecasts for natural resources and energy; construction and related industries; industrial materials and components; production and manufacturing equipment; information and communication; the consumer economy; transportation and travel; health care; and financial, business, and professional services.
S/N 003-009-00635-0, ISBN 0-16-043003-8. $37.00

United States Trade Shifts in Selected Industries (1994)
Analyzes changes in imports, exports, and trade balances of key agricultural and manufactured commodities, including for the first time the US service sector as a whole and by selected industries; also analyzes significant shifts in US bilateral trade balances in 1993; and summarizes the significant factors affecting the US trade balance over a 13-year period (1980-1993), highlighting selected industries.
S/N 049-000-00070-7. $15.00

International Agency Publications

European Union

Market Services and European Integration: The Challenges for the 1990s (1994)
Edited by P. Buigues, et al. Order no. CM-79-93-267-EN-C.

Published by the Office for Official Publications of the European Communities. Available in the United States from Unipub, 4611-F Assembly Drive, Lanham, MD 20706; Tel: (800) 274-4888.

Organization for Economic Cooperation (OECD)

The following publications are available from OECD Publications and Information Center, 2001 L Street NW, Suite 700, Washington, DC 20036-4910; Tel: (202) 785-6323; Fax: (202) 785-0350; Web site: www.oecd.org:

International Trade in Professional Services: Assessing Barriers and Encouraging Reform (1996)
ISBN 92-64-14873-6. $59.00

Services in Central and Eastern European Countries (1991)
ISBN 92-64-13909-5. $28.00
By Statistics Directorate Organization for Economic Cooperation and Development. ISBN 92-64-03681-4. $60.00

Services: Measuring Real Annual Value Added (1996)
By Statistics Directorate Organization for Economic Cooperation and Development. ISBN 92-64-03681-4. $60.00

Services: Statistics on International Transactions, 1970-1993 (1996)
By Statistics Directorate Organization for Economic Cooperation and Development. ISBN 92-64-04836-7. $67.00

Trade in Information, Computer and Communication Services (1990)
By the Organization for Economic Cooperation and Development. ISBN 92-64-13327-5. $13.00

Trade, Investment, and Technology in the 1990s (1991)
Published by the Organization for Economic Cooperation and Development. ISBN 92-64-13480-8. $30.00

OECD Economic Outlook (Semiannual)
Economic summaries of OECD's 24 member countries. ISSN 0474-5574. $30/issue or $46.00/year.

United Nations

The following publications are available from United Nations Publications, Room DC2-0853, New York, NY 10017; Tel: (212) 963-8302, (800) 253-9646; Fax: (212) 963-3489; Web site: www.un.org:

U.N. Statistical Yearbook (Annual publication)
Economic and demographic data for approximately 250 countries. Data on world economy, structure, trends and performance, population, unemployment, inflation, energy production, food supply, external debt, education, housing and more. Also available on CD-ROM. $110.00

International Trade Statistics Yearbook (Annual publication)
Statistical analysis of overall foreign trade by regions and countries, as well as world exports by origin, destination and product category. Published in two volumes. $135.00

Demographic Yearbook (Annual publication)
Demographic statistics on size, distribution, and trends in population, fertility, and mortality rates for about 250 countries and regions. $125.00

Liberalizing International Transactions in Services: A Handbook (1994)
By the United Nations Conference on Trade and Development in association with the World Bank. UN Sales Number E. 94.II.A.11, ISBN 92-1-104432-4. $45.00

United Nations Education, Scientific & Cultural Organization (UNESCO)

UNESCO *Statistical Yearbook*
Economic and demographic data for 200 countries. $95.00 Published by UNESCO and Bernan Press. Available from: Bernan Press, 4611-F Assembly Drive, Lanham, MD 20706; Tel: (800) 274-4888.

World Bank

The World Bank
Box 7247-8619
Philadelphia, PA 19170-8619
Tel: (202) 473-1155
Fax: (202) 522-2627
Web site: www.worldbank.org

World Bank Atlas (Annual publication)
Gives population, gross domestic product and average growth rates for 209 countries. 1995 edition: ISBN 0-8213-3287-2. Order # 13287, $7.95

Liberalizing Trade in Services (1994)
By Bernard Hoekman and Pierre Sauve. World Bank Discussion Paper 243. ISBN 0-8213-2858-1. Stock No. 12858, $8.95

Emerging Stock Markets Factbook 1996 (1996)
By the International Finance Corporation. ISBN 0-8213-3649-5. Order # 13649. $100.00

Periodicals

Export Today
733 15th Street
N.W., Suite 1100
Washington, DC 20005
Tel: (202) 737-1060
Fax: (202) 783-5966
The "how to" international business magazine for US exporters. 8 issues/year, $95.00

The Exporter
Trade Data Reports
34 West 37th Street
New York, NY 10018
Tel: (212) 587-1340
Fax: (212) 587-1344
Monthly reports on the business of exporting. Monthly, $160.00/year.

Foreign Trade
6849 Old Dominion Drive
#200, McLean, VA 22101
Tel: (703) 448-1338
Fax: (703) 448-1841.
Features trade briefs, information on financing, shipping, air cargo, trucks and rails, and current legislation. 10 issues/year. $45.00

International Business
IB Communications Inc.
9 East 40 Street
10th Floor
New York, NY 10016
Tel: (212) 683-2426
Fax: (212) 683-3426
Subscription Service: (512) 873-7761
Reports on overseas market opportunities, global corporate strategies, trade and political developments to assess their impact on US imports, exports, joint ventures and acquisitions. Monthly, $48.00/year

Journal of Commerce
P.O. Box 5570
New York, NY 10087
Tel: (800) 222-0356
Fax: (908) 859-1300
Information on domestic and foreign economic developments plus export opportunities, agricultural trade leads, shipyards, export ABCs and trade fair information. Feature articles on tariff and non-tariff barriers, licensing controls, joint ventures and trade legislation in foreign countries. Daily Monday–Friday, $295.00/year

Services Marketing Today
American Marketing Association
250 S. Wacker Dr.
Suite 200
Chicago, IL 60606
Tel: (800) AMA-1150, (312) 831-2742
Fax: (312) 993-7542
Bimonthly. Members: $20.00/year, Nonmembers: $28.00/year

World Trade
World Trade
4199 Campus Drive, #230
Irvine, CA 92715
Tel: (714) 725-0233
Fax: (714) 725-0306

Books and References

Asian Capital Markets: Market Access Restrictions and Regulatory Environment Facing US Securities Firms in Selected Asian Markets (1994)
Published by the Securities Industry Association, 120 Broadway, New York, NY 10271; Tel: (212) 608-1500; Fax: (212) 608-1604

Basic Guide to Exporting, Second Edition
Published by World Trade Press, 1505 Fifth Ave., San Rafael, CA 94901; Telephone (415) 454-9934; Fax (415) 453-7980

Business International's Guide to International Licensing: Building a Licensing Strategy for 14 Key Markets Around the World (1993)
By Thomas J. Ehrbar. ISBN 0-07-009332-6. $39.95
Published by McGraw-Hill, 1221 Ave. of the Americas, New York NY 10020; Tel: (800) 722-4726, (212) 512-2000.

Coalitions and Competition: The Globalization of Professional Business Services (1993)
Edited by Yair Aharoni. ISBN 0-415-08228. $65.00
Published by Routledge Press, 29 W. 35th St., New York NY 10001; Tel: (212) 244-3336.

Europa World Year Book (Annual)
Information on every country and major international organizations; includes statistics and directories. 2 vols. $670.00.
Published by Europa Publications Ltd. Available from Gale Research, P.O. Box 33477, Detroit, MI 48232-5477; Tel: (800) 877-GALE (800-877-4253); Fax: (800) 414-5043; Web site: www.gale.com/gale.html.

Exporters' Encyclopedia (Annual)
Covers more than 220 world markets. $565.00
Published by Dun's Marketing Services, 3 Sylvan Way, Parsippany, NJ 07054-3896; Tel: (800) 526-0651, (201) 605-6000.

Exportise
Instructional manual on conducting international business, with detailed information on exporting. $19.95
Published by The Small Business Foundation of America, 722 12th St. NW, Washington, DC 20005; Tel: (202) 628-8382; Fax: (202) 628-8392.

The Growth of Global Business (1993)
Edited by Howard Cox, Jeremy Clegg, Grazia Ietto-Gillies. $65.00
Published by Routledge Press, 29 W. 35th St., New York NY 10001; Tel: (212) 244-3336.

Handbook of International Management (1988)
Edited by Walter Ingo and Tracy Murray. ISBN 0-471-60674-X. $105.00
Published by John Wiley & Sons, 1 Wiley Dr., Somerset NJ 08875-1272; Tel: (800) 225-5945, (908) 225-5945.

Handbook of Successful Franchising, 3rd Edition (1989)
By Mark P. Friedlander, Jr. and Gene Gurney. ISBN 0-8306-4090-8.
Published by TAB Books, P.O. Box 40, Blue Ridge Summit PA 17294; Tel: (800) 233-1128, (717) 794-2191.

International Commercial Agreements: A Primer on Drafting, Negotiating and Resolving Disputes (1992)
By William F. Fox, Jr. ISBN 90-6544-587-0. $70.00
Published by Kluwer Law and Taxation Publishers, P.O. Box 358, Accord Sta., Hingham MA 02018; Tel: (617) 871-6600.

International Trade in Services (1989)
By Ken Tucker and Mark Sundberg. ISBN 0-415-02549-4. $62.50
Published by Routledge Press, 29 W. 35th St., New York NY 10001; Tel: (212) 244-3336.

Investing, Licensing and Trading Conditions Abroad
Includes information on operating conditions and practices for 60 countries. $1,975.00
Published by Economist Intelligence Unit, 111 W. 57th St., New York, NY 10019; Tel: (800) 938-4685, (212) 554-0600.

Joint Ventures and Other Alliances: Creating a Successful Cooperative Linkage (1990)
By Alan I. Murray and Caren Siehl. ISBN 0-910586-76-4. $12.00
Published by Financial Executives Research Foundation, P.O. Box 1938, Morristown, NJ 07960-1938; Tel: (201) 898-4608; Fax: (201) 898-4649.

Managing Services as a Strategic Profit Center (1991)
By Donald F. Blumberg. ISBN 0-07-006189-0. $22.95
Published by McGraw-Hill, 1221 Ave. of the Americas, New York NY 10020; Tel: (800) 722-4726, (212) 512-2000.

Marketing Services: Competing through Quality (1991)
By A. Parasuraman and Leonard L. Berry. $32.95
Published by The Free Press, c/o Simon & Shuster Ordering Department, 200 Old Tappan Rd., Old Tappan NJ 07675; Tel: (800) 223-2336.

Marketing Strategies for Services: Globalization, Client-orientation, Deregulation (1994)
Edited by M.M. Kostecki. ISBN 0-08-042389-2. $65.00
Published by Elsevier Science, P.O. Box 945, New York, NY 10159-0945; Tel: (888) 437-4636, (212) 633-3730; Fax: (212) 633-3680; Web site: www.elsevier.com.

The New Social Economy: Reworking the Division of Labor (1992)
By Andrew Sayer and Richard Walker. ISBN 1-55786-280-X. $21.95
Published by Blackwell Publishers, 238 Main St., Cambridge MA 02142; Tel: (800) 216-2522, (617) 547-7110.

Operations Management for Service Industries: Competing in the Service Era (1992)
By Glenn A. Basset. ISBN 0-89930-746-9. $55.00
Published by Quorum Books, 99 Post Rd., Box 5007, Westport CT 06881; Tel: (800) 225-5800, (203) 226-3571.

Post-Capitalist Society (1994)
By Peter F. Drucker. ISBN 0-88730-661-6. $13.00
Published by Harper Business Press, 10 E. 53rd St., New York NY 10022; Tel: (800) 242-7737, (212) 207-7581.

Profitable Exporting: A Complete Guide to Marketing Your Products Abroad, Second Edition (1993)
By John S. Gordon and J.R. Arnold, ISBN 0-471-575143.1 $85.00
Published by John Wiley & Sons, 1 Wiley Dr., Somerset NJ 08875-1272; Tel: (800) 225-5945, (908) 225-5945.

Service America! Doing Business in the New Economy (1990)
By Karl Albrecht and Ron Zemke. ISBN 0-446-39092-5.
$13.99
Published by Warner Books, c/o Little Brown & Co., 200 West
St., Waltham MA 02154; Tel: (212) 522-7200.

*Service-Led Growth: The Role of the Service Sector in World
Development* (1987)
By Dorothy I. Riddle. ISBN 0-275-92728-8. $16.95
Published by Greenwood Press, 99 Post Rd., Box 5007,
Westport CT 06881; Tel: (800) 225-5800, (203) 226-3571.

*Service Quality: Multidisciplinary and Multinational Per-
spective* (1990)
Edited by Stephen W. Brown. From the Issues in Organiza-
tion & Management Series) ISBN 0-669-21152-4. $49.00
Published by The Free Press, c/o Simon & Shuster Ordering
Department, 200 Old Tappan Rd., Old Tappan NJ 07675;
Tel: (800) 223-2336.

Services Marketing, Third Edition (1996)
By Christopher H. Lovelock. ISBN 0-13-455841-3.
Published by Prentice-Hall Business Publishing; Tel: (800)
643-5506; Fax: (800) 835-5327; Web site: www.prenhall.com.

Services Marketing: Principles and Practice (1995)
By Adrian Palmer. ISBN 0-02-390563-8. $68.00
Published by Prentice-Hall Business Publishing; Tel: (800) 643-
5506; Fax: (800) 835-5327; Web site: www.prenhall. com.

*Servicing International Markets: Competitive Strategies of
Firms* (1992)
By Peter J. Buckley, et al. ISBN 0-631-18189-X. $59.95
Published by Blackwell Publishers, 238 Main St., Cam-
bridge MA 02142; Tel: (800) 216-2522, (617) 547-7110.

Trade Shows Worldwide (Annual publication)
Over 6,800 scheduled exhibitions, trade shows, association
conventions, and similar events are listed. $245.00
Published by Gale Research, P.O. Box 33477, Detroit, MI
48232-5477; Tel: (800) 877-GALE (800-877-4253); Fax:
(800) 414-5043; Web site: www.gale.com/gale.html.

*Understanding Services Management: Integrating Market-
ing, Organisational Behaviour, Operations and Human
Resource Management* (1995)
Edited by William J. Glynn and James G. Barnes. $33.00
Published by John Wiley & Sons, 1 Wiley Dr., Somerset NJ
08875-1272; Tel: (800) 225-5945, (908) 225-5945.

World Business Directory, Third Ed. (1995)
By the World Trade Centers Association. ISBN 0-8103-
5677-5. 4 volumes. $520.00
Available from Gale Research, P.O. Box 33477, Detroit, MI
48232-5477; Tel: (800) 877-GALE (800-877-4253); Fax:
(800) 414-5043; Web site: www.gale.com/gale.html.

Worldcasts (Quarterly)
Abstracts over 60,000 forecasts for products and markets in
countries outside the United States. Two editions, organized
by region and by product, $975.00 each.
Published by Predicasts, 11001 Cedar Avenue, Cleveland,
OH 44106; Tel: (800) 321-6388; Fax: (216) 229-9944.

World Market Share Reporter (1995)
Published by Gale Research, P.O. Box 33477, Detroit, MI
48232-5477; Tel: (800) 877-GALE (800-877-4253); Fax:
(800) 414-5043; Web site: www.gale.com/gale.html.

World Trade Almanac
Published by World Trade Press, 1505 Fifth Ave., San Rafael,
CA 94901; telephone (415) 454-9934; fax (415) 453-7980

World Trade Resources Guide (1991)
ISBN 0-8103-8404-3. $169.00
Published by Gale Research, P.O. Box 33477, Detroit, MI
48232-5477; Tel: (800) 877-GALE (800-877-4253); Fax:
(800) 414-5043; Web site: www.gale.com/gale.html.

Worldwide Government Directory (Annual publication)
Published by Worldwide Government Directories, Inc. $347.00
Available from Gale Research, P.O. Box 33477, Detroit, MI
48232-5477; Tel: (800) 877-GALE (800-877-4253); Fax: (800)
414-5043; Web site: www.gale.com/gale.html.

Articles

"Asia, At Your Service"
The Economist; February 11, 1995 (v335, n7901), page 53.

"The Coming Boom in Services Trade: What Will It Do to
Wages?"
By Gary Clyde Hufbauer
Law and Policy in International Business, Winter 1994 (v25, n2).

"Developing Global Strategies for Service Businesses"
By Christopher H. Lovelock and George S. Yip
California Management Review; Winter 1996, v38, n2, page 64.

"Duel to the Death? (Cable Television Industry in France)"
By Kenneth Scott Hart
Communications International (London), May 1994 (v21, n5).

"EMCs/ETCs: What They Are, How They Work"
By Richard Barovick and Patricia Anderson
Business America; July 13, 1992.

"Exporting Know-How: Service Companies Are Keeping the US
Competitive in Foreign Markets"
By Warren Cohen
US News & World Report; August 30, 1993 (v115, n9), page 53.

"Exporting Services"
Caribbean Business; June 22, 1995 (v23, n25), page 27.

"Exporting Services: Developing a Strategic Framework"
By Jack S. Goodwin and Clifford J. Elliot
Advanced Management Journal; Winter 1995 (v80, n1),
page 21.

"Exporting 'Soft' Technologies"
By James I. Walsh
Business America; August 1994 (v115, n8); page 30.

"Exporting Strategies: Developing a Strategic Framework"
By Jack S. Goodwin and Clifford J. Elliott
SAM Advanced Management Journal, Winter 1995
(v60, n1), page 21.

"GATS Battle Tests Barriers to Global Financial Competition"
By Kenneth Silverstein
Corporate Cashflow Magazine, August 1995 (v16, n16).

"GATS: The Uruguay Round Accord on International Trade
and Investment in Services"
By Harry G. Broadman
World Economy, May 1994 (v17, n3).

"The Global Service 500"
Fortune, August 22, 1994 (v130, n4); page 194.

"Global Strategy in Service Industries"
By Ravi Sarathy
Long Range Planning, December 1994 (v27, n6), page 115.

"Global Telecommunications and Export of Services:
The Promise and the Risk"
By Vary T. Coates, Todd M. LaPorte and Mark G. Young
Business Horizons, Nov–Dec 1993 (v36, n6), page 23.

"The Globalization of Service Multinationals"
By Alexandra J. Campbell and Alain Verbeke
Long Range Planning; April 1994 (v27, n2), page 95.

"The Good Word in Trade is Services"
By Daniel J. Connors and Douglas S. Heller
The New York Times, September 5, 1993.

"Hot Exports!"
By Neal Weinstock
World Trade; April 1994 (v7, n3), page 30.

"How Do I Go International?"
By Marc J. Chittum
Journal of Management Consulting; Fall 1992 (v7, n2), page 30.

"Internationalization By Business Services: A Methodological Critique of Foreign-Market Entry-Mode Choice"
By P.N. O'Farrell and L. Moffat, et. al.
Environment & Planning; May 1995 (v27, n5), page 683.

"International Trade Organizations and Economies in Transition: A Glimpse of the Twenty-first Century"
By Gary Clyde Hufbauer
Law and Policy in International Business, Summer 1995
(v26, n4)

"An Introductory Guide for US Businesses on Protecting
Intellectual Property Abroad"
Business America; July 1, 1991; page 2.

"Knowledge, Power and International Policy Coordination"
By Peter M. Haas
International Organization; Winter 1992 (v46, n1).

"Liberalizing International Trade in Telecommunications
Services"
Harry G. Broadman and Carol Balassa
Columbia Journal of World Business, Winter 1993 (v28, n4).

"Managing Services Exports: The Key Issues"
By Jack S. Goodwin and Clifford J. Elliott
American Business Review; January 1996 (v14, n1), page 46.

"The NAFTA: Exports, Jobs, Wages"
Business America; October 18, 1993.

"National Export Strategy Services Initiative Unveiled at
Services Export Conference"
Business America; August 1995 (v116, n8); page 24.

"North Carolina DEC Develops Directory of International
Service Providers"
By Greg Sizemore
Business America; March 1995 (v116, n3), page 26.

"The Political Economy of Service Sector Negotiations in
the Uruguay Round"
By Vinod K. Aggarwal
The Fletcher Forum of World Affairs; Winter 1992 (v16, n1),
page 35.

"Protecting Free Trade in Audiovisual Entertainment,"
By Kirsten, L. Kessler,
Law and Policy in International Business, Winter 1995 (v26, n2).

"Reform Tide Erodes Trade Barriers (Maritime)"
By Ken Cottrill
Distribution (Germany), July 1995 (v94, n7).

"Sectoral Trends in World Employment and the Shift
Towards Services"
By Jaroslaw Wieczorek
International Labour Review; 1995 (v134, n2), page 205.

"Services in a Shrinking World"
By Peter Daniels
Geography; April 1995 (v80, n2), page 97.

"Service Exports"
Business America; October 1994 (v115, n9), page 87.

"Service Statistics: Too Important to Ignore"
By Julian Arkell
The Service Economy (Coalition of Service Industries, Inc.)
April 1995 (v9, n2).

"Services"
By John Siegmund
Business America; January 1994 (v115, n1), page 8.

"Service Sector Trade in the Asia-Pacific Region"
The Service Economy (Coalition of Service Industries, Inc.),
November 1994.

"Services, Especially Business, Professional and Technical,
Are a Success Story of the US Trade Balance"
By Lian Von Wantoch
Business America; August 1994 (v115, n8), page 31.

"Services Exports and the US Economy"
Business America; August 1995 (v116, n8), page 25.

"Suddenly, Services Aren't Such World-Beaters: Exports Are Stalled—Bad News for the Overall Trade Deficit"
By Amy Borrus
Business Week; September 18, 1995 (n3442), page 45.

"Trade Lessons Form the World Economy"
By Peter F. Drucker
Foreign Affairs; Jan/Feb 1994 (v73, n1), page 99.

"The Uruguay Round Agreement: Trading on the Future,"
By Dean R. O'Hare
The Service Economy (Coalition of Services Industries, Inc.), October 1994 (v8, n4).

"US International Sales and Purchases of Private Services"
By Michael A. Mann and Sylvia E. Bargas
Survey of Current Business; September, 1995 (v116 n9), page 68.

"Venturing Into Foreign Markets: The Case of the Small Service Firm"
By M. Krishna Erramilli and Derrick E. D'Souza
Entrepreneurship: Theory & Practice; Summer 1993 (v17), page 29.

NOTES